'An engaging romp, a careful dissection, and a radical indictment of what's wrong with journalism. Smart suggestions for where to find signs of renewal and hope, too. Vintage Toby Miller.'

Silvio R. Waisbord, *The George Washington University, USA*

'This powerful book is a devastating critique of the failures of Anglo-American journalism. It provides endless examples of the gap between normative accounts of truth-telling and actual practices of stenography, clientelism and complicity with elites. From reporting on everything from food to climate and from sports to war, Miller's polemic situates journalism closer to misinformation than the democratising practice we desperately need it to be.'

Des Freedman, *Goldsmiths, University of London, UK*

'From a starting point of "cosmic ambivalence about the news today" Miller and his co-authors take us on a political economic and cultural analytic romp through mainstream journalism's failures. Questioning its moral and material basis from sports journalism to free speech; weaving philosophical and ideological critique with an analysis of journalistic practice defined by a methodological individualism, nationalism and absolutism – *Why Journalism* is far more than a polemic but it is a rollicking good read!'

Natalie Fenton, *Goldsmiths, University of London, UK*

WHY JOURNALISM?
A POLEMIC

This new book from Toby Miller engages with journalism from within the cultural studies tradition, addressing fundamental claims for the profession and its biggest contemporary challenges: critiques, objectivity, and insecurity.

Why Journalism? A Polemic considers four key aspects of contemporary journalism in terms of theoretical relevance and historic tasks that are not usually considered in parallel:

- Citizenship: political, economic, and cultural
- Environment: the climate crisis and reporters' material impact
- Sports: the importance of the popular; and
- Technology: its former, current, and future significance

With examples drawn from Latin America, Spain, and France as well as the US and Britain, the query animating these investigations returns again and again, implicitly and explicitly: why journalism? Miller argues for an answer to that dilemma that will involve a fundamental shift in how reporters, proprietors, professors, students, and states view the profession.

This is essential reading for scholars and students of media and cultural studies as well as journalism studies.

Toby Miller is Profesor Visitante at Universidad Complutense de Madrid, Profesor Cátedra de Comunicación y Teoría Crítica at Universidad de la Frontera, and Research Professor in the Graduate Division, University of California, Riverside.

WHY JOURNALISM?
A POLEMIC

Toby Miller

LONDON AND NEW YORK

Designed cover image: © Roberto Gamonal

First published 2024
by Routledge
4 Park Square, Milton Park, Abingdon, Oxon OX14 4RN

and by Routledge
605 Third Avenue, New York, NY 10158

Routledge is an imprint of the Taylor & Francis Group, an informa business

© 2024 Toby Miller

The right of Toby Miller to be identified as author of this work has been asserted in accordance with sections 77 and 78 of the Copyright, Designs and Patents Act 1988.

All rights reserved. No part of this book may be reprinted or reproduced or utilised in any form or by any electronic, mechanical, or other means, now known or hereafter invented, including photocopying and recording, or in any information storage or retrieval system, without permission in writing from the publishers.

Trademark notice: Product or corporate names may be trademarks or registered trademarks, and are used only for identification and explanation without intent to infringe.

British Library Cataloguing-in-Publication Data
A catalogue record for this book is available from the British Library

Library of Congress Cataloging-in-Publication Data
Names: Miller, Toby, 1958– author.
Title: Why journalism? a polemic / by Toby Miller.
Description: Abingdon, Oxon; New York, NY: Routledge, 2024. |
Includes bibliographical references and index.
Identifiers: LCCN 2023047621 (print) | LCCN 2023047622 (ebook) |
ISBN 9781032701646 (hardback) | ISBN 9781032701622 (paperback) |
ISBN 9781032701660 (ebook)
Subjects: LCSH: Journalism.
Classification: LCC PN4731 .M486 2024 (print) |
LCC PN4731 (ebook) | DDC 070.4—dc23/eng/20231025
LC record available at https://lccn.loc.gov/2023047621
LC ebook record available at https://lccn.loc.gov/2023047622

ISBN: 978-1-032-70164-6 (hbk)
ISBN: 978-1-032-70162-2 (pbk)
ISBN: 978-1-032-70166-0 (ebk)

DOI: 10.4324/9781032701660

Typeset in Sabon
by codeMantra

CONTENTS

Acknowledgments   *viii*

Introduction—why journalism?   1

1   Citizenship (with Bill Grantham)   33

2   Environment (with Richard Maxwell)   64

3   Sports (with David Rowe)   91

4   Technology   117

Conclusion   140

References   *151*
Index   *225*

ACKNOWLEDGMENTS

I'd like to thank people who have helped develop my thinking on the subject and/or contributed to this work: three anonymous reviewers, the workers involved in producing and circulating the book, and Eva Aladra Vico, Jesús Arroyave, Marta Milena Barrios, Sarah Berry, Mick Burton, Jim Carey, Jennifer Craik, André Dorcé Ramos, Elisabeth Eide, Mark Falcous, Natalie Foster, Bob Franklin, Des Freedman, Roberto Gamonal Arroyo, Néstor García Canclini, Kelly Gates, Nancy Regina Gómez Arrieta, Bill Grantham, Maggie Gray, John Hartley, Joe Heumann, Richard Higgott, James Jacobs, Roy Krøvel, Keith Larsen, Marie Leger, Meg Le Masurier, Justin Lewis, Jorge Mariscal, Randy Martin, Richard Maxwell, Vicki Mayer, Jim McKay, Caitlin Miller, JDB Miller, Lainey Paloma Miller, Jed Novick, Kelly O'Brien, Henrik Örnebring, Guillermo Orozco, Rune Ottosen, Joan Pedro Carañana, Isabel Cristina Ramírez, Paula Requeijo Rey, Kristina Riegert, Andrew Ross, David Rowe, Jorge Saavedra Utman, Alfredo Sabbagh Fajardo, Víctor Sampedro Blanco, Anita Schiller, Dan Schiller, Herb Schiller, Annika Egan Schölander, Federico Guillermo Serrano-López, Olga Lucía Sorzano, Rob Steen, Will Straw, Anamaria Tamayo Duque, Enrique Uribe Jongbloed, and Barbie Zelizer.

INTRODUCTION—WHY JOURNALISM?

Why journalism? For many of us, it's a dying profession, imperiled by populist amateurism, new technology, and corporate and state financial and propagandistic distortion; and cheapened by strategic communications, the contemporary euphemism for public relations (PR). For others, journalism remains a part of daily life, like waking up or cleaning our teeth. Retrieving the paper from the front lawn, dining in front of TV news, reading wire reports on laptops, discerning trends in real estate, or following football scores by phone—each one relies on journalism.

Journalism tells contemporary stories that are meant to be based in fact. It operates within certain values of open knowledge, blended with ideas of privacy, the public interest, and what interests the public. Sometimes those things overlap, sometimes they are contradictory or complementary, and sometimes simply separate. In Ferdinand Tönnies' words from a century and more ago, '[j]ournalism is the small change of literature, which penetrates every corner of the home, multiplies knowledge, stimulates thought, repeatedly communicates truth and untruth, authenticity and inauthenticity, evokes passionate feelings, confirms attitudes, forms opinions, and supports conversation' (2000: 146).

For me, journalism has been, and remains, both a mundane and a vital quotidian thing, as well as part of my professional life. As a child, I awoke each day to newspapers delivered to home, and dined each night to radio current affairs. I exhibited frustration when my father would be called to the phone by a *Times* leader writer seeking help. I should have been more understanding, because my dad worked as a foreign correspondent for *The Economist, inter alia*. My mother took down its cables in shorthand in the middle of the night, instructing him on the desired story the following morning.

DOI: 10.4324/9781032701660-1

He and I would go to the post office that evening to send his typed article by telegram. It gave me an appreciation that a 'condensed form of writing' (Innis, 1986: 161) could be precious if done well.

As an adult, for four and a half years I read the daily news and weather on radio networks, ran a sports desk on weekends, and worked at live events, outside broadcasts. In the decades since, I have been a speechwriter, a weekly radio and television film reviewer and commentator on the popular, a columnist for magazines[1] and newspapers,[2] and a vacation replacement radio talk-show and TV current-affairs host.[3] Some of these experiences were one-offs. Some endured—then ended—with the chilly advent of new editors, economic crises, or 'musical differences.' Few were paid, and some outlets denied me free access to what was published. For two decades, I was a frequent interviewee across the principal media forms,[4] until I stopped working at élite US universities. And I've taught in Colombian and Spanish journalism schools.

But the truth is, I never studied the topic in college or grad school and might be considered a mere adjunct to both journalism and its academic field: a *dilettante*, an unqualified, part-time *arriviste*, some distance from those Marx described as 'engaged in journalism in the proper sense' (1996: 162). Even my radio days saw me cataloged as a 'JAFA' (just another fucking announcer). I'd certainly not get France's identity card issued to professional reporters.[5] Perhaps I'm a fellow-traveler, like Hegel, who funded his other work by 'compiling reports on royal boar hunts' for Bamberg readers (Oltermann, 2020)—one version—or as a powerful local editor (Häberlein and Schmölz-Häberlein, 2020)—another.

I remain fascinated and frustrated by the profession, in all its duty of care, its bloviation,[6] its pomposity, its *faux* objectivity, its economism, its linguistic and other cultural biases, its reductionism, its *machismo*, its trivialization—above all, the tendency to promote journalism in one country rather than something truly international as well as local. I think it can be better. So this is a polemic, written by a disappointed follower and occasional practitioner, with hope for the future and a call to reconsider the purpose of journalism—its reason to be. I take my inspiration from Charlotte Brunsdon explaining that critical readers, listeners, and viewers engage with the news 'to find out about what was happening in the world and to scrutinize how it was or wasn't being presented' (2021: 11), very much per Roger Chartier's wish to identify 'the strategies by which authors and publishers tried to impose an orthodoxy or a prescribed reading on the text' (1989: 166).

This polemic is a call to reinvigorate journalism, to impel it toward a fundamentally democratic, progressive search for knowledge and how to share it, the better to eradicate and prevent inequality, violence, and climate disaster. Reporters can assist in meeting those crucial needs, helping to structure how people engage with overtly political—'capital-P' political—as well as environmental, cultural, and social arenas of life. I favor a profoundly contextual approach that is also alert to the material practices of reporting: how political-economic conjunctures of both prevailing and subordinate social forces could be articulated to the discourse, survival, and amelioration of the profession.

The remainder of this Introduction addresses fundamental claims for journalism and its biggest contemporary challenges: critiques, objectivity, and insecurity. Throughout the book, I'll include many international examples, though my primary focus will be on the US and Britain, with a secondary look at Colombia and México. I do so because I know those societies best, and because the Anglo ones are often taken as exemplars, however bizarre that may be.[7]

Claims

The foundational query 'why journalism?' has preoccupied philosophers, politicians, and hacks themselves for centuries. If we look back at oddly revered stale-pale-male accounts of what journalism can do, we find fragments from centuries past that continue to haunt the belief systems of today—for good and otherwise. In 1644's *Areopagitica*, the Anglo world's *ur*-text on these matters, John Milton avowed that 'when complaints are freely heard, deeply considered, and speedily reformed, then is the utmost civil liberty attained' (1909–14: 1). A century later, Immanuel Kant saw *Aufklärung* [the Enlightenment] as a riposte to the military, taxes, and religion, which insisted on obedience; the new way placed its faith in the '*public* use of reason' presented to 'the *reading world*' (1996: 60–61). It could generate 'morally practical precepts' by schooling people to transcend particular interests via the development of a '*public* sense, *i.e.* a critical faculty which in its reflective act takes account (*a priori*) of the mode of representation ... to weight its judgement with the collective reason of mankind' (Kant, 1987). Kant envisaged an '*emergence from ... self-incurred immaturity*,' independent of superstition, government, and commerce (1991: 54). For Thomas Jefferson, 'the basis of our governments being the opinion of the people, the very first object should be to keep that right; and were it left to me to decide whether we should have a government without newspapers, or newspapers without a government, I should not hesitate a moment to prefer the latter' (1787). The 18th-century Nordic pamphleteer Peter Forsskåll argued that 'the life and strength of civil liberty consist' in 'unlimited freedom of the written word' (n.d.).

Perhaps drawing on his experience covering boars, Hegel drew a complex, suggestive contrast between secular reportage and sacerdotal fantasy to explain why journalism matters: 'Reading the morning newspaper is the realist's morning prayer. One orients one's attitude toward the world either by God or by what the world is. The former gives as much security as the latter, in that one knows how one stands' (2002: 47). Hegel's binary opposition of religion versus reportage has some historical weight: Sunday newspapers took over from sermons for many people across 18th- and 19th-century Western Europe and the Americas. This 'displacement of pulpit by press' saw God-bothering priests abandon earlier themes, such as real-estate prices, international relations, and domestic politics, in favor of biblical exegeses and moral pronouncements (Eisenstein, 2005: 104–05).

Henri de Saint-Simon insisted on 'liberty of the press' (2015: 70). Jeremy Bentham referred to journalism as a 'check to arbitrary power ... upon the conduct of the ruling few' (2012: 8, 13). James Mill invited people to '[d]raw a picture, in the most glowing colours, of a society in which freedom of the press had full scope; how virtue, how public spirit would flourish—what happiness, what peace would flow' (n.d.: 105r). John Stuart Mill defended newspapers 'as one of the securities against corrupt or tyrannical government' (1859), while Simón Bolívar called for 'freedom of the press' and an independent media as cornerstones of South America's autonomy from Spain—part of 'all that is sublime in politics' (2003: 21, 42, 73). For Alexis de Tocqueville, the 'sovereignty of the people and the liberty of the press' were 'correlative institutions' (2000: 320).

Journalism joined religion, oligarchy, and labor as a *Fourth Estate,* linking writing, and hence easily shared knowledge, to lawmaking (Carlyle, 1908: 189). Thomas Carlyle summed up its claims to authority in demagogic and economic terms: 'Great is Journalism. Is not every Able Editor a Ruler of the World, being a persuader of it; though self-elected, yet sanctioned, by the sale of his Numbers?' (1930: 955). Thomas Macaulay emphasized expertise; he called newspapers a crucial safeguard of 'public liberty,' authorized by a phalanx of the great and the good and legitimized by readers (1848: 210). In 1910, Max Weber said: '[o]ne hundred fifty years ago the British Parliament forced journalists to apologize on their knees for breach of privilege after they reported about its sessions ... today a mere threat from the press not to print the speeches of representatives forces Parliament to its knees' (1976: 97).

On the left, Rosa Luxemburg held that '[w]hen such things as subscribing to a newspaper or buying pamphlets become part of a worker's everyday habits, his [sic] economic maintenance rises, and correspondingly so do wages' (2014: 255). Lenin's list of revolutionary tasks placed the foundation of national newspapers at its core (1975: 61, 92–101). They could form 'an enormous pair of smith's bellows that would fan every spark of the class struggle and of popular indignation into a general conflagration' (1975: 105).

At its best, the profession enables cosmopolitan empathy through the concept of 'meanwhile,' the understanding that at the same time—but in another place—other people and life forms exist in ways that are different from, yet akin to, one's own. Hence Hegel placing daily journalism alongside personal landmarks: 'we were born at a specific time … we die at a specific time, we even get news daily through the newspapers about what happens in the world in places where we are not' (2002: 233). That discourse of simultaneity is a prerequisite for national and international identification, a fundamental precept of modernity that connects people who would otherwise be out of touch with each other's concerns. It enables them to scrutinize private and public institutions, appreciate social problems, enjoy debate over values, animate the radical power of reason, and belong somewhere beyond the immediate (Anderson, 2006; Sen, 2009: 335–37).

Reactionaries argue that nations are constants across history, albeit changing morphology with time and circumstance. They are sustained through supposedly indelible ties: origin myths, languages, customs, races, and religions (Herder, 2002; Smith, 2000). For those more in thrall to modernity, such 'ties' are invented traditions (Hobsbawm and Ranger, 2002). Far from being the outcome of abiding mythologies, the materiality and idea of the nation derive from the Industrial Revolution and imperialism, which brought places together that had not previously deemed themselves linked in any way. Relatively isolated, subsistence villages were transformed by the interdependence engendered by capitalist organization, the commodification of everyday relations, and the sense of unity generated from nation-binding technologies and institutions, most notably print and public education (Gellner, 1988).

Pamphlets, novels, manifestoes, and newspapers 'provided the technical means for "re-presenting" the *kind* of imagined community that is the nation.' Readers could compile views of the world from beyond their personal experience, thanks to categorizations, choices, affinities, differences, inclusions, and exclusions determined by editors and writers, as well as the people and issues that were the objects of reportage. Then as now, audiences and journalists were bound together by simultaneity, newsworthiness, professional norms, and paradoxical tendencies of ephemerality and reputation (Anderson, 2006: 24–25, 33; also see Pettegree, 2014). These qualities have stimulated, and relied upon, 'a gregarious curiosity' that is paradoxically evident in readers' 'silent perusal,' which encourages 'adherence to causes whose advocates could not be found in any one parish and who addressed an invisible public from afar' (Eisenstein, 2005: 104, 107); hence Walter Lippmann speaking of 'the continuous reporting of an unseen environment' unveiling 'distant complexities' (1998: 261).

Terry Eagleton suggests that '[i]t is impossible for us now to recreate the excitement and bemusement of the first readers … at encountering a narrative which seemed to find everyday existence extraordinarily enthralling.' For this 'was early capitalist existence, in which frenetic change, sickening instability and the thrills and spills of survival in a predatory world were the name of the game' (2006: 269). Little magazines of social and literary criticism were emerging (Eagleton, 2005), promoting 'an idiom of taste and conduct' that fanned outward from journalists to novelists and the reading public (Leavis, 1939: 124), predating the emergence of university domination over philology, literary criticism, and so on; initial advances in those fields were made by reporters (Hohendahl, 2016). Politics was being discussed in the coffee shops of 18th-century Europe—3,000 in London alone. They are revered by latter-day theorists as sites of *bourgeois* formation and news (Habermas, 2011: 56). For the people who worked in these places, they could be nightmarish; reporters jostled with employees to obtain personal, damaging gossip or business news for sale (Coffee-man, 2016: 183). And the shipping merchants who were forming counter-public spheres in these shops—a new class yearning for political power—were awaiting news of the enslaved and free labor they had dispatched around the globe as much as they were discussing ideas.

Some analysts argue that the media stand for the expansion of civil society, a moment in history when the state became receptive to, and part of, the general population, coinciding with other changes, such as diminished traditional authority, the promulgation of individual rights and respect, and human interaction that was newly intense and interpersonal, yet on a large scale (Shils, 1966; Hartley, 1992). Perhaps the most noteworthy recent claim is the link drawn by Amartya Sen between a free press, multi-party democracy, and the avoidance of famine, per India's food insecurity immediately prior to 1947 versus relative abundance once democracy had vanquished the British (2000). And data from across the world confirm journalism's crucial role in opposing corruption, potentially improving the economic circumstances of ordinary people (Ambrey et al., 2016). CP Scott, who edited the *Guardian* for well over half a century, saw twin sides to such work: 'a business, like any other,' that 'has to pay in the material sense in order to live. But it is much more than a business; it is an institution; it reflects and it influences the life of a whole community; it may affect even wider destinies' (2017).

Critiques

Despite these heady assertions about the value of news, reporters have long been regarded as disposable and unworthy. If we go back to the profession's origin myths in the 17th- and 18th-century European occupations of gazetteer and newsman, we find they were derided as unreliable and given to sensationalizing. Such complaints indexed their contradictory roles as spokespeople for traditional sources of ecclesiastical and state authority or rivalrous emergent *bourgeoisies*—for the earliest journalists were passionate observers and partisan chroniclers of an urbanizing Europe, whether as roving anonymous reporters or sedentary philosopher-anthropologists named Kant (Foucault, 2007: 48).

These writers were describing the Industrial Revolution as it deepened and spread (Briggs and Burke, 2015), bringing with it new communications technologies, democratic urges, class anxieties, education systems, and forms of knowledge, as well as new forms of imperialism and slavery. As print proliferated at home and abroad, European critics feared a return to the 'barbarism' of the post-Roman Empire. Erudition would be overwhelmed by popular writing as well as war (Chartier, 2004) and there was the prospect of an 'ochlocracy' of 'the worthless mob' (Pufendorf, 2000: 144). Spirited debate ensued over whether the press was breeding anarchic readers who lacked respect for the traditionally literate classes—that a *Leserevolution* [reading revolution] was producing chaotic, permissive practices of reading in place of the continuing study of a few important hermeneutic texts (Davidson 1989: 14–16).

In the wake of the French Revolution, Edmund Burke was animated by the need to limit popular exuberance via a 'restraint upon … passions' (1994: 122). Jefferson was appalled by 'the malignity, the vulgarity, and mendacious spirit' of reporters (quoted in Graber, 2017: 239). JS Mill derided them as engaged in the 'more troublesome and disagreeable kinds of literary labour' (2004: 159). Friedrich Nietzsche held newspapers partly responsible for the 'palpable *desolation* of the German spirit' (2006: 117) and DH Lawrence said they created the 'shallow consciousness' of 'an inert lump' (2004: 22, 138)—the humble reader. By the 1920s, Lippmann discerned public and academic 'disdain for the professionals' (1998: 320). Scribes were often accused of generating 'a debased synthetic commercial culture' (Williams, 1970: 28). Weber argued that journalism's social standing was 'always estimated by "society" in terms of its ethically lowest representative' (1946: 96–98).

Such disparagement recurs over and over again in Western European and Yanqui democracies (Hargreaves, 2014). Consider this fragment from Hildy Johnson in *His Girl Friday* (Howard Hawks, 1940):

A journalist? What does that mean? Peeking through keyholes, chasing fire engines … waking people up to ask them questions … stealing pictures off old ladies? I know about reporters. Buttinskies running around with no money, and why? So a million people will know what's going on.

Or 'The Voice's' oration for *Citizen Kane* (Orson Welles, 1941):

Kane is dead. He contributed to the journalism of his day—the talent of a mountebank, the morals of a bootlegger, and the manners of a pasha [*sic*]. He and his kind have almost succeeded in transforming a once noble profession into a seven percent security—no longer secure.

Former Conservative Party hegemon Alan Clark claimed reporters mostly led 'squalid and unfulfilling lives,' were 'insecure in their careers,' exhibited 'a considerable degree of dependence on alcohol and narcotics,' and were urged by their editors to apply 'crude vindictiveness' when covering private life (1999). Today's conservatives lament that 'the vampire of postmodern politics' has left them 'without a crucifix' to counter wild demagogues (Carey, 1993: 2). The political center maintains that '[o]utstanding reporting and writing mingle with editing and reporting that smears, sneers and jeers, names, shames and blames' (O'Neill, 2002: 90). On the left, we express concern that journalism is dominated by the drive to prepare populations for insertion into the world system of labor and consumption rather than explaining democratic rights, culture, science, and society in a universalist frame.

The prevailing political economy has always affected what counts as news and journalists' liberty to report it. Leigh Hunt's satirical 'Rules for the Conduct of Newspaper Editors with Respect to Politics and News' from 1808 insist that:

> If you are proprietor as well as editor of your paper, you have the truly English freedom of saying what you please for your patron: but if you are editor only, it becomes you to say every thing which the proprietors may dictate, and nothing to which they may object. This restriction may appear hard, but in difficult times you must be hardened to meet difficulties; you are the servant of the proprietors, and inclination must be sacrificed to duty. What is called spirit will not pay your bills.
>
> *(2003)*

For August Bebel, papers 'fall in with the business interests of the bourgeoisie' and hence seek 'to make the bourgeois world ... appear as the best of all possible worlds' (1971: 104–05). Walt Whitman referred to 'kept-editors' as akin to 'spaniels well-train'd to carry and fetch' (2004: 120). In 1909, 'An Independent Journalist' wrote of Gringo newsrooms' failure to create and sustain barriers between Mammon and fact:

> The counting-room is too close to the sanctum; there is too much fear of the big advertiser, too much dread of "making enemies," too much thought of circulation and the danger of offending this or that element. ... Editors pass over subjects they would like to discuss because they anticipate criticism, complaint, withdrawal of patronage. ... they occasionally express opinions that are not theirs at all, but the known or supposed opinions of certain interests whose good will is desirable if not essential ... there are newspapers which serve as the special organs of special interests, of plutocracy, privilege, and monopoly.
>
> *(1909: 327)*

For Robert Park, '[t]he nerve of the press situation is revenue.' Understanding 'sources of income' usually explains how the news is controlled and by whom. The media 'become independent only when the editor is so situated that his [sic] opinions are not dictated by the exigencies of party or institutional interests and are not preordained by party doctrine or dogma' (1922: 360). Walter Benjamin despaired that newspapers could ever be 'a suitable instrument of production in the hands of the writer' because they 'belong to capital.' Reporters may harbor ideological sympathies with workers, but cannot truly empathize and incarnate class struggle absent an equivalent drive of their own to control the means of production (1970: 87–88). Decades later, AJ Liebling saw a 'monovocal, monopolistic, monocular press' (1964: 3). Today, Heather Gautney is forced to say:

> News outlets that once played down the middle to capture the broadest possible audience, now, in the era of twenty-four-hour cable TV and deregulated media, gain market share by targeting specific consumer segments and tailoring the news to their consumer tastes … hooking audiences through spectacle and affirmations meant to stoke social and political division. With just a handful of conglomerates competing to rule the airwaves, journalists and their editors have little incentive to factually report the news when it conflicts with what their audiences, and benefactors, want.
>
> *(2022: 200)*

Of course, in the US owners are often not locals these days, or folks who have a sense of duty aligned with journalism, but hedge funds, which regard the news world as one more profit center, to be trimmed wherever possible. They run more than half the country's papers (Helmore, 2021) and are responsible for a 'toxic commercialism that prioritizes profit over democratic imperatives' (Pickard, 2020: 1).

These political-economic problems led Weber to admire reporters, because of the extraordinary responsibility that came with their role and the factory-like discipline of the deadlines they faced, which both demanded and constrained creativity. This was especially true at times of intense conflict (he was writing just after the Great War and during the November Revolution). Journalists were 'propertyless and hence professionally bound,' their occupation 'an absolute gamble in every respect and under conditions that test one's inner security.' The sense of being obligated to employers was connected to the priority placed on advertising revenue over true independence and the absence of both 'genuine leadership' and 'the responsible management of politics' (1946: 96–98). In Tönnies' words, reporters 'must balance the interests of the owner and the party or the government and look out for the public at the same time' (2000: 158).

Across the globe, journalists today are troubled by misbehaving owners, conflicts of interest, disempowerment, and disemployment. They point to the eroded boundary between the editorial and advertising sections of press work (Artemas et al., 2018; Bærug and Harro-Loit, 2012; White, 2017). This was disclosed most shockingly in the *New York Times' Innovation* report of 2014. Propelled by Mark Thompson, the former BBC and future CNN oligarch known for biting a news rival and cutting (others') salaries, it declared an end to that once-prized frontier (Wells and O'Carroll, 2005). The wall between these genres and segments has become 'a curtain,' if it is anything at all (Coddington, 2015).

Critical coverage of business has also been severely impeded by this ethical breakdown (Rafi Atal, 2018). For while corporations and governments that advertise have always sought to wield influence over the press, the extent is becoming greater and more overt, to the point of a 'culture of collaboration' (Li, 2022: 31). Take a peek at newspapers today by contrast with the past and you'll see 'native advertising' perform this function textually, matching occupational misconduct. All content is graphically similar, with minimal efforts to distinguish greed from reportage. Claims to the contrary about differentiation between the categories abound (Sullivan, 2013) but the visual evidence counters those arguments. This amounts to 'an involuntary but fatal censorship whereby, for reasons that are entirely legitimate in themselves (such as advertising revenue, product sales, and so forth), an excess of information is transformed into noise' (Eco, 2020: 54).

Consider these examples. Most young Colombian newspaper and magazine reporters are initially hired through employment exchanges. They are not formally tied to media outlets, instead working with sub-contractors for between six months and a year. If the relevant media outlet considers their work valuable, these jobbing journalists are directly employed. Even then, few receive a living wage or the social benefits of Colombian workers. Reporters therefore take a second job within the same magazine or newspaper: selling advertising space and time to the very officials or business leeches who may also be their sources of information and targets of research. As a consequence, many journalists receive only a small portion of their income directly from their occupation, which they supplement through advertising quotas via a percentage of each sale or by directly charging clients. There is no barrier between editorial and advertising content. And there are more spectacular instances: Colombia's *El Espectador* reported extensively on white-collar crime in the 1980s, focusing on Grupo Grancolombiano, a corporation with interests across finance, manufacturing, and the media. It took a decade for the paper to recover from the resultant loss of advertising revenue—and having its offices bombed (Duzán, 1994; Rathbone, 2013).

In the UK, Peter Oborne left his job as the *Telegraph*'s chief political commentator after a story he was working on about Europe's biggest bank, HSBC, discriminating against Muslim accountholders remained unpublished. The US Department of Justice had labeled HSBC 'the preferred financial institution for drug cartels and money launderers' (2012).[8] Yet the bank's breathtaking money laundering and tax evasion barely rated (or rate) mention in the paper (Boland-Rudder, 2019; Jolly and Agencies, 2021). Meanwhile, the *Telegraph* gave a Cunard liner significant coverage and Hong Kong freedom protests were rendered virtually invisible. The link? HSBC, Cunard, and China's Leninists were among the paper's key advertisers, and the bank had just lent the ailing paper's owners £250 million (Oborne, 2015; Bowers, 2015). Dozens of *Telegraph* journalists expressed outrage about cover-ups by their employer (Cook, 2015). For its part, HSBC has gone merrily on, endorsing suppression of democracy because of the need to 'stabilise Hong Kong's social order' (quoted in Chatterjee and White, 2020). The *Telegraph* loftily denounces 'the way banks intrude into the private lives of customers … to push out customers who do not conform to a political outlook deemed permissible by self-appointed arbiters' ("Banking's," 2023). It remains silent over a preferred lender-advertiser shutting down or refusing to open Muslims' accounts, as does almost the entirety of Anglo journalism (Versi, 2023; Oborne, 2023). To its credit, the paper has at least reported HSBC's East Asian political disgrace (Foy, 2023). But when the *Telegraph*'s mind-boggling mismanagement made it subject to a takeover in 2023 by Abu Dhabi money, the paper had the astonishing hubris to object to the deal because it claimed to prize its reporters being 'independent purveyors of fact and analysis' (Daley, 2023), denouncing the bid as a risk to national security (Williams, 2023). Unlike its bigotry against Islam and funding from the PRC, presumably. The notion of a conflict of interest has been fatally compromised.

Objectivity

A primary justification for journalism is that it claims to tell people the truth, often based on a notion of objectivity. The goal is to advise citizens in a balanced way so they have relevant facts about the world and can intervene in it by lobbying, voting, or otherwise participating. This shibboleth is especially strong in the US, but similar terms, such as professionalism and impartiality, are deployed everywhere. Reporters hold on to these notions with a breathless commitment. It is argued that the discourse of professional objectivity can counter the power of media moguls and political leaders who pour scorn on the notion of a *cordon sanitaire* between state and press (Waisbord, 2013). For many true believers, the Global North's commitment to objectivity is the one precept making journalism worthwhile (Gauthier, 1993). But it relies on problematic theory, political economy, and history.

In ancient, medieval, and modern philosophy, the possibility of objective truth was clear. Finding out what was true was not easy, but it *was* desirable and attainable. There came to be dual models for establishing the nature of reality, namely correspondence and coherence theories. They matched representations against the social world and their own logical systems respectively. Correspondence theories aimed to *present* information, not merely *re*present it; they depended on external corroboration. By contrast, coherence theories assumed the implausibility of a perfect match between reality and understanding, relying instead on a consistent, transparent intellectual method that could be replicated (Malpas, 1992; Rorty, 1981: 178, 333–42). Then came 19th-century empiricism, which supposedly bore 'no trace of the knower' (Daston and Galison, 2007: 17). Researchers disappeared from view, transformed into sightless, invisible recording machines that incorporated information and norms from their more overtly present antecedents. Human values were deemed incapable of verification, as they were hopelessly subjective—intrinsically 'other' than facts (Putnam, 2002: 1).

Against that, we all know the grand yet avowedly *anti*-grand narrative of the 1980s and 1990s that questioned these logics: the postmodern. Originating as a set of bracing intellectual, artistic, and architectural movements, it encouraged the widespread and profound rejection of expertise (Lockie, 2017) and compromised hitherto-dominant means of establishing truth. Supposedly compelling fields of knowledge, such as science, history, religion, and philosophy, lost credibility due to their longstanding service in support of imperialism, slavery, colonialism, capitalism, Maoism, Leninism, fascism, misogyny, inequality, and war (Ross, 1996).

In their place came the *différend*. Certain modes of speech were deemed incommensurate with one another, and deciding between them violated their respective codes of communication (Lyotard, 1988: xi). Denying this irreconcilability ignored one's own conditions of existence to pronounce on fundamentally opposed genres of speech or force them to cohere. Eschewing that, all thought became contingent and multi-perspectival, including scientific method itself. And it is true that even amongst analytic philosophers, attempt after attempt to define truth to their arcane satisfaction failed. Many understand truth relationally rather than axiomatically, in dynamic relation to 'belief, desire, cause, and action' (Davidson, 1996: 265).

These issues are closely linked to objectivity, which is often juxtaposed to commitment (what Gringo J-schools like to call 'advocacy'). That opposition is problematic. Consider academia. The most conventional of professors repeatedly work for and in the name of extramural institutions, such as city governments or companies, and concepts, from military security to political participation. Many US scientists are happy to communicate with journalists to promote their employers and their work (Pew Research Center, 2015). They consider it central to their calling rather than separate from the pursuit of truth, which they always already see as contingent.

Engineering schools produce value-laden notions of urban and rural life and efficiency and effectiveness about everything from buildings to bridges to dams. Business schools forward ideas about capitalism and entrepreneurship as the core of their mission. Biochemistry departments seek corporate partnerships to develop pharmaceuticals. The ties between research universities and the energy sector are manifold, massive—and finally manifest; they are normal (Washburn et al., 2010). The humanities' search for relevance propels it into the imaginary embrace of the creative industries.

These are the lineaments of faculty driven by a desire to transform the world rather than undertake pure research. And so it is in journalism: war correspondents are not impartial about the people they meet in battle, who protect them and whose loved ones they seek to interpellate; food critics like to eat out; sports reporters are fans.

Accounts of the history of objectivity and journalism change with prevailing currents of theory and historiography (Brewin, 2013; Calcutt and Hammond, 2011), but even though contemporary reporters may acknowledge the impossibility of an unvarnished truth, many hold to it as a guide and a prospect. The Anglo world remains wedded to the notion that objectivity is attainable and vital, 'promoting faith in an external truth or ideal, an individualistic viewing position' (Maras, 2013: 1). In lockstep with that, journalism research largely eschews political-economic critiques (for example, St. John III and Johnson, 2012), albeit with honorable exceptions (Schiller, 1981; McChesney, 2003, 2013).

Accounts of newsgathering produced in the Anglosphere often ignore the world history of journalism, professionalism, and objectivity, thanks to a nativist self-absorption that assiduously eschews international political economy (a recent instance is Wallace, 2019). But the idea of journalistic objectivity as a guarantee to readers has an international lineage, with Japanese periodicals boasting of impartiality from the 1870s and their Chinese equivalents from the 1910s. A sweetly romantic notion of capitalism asserts that the commodification of news by wire agencies seeking to sell stories to all points on the political spectrum stimulated objectivity. A similarly romantic notion of socialism sees anti-*bourgeois* reportage requiring the same, albeit with an obsession about eschewing 'tendentiousness' (Tong, 2021). One key geopolitical difference is that reporters in the Global South have focused on nation-building and global and regional inequality more than their equivalents in the rich world. They also tend to debate journalism's unequal creation and exchange of ideas, systematic distortions of international news, and lopsided historiography and theory (Loo, 2019; Cheruiyot, 2021; Mutsvairo et al., 2021).

Since the earliest days of the media in the Global North, truth 'has in effect always been more of a brand than a promise—more of a sales pitch and marketing slogan than any sort of reliable descriptor of product' (Winston and Winston, 2021: 4; also see Earns-Branaman, 2016). The discourse of professionalism and objectivity was not part of 18th- and 19th-century Gringo newspapers. Proprietors and staff were aligned with a wide variety of political, economic, and cultural interests (McChesney, 2013: 204; Park, 1922: 364). But along came diminished costs, increased literacy, and large-scale advertising. The Gilded Age saw periodicals shift from openly expressing political preferences to becoming profit centers. Ease of entry for policy dissidents lessened as major capitalists invested. With concentrated ownership, the new class of mogul feared regulation in a moment of emergent trust-busting. Proprietors developed twin ideas—journalistic independence and professional objectivity—as bulwarks against democratic threats (McChesney, 2003) despite inventing sensationalist journalism, which they legitimized as a response to readers; wishes. Hence the Association of National Advertisers producing its 1913 *Baltimore Truth Declaration*, a code of conduct that specified and denounced misleading marketing. This commitment also coincided with anxiety about state regulation (Lears, 1983: 20).

And on they go. Consider the notorious assertion by the then-president of CBS News, Richard S Salant, that the company's journalists 'cover stories … from *nobody's* point of view' (quoted in Epstein, 1974: ix). This *nostrum* still matters. In practical terms, it means reporters must hide themselves: 'you are, in fact, not "you," but the paper itself.' That necessitates journalists pretending their own positions, desires, theories, methods, and processes are of no import (Wolfe, 2021); nor are those of proprietors, managers, educators, or prevailing ideologies. Objectivity remains a tool, a claim, a desire, and a falsehood, rooted in a mystical, magical potion or process by which 'the news somehow discovers itself,' its definition and treatment determined by political prominence and professional practice, with journalists mediating between institutions and audiences, between public and private, between immediacy and history (Hall, 2021: 235–36).

Whereas commodity signs on show in the media might have begun as reflections of reality, they displace representations of the truth with representations of themselves ('how to describe the weather in a newscast'). Then these two delineable forms of truth and genre grow indistinct. With underlying reality lost, signs become self-referential, with no residual correspondence to the real: they adopt the form of their own simulation (Baudrillard, 1988) ('the weather is what the newscast says it is; the newscast is the thing that describes the weather').

The reality is that the media are industrial products ruled by dominant economic forces that diminish ideological and generic innovation in favor of standardization—a blend of political and economic calculation. Reporters mostly write and speak in ways that are customized to the requirements of the economy and media production: maximization of repetition and minimization of innovation, to diminish risks and costs (Adorno and Horkheimer, 1977).

A particular event blighted Yanqui TV news: Don Hewitt originating *60 Minutes* in 1968. The weekly program soon gained the highest ratings on television, making CBS News profitable for the first time. Decades later, Hewitt admitted that his creation had 'single-handedly ruined television' by establishing the expectation that news reporting make money through an entertainment-based cult of personality (quoted in Barkin, 2003: 53). As a consequence, we get a news world aptly satirized in *Network* (Sidney Lumet, 1976), where TV programming executive Diana Christensen tells reporters what she thinks of their work as she details plans to transfer journalism to the entertainment division:

> It's straight tabloid. You had a minute and a half on that lady riding a bike in Central Park. On the other hand, you had less than a minute of hard national and international news. It was all sex, scandal, brutal crimes, sports, children with incurable diseases and lost puppies. So I don't think I'll listen to any protestations of high standards of journalism. You're right down in the street soliciting audiences like the rest of us.

The news always confronts this 'collective action' problem: sizable groups of people, such as citizens affected by public policy or reporters at work, frequently do not act in rational solidarity, despite their seemingly shared concerns. Such commitments and possibilities are trumped by perceived individual self-interest (Olson, 1971):

> If the television newscasts were watched or newspapers were read solely to obtain the most important information about public affairs, aberrant events of little public importance would be ignored and the complexities of economic policy and quantitative analyses of public problems would be emphasized. When the news is, by contrast, largely an alternative to other forms of diversion or entertainment for most people, intriguing oddities and human-interest items are in demand.
>
> *(Olson, 2000: 94)*

The argument runs that because 'the media are driven by the power and wealth of private individuals,' it becomes normative for them to 'turn private lives into public spectacles. If every private life is now potentially public property, it is because private property has undermined public responsibility.' This is a grand paradox of the contemporary, per newspapers spying on famous people: 'our respect for human privacy ... makes phone hacking ... repugnant, and our respect for private profit ... allows it to flourish' (Eagleton, 2011).

Apart from that trivialization, the news process in capitalist democracies always already involves particular choices, assumptions, and preferences that obscure any notion of objectivity. These include support for free speech, rejection of authoritarianism, presence of high educational levels, and a set of values associated with liberalism and business interests. As such, journalism is dedicated to processes and institutions of inequality, *inter alia*. Its putative guarantee of objectivity becomes a cage, in the sense of a political-economic dependence on highly placed sources and their agendas, and a failure to focus on etiological explanation that does not suit ideological or company priorities (Carey, 1997: 138–39, 161). It also ignores varied news audiences, who have their own versions of facts, as Helen MacGill Hughes explained 80 years ago (1981).

In the 1970s, Raymond Williams developed the idea of residual, dominant, and emergent hegemonies to describe the process whereby economic formations compete over media narratives that legitimize social control and hierarchy. At the time he wrote, core instances of these categories were the remains of empire (residual), a modern mixed economy (dominant), and neoliberal transformation (emergent) (1977). We shall revisit that kind of work in Chapter 1. No Marxist he, but Jim Carey saw the commodification and governmentalization of information during the same period enabling increasingly centralized forms and norms of élite power via professionalism (2009: 129). He recognized that objectivity was an alibi, a ruse, for utilitarian guardians of 'the given social order' (1997: 68).

No wonder Upton Sinclair's self-published critique of press consolidation and its silencing of socialist voices (1919) was wildly popular and influential—other than with the dominant media and academia. No wonder Hunter S Thompson said '[t]he only thing I ever saw that came close to Objective Journalism was a closed-circuit TV setup that watched shoplifters in the General Store at Woody Creek, Colorado. I always admired that machine' (2012: 153).

Thirty years of working in very different societies—the US, Britain, México, Spain, and Colombia—have left me alarmed by the poverty of journalism, especially in Gringolandia, and in particular its claims to objectivity. From listening incredulously in Gotham seminars during the immediate post-Cold War period to hegemons announcing they would re-educate former Soviet reporters on everything from political to economic coverage, to experiencing a vast array of people intoning on topics about which they were spectacularly unqualified to do more than write shoddy first drafts for Wikipedia, I have seen and heard too much.

Mainstream Yanqui news places abundant faith in poorly accredited pseudo-experts; governmental and think-tank press releases; Twitter/X pronouncements from the not-very-great, good, or representative; wire-service *nostra*; scientific 'advances' promising to keep wealthy people alive, slim, and sentient for longer; and foci on psychic interiority. And again and again, as Gaye Tuchman observed six decades ago, the discourse of 'professionalism serves organizational interests by reaffirming the institutional processes in which newswork is embedded' (1980: 12). The news 'is defined not by being, of itself, information, but by being published as such' (Winston and Winston 2021: 4), with objectivity an 'invisible frame' that conceals a multitude of decisions (Schiller, 1981: 2). In Lippmann's words, 'news and truth are not the same thing.' One signals an event as meaningful; the other provides explanatory context. Reporters must confront the fact that they have 'a very small body of exact knowledge' (1998: 358–59). 'Journalism is not a school of perfection'; rather, it 'consists of defining each day in the light of present circumstances' (Camus, 1991: 61, 80).

Yet there have always been alternatives. Until the Second World War, Lettish-, German-, Italian-, and Spanish-language US papers differed from 'the individualism of the commercial press.' Featuring a wide array of socialist and anarchist views, they were not 'business institutions' per the Anglo model (Park, 1922: 361–63, 365). Ethnic broadcasters were at work from the 1920s, and a decade later, Chicago sported basement radio clubs run by second-generation migrant youth in search of cultural experimentation (Cohen, 1989: 17–18). By the 1940s, there were over a hundred non-English-language stations in North America (Barlow, 1988: 84). But the struggle for hegemony between a reactionary nativist capitalist press and a more radical immigrant one was always unequal. Today, only the Spanish language has a thriving news presence, on television, and is similar in tone to English-language norms, albeit less xenophobic and more interested in minority concerns.

Gabriel García Márquez's foundation avows that journalism matters 'como registro histórico, como expresión de la sociedad, como desarrollo del conocimiento y porque fundamenta la libertad de personas y de sociedades' [as an historical register, an expression of society, the development of knowledge, and individual and collective freedom] (Blázquez, 2016). A few hours reading El Salvador's *El Faro* show how remarkable such writing can be when it details and explains violence and corruption (Wallace, 2018).[9] *Ojo Público*[10] in Perú does the same, while *Salud con Lupa* specializes in medical investigations.[11] For those who pursued investigative reporting in the US during the 1960s and 1970s, state and capitalist corruption were so obvious and profound that the idea of presenting two sides to a story in order to appear objective was always already an absurdity. But the long tradition of muckraking and investigative reporting may be dying in the light as it struggles with rapacious institutional owners and the fantasy of impartiality. Most progressive Yanqui reporters find the press closed to their work. It is far from 'free.' Their sense of solidarity is compromised by the capitalist competitiveness generated by the fight to be first to a story, while reporting on deeply political uses of power by the state and others risks disemployment (Borjesson, 2002).

When I lived in Manhattan, the only credible coverage of the country's working class in the *New York Times* was its local section.[12] The Anglo world has no left-wing daily paper per *Libération*,[13] *El Periódico*,[14] *La Jornada*,[15] *Taz*,[16] *l'Humanité*,[17] *La República*,[18] *Chunichi Shinbun*,[19] *Indoleft*,[20] *junge Welt*,[21] *MediaPart*,[22] or *Público*,[23] which are excellent on their own turf. *Rebelión* is a global digest that blends new information and opinion.[24] *MediaPart*, available in French, Spanish, and English, does not include advertising or give editorial power to its board, operating from the perspective that 'Seuls nos lecteurs peuvent nous acheter' [Only our readers can buy us].[25]

I find the progressive English-language press dominated by position-taking, just like its opponents, and lacking actual reporting. There are important exceptions, such as work done by environmental journalists, but liberal and leftist magazines like *Mother Jones*,[26] *The Nation*,[27] *CounterPunch*,[28] *Huffington Post*,[29] *Slate*,[30] *Common Dreams*,[31] *openDemocracy*,[32] *The Progressive*,[33] *ZNet*,[34] *AlterNet*,[35] and *The New Statesman*[36] are laden with belief and argument in place of research. No doubt this is due to lack of funds rather than competence, but the result is demoralizing. *The Guardian*,[37] the one brightish beacon for English-only newspaper readers in the UK, the US, and Australia, embodies 'a liberalism that can pursue equality, celebrate diversity and extol emancipation whilst simultaneously defending the institutions that give rise to inequality, discrimination and militarism' (Freedman, 2021: 15–16). *The Toronto Star* is similar.[38]

The British print media on the whole are profoundly reactionary, whether aimed at the white ruling or working classes. As one insider has come to admit, they amount to 'a venal Tory-supporting press' (Oborne, 2021: 66). The opinion pages of both UK and US financial papers are intensely reactionary, most oleaginously in the case of the *Wall Street Journal*,[39] as exposed by hundreds of its own, horrified employees (Moreno, 2020). Conversely, actual reporting done by *The Financial Times*[40] and *The Economist*[41] can be excellent when propelled by particular liberal virtues: against dictatorship, violence, and demagoguery; for the environment, democracy, and scholarly knowledge. The clue to their value lies in the way Gringo journalists denounce *The Economist* for not doing what they deem 'real' journalism (Zevin, 2019: 4) and the fact that Marx regarded it as required reading, the better to comprehend the 'financial aristocracy' (1996: 100). But like the *Guardian*, those titles fail to problematize capital and its political and intellectual servants.

Consorting with the powerful because they are deemed newsworthy and provide scoops works. Conversely, 'those who are prepared to be critical of the ruler if this is merited, will not have the ruler's confidence … and so will not have access to the source of the relevant information' (Gaukroger, 2012: 126). As a consequence, vital dissenting questions of politics and economics remain uncovered. Witness struggles to publish revelations about espionage, due to the complicity of journalism with spying. Thousands of BBC employees have been vetted by the security services to exclude radicalism from its serried ranks, while the CIA advised the US media for decades on what to cover and how to do so, received detailed information on foreign affairs from complicit journalists, and planted operatives within the press corps (Milne, 2015; Norton-Taylor, 2020; Bernstein, 1977).

In addition, all too often, and across the Anglo world, avowedly objective reportage falls into a bargain-basement-binarism-balance dilemma. Reporters look to sources of authority based on conservative versus liberal positions to claim they are providing accounts from 'both' perspectives. In the US, this feeds into an acceptance of the Democrat-Republican bifurcation of the world (Carey, 1997: 137); '[m]any journalists are comfortable in the apparently centrist terrain between Republicans and Democrats—it coincides, after all, with a notion of objectivity in which the reporter is placed in between the two protagonists' (Lewis, 2001: 86). This serves as a defense against reactionary accusations of dastardly liberalism (Gabler, 2013). The working norm is:

> presentation of "both sides" of an issue with little recourse to independent forms of verification. Thus environmentalists present one set of facts, and corporate interests present another set of facts. … journalists who systematically attempt to verify facts—to say which set of facts is more accurate, for example—run the risk of being accused of abandoning their objectivity. Indeed, when journalists are asked to evaluate competing claims, they invariably fudge the issue by referring to instances of truth and veracity on both sides—a relativist cop-out of the most facile and predictable kind.
> *(Lewis, 2001: 15–16)*

The relevant research shows that while most US journalists say they personally lean toward liberalism and the Democratic Party, this is not reflected in their reporting, so strong is the drive to give two sides to any and every political topic (Hassell et al., 2020).

What Barack Obama has called the 'antiseptic notion of objective journalism' (2008: 73) may offer Gringo reporters a comfortable ideological life. But it diminishes their connection to the real demography of the country, where registered independents comfortably outnumber dedicated followers of the Republican Party, and possibly Democrats, too (Reich, 2023).[42] That binarism is duly repeated by the British, despite the BBC claiming to prefer a doctrine of impartiality, which putatively avoids simplistic bifurcation (Wahl-Jorgensen et al., 2017). In fact the Corporation has always clung to the notion of mediating like a kind parent between competing factions of the body politic/familiar (Hall, 1974).

Weber explained that '[s]*cientifically the middle course is not truer even by a hair's breadth*, than the most extreme party ideals of the right or left. Nowhere are the interests of science more poorly served in the long run than in those situations where one refuses to see uncomfortable facts and the realities of life in all their starkness' (1949: 57–58). Such purported even-handedness does not function in the interests of majorities or minorities, of dissonance or science (Sampedro Blanco, 2023).

The journalist-born-a-slave Ida B Wells, a foundational figure in the struggle for civil rights, sought 'to spread the truth of our cause and insure its success' against a 'Malicious and Untruthful White Press.' She regarded this as a duty for 'wielders of the pen belonging to the race which is so tortured and outraged' (2014: 119, 197, 232). Albert Camus heralded the 'courage and determination' shown by 'journalists of the Resistance' during the fascist occupation of France (1991: 45) and sought 'a journalism of ideas' (1991: 52). Presenting varying sides to a story should see a dialectical analysis that explained to readers the evidence, theories, and methods underpinning perspectives on events (1991: 53). Carl Bernstein insists 'that when you see and hear the widow of one of the three men shot to death and put under a levee in Mississippi, there aren't two sides to that story. In journalism I think we're burdened by the myth of objectivity' (quoted in O'Hehir, 2022).

Brazilian critics equate *doisladismo/jornalismo de dois lados* [two sideism/ journalism of two sides] with totalitarianism, because it insists on fascist and anti-scientific lies and distortions being heard, per coverage of #VidasNegrasImportam [Black Lives Matter][43] by Globonews and CNN Brasil, which also juxtaposed 2020's important syndemic isolation with the desire for a return to football. The networks' interlocutors on such issues include diehard racists and right-wing terrorists (Kartz, 2019; Tsavkko Garcia, 2020).

The white Anglo fetish of 'emotional detachment' ironically 'produces, regulates, amplifies, and mediates' feelings (Lünenborg and Medeiros, 2023: 80). A reliance on problematic but institutionally established 'experts' severely disadvantages civil society, so longstanding and emergent popular concerns may alienate or simply elude mainstream journalism (Sampedro, 2021: 92). We shall see the result in stark relief in Chapters 1 and 2.

Reporters miss out on the knowledge produced by social movements, academia, business, unions, and so on that transcends binaries or gives definitive answers inimical to major parties and the fractions of capital they represent—hence the value of 'movement journalism' per Project South (Simonton, 2017) and Press On, which do not privilege 'turning journalists into soapboxes for activists,' but favor 'collaboration between journalists and grassroots movements' and 'journalism created by oppressed and marginalized people.'[44]

The gadfly Oborne, a Tory who belatedly renounced his support of Brexit and devotion to the right-wing media, learnt the hard way that '[w]e should not go into our trade to become passive mouthpieces of politicians and instruments of their power.' But it happens. During the 2019 British election campaign, UK Prime Minister Boris Johnson told numerous lies on television about both his administration and the opposition; not one was picked up by the journalists involved. Repeated falsehoods were then headlined uncritically by a docile press corps (Oborne, 2021: 18, 31–40).

Biased political coverage from the BBC during the life of administrations and election campaigns discloses its profound commitment to reactionary politics (Lewis, 2014, 2015; Berry, 2013b; Milne, 2015). The Corporation's vast resources[45] produce patchy national reporting (and sub-editing) but fine overseas work, when conducted by local people and outsiders with appropriate linguistic capacities. For example, BBC Mundo's few journalists do excellent reporting, and the World Service is valuable.[46]

But the BBC has long failed to cover the basics of EU policy and its impact on Britain, and decades of mendacious coverage by the *bourgeois* press mean all sources ignore left-wing positions in favor of membership. No wonder popular British knowledge of Europe lags so far behind that of member nations (Hix, 2015). TV coverage of the 2016 plebiscite on leaving the Union gave equal weight to conventional arguments pro and con, but independent experts were only interviewed within that binarism, excluding progressive arguments (Cushion and Lewis, 2017). As the process moved from critique to campaign to implementation, Tory lies were repeated over and over by mainstream journalism (Oborne, 2019). Pro-Brexit voters duly followed the script written by the right, opposing immigration and welfare for fellow-EU citizens, fearing loss of sovereignty, and luxuriating in white imperial fantasies of past and present (Berry et al., 2021).

Others have known about the problem of objectivity for rather longer than those caught up in the particularly dirty world of early 21st-century Anglo politics:

> The ideas of the ruling class are in every epoch the ruling ideas, i.e. the class which is the ruling material force of society, is at the same time its ruling intellectual force. The class which has the means of material production at its disposal, has control at the same time over the means of mental production, so that thereby, generally speaking, the ideas of those who lack the means of mental production are subject to it. The ruling ideas are nothing more than the ideal expression of the dominant material relationships, grasped as ideas.
>
> *(Marx and Engels, 1995)*

The Anglo press has always provided ideological accompaniment to capital, ever since the moment when the *bourgeoisie* 'developed materially' and 'weaned the intelligentsia to its side and created its cultural foundation' (Trotsky, 1977: 44).

Deviating from that path has consequences. I recall being interviewed by network TV about performance-enhancing drugs in baseball. During recording, I spoke of the cavalier use of medication, surgery, and exhortation to make athletes 'play hurt' and other corporate malfeasance that I viewed as the backdrop to substance abuse. Afterward the reporter asked me rather pointedly whether I was part of a movement to legalize recreational drugs. The interview did not go to air. When I appeared live on New York 1, a local cable news channel, shortly after the September 11, 2001 attacks on the US, I was asked to comment on the psychology of terrorists, per 'What makes people do these things?' and 'Are they maladjusted?' I endeavored to direct the conversation toward US support of totalitarian regimes in the Middle East that restricted access to politics and turned religion into a zone of resistance. I spoke of TV journalists' sparse and prejudicial narrative frames and background knowledge. The production staff thanked me for saying the *non dit*, told me that the board lit up with supportive reaction when the program accepted phone calls from the public, and said I'd be invited back. I wasn't.

But even true-believer US journalists are belatedly abjuring 'bothsidesism' (Forman-Katz and Jurkowitz, 2022). The Yanqui news élite has come to acknowledge that the quest for objectivity was defined, anointed, and deployed by a white male enclave that cordoned off both lead stories and executive suites from people of color, who were assigned 'penny crimes' (black-on-black violence) and junior positions (French, 2016; Downie Jr., 2023; Downie Jr. et al., 2023). Just 6% of US journalists are African American and 8% Latin@ (Tomasik and Gottfried, 2023)—groups that comprise a third of the country's population.[47] The recent past has seen uproar among journalists about their oligarchs' racial attitudes, over everything from hiring and firing to reporting and ignoring (Mergerson, 2023; Schmidt, 2023). A 2022 survey of 12,000 Gringo reporters found serious dissatisfaction with the industry's commitments to diversity (Gottfried et al., 2022).

Right across the country, women of color experience marginalization and struggle in their daily work as reporters (Women's Media Center, 2018). TV news sees diversity on camera, in a marketing attempt to match real demography, but off-screen there is much less equitable representation in decision-making positions. White editors and owners in the US publicly applaud/pillory themselves for inclusiveness or its absence (for example, Eller, 2020) without acknowledging their role in resisting diversity, often to the disgust of employees (Waxman, 2020).[48] Much work remains to be done: the *New York Times*[49] and the *Wall Street Journal* found themselves unable to describe Donald Trump's remarks as racist when he proposed dispatching congresswomen of color to what he termed the 'crime-infested places from which they came' (quoted in "How Objectivity," 2020), and NPR stories about communities of color are infrequent, due to the routine invocation by executives of a white, middle-aged, middle-class audience that must not be alienated (Garbes, 2020).

Britain's rhetoric of journalistic inclusion fudges its reality of systematic exclusion (Douglas, 2022). BBC radio producers I have known speak of prejudice against women and people of color in what former Director-General Greg Dyke termed a 'hideously white' workforce, particularly at the managerial level (quoted in "Dyke," 2001). Corporation supporters claim it has made strides to feature more diverse voices as both reporters and experts (Rattan et al., 2019) but women of color still leave the place in significant numbers, exhausted by its barriers to inclusivity (Yossman and Ravindran, 2022). The UK media in general discriminate interpersonally and structurally against black reporters (Al-Kaisy, 2023), and rarely address or recruit those who are basically excluded from British notions of diversity—the hundreds of thousands of French, Polish, Chinese, and Latin American UK residents who are left outside that discourse.

Racism is a problem in other countries with histories of invasion and slavery, such as Colombia and Brazil. Despite their demography, they have comparatively few Afro-descended and indigenous reporters, media executives, politicians, lawyers, or academics. Latin American capital's preference for light-skinned *mestizaje* [mixed-race cultures], combined with the absence of effective affirmative action, militate against generating a sizable black middle class (Tamayo Gaviria, 2022; Instituto Interamericano de Derechos Humanos, 2007; Ferreira, 2021; Jornalistas and Cia, 2021).

Gender is another prejudicial determinant in journalism's division of labor. In US newsrooms, women dominate education, health, and social policy. Men hold sway over politics and economics—the headline fields (Tomasik and Gottfried, 2023). A 2020 study of reporters in Africa, South Asia, Britain, and Gringolandia discloses that fewer women are hired, quoted, and discussed by the *bourgeois* media today than last century, especially in the field of politics (Kassova, 2020). NPR is notorious for interviewing pale males (Jensen, 2019); hence the necessity for resources such as 'Women Also Know Stuff. You Should Ask Them About It.'[50] That pattern also applies in contemporary Europe (Council of Europe, 2020) and to centuries of British journalism (Lansdall-Welfare et al., 2017). French women reporters report discrimination at work and intimidation for publicizing the threats they receive (Montañola et al., 2022).

In sum, the record of objectivity as a practice discloses a tendency to conceal rather than be transparent; to draw on binaristic accounts of the truth, to the exclusion of definitive findings and profound uncertainty alike; and to provide a cloak for parthenogenetic corporate and managerial policies and preferences. This is a story of restricted occupational opportunities, unrestricted work harassment, and misogynistic coverage. The pattern repeats again and again (Byerly, 2013; Shor et al., 2015; Marron, 2021). A new journalism can only be built from the ruins of such failures.

Insecurity

We are often told today that journalism is in crisis. This is variously attributed to the folly of newspapers making copy available free online while charging for it in print; advertisers moving their money elsewhere; the charge of finance-based conglomerates into media ownership, driven by Wall Street stock valuations rather than the public interest; the spread of fake news; the role of aggregating communications firms masquerading as 'social' media; and the notion that anyone, anywhere, any time is a reporter because they can tap their thumbs.

The profession is running scared in the Global North, as proprietors cut costs; interlace entertainment, advertising, sports, and news; lose their commitment to the public interest; turn covetous eyes to opportunity cost's alternative valuations; and behave abominably to their workers. The contradiction between the supposed relative autonomy of the profession versus paymasters' and governments' desires sees sovereign expression severely compromised (Galtung, 1995). More and more journalists face precarity and rely on wire services and press releases to select topics and produce news, all the while writing and speaking in different outlets owned by their masters (Lewis et al., 2008).

There was a 26% drop in US news employment between 2008 and 2021, principally due to the closure of small titles. The decrease hasn't been compensated by online positions (Walker, 2021). It can hardly be a surprise, then, that 87% of journalism grads in the US wish they could change their major. That is far and away the worst record of any discipline, though it is a comment on the quality of their education as well as its vocational success (Dickler, 2022). In France, the profession has become more female, more precarious, and less numerous (Charon, 2018). Across Latin America, the COVID-19 syndemic was matched by another—the disemployment of journalists and erosion of their working conditions, as national radio and TV reporters labored without contracts and print journalists outside the metropoles were paid insufficient salaries to survive. Minus public-health protection, hundreds died from the coronavirus. Why? Argentina, for example, has no union representation and workers confront severe reprisals when they seek to organize ("Los derechos," 2022).

Meanwhile, more and more news organizations that once dismissed the 'legacy' media as anachronistic are in the 'internet graveyard' (calling *Gawker, Toast, BuzzFeed News, Input, Refinery29* [described by former employee Sesali Bowen as 'the official publication of White Feminism™'], *Outline, Splinter, Vice,* and numerous others that may have begun with politics but quickly—and fruitlessly—articulated themselves to the lifestyle purchases of the youthful US *bourgeoisie*) (Bowen quoted in Flynn, 2020). As Google has claimed their audiences, these self-styled disrupters' stock-market 'valuations' have plunged, in some cases from the billions to the nugatory, their long lunches no longer funded by investors (Demopoulos, 2023; Sweney, 2023; "Declaration of Frank A Pometti," 2023).

Around the globe, there is self-censorship in newsrooms, for professional, procedural, organizational, reference-group, economic, and political reasons (Hanitzsch et al., 2010).[51] '[M]edia capture' jeopardizes independent reporting, as journalists concentrate on satisfying oligarchs and oligopolists (Schiffrin, 2017; Dragomir, 2018). The spread of 'fake' news through churnalism and trolling has become a topic of critique in the Oval Office, the UK Parliament, EU headquarters, and everywhere in-between (Barclay, 2018; Marcos Recio et al., 2017; House of Commons, 2019; Renda, 2018).

Reporters Without Borders' *World Press Freedom Index* makes it clear that the use of false information by PR/strategic communications, journalism's 'evil twin' (Ehrenreich, 2006: 16), has reached catastrophic levels in terms of polarization within and between countries (2022). The US Bureau of Labor Statistics predicts job growth for the evil twin of 8% through 2031, amounting to over 25,000 openings a year—well above occupations in general (2023a). By contrast, the decade is expected to see a 9% decline in the number of journalists (2023b) and the respective starting salaries show a disparity commensurate with corporate valuation (2023a, 2023b). The trend is dramatic—a move away from critical public-interest work and into promotion. The PR labor force is overwhelmingly female. As labor market signals travel, men may move into the field (Sherwood et al., 2018).

When I was 'coming through,' as my fellow Americans like to put it, those of us on the US left were prone to distrust the *bourgeois* media. Now the far right and the conservative white working class often evince a proverbial loathing for mainstream reporters, based on the stance of reactionary TV, radio, and news outlets themselves, amateur media, and paid propaganda posing as organic protest. In most other countries, this is not the case, but it is so in similarly provincial right-wing places like South Korea, Japan, and Hungary (Newman et al., 2019).

All too often, the news incarnates 'the specious present' (Anon, 1882: 168), an imagined world that appears to be contemporary, but is forged from partial knowledge of the very recent past (Park, 1940: 676); hence the tricks of 'news management':

> I have always taken the view that if, by some chance, I discovered that tomorrow's newspapers were going to take up some wrong I had committed that would cause me serious harm, the first thing I'd do would be plant a bomb outside the local police headquarters or railway station. The next day the newspaper front pages would be full of it and my personal misdemeanour would end up as a small inside story.
>
> *(Eco, 2020: 46–47)*

The overall impact is telling. Gallup has polled Gringos over 50 years about their trust in the *bourgeois* media. The cumulative results show a very significant decline, from two-thirds to three-quarters believing reportage in the 1970s to 40% in 2020 and 26% in 2022, with the right being the principal doubters (Brenan, 2020; Gallup and Knight Foundation, 2023). In Spain, France, Italy, and the UK, just a quarter of the population trusts the news media (Pew Research Center, 2018).

There is a clear correlation between the demise of the local press in the US and citizens' declining participation in municipal politics (Hayes and Lawless, 2021): 'the information they needed to self-govern' is no longer available through a journalism 'decimated by economic and technological challenges' (Pian Chan, 2017: 1). More than half of US counties have no credible source of local news, and the country as a whole is on track to have lost a third of the newspapers it had boasted in 2005 within two decades. Working-class communities suffer disproportionally (Abernathy, 2023). That experience is not universal, but it resonates with many other countries (Gulyas and Baines, 2020). For example, in Colombia, *Cartografías de la Información* [Information Maps] produced by the Fundación para la Libertad de Prensa [Foundation for Press Freedom] have identified 'el periodismo local se extingue' [the extinction of local journalism].[52]

The concept of 'meanwhile' still applies, but the idea of journalism as something experiential, based on walking, talking, and observing—so central to its long history—is compromised (Carey, 2007; O'Hehir, 2022). This trend coincides with US journalists becoming more urban, disproportionately educated at fancy schools by contrast with the overall population, and associated with centers of power, as opposed to when local news mattered and journalists were seen, heard, and read within specific communities. Unsurprisingly, Yanqui reporters are liable to attack by nativist news outlets that claim to represent the flyover states and their purportedly neglected interests (Kreiss, 2019). That in turn relates to the US public's skepticism about cherished journalistic principles: while two-thirds of the adult population think knowing facts is helpful, well under a third agree that identifying and explaining social problems is of value. There is a widespread preference for hierarchy and loyalty over expertise and problematization (American Press Institute, 2021).

The same applies in Britain, where journalism is increasingly middle class; two-thirds of reporters are from powerful backgrounds, behind only medicine among the professions. This is a product of requiring graduate-school education, interning for free, and working on a freelance basis (Social Mobility Commission, 2016; Sutton Trust and Social Mobility Commission, 2019). Jon Snow, for decades one of the nation's foremost TV news anchors, confessed in 2017 that 'in an increasingly fractured Britain, we are comfortably with the elite, with little awareness, contact, or connection with those not of the elite.' Hostility flows from this disarticulation, as well as incomprehension.

Threats confronting the profession are not only about ownership, the labor process, and popular attitudes. There is also violence. Reporters

> often venture into the darkest corners to shed light on current events. A considerable number of them are subjected to intimidation, physical violence, kidnapping or illegal detention in direct relation to their work and, in extreme cases, they can be killed because of their professional activity. Some are killed in war or conflict zones or in situations of civil unrest, while others are the specific targets of homicidal violence.
> *(United Nations Office on Drugs and Crime, 2013)*

The 'killing of a journalist is a sign of deteriorating respect for human rights.' It frequently generates additional repressive reactions by the state, furthering the frequency of violent political crimes (Gohdes and Carey, 2017). Countries that lack truly independent judiciaries and a separation of powers in particular lurch toward such violations (Whitten-Woodring, 2009).

Given discrepancies in the collection of data, it's difficult to establish the global incidence of violence against journalists and responses to it. The Committee to Protect Journalists estimates almost 2,000 reporters were killed worldwide between 1992 and 2022.[53] And no, it's not principally a problem for white war correspondents from wealthy countries who venture into lands of which they know little or nothing, what a self-critical Fergal Keane came to realize was a 'neo-colonial form of journalism' (quoted in Anderson, 2023).

Although such deaths are often heavily reported as headline stories, local investigative reporters are much more vulnerable: 93% of journalists murdered between 2002 and 2013 were working in their own countries, often executed by criminal gangs threatened with media exposure (González de Bustamante and Relly, 2016; Gohdes and Carey, 2017; International Federation of Journalists, 2019). Such violence occurs both in overtly conflicted nations and putatively peaceful ones (von der Lippe and Ottosen, 2016; González de Bustamante and Relly, 2016; Löfgren Nilsson and Örnebring, 2017; Jungblut and Hoxha, 2016; Garcés and Arroyave, 2017): 'aggression against those who tell the truth does not discriminate between times of peace and war, professional journalists or citizens, not even the channel through which they send their messages' (Suárez Serrano, 2016: 27).

Latin America is a key site,[54] with 139 reporters killed between 2011 and 2020, the majority in Colombia, Brazil, Honduras, and México, generally in small towns where they were dutifully covering corruption, criminality, and politics. Only a few were active in zones of conventional military conflict. Most were precariously employed, freelancing for various media organizations. They were targeted individually, close to home, and professionally (Reporters Without Borders, 2021; del Palacio Montiel, 2015). Meanwhile, the Council of Europe rates press freedom across that continent 'more fragile than at any time since the end of the Cold War' because of violence and obstructiveness. Death threats doubled in 2018 on the previous year, as did impunity (2019: 5, 8, 16). Those numbers looked insignificant by contrast with 2021, when physical assaults on journalists grew 61% year on year (Council of Europe, 2022: 9–10). In the US, hundreds of journalists are assaulted each year, mostly by police and far-right protestors.[55] The first few weeks of the Israeli Defense Force's incursions into Gaza saw 63 media workers/reporters murdered, of whom 56 were Palestinian. The invasion had killed as many in two months as died in 20 years of the conflict in Việt Nam ("Journalist Casualties," 2023; Ricchiardi, 2006).

The proliferation of online platforms means reporters 'are more visible and accessible than ever, and audience members have an unprecedented opportunity to (anonymously) express whatever sentiments they wish to journalists, in particular in the online context' (Löfgren Nilsson and Örnebring, 2016: 881; also see Yardi and Boyd, 2010). Prevalent forms of harassment have expanded from physical attacks to swearing, defamation, calumny, trolling, stalking, and threats of sexual assault and murder. Pressure comes not only from systematically violent groups, or parties to particular disputes, but everyday citizens who dislike what they read (Cook and Heilmann, 2013). Such aggression stimulates cultural and emotional differences; some reporters react to threats with greater resilience—or foolhardiness—than others (Høiby and Ottosen, 2015). Across the globe, the frequently gendered nature of threats is clear; an international survey of women journalists saw three-quarters of respondents indicate they had encountered online violence (Ferrier, 2019; Posetti and Shabbir, 2022). And while women war correspondents sometimes gain unique *entrée* to human-interest stories, personal confessions, and family perspectives, they are routinely excluded and patronized by everyone from translators to editors-in-chief—told that the front is no place for them (von der Lippe and Ottosen, 2016).

Conclusion

In keeping with what I have outlined above, the backdrop to much of this volume is a conjuncture of binarism, labor exploitation, proprietorial malfeasance, negative public opinion, and rampant violence. The chapters to come are equally driven by a cosmic ambivalence about the news today, a dissatisfaction with reportage of crucial elements of quotidian and conjunctural life, and a desire for professionals in the wealthy world to depart from their business-as-usual parthenogenesis. My attempts to do so are trans-historical and trans-geographical, drawing on numerous influences from philosophy, sociology, anthropology, political science, communications, and cultural and media studies, notably international political economy.

Where this Introduction has focused principally on historical and philosophical issues, the chapters to come are both theoretical and applied. I'll consider four key aspects of contemporary journalism in terms of theoretical relevance and historical tasks:

- Citizenship: political, economic, and cultural
- Environment: the climate crisis and reporters' material impact
- Sports: the importance of the popular; and
- Technology: its former, current, and future significance

Why those four subjects? In each case, they are central journalistic topics and involve the complicity of reporters. As this Introduction has shown, notions of citizenship legitimize journalism in its core mission. The particular issues addressed in Chapter 1 focus on limit cases of the relationship between the news and other institutions, namely the devastation of war and the interaction of free speech and religion. I have selected the environment as Chapter 2, because it has become a public-policy emergency, and journalism's role in that crisis has been crucial. Sports are selected for Chapter 3 because, for many people, they *are* the news, the section of the paper or application most regularly and passionately devoured, several times a day. Again, social, political, and cultural pressures both bear on journalism and are incarnate in it. Chapter 4 is on technology, important on its own terms and both heralded and feared by reporters.

I write as someone in favor of a democratic socialism driven by feminist, queer, and postcolonial urges, recognizing that 'all politics requires economic, political and cultural conditions of existence' (Hall, 2013: 2). Journalism well done is critical to any such endeavor. It is the cultural opportunity *par excellence* to reimagine society based on actually existing circumstances, thanks to what should be a blend of political economy, ethnography, and textual analysis that 'remains fundamentally open to the contingency of historical movement and change' (Hall, 1995: 33).

The query animating my investigations here returns again and again, both implicitly and explicitly: why journalism? The Conclusion argues for an answer to that dilemma. It will involve a fundamental shift in how reporters, proprietors, professors, students, and states view and reproduce the profession, in the spirit of Umberto Eco's words: '[l]a función del cuarto poder es ciertamente la de controlar y criticar a los otros poderes tradicionales' [The function of the fourth estate is to control and criticize the other traditional powers] (1995).

It's become a *donnée* that for democracies to function, reporters must provide 'organized, expert scrutiny of government' (Stewart, 1975: 634) and cover human rights, economy, society, government, science, and culture. The fundamental idea is to draw citizens into the electoral and policy process, ensuring informed public consent and dissent; journalism should engage wider questions than the deracinated world of Anglo political science (Renwick

Monroe, 2005). For now, things are all too often just as they were 60 years ago: '[f]reedom of the press is guaranteed only to those who own one' (Liebling, 1964: 30). Scott maintained that the news 'may educate, stimulate, assist, or it may do the opposite. It has, therefore, a moral as well as a material existence, and its character and influence are in the main determined by the balance of these two forces. It may make profit or power its first object, or it may conceive itself as fulfilling a higher and more exacting function' (2017).

For those of us working in the Marxist tradition, this means reportage is 'embedded as a social practice,' a process that sees 'events in the socio-historical world' become news via 'ideological production' (Hall, 2021: 105). The interrelationship of the moral and the material, the ideological and the practical, is hence the key to answering 'why journalism?'

Notes

1 *Huffington Post, Inland Empire, Frente Transversal, O Globo Revista da TV, Outsports, Rezagos, Desde Abajo, European Financial Review, ZNet, openDemocracy, The Conversation, Chronicle of Higher Education, Campus Review, Printasia, Zócalo, EduFactory, Los Angeles Review of Books, Screen International, Times Higher Education, Arena Magazine, Business Review Weekly, The Thumb Print, The Advocate, Le Partage, Asia Sentinel, Daily Telegraph, Ground Report, Science 2.0, The Spectator Australia, Miller-McCune, Filmnews, Australian Left Review*. One regular column lasted a decade (*Psychology Today*, with Richard Maxwell).
2 *New York Times, Guardian, Press-Enterprise, The Age, The Australian, Página 12, Sydney Morning Herald, New Zealand Herald.*
3 KPFK *Background Briefing* 2011–13; BBC World Television 1999.
4 For example, the BBC, *La Diaria, The Telegraph, Guardian, Financial Times, Radiocatalunya, La Vanguardia, West Australian,* SBS, *El Punto, Australian Financial Review, El Universal, Australian, Salon,* NPR, *Lima Cultura, Techworld, Computerworld,* PC World, *Sky News, Globo, Magis, Windsor Star, Monitor Universitario, La Jornada Jalisco, Los Angeles Review of Books, La Jornada, Press-Enterprise, Hollywood Reporter, Montreal Gazette, Kansas City Star, San Jose Mercury, Sacramento Bee, Christian Science Monitor,* France 24, *Globouniversidade,* CNN, PBS, *Vancouver Courier,* CBS, *New York Times, Philadelphia Inquirer, Washington Post, Star Phoenix, Boston Globe, St. Louis Post-Dispatch, USA Today, Los Angeles Times, Sydney Morning Herald, Courier-Mail, San Francisco Chronicle, Seattle Times, El País, The Hindu, Seoul Times, Newsday, Toronto Star, The Age, Denver Post,* Tercer Canal, Canal 44, Channel Seven, Channel Ten, ZDF, Al Jazeera, CCTV, Canal Plus, Food Network, ESPN, NBC, New York 1, Metro, The History Channel, CNBC, A&E, Fox News, ABC, KPFK, RCN, Caracol, KCBS, Sveriges Radio, CBC, All-India Radio, Radio Free Europe, *inter alia.*
5 http://www.ccijp.net/article-69-definition-du-journaliste-professionnel-et-contrat-de-travail.html.
6 Bloviation refers to pompous speech—it has been in journalistic use for a century, supposedly typifying the addresses of Yanqui President Warren Harding.
7 The work is also limited by the fact that I can only review materials in four languages.

8 In the interests of full disclosure, I should mention that when I returned to live in the UK after four decades away, HSBC was the only bank that would permit me to open an account. I was a British citizen and had full-time employment, but only a kindly Iranian immigrant banker employed there was willing to help me. Other British banks turned me away, and unpleasantly.
9 https://elfaro.net/es?rf=portada.
10 https://ojo-publico.com/.
11 https://saludconlupa.com/comprueba/.
12 I owe this insight to my late friend Randy Martin.
13 https://www.publico.es/.
14 https://www.elperiodico.com/es/.
15 https://www.jornada.com.mx/.
16 https://taz.de/.
17 https://www.humanite.fr/.
18 https://larepublica.pe/.
19 https://www.chunichi.co.jp/.
20 https://www.indoleft.org/.
21 https://www.jungewelt.de/.
22 https://www.mediapart.fr/.
23 https://www.liberation.fr/.
24 https://rebelion.org/.
25 https://www.mediapart.fr/journal/france/020719/mediapart-rend-son-independance-irreversible?userid=ff1ceb71-e66f-4e91-b4ce-3f6546e67d52.
26 https://www.motherjones.com/.
27 https://www.thenation.com/.
28 https://www.counterpunch.org/.
29 https://www.huffpost.com/.
30 https://slate.com/.
31 https://www.commondreams.org/.
32 https://www.opendemocracy.net/.
33 https://progressive.org/.
34 https://znetwork.org/.
35 https://www.alternet.org/.
36 https://www.newstatesman.com/.
37 https://www.theguardian.com/international.
38 https://www.thestar.com/.
39 https://www.wsj.com/.
40 https://www.ft.com/.
41 https://www.economist.com/.
42 https://worldpopulationreview.com/state-rankings/registered-voters-by-party.
43 https://www.instagram.com/explore/tags/VidasNegrasImportam/.
44 https://www.presson.media/.
45 https://www.bbc.co.uk/news.
46 https://www.bbc.com/mundo;https://www.bbc.co.uk/sounds/play/live:bbc_world_service.
47 https://www.census.gov/library/visualizations/interactive/racial-and-ethnic-diversity-in-the-united-states-2010-and-2020-census.html.
48 https://twitter.com/PiyaSRoy/status/1268374028634386436?ref_src=twsrc%5Etfw%7Ctwcamp%5Etweetembed%7Ctwterm%5E1268374028634386436%7Ctwgr%5E361c030b48c7624bbf13372dbe23d6518cb93e05%7Ctwcon%5Es1_&ref_url=https%3A%2F%2Fwww.thewrap.com%2Fclaudia-eller-exits-variety%2F.
49 https://www.nytimes.com/.
50 https://www.womenalsoknowstuff.com/.

51 This is discernable through numerous methods, from the ethnographic to the textual (Tao et al., 2017).
52 https://flip.org.co/cartografias-informacion/.
53 https://cpj.org/data/killed/?status=Killed&motiveConfirmed%5B%5D=Confirmed&motiveUnconfirmed%5B%5D=Unconfirmed&type%5B%5D=Journalist&type%5B%5D=Media%20Worker&start_year=1992&end_year=2023&group_by=year.
54 https://cpj.org/americas/.
55 https://pressfreedomtracker.us/.

1
CITIZENSHIP (WITH BILL GRANTHAM)

This chapter examines citizenship and journalism. It makes particular reference to two countries renowned for their democratic rebellions and journalistic histories—the US and France.[1] The first section looks at theories of citizenship, then sees how they have been incarnated in Anglo reportage, with a particular focus on politics, economics, and culture. The second considers the biggest contemporary controversy over free speech—the right of the Parisian satirical magazine *Charlie Hebdo*[2] to represent a prophet, a veritable limit case. The point is to show how traditional justifications for journalism, based on communicating knowledge of public-policy questions to citizens, extend beyond the conventions of capital-P politics to engage the economy and culture in both obvious and surprising ways.

The last 200 years have produced three zones of citizenship, with partially overlapping but somewhat distinct historicities. Classical political theory accorded representation to citizens through the state. The modern, economic, addendum was that the state promised a minimal standard of living. The postmodern, cultural, guarantee was access to the technologies of communication. The political covers the right to reside and vote; the economic, the right to work and prosper; and the cultural, the right to know and speak. The first category concerns political rights; the second, material interests; and the third, cultural representation. This chapter examines them serially.

One might assume that in journalistic terms, the three kinds of citizenship refer to distinct beats, respectively congress or a chamber of deputies (politics), stock exchanges or board rooms (economics), and theater or cinema (culture). There is a germ of truth in this distinction, but the categories inflect and overdetermine one another as their relative importance shifts over time.

They also help to account for the condition of much journalism, along with the pressures imposed by new kinds of shareholders and technologies.

Political citizenship

Democracy is conventionally said to arise and thrive in the interactions of governments and populations, with the US and French Revolutions as its model. Political citizenship confers the right to vote, to be represented in government, and to enjoy physical security. That notion is bounded by countries whose inhabitants recognize one another as political citizens and use that status to invoke the greater good.

The journalistic corollaries of political citizenship are regular reportage of domestic political affairs, with a focus on lawmakers' deliberations and judicial review; the associated notion that representative government depends on an open press to explain social issues as defined by popular movements, technocrats, and parliamentary parties; electoral coverage; and a concentration on international relations in terms of local and global security. The intent is to draw citizens into policy processes through informed public comment, dissent, and consent that:

> subjects citizens' beliefs and opinions to critical scrutiny, assists the formation of an informed public opinion and collective will, provides the only effective check on the government, enables citizens to create a vibrant civil society, and in general ensures an easy and constant flow of ideas among citizens and between them and the government.
>
> *(Parekh, 2017: 932)*

The idea of free speech as central to citizenship is often linked to the British journalists John Trenchard and Thomas Gordon, whose *Cato's Letters* columns of the 1720s maintained that '[w]ithout freedom of thought, there can be no such thing as wisdom; and no such thing as publick liberty, without freedom of speech: Which is the right of every man [*sic*], as far as by it he does not hurt and control the right of another; and this is the only check which it ought to suffer, the only bounds which it ought to know' (1723: 336). Trenchard and Gordon were extensively quoted in Britain and North America, not least because they shared with imperialists and colonists an insistence on reserving the right of political speech to free men. Speech was a sign of racial and gender supremacy (Dabhoiwala, 2022, 2023).

The US represents itself as the bastion of expressive totality via its 18th-century project of untrammeled noise made by white, property-owning men. That has expanded over time to include all free adults. To live there, as we both did for more than two decades, is to experience a constantly replenished fantasy of unrestricted speech, where competing perspectives allegedly forge the truth, unencumbered by censorship. For its part, France, where Bill also resided, takes open expression as a founding *donnée* of the Republic. But the reality in both countries is very different. We therefore pose queries that may both underpin and undermine journalism: what *is* 'free speech' and how does it relate to the prevailing political economy?

Some protection for speech existed in the various US state charters enacted prior to the Federal Constitution, but its *locus classicus* is the latter's fabled First Amendment, when the founding parents sought 'to create a fourth institution outside the Government as an additional check on the three official branches' (Stewart, 1975: 634). The Amendment says:

> Congress shall make no law respecting an establishment of religion, or prohibiting the free exercise thereof; or abridging the freedom of speech, or of the press; or the right of the people peaceably to assemble, and to petition the government for a redress of grievances.[3]

Its original six guarantees—against the creation of a state religion and for freedom of worship, speech, the press, assembly, and the right to seek redress from the government—have evolved into more general protections of expression and activism. The apparently limiting language of the Amendment—'Congress shall make no law'—has been taken by successive Supreme Courts to cover all three levels of government and to protect not only individual people but also media institutions, so crucial is their role in democracy (Stewart, 1975: 634). The state went further to enable this watchdog function. Per longstanding British norms, from the 19th century, the US Post Office Department, as it was then known, facilitated political conversation by underwriting the transportation of newspapers and magazines, while the Federal Government once took on the responsibility of enabling free speech by subsidizing its distribution—not just getting out of the way or regarding it as identical to other commodities. This helped produce diverse reportage and opinion (McChesney, 2013; Silberstein-Loeb, 2014).

In US jurisprudence, the historical means of regulating expression is to say that a particular form does not constitute speech. Examples have included defamation, blasphemy, sedition, 'fighting words,' pornography, and motion pictures. Some of those genres have since been re-anointed within First Amendment protection. Others have not. Many issues continue to stem from the quandary 'What is speech?' So, is burning the national flag a speech act? (yes). Is legislation nominating English as the national language unconstitutional? (yes). Can governments erect religious statuary? (no). May a person who peacefully urges citizens to refuse the draft in wartime be treated as a criminal? (yes, because that is the equivalent/obverse of shouting 'Fire!' in a theater when there is none, which frightens crowds and draws in public resources for no good reason). Hate speech and Holocaust denial are illegal in France, whereas in the US, they are more the province of social censure, albeit with some state sanctions (Tourkochoriti, in press). Most notably for this chapter, satire is accorded special protection in France because it is associated with individual freedom to express oneself, which trumps collective notions such as religious solidarity or hurt feelings (Alicino, 2015). It forms part of the French Revolution's 1789 *Déclaration des Droits de l'Homme et du Citoyen* [*Declaration of the Rights of Man and of the Citizen*].[4] The right to free speech for the press was enshrined legislatively in 1881 and blasphemy became a right rather than a crime (Janssen, 2015; Fourest, 2015: 13).

For critics like Stanley Fish, limits to speech emerge not only in cases when governments must deal with the damage that open discourse can cause (1994). Rather, the *very idea* relies on limits: the notion that speech has no material consequences other than the exchange of views does not guarantee protection if it promotes actions that may affect others. Consider the complexities posed by speech-act theory's notion of the performative, which creates something, versus the constative, which describes it. 'I thee wed' are not just words. They enact a legal relationship, with lasting implications not only for the parties concerned, but taxation, public expenditure, healthcare, divorce, alimony, and inheritance, *inter alia*. The distance between action and speech is compromised (Austin, 1962).

Limitations on expression flourish in every home of free speech. In Britain, Milton was happy 'to suppress the suppressors themselves'—a means of denying Catholics the free-speech rights he claimed for his own sect.[5] The *Déclaration* avows that 'No man [sic] ought to be molested on account of his opinions, not even on account of his religious opinions, provided his avowal of them does not disturb the public order established by law' and '[t]he unrestrained communication of thoughts and opinions being one of the most precious rights of man, every citizen may speak, write, and publish freely, provided he is responsible for the abuse of this liberty, in cases determined by law.'[6] JS Mill famously put it this way:

> opinions lose their immunity [from sanction], when the circumstances in which they are expressed are such as to constitute their expression a positive instigation to some mischievous act. An opinion that corn-dealers are starvers of the poor, or that private property is robbery, ought to be unmolested when simply circulated through the press, but may justly incur punishment when delivered orally to an excited mob assembled before the house of a corn-dealer, or when handed about among the same mob in the form of a placard.
>
> *(1859)*

Then as now, free-speech supporters confront difficulties to do with defining speech, assessing whether it is in the public interest and determining how it is phrased—as information, opinion, or demagoguery. And further restrictions apply to who *owns* speech. For instance, the US Copyright Act of 1976 as subsequently amended incorporates the doctrine of Fair Use to manage restrictions on free speech generated by intellectual property (17 U.S.C. §§ 107). It grants limited rights, for instance, to comment on and even *through* texts produced by others.

It is crucial that citizens of past, present, and future empires and countries ponder the relationship between political economy and speech. Here, we address coverage of a universal aspect of political citizenship—collective security/militarism.

War

The Anglo media have an undistinguished history of fanning chauvinistic flames at times of war, potential and actual (Innis, 1986: 163). As Jack London understood, 'American journalism has its moments of fantastic hysteria … when it is on the rampage' (2010: 67). US news relies on official sources, dating from the evolution of journalistic codes and norms mentioned in the Introduction—tools for monopolistic owners to distract attention from their market domination by proclaiming a non-partisan professionalism while shadowing powerbrokers who could theoretically exercise anti-trust tools (Clark and McChesney, 2001; McChesney, 2003; Herman, 1999: 83, 87, 158). Reporters refer to the White House, the State Department, and the Pentagon as their 'Golden Triangle' of sources (Love, 2003: 246). Those relationships are mobilized as required by *raison d'état*.

That said, 50 years ago, newspaper revelations about governmental lies re the American War in Việt Nam saw Supreme Court justice Hugo Black proudly announce that 'paramount among the responsibilities of a free press is the duty to prevent any part of the government from deceiving the people and sending them off to distant lands to die of foreign fevers and foreign shot and shell' ("*New York Times* Company," 1971 403 U.S. 713).[7] What happened to denature that record?

The legacy of *60 Minutes* has been a race to domestic ignorance in search of commercial success. US TV coverage of governmental, military, and international affairs dropped from 70% of network news in 1977 to 60% in 1987 and 40% in 1997.[8] In 1988, each network dedicated about 2,000 minutes to international news. A decade later, that figure had halved, with about 9% of the average newscast covering anything 'foreign.' By 2019, the figure was a third by contrast with 1988. Between May 2000 and August 2001, just 22% of network news was international—ten points below, for example, its British and South African equivalents, and 20 points below Germany—and 3% of US coverage addressed foreign policy. In 2000, three stories from beyond the US (apart from the Olympics) made it into the networks' 20 most-covered items, and they were tightly linked to domestic issues: the Miami-Cuba custody dispute over Elián González, the second Intifada, and the bombing of the USS Cole off Yemen. The main broadcast networks closed most of their investigative sections and foreign *bureaux*. Whereas ABC News had once maintained 17 offices overseas, that number fell to seven. CBS had eight journalists covering the rest of the world (Miller, 2006; *Tyndall Report*, 2019). Africa was essentially invisible (Golan, 2008).

Because what was defined as terrorism mostly occurred outside the US prior to 2001, it was not rated as newsworthy: throughout the 1970s and 1980s, *New York Times* reportage of overseas terror took up less than 0.5% of the paper (Love, 2003: 248). In the first days after September 11 that year, 68% of the US population understood that the attack was linked to their country's ties to Israel. Within a month, the proportion had fallen to 22% (Abrahamian, 2003: 538). In the next seven months, *US News & World Report*'s explanations focused entirely on Al-Qaeda and domestic security failings (Gerges, 2003: 79, 87 n. 9). From September 2001 to December 2002, network news coverage of the attacks and their aftermath basically ignored a stream of relevant topics: Zionism, US foreign policy and business interests, and life after the invasion of Afghanistan (McDonald and Lawrence, 2004: 336–37; Traugott and Brader, 2003: 186–87, 183–84; *Tyndall Report*, 2003).

At the height of imperialistic fervor came ABC's *Profiles from the Front Lines* (2003), a 'reality' series produced by Hollywood action-adventure maven Jerry Bruckheimer about troops fighting for empire that modeled the subsequent embedding of reporters in Iraq (Livingston et al., 2005: 49).[9] Conversely, thousands of civilian Afghan deaths covered by South Asian, South-East Asian, Western European, and Arabic news services went essentially unnoticed by Gringos, because they could not be 'verified' by US journalists and officials (Miller, 2007). CNN instructed presenters to mention September 11 whenever Afghan suffering was discussed, and Walter Isaacson, the network's president, deemed it 'perverse to focus too much on the casualties or hardship' (quoted in Kellner, 2003: 107, 66). His rewards have been many, the latest including an endowed chair at Tulane University in 'American History and Values' and the National Humanities Medal.[10]

By contrast with the expert in 'American History and Values,' in 2004, Arizona State University art professor John Jota Leaños was berated for generating a poster, 'Friendly Fire,' about Pat Tillman, a sports star who died fighting as a recruit in Afghanistan and was heroized by the authorities. The Pentagon was trying to conceal two facts: that Tillman had become antiwar, and was inadvertently killed by his own side. The poster questioned 'the quasi-religious and dogmatic adherence to Tillman's mythological heroic image by mainly conservative male Americans.' Leaños was immediately subject to excoriating scrutiny by CBS, CNN, and ABC, which in turn produced hundreds of violent, splenetic emails and threats directed at him by viewers;

an inquiry into the artist by his employer; and denunciations by the school's educrats (Leaños, 2009). Yanqui '[j]ournalists simply could not write about Tillman without evoking his role as a protagonist of mythic proportions' (Chidester, 2009: 366).

That said, the invasion and occupation of Afghanistan quickly ceased to interest. By 2020, the country was granted five minutes of coverage across 233 hours of network news (Tyndall, 2021). Iraq overtook it in the playbook of media adventurism.

Susan D Moeller's study of mainstream Yanqui media coverage of state violence between 1998 nuclear tests in South Asia and the 2003 occupation of Iraq found that a wild array of *matériel*, policies, and practices was essentialized under the emotive sign 'Weapons of Mass Destruction.' That syntagm became a 'monolithic menace,' with few distinctions drawn between radiological, nuclear, chemical, or biological weaponry, and no recognition that many of those items were made, held, and sold by the very countries that were most moralistic about their manufacture, possession, and sale—the US and Britain (2004).

The quest for such items in Iraq was romanticized and heroized by Yanqui journalists. In the aftermath of invasion, the *Washington Post*'s Karen Young said '[w]e are inevitably the mouthpiece for whatever administration is in power,' while the paper's Pentagon correspondent, Thomas Ricks, acknowledged that his editors' position could be summarized as: 'Look, we're going to war, why do we even worry about the contrary stuff' (quoted in Mitchell, 2004). The *Post* ran 140 front-page articles promoting invasion in the months prior to the assault. Arch martinet Rupert Murdoch, the ever-Oedipal son of an embedded journalist on the Somme, promised 'We'll do whatever is our patriotic duty,' later intoning that removing صدام حسين عبد المجيد التكريتي [Saddam Hussein] would reduce the price of oil: 'The greatest thing to come out of this for the world economy' (quoted in Solomon, 2001). Each of the 175 newspapers Murdoch owned across the world endorsed the war (Greenslade, 2003). Beyond the 'Dirty Digger,' as he is known to *Private Eye*,[11] coverage from the *New York Times* during the prelude was so supportive that Vice President Dick Cheney quoted it approvingly on network television (Herman and Chomsky, 2008: 788). Viacom, CNN, Fox, and Comedy Central refused to feature billboards and commercials opposing the invasion (Hastings, 2003).

UN activities in the region, including weapons inspections, were the least-covered relevant items on network news (Huff, 2003). CNN's international stations, supposedly cosmopolitan by contrast with their Gringo incarnation, deferred to Administration propaganda (Mhamdi, 2017). Domestically, Fox News increased its ratings lead in cable news (Ponce De Leon, 2015). These are very small segments of the population by contrast with network television audiences, but they bring in ongoing advertising revenue, regardless of Fox distorting the truth again and again (Aday et al., 2005) and later revelations that their broadcasters lied about the 2020 General Election (Marcotte, 2023). Bitter nationalism gains attention.

In the opening stanza of the assault, half the reports from the 1,000 Yanqui journalists embedded with invaders depicted combat. They studiously avoided filming or commenting on the carnage they were witnessing. As the war progressed, the most US residents saw were deeply sanitized images of the wounded from afar, in keeping with 50 contractual terms required of reporters in return for 'access.' Even injured US soldiers were left unnoticed, with no bedside interviews from hospitals; fallen men and women became 'the disappeared.' News photography commemorated them only via highly misleading, romantic imagery, in stark relief to battleground pictures from World War II and Việt Nam (Aday, 2005).

NBC correspondent David Bloom boasted that the media were so keen to become adjuncts of the military that they were 'doing anything and everything that they can ask of us' (quoted in Carr, 2003). WABC radio's NJ Burkett compared the Yanqui soldiers preparing their weapons to 'an orchestra on an opening night' (quoted in Rutenberg, 2003). During the occupation, General Motors—the country's biggest advertiser at the time—and other major firms announced they 'would not advertise on a TV program about atrocities' (quoted in McCarthy, 2004). Yanquis were offered human-interest stories about happy Iraqis, though that did not stop the Administration from complaining about negative news (Aday, 2010).

The sanctimonious certainty was part of a profound belief among US élites in the doctrine of pre-emptive 'just war,' via a genealogy that takes World War II's struggle against fascism as the acme of pure, even saintly, motives. It is cited again and again to legitimize invasion and empire (Walzer, 2015). The rest of the world addressed the political economy of what invading forces had done in Afghanistan and Iraq (Kolmer and Semetko, 2009), relegating military maneuvers behind civilian suffering. Even the Leninists running Beijing allowed news audiences serious discussion of the Iraq invasion in terms of nationalism and geopolitics. The British, cowering behind their fantasy of ensuring a continued 'special relationship' with Washington (Burns and Morrison, 2021; Churchill, 1946), nevertheless permitted some diversity of media coverage, albeit less on TV than in print (Guo et al., 2015; Goddard et al., 2008; Lewis, 2004).

In 2005, US authorities finally admitted that no weapons of mass destruction had been found in Iraq. Only ABC made it a lead story. Fox News barely touched on the topic, and CBS and NBC relegated it to a minor item—fewer than 60 words on the nightly news. The *New York Times* claimed the admission was 'little noted' around the world (Whiten, 2005). This was not only an indictment of US reporters; it was the apotheosis of war journalism's emphasis on the need for violence, a desire for victory, a faith in élites, and the credulous reproduction of propaganda (Nohrstedt and Ottosen, 2022; Perez de Fransius, 2014).

Some continue to claim that the twin imperial disasters of Afghanistan and Iraq were caused by governmental misjudgment and public opinion alone, excluding the media from responsibility, or even discussion (Doherty and Kiley, 2023). The reality is that US journalism has turned away from being a central element of political citizenship. And purely web-based outlets mirror the mainstream media's refusal of international stories (Himelboim et al., 2010). The country with the greatest global impact of any nation in history is simply not committed to informing its residents of basic geopolitical facts or the conduct of their military. It follows that the average US citizen is ignorant of world events, in contradistinction to other wealthy countries (*National Geographic* and Council on Foreign Relations, 2019; Aalberg et al., 2013). When Yanquis have some knowledge of foreign affairs, it is largely colored by the univocal views of their preferred sources (Silver and Shearer, 2021).

For this is an era marked by conflicts of interest in the 'career path' of officials-cum-journalists, a 'recycling between those in government who often deceive, and those in media who have a follow-up career.' Together they form a 'deception chain' (Jackson, 2023). During the dual invasions, US television news effectively diminished the dominant discourse to technical efficiency and state propaganda. More than half of studio guests talking about the impending action in Iraq in 2003 were superannuated white males ("In Iraq," 2003), 'ex-military men, terrorism experts, and Middle Eastern policy analysts who know none of the relevant languages, may never have seen any part of the Middle East, and are too poorly educated to be expert at anything' (Said, 2003). Of 319 mavens giving 'analysis' on ABC, CBS, and NBC in October 2003, 76% were current or previous officials. Of the civilians, 79% were Republicans. And 81% of sources were Yanquis. A sample of NPR's guest list on all topics over one month shows 64% were officials or corporate leeches. Local news coverage was similarly lopsided (Whiten, 2004; Rendall and Butterworth, 2004; Grand Rapids Institute for Information Democracy, 2005). By contrast with the professoriate, and when controlling for ideological preferences, then as now, guests endorsed military adventurism, in part because their proximity to DC hegemons prejudices them in favor of imperial violence (Hanania and Abrams, 2023).

This is part of a wider domination of conservative perspectives over the Gringo airwaves. During the 1990s, progressive think tanks obtained a sixth of media quotations and appearances compared to reactionary institutions. In the decade to 2005, progressives averaged 14% of citations. In 2012, the right and center had 81% of coverage. Media attention does not correlate with scholarly esteem or achievement, and the academics most likely to be interviewed have worked in government or for Mammon. These public intellectuals are general rather than specific in their remarks, and disdainful of both theory and fact—an unusual combination (Miller, 2007).[12]

Herbert Gans explains how this increasingly abject failure of Yanqui reportage came to pass:

> State, Defense, and the FBI as well as the CIA ... are thought newsworthy because they defend the nation. ... Since the end of the Cold War, federal agencies relevant to banking, investment, and the global economy, notably Treasury and the Federal Reserve Bank, have become newsworthy as well, but Commerce and Labor have not. Even though there are more workers in the country than bankers, the highest officials in the Treasury and the Federal Reserve Bank regularly supply the national news about work and workers.
>
> *(2003: 46)*

The tendency to rely on these pillars of conservatism as sources of knowledge must be put in reverse. And the trend goes beyond politics. As Gans explains, it is not only warmongers who are taken to be experts but also servants of capital. That takes us to the financialization of journalism, which has occurred under the sign of the second type of citizenship—the economic.

Economic citizenship

Like political citizenship, economic citizenship has been alive for a long time, via the collection and dissemination of information about the public through the census and related statistical devices and policies. When paupers came to be marked as part of the social world during 19th-century transformations of capitalism, poverty became an interventionist category, with well-being a right, a problem, and a number, and society more than a market (Polanyi, 2001).

Economic citizenship developed further in the Global North during the Depression, and the Global South during decolonization. It redistributed capitalist gains across society to secure employment, health, and retirement, and the state invested in areas of market malfunction. The great task of the New Deal was 'to find through government the instrument of our united purpose' against 'blind economic forces and blindly selfish men' via 'a new chapter in our book of self government' that would 'make every American citizen the subject of his [sic] country's interest and concern' (Roosevelt, 1937). In the words of Australia's World War II Prime Minister John Curtin, 'the masses should be lifted up' (quoted in van Creveld, 1999: 35). The state effectively said 'we are asking you to get yourselves killed, but we promise you that when you have done this, you will keep your jobs until the end of your lives'

(Foucault, 2008: 216). Two historic promises were made by established and emergent governments: to secure the political representation and economic welfare of citizens.

Universal sovereignty following World War II required concerted international action to convince colonial powers that the peoples they had enslaved should be given the right to self-determination. The ensuing postcolonial governments undertook to deliver economic welfare via state-based management of supply and demand and the creation of industries that would substitute imports with domestically produced items. For Ghanaian President Kwame Nkrumah, the legacy of economies in which 'one class of citizen toils and another reaps' (1970: 71) was clear: emerging states' economic development had been 'subordinated … to the needs of the colonial powers.' As a consequence, they required 'a new type of citizen … who submerges self in service to the nation and mankind' (1964: 150, 130)—an Afrocentric belief in communitarianism (Mamdani, 1996). But most new states have remained dependent on the metropole and not grown economically. Their formal *political* post-coloniality has rarely become *economic*, apart from some Asian countries that pursued trade-based capitalist manufacturing, aided by favorable tariff policies designed to discourage them from Marxism/Maoism.

After the global economic crises of the 1970s, even places in the Global North that had *bourgeoisies* with sufficient capital formation to fund social welfare no longer hedged employment against inflation by influencing demand, and their overseas development policies were wholly or partially dismantled when state socialism and social democracy alike eroded. As rich petrostates like Britain, France, and the US were exposed to increasing costs for natural resources and decreasing employment because of a global labor supply, a new imaginary arose: supply-side and monetarist economics (Mitchell, 1998). Economic citizenship was turned on its head through policy renegotiations conducted by capital, the state, and their intellectual servants in economics. Anxieties over unemployment were trumped by anxieties over profits, with workers called upon to identify as stakeholders in business.

Reforms redistributed income back to the domestic ruling classes. Metropoles and corporations became privileged economic citizens, with individuals conceived of as self-governing consumers. Consider British Prime Minister Margaret Thatcher's infamous interview in *Woman's Own*:

> I think we have gone through a period when too many children and people have been given to understand "I have a problem, it is the Government's job to cope with it!" or "I have a problem, I will go and get a grant to cope with it!" "I am homeless, the Government must house me!" and so they are casting their problems on society and who is society? There is no such thing!
>
> *(quoted in Keay, 1987: 9)*

Or the moment when Mexican President Vicente Fox challenged reporters asking him about responsibility for the state of the nation with: '¿Yo por qué? ... ¿Qué no somos 100 millones de mexicanos?' [Why me? ... Aren't there a hundred million Mexicans?] (quoted in Venegas, 2003).

These microeconomic assumptions of ratiocinative consumption have dominated for decades, gleefully celebrating technological innovation, buoyant demand, the quest for growth, mendacious marketing, and conventional property relations in the name of capitalist efficiency and governmental normativity. The accompanying doctrine of neoliberalism has been one of the most successful attempts to reshape individuals in human history. Its achievements rank alongside such productive and destructive sectarian practices as state socialism, colonialism, nationalism, and religion. Neoliberalism's lust for market regulation was so powerful that its prelates opined on every topic imaginable, from birth rates to divorce, suicide to abortion, performance-enhancing drugs to altruism. Rhetorically, it stood against elitism (for populism); against subvention (for markets); and against public service (for philanthropy) (Hall and Massey, 2010). Hobbes' warnings about 'a war of all against all' lay largely unheeded (2017: 139) as faith grew in charity based on religious mandate and personal choice—not political-economic citizenship (Hall and Held, 1989).

There are significant problems with such reasoning and its basis in the notion that supply and demand set prices and produce positive outcomes, unfettered by democratic regulation. The notion rests on abstract concepts such as choice and freedom, without acknowledging the material conditions of existence needed to appreciate and exercise such rights (Hall and Held, 1989). As Stuart Hall explains, markets:

> do not work mysteriously by themselves or "clear" at their optimum point. Only by bracketing out of the calculation the yawning differences between the relative wealth which buyer and seller bring into the exchange can they be called "fair." No "hidden hand" guarantees the common good. They require the external power of state and law to establish and regulate them. But the discourse provides its subjects with a "lived" "imaginary relation" to their real conditions of existence. This does not mean that markets are simply manufactured fictions. Indeed, they are only too real! They are "false" because they offer partial explanations as an account of whole processes.
>
> *(2011: 716)*

Journalism has been neoliberalism's willing spokesperson and servant. We focus next on the profession's part in these shifting discourses, notably the triumph of corporate idioms under the sign of putative economic freedom.

Business heroism

English-language media references to 'the economy' as a living entity, with needs and desires, derive from the Great Depression, when press attention shifted from relations between producers and consumers of goods (a labor-process discourse of popular newspapers that dissented from marginalist economics) and onto relations between different material products *of* labor. There was a similar change in emphasis from use- to exchange value and the discursive commodities 'the economy' and 'the market' were anthropomorphized and valorized (Emmison, 1983; Emmison and McHoul, 1987). 'The economy' as we know it entered popular knowledge at a high point of Keynesianism, but with terminology that would suit the coming reactionary turn in economic citizenship.

Today's journalistic incarnations of economic citizenship focus on national and multinational corporations and the stock market, along with a residual, romantic account of small business and the discourse of life-as-competition and the self as a rational subject ready to build its capacities. Gary Becker is an informal deity, thanks to his doctrine of human capital (1993). People are intelligible through the precepts of selfishness, as they are supposedly governed by market imperatives. Internally divided—but happily so—each person 'is a consumer on the one hand, but … also a producer' (Foucault, 2008: 226). In Alexander Kluge's words, this is capitalism constituting each citizen as 'a commodity owner: like a miser grasping every detail and collecting surplus on everything' (1981–82: 210–11). Coin-operated think tanks are the intellectual handservants of this perspective. These vocalists of a 'permanent criticism of government policy' (Foucault, 2008: 247) do 'research' in order to pen op-eds in newspapers and provide talking points on cable news, with reporters genuflecting to their pseudo-academic bloviation. We shall learn more of their dread work in the next chapter.

The news parrots the market's vocabulary. It 'internalizes the thinking of the executive suite' (Schiller, 2014: 7), assuming a community of commitment to fictive capital. Leading sources of wholesale video news make most of their money from reporting finance. Political journalists at Reuters refer to themselves as 'cavaliers' and their business counterparts as 'roundheads'—severe metaphors from the English Civil War (Palmer et al., 1998). The roundheads won. From Ireland to Italy, from Germany to Greece, PR sections of corporate interests give reporters inside information on how élites wish to reshape the distribution of income upward. These 'scoops' are lapped up by editors and owners (Tambini, 2010; Reich, 2012; Rafter, 2014; Mylonas, 2015; Mazzoni and Barbieri, 2014).

Journalistic heroization of business executives saw a doubling of time dedicated to them by US TV across the 1990s. In 2000, finance was the principal topic on ABC, NBC, and CBS nightly news, and second only to terrorism in

2002. Promoting stocks where one had a personal financial interest became *de rigueur* for anchors and pundits. The New York Stock Exchange called for regulation requiring reporters to disclose their investments, so egregious had been their complicity with the dotcom disasters of the 1990s (Miller, 2007; Thompson, 2013). Business advisors continue to dominate discussion on dedicated finance cable stations like CNBC and Bloomberg, where they are granted something akin to the status of seers.

During his time as Chair of the Federal Reserve, Alan Greenspan was filmed getting in and out of cars as if *en route* to decide the fate of nations, each upturned eyebrow or wrinkled frown subject to hyper-interpretation by a bevy of needy followers. The focus fell on share prices in Asia, Europe, and New York; reports on company earnings, profits, and stocks; and portfolio management (Martin, 2002; Martin, 2004). That obsessive pattern repeated as farce in the latter part of the decade, when financial markets crumbled into fury and tears before their failed capitalism was bailed out by taxpayer-financed socialism, with upwards of 30 million Gringos disemployed and/or dispossessed along the way (Starkman, 2014). This was per the theory that certain financial institutions must be protected at all (public) cost because of their value to the ruling class. That generated the slogan 'too big to fail' in the 1970s, which was invoked repeatedly over the decades (Nurisso and Prescott, 2017). Conversely, the disemployed and dispossessed are always permitted to 'fail.'

The role of US journalists in the sub-prime crisis was masked by a series of tactics focused on identifying other blameworthy actors and accepting little if any responsibility (Usher, 2013). Per tendencies across the European world, in the UK, 'the City' provided expert opinion in dominant news sources, to the exclusion of progressive critique (Knowles et al., 2017; Sobieraj, 2022; Berry, 2013a, 2013b). Cultural stereotypes were also put in play. For example, German coverage of Greece's place in the Eurozone crisis focused on supposed differences in national character between industrious European Northerners and feckless Southerners (Bickes et al., 2014).

The Anglo world has a barely breathing labor beat. Economic news has been reduced to corporate and shareholder stories. Public policy is measured in terms of its reception by business. Markets stalk politics, ready to punish activities that might restrain capital. Journalists' veneration of stock movements remains ever-ready to point to infractions of an anthropomorphized, yet oddly subject-free sphere, a means of constructing moral panics around the conduct of whoever or whatever raises its ire. Across capitalist economies, national élites are treated as knowledgeable, critics ignored (Rios-Rodríguez and Arrese, 2021). Again and again, reporters attribute expertise to people and institutions that should be regarded as very partial sources (Manning, 2013). In place of history, geopolitics, and critical economics, coverage focuses on popular and individual 'irresponsibility' as the *casus belli* whenever capitalist crises occur—as they inevitably, inexorably do (Basu, 2018). During the UK's long, catastrophic era of austerity that commenced in 2010—better understood as diminished democracy and accelerated profits—the large number of academic economists offering alternatives was ignored by the *bourgeois* media (Wren-Lewis, 2018). Heaven forfend that critical scholars or union officials be viewed as experts. This tendency, so deeply instilled in journalistic practice, needs reversing.

The second half of this chapter turns to the sphere of culture. As we shall see, it overlaps with political and economic citizenship, whether the topic be consumption or cartooning, and incarnates the transformations and crises characterizing journalism.

Cultural citizenship

The 'ideal' citizen, able to mediate differences and struggles, is frequently understood to be a clear-headed, dispassionate subject who knows when and how to set aside personal and sectarian preferences in search of the greater good. This sounds universal rather than culturally specific, but it has frequently corresponded, in both rhetorical and legal terms, to white, male, property-owning subjects protecting their interests from the wider population under a cloak of collective prosperity.

In fact, citizenship is increasingly linked to cultural differences. For instance, the Ottoman Empire offered rights to non-Muslims, and the first constitutional guarantees of culture appeared in Switzerland in 1874. But that was unusual until after World War II and mass decolonization. Today, cultural provisions are standard in post-dictatorship charters, blending artistry and ethnicity. Concerns with language, heritage, religion, and identity respond to histories structured in dominance through cultural power and the postcolonial incorporation of the periphery into an international system of 'free' labor. In Jesús Prieto de Pedro's words:

> The European liberal constitutions of the nineteenth century were political constitutions. … The constitutions of the first third of the twentieth century … were devoted to economic and social issues. … another stage is evidenced in the decade of the 1970s in the eruption of cultural concerns: this generates lexical forms and doctrinal categories such as "cultural rights" … the free existence of culture, cultural pluralism, and the access of citizens to culture are guaranteed in intensified forms.
>
> *(1999: 63)*

Europe was forged in bellicose encounters North, South, East, and West, starting with African Islamic and Spanish Christian imperialism, followed by global invasion, occupation, and colonization and funded through enslaved labor. Unlike North Africa's Umayyad in Hispania, words as well as swords arched across the globe via the missionary and military fervor of Spain's *conquista de América*, Portugal's *missão civilizadora*, France's *mission civilisatrice*, and Britain's civilizing mission (Rojas, 2002). For instance, Queen Isabella's functionaries established Castilian as a mode of conquest and management. Indeed, her imperial grammarian, Antonio de Nebrija, argued that 'language was always the companion of empire.' Along with Christianity, it would enable the Queen to 'put under her yoke many barbarous peoples and nations of alien languages' (2016: 202, 204). Conversion was paramount.

Europe's religious hegemony was a 'complement' to 'positivist nation-building at home,' its bloodletting legitimized by capitalism and nationalism (Asad, 2005: 2). That deployment of ideology and *matériel* to transfer beliefs and seize land and goods is wryly troped in the postcolonial African saying, 'When the white man came, he had the Bible and we had the land. When the white man left, we had the Bible and he had the land' (quoted in McMichael, 2017: 17).

Formerly colonizing nations have been altered by their post-war migrant populations' languages, religions, cuisines, clothing, and senses of self, especially when they come from formerly enslaved/colonized lands; hence the famous 1970s British slogan popularized by the immigrant activist and Marxist theorist Ambalavaner Sivanandan: 'We are here because you were there' (Patel, 2021; Sivanandan quoted in Gordon, 2014).[13]

The 'history of individual peoples, and indeed of whole continents, is now being written in terms of a cultural formation defined by something outside, "the other"' (Halliday, 2001: 113). Working in Madrid, London, or Paris means routinely confronting the end-game of these interactions, including reactions from nativists who deny their own bloody past; hence the British seeking to send asylum seekers to authoritarian states rather than provide them with shelter (Goodwin-Hill, 2022).

So whereas debates about religion within Europe were historically about the commensurability of Protestantism and Catholicism within and between states, the issue today is Islam, as a racial referent, a governmental alternative to secularism, and a source of highly identifiable migratory status. Habermas explains that longstanding anti-Islamic Western violence, taunts, and fiefdoms stimulate a de-territorialized terrorism by non-state as well as state actors, in a potent mixture of faith, fraud, ethnicity, and economics (2006a). In response, the liberal wing of the EU expects the press to inform and represent Muslim immigrants, right the wrongs of stereotypes, and encourage identification with Europe. Migrants are dual targets: of the state, to ensure credulous fealty, and of commerce, to ensure work and consumption (Mattelart and d'Haenens, 2014). The UK remains a center of anti-Muslim sentiment; although physical and verbal violence soar (Tell MAMA, 2023), the data are barely covered by the *bourgeois* media.

Former slave-holding and currently imperialistic countries have not even begun the necessary task of paying reparations to descendants of the people whose homes and lives they besieged, occupied, and seized. Any project redefining national identity in the light of latter-day migration from former colonies and elsewhere remains incomplete and forever in jeopardy from reactionaries. Populist reporters and white nationalists in the US and many European countries fan a tumultuous parthenogenetic anxiety, per the 'great replacement theory.' Originating from the French writer Renaud Camus, it holds that 'white' culture and society are at risk from attempts to supplant their racial hegemony through mass immigration by people of color and Islamic faith, orchestrated by a global élite (Camus, 2012). This belief is prevalent wherever the 'social' media denounce what they claim are massive conspiracy theories underpinning immigration (Gaston with Uscinski, 2018). Fox News is the principal conventional media organization spreading the theory; it has done so hundreds of times. The network's journalists argue that the Democratic Party seeks increased immigration by people of color to advance its electoral prospects (Trilling, 2021; Rose, 2022).

There is a further aspect to culture and citizenship. For new sovereign realities are influenced and indexed by the wider political economy, which has seen a turn to culture not just as a pleasurable pastime, a source of integration, or an article of faith, but as a core material concern—superstructure and substructure intertwined. In the 1980s, the Global North recognized that its economic future lay in finance capital and ideology rather than agriculture and manufacturing and the Global South sought revenue from intellectual property as well as minerals and masses. Such changes continue to be touted as routes to economic development as much as cultural and political expression. Between 1980 and 1998, annual world exchange of electronic culture grew from US$95 billion to US$388 billion. In 2003, those areas accounted for 2.3% of Gross Domestic Product (GDP) across Europe, to the tune of €654 billion—beyond real estate, equal to chemicals, plastics, and rubber. Trademarks, copyright, and patents alone are worth US$360 billion a year in the US, more than aerospace, automobiles, and agriculture. They employ 12% of the workforce, up from 5% a century ago, providing some 35% of GDP and 19% of employment. The entertainment industries alone—film, television, music, and publishing—made US$1.8 trillion in 2021, accounting for 7.76% of GDP and 9.6 million jobs, or 4.88% of the labor force. Annual growth in film and television between 2018 and 2021 averaged 6.15%, as opposed to 1.76% for the economy overall. Copyright, royalties, and licensing concentrate most of that wealth among high-level executives and actors, of whom there are many, such that the sector proclaims an average annual salary of US$121,583—51% higher than the overall national norm. Their contribution to overseas trade in 2021 amounted to US$230.3 billion (Stoner and Dutra, 2022).

Internationally, the culture industries account for nearly 50 million jobs and annual revenue of US$2.25 trillion (Collins, 2008; Miller, 2009; OECD, 2021; United Nations Conference on Trade and Development, 2022a). Perhaps its most famous catch cry is '从中国制造到中国创造' [From Made in China to Created in China], the Communist Party's desideratum for restructuring its economy away from manufacturing and toward intellectual property.[14] The African Union avows that a Pan-African future can be achieved in part through culture,[15] the Inter-American Development Bank (IADB) has pledged allegiance,[16] the European Union is keen,[17] the Association of Southeast Asian Nations has a formal declaration on the subject (2022), the UN General Assembly proclaimed 2021 the 'International Year of Creative Economy for Sustainable Development,'[18] and the United Nations Conference on Trade and Development (UNCTAD) published *Creative Industry 4.0: A New Globalized Creative Economy* the following year (2022b).

The journalistic corollaries of the social forces described in this section include an increased focus on religion and race as unifying and dividing forces, culture's importance to the economy, lamentations for lost industries, additional space dedicated to such topics as cuisine and health, and expanded but still restricted access for readers to create texts—old-style newsroom tips and letters to the editor have turned into almost-live images from cellphones of restaurant dishes and recipes on blogs (excellent sources of free intellectual property). We investigate some of these tendencies, examining how media coverage of food has changed at a time when lifestyle can trump politics. Then we return to France, free speech, and religion.

Food

Food is materially crucial to life. An index of power, it was the basis of the earliest class systems, symbolized by work and consumption, and religion, organized around harvesting and prayer. And if the Habermasian coffee house mentioned in the Introduction depended on caffeine as its fuel, gastronomy was also, perhaps equally, a site for launching social critique and spice-driven slavery during the Enlightenment (Mennell, 2003). The three types of citizenship map onto food: the political (food policy); the economic (food resources); and the cultural (food symbolism). Secure nutrition is one of the fundamental guarantees made to citizens by their governments.

Macroeconomic transformations have stimulated corporate trade in agriculture and a new international division of food labor. The last three decades ended 200 million food jobs in the Global South. The latest predictions are for another 120 million by 2030 (Brondizio et al., 2023). As capitalism pushes people away from suddenly unsettled rural life and toward unprepared urban worlds, there are breakdowns in community life unparalleled other than in times of war. Biodiversity sustained through local knowledge crumbles. Climate change intensifies pressure and poverty.

As noted in the Introduction, functioning democracies with a free press do not experience famine, because information about shortages can move around the country courtesy of local, regional, and national news, outwitting corporations and states that try to deny problems (for example, there have been no famines in post-independence Australia or India) (Sen, 2000). But with the displacement of national by global forms of regulation that match business mobility, the idea of localism and reportage dealing with food issues has become less plausible (Atkins and Bowler, 2001: 38–39, 43). The international food rebellions of 2007–12 were covered in the global media by interviewing distant 'experts,' to the exclusion of participants' perspectives (Hossain, 2018).

'Despite' the technologies of modernity, from instantaneity to transportability, food security and sovereignty remain as distant for much of the world as ever (Wilson, 2017). Innovations once hailed as triumphs are now seen as unsustainable drives to control/overcome nature and feed the wealthy (Food and Agriculture Organization of the United Nations et al., 2020). Even anthropocentric interpretations agree with this account, given the disastrous impact on diet and the environment of industrialized farming and marketing, per the findings of scientific academies across Africa, the Americas, Asia, and Europe (Fears et al., 2019). We now know that food loss and waste are responsible for more greenhouse emissions than all but two countries (United Nations Environment Programme, 2021).[19]

Since the late 1980s, more and more nations import cuisine from around the globe. Food at the point of consumption has become radically disaffiliated from its conditions of production and circulation. For example, restaurant customers are not told of the complex economics and politics behind their purchase. Instead, they are given a spice of difference to do with the geographic origin of items on the menu. And while food is often produced in rural settings, it is increasingly an urban problem and pleasure—literally a moving feast, traveling great distances and accreting and attenuating power and signification, with a noteworthy media presence. Tragically and irresponsibly, the interplay of journalism and food has become largely a matter of identity and cookery, not public health or political economy. Regrettably, journalism historians and other scholars have shown little interest in the genre. They are fascinated by certain food identities—but not those of workers or patients (Voss, 2014: 13; Fusté-Forné and Masip, 2018).

Food has long been a theme and a source for writers. European advice books from the mid-1600s detailed table settings, measured distances between diners, and explained the need for tablecloths to hide the lower body while eating. The earliest cookbooks date from this time, explaining how the élite comported itself as a model for the slightly lower orders. By the mid-19th century, Mrs Beeton's thousand-page *Book of Household Management* had thoroughly textualized food custom, blending the political economy of daily life with manners and recipes—cultural citizenship. US newspapers first started publishing articles about food in the 1840s. By the 1880s, these columns had become social-advice guides, with instructions on the behavioral correlatives of class mobility (Miller, 2007: 118). In the post-World War II period, US publishers discerned a variety of markets for food media, notably single working women. In 1961, 49 cookbooks were published; in 2001, over 1,700, and with cross-media links—by 2004, half the 25 top-sellers were 'written' by Food Network TV presenters. All in all, 530 million books on food and alcohol were sold in the US in 2000. Fifty years ago, the US had about 20 food magazines; by 2002, the number was 145. In the decade from 2011, annual compound growth rate in US sales of culinary books was 11%, while the first full year of the COVID-19 syndemic saw a 42% increase (Ballard, 2021; "The Great," 2021).

We saw in the Introduction that by the mid-19th century, the concept of 'meanwhile,' linking hitherto-unconnected people across a country, flourished through journalism, along with the notion of a disinterested duty of care, a sense of belonging and responsibility that could transcend personal experience. Hunger quickly became a key aspect of this capacity to identify with the unknown. Reporters wrote human-interest stories that showed the folly of ascribing responsibility for hunger individually, empowering critics of British poverty by highlighting the lives of skeletal child workers who perished agonizingly before adulthood, and the cynical creation of Ireland's Great Hunger. By the turn of the century, the UK had what it called 'New Journalism,' an investigative genre of intense commitment that warned of class unrest deriving from mass hunger. Its vista expanded to include victims of empire in South Asia and Africa (Vernon, 2007: 18–34).

But that focus diminished. The newspaper food coverage that gradually emerged in its stead was consumer-oriented, in what were known as women's sections. In 1940, the *New York Times* published 675 food stories, of which just 4% were light background fare (now known as 'foodie' news: reviews, recipes, and profiles). The remainder reported on poisoning, nutrition, or famine. Twenty years on, the corollary proportion of 'foodie' coverage had doubled to 9%. By the 1970s, food journalism and editorship were male-dominated (Voss, 2014: 13, 22).

Approximately 25% of US newspapers added 'Style' pages between 1979 and 1983, of which 38% had circulations of more than 100,000. That helps contextualize the shifting discourse on cuisine in the *Philadelphia Inquirer* and *Philadelphia Magazine*. In the early 1960s, the *Inquirer* ran recipe columns and advertisements related to home dining, with women the target. Practical artistry was articulated with home economics: simplicity and thrift were called for, other than on special occasions. In the 1970s, a section appeared in the Sunday *Magazine* on places to go, displacing 'Food and Family.' Restaurants were described as public, commercial, cultural sites of urban sophistication. By the 1980s, the Sunday food section included a wine guide and food writers were dubbed 'critics.' They offered instruction on enjoyment, not investigations of production. Aesthetics had displaced functionality. Across the US, 36% of food stories papers were about lifestyles. Fairly rigorous distinctions were drawn between *dining* out (costly, occasioned, planned, and dressed for) and *eating* out (easy, standardized, and requiring minimal presentational effort). In 2000, 80% of the *New York Times*' 1,927 food stories were about chefs and recipes. The 'foodie' trend in reportage and interest is celebrated as a response to affluent consumers, a skilled working class, efficient and effective transportation, and cosmopolitanism (Hanke, 1989; Jones, 2003; Barnes, 2004; Danford, 2005; Harris, 2003: 55; Makala, 2005; Finkelstein, 1989: 38; Fine and Leopold, 1993: 167; O'Neill, 2003; Fattorini, 1994).

Newspaper food writers are mostly critics—not of diet, social relations, or climate crisis—but personal tastes that duel with the flavors served up to them in fancy restaurants (Cruz López, 2021). They curate a middle-class readership with romantic tales of life in food preparation, to the frustration of actual workers. In the words of the noted cookbook author and columnist Molly O'Neill (2003), '[s]ome of the most significant stories today are about food. But you won't find them in the food section, where journalism has been supplanted by fantasy.'

Key links between food and the audiovisual media date from the telegraph and the radio providing data on commodity prices and weather, and overproduction leading to mass advertising. What began as cooking shows in the earliest days of television, and occasional newspaper investigations of food's insidious labor process, has burgeoned into a proliferation of screen networks, textual criticism, and celebrity chefdom (O'Connell, 2019; Chan, 2022). Connections to tourism and celebrity culture tie food reporters ever-closer to uncritical promotions of capitalism and nationalism, neglecting the labor beat (Fusté-Forné and Masip, 2020). No surprise, then, that while US TV news provided exhaustive coverage of miners on strike in the Soviet Union in 1989, pronouncing them paragons of virtue struggling against an authoritarian regime, a few years later, when McDonald's violated post-Soviet Russian law by refusing to recognize the relevant union, restive workers were granted no such coverage (Martin, 2004: 16–17).

Journalistic trivialization of food has come at a time of serious public-health crises: in the 1970s, food-borne disease was rare in the US, and generally attributable to cutesy-pie events like church picnics. Today, 48 million people are laid low through infected food each year. Three thousand die and 128,000 hospitalized, at a public-health cost in the billions.[20] The Federal Government makes a quarter of the food-safety inspections it did two decades ago, with the percentage of imported food examined dropping from 8% in 1993 to 2% ten years on and 1.3% in 2007. The proportion of food stories that engages this political economy is minuscule (Eyck, 2000; Miller,

2007; "U.S. Food," 2007; U.S. Government Accountability Office, 2021). Environmental issues associated with food are largely invisible in the *bourgeois* media. And this is not just a Gringo story. Elsewhere, food writers blissfully ignore sustainability in favor of addressing and cultivating middle-class tastes (Brüggemann et al., 2022; Jones and Taylor, 2013). Singapore sees a food vision of ethnic national identity served up by governments and reiterated glowingly by journalist after journalist (Duffy and Ashley, 2012). In China, where food-related horrors are increasing and public knowledge of them is hampered by state and corporate mendacity, food journalism seems to do better than in the Anglo world (Yang, 2013).

Average caloric intake in the US increased from 2,080 to 2,347 between 1980 and 2000. Adult obesity grew by 80%, leading the Surgeon-General to place overeating alongside smoking as the principal lifestyle killer in the country (Sturm and Datar, 2005; Saad, 2003). Discussion of the topic in the national media has increased fivefold since 1992. Despite clear correlations between youth obesity and local prices of fresh fruit and vegetables—nothing to do with consumer choice—the high moralism so prevalent in the Yanqui media, and characteristic of neoliberal economic citizenship, has led to a doctrine of personal responsibility, militating against both collective identification and action. Journalists cover the topic as a matter of individual preference and medical definition, measurement, and treatment (Lawrence, 2004). Only a third of the public holds multinationals responsible for obesity (Sturm and Datar, 2005). Right-wing British reporters are equally prey to blaming obesity on personal irresponsibility; the left focuses on institutions (Brookes and Baker, 2021). In Australia, which has no progressive daily media, journalists writing about obesity routinely break their own codes of fairness. TV news places the blame on consumer choices (Bonfiglioli, 2020; Bonfiglioli et al., 2007).

Serious conflicts of interest are generated by the interlocking directorates of media and food corporations. General Electric (then NBC's owner) and the *Washington Post* shared company directors with Coca-Cola, and Pepsi's board featured people from equivalent groups within the *New York Times*, Gannett, and the Tribune Company. Tribune has had directors in common with McDonald's and Quaker Oats, while General Electric was represented at Anheuser-Busch and Kellogg (Raphael et al., 2004; Phillips, 2008). Isolated attempts by investigative journalists to reveal corporate malfeasance in food are met with litigation PR: corporations seeking to discredit revelations of their venality through clandestine newsgathering designed to discredit potential jurors, attorneys, judges, and journalists (Bradley, 2016).

Nevertheless, there are many signs of increased public interest in food in terms of consumer movements, concerns regarding new technology, struggles over state regulation, criticisms of multinational takeovers of family farms, the search for 'natural' brands, the emergence of agricultural cooperatives, animal-rights discourse, non-traditional medicine, the sexual politics of eating disorders, and Global South poverty. These issues offer abundant evidence of a potential audience for a more responsible, politicized approach. Thankfully, scholars and food writers alike are awakening to the crucial politics of their tastes and fancies, albeit with the kind of cybertarian utopianism that will be engaged in Chapter 4 (Fakazis and Fürsich, 2023). But journalism has a great distance to go if it is to provide readers with knowledge of one of the most elemental components of citizenship.

Cartooning

This final part of the chapter discusses free speech, journalism, and religion via the 2015 case of *Charlie Hebdo*, when a dozen Parisian workers associated with the periodical were murdered in the name of Islam. Their assassination was justified on the grounds that the magazine's cartoons of Mohammed were blasphemous—an instance where the political and the cultural collide. Subsequent reactions included Latin American cartoonists drawing multifaceted, paradoxical responses that shared a horror of violence ("Caricaturistas," 2015); increased cardiovascular incidents in a French hospital, leading to connections being adduced between heightened media coverage, intense illness, and stress (Della Rosa et al., 2016; Chatignoux et al., 2018); reports of severe distress by Italian students through vicarious identification with 2015 terrorism (Raccanello et al., 2018); and massive protests against the magazine across much of the Islamic world (Sreberny, 2016; Mueller and Matthews, 2016).

The immediate aftermath of the *Charlie* killings was a surfeit of expressive totality, from then-French President François Hollande and 50 heads of state (2015) marching and militarizing to lapsed-Trot Tariq Ali and colleagues (2015) marching and moralizing. Four million French residents demonstrated in support of the slain and what they supposedly represented—post-Revolutionary ideals of republican nationhood (Weston Vauclair, 2015: 6; Eko, 2019). For many analysts in the Global North, the attacks on *Charlie* were assaults on all reporters 'in their role of advocates of free speech' (Sumiala et al., 2018: 121). Britain's National Union of Journalists described the murders as 'an attempt to assassinate the free press ... to suppress democracy and freedom of speech' (quoted in Wolska-Zogata, 2015: 355–56).

But the Organisation of Islamic Cooperation (OIC),[21] which represents 57 countries over four continents that define themselves as Muslim, had already condemned cartoons of Mohammed that appeared in the Danish broadsheet *Jyllands-Posten* in 2005–06 (Howden et al., 2006), reprinted in *Charlie*, along with 19 other European papers (Ervine, 2019: 24, 28). (The editor of *France Soir* lost his job for doing so.[22]) The Pakistani press had reacted angrily to those representations, asking whether free speech was being misused in a provocative, conspiratorial form (Eide, 2010). Several states boycotted Danish products, Denmark's diplomatic missions were set alight, its representatives and aid workers were withdrawn from certain countries, and the public was warned against much international travel (Klausen, 2009: 1).

It makes sense to consider some of the distinctions between how press freedom is conceived, which depends on varying conceptions of civil society, the state, and liberty, albeit with some universal elements. Beginning with speech and blasphemy, we go on to address the cartoons and assassinations in the context of debates about speech in the name of liberalism, and violence in the name of Islam.

The preamble to the United Nations' Universal Declaration of Human Rights calls for 'a world in which human beings shall enjoy freedom of speech and belief and freedom from fear and want … the highest aspiration of the common people.' Article 19 avows that '[e]veryone has the right to freedom of opinion and expression; this right includes freedom to hold opinions without interference and to seek, receive and impart information and ideas through any media and regardless of frontiers.'[23]

But even the human rights group 'Article 19' offers *'Hate Speech' Explained: A Toolkit* to guide governments on circumscribing the very thing their eponym seeks to guarantee.[24] The organization favors limits to speech when applied to individuals' dignity, though not in the name of collective notions, such as national security, morality, or public order. It accepts the category 'hate speech,' while recognizing that this varies in its definition and legal status across jurisdictions and philosophies. For example, YouTube and the South African state both link hate speech to violence, but the European Court of Human Rights does not. Hence the Article 19 group arguing that '[p]luralism is essential, as one person's deeply held religious belief may be offensive to another's deeply held belief and vice versa. By privileging one belief system over another, either in law or in effect, restrictions on blasphemy inevitably discriminate against those with minority religions or beliefs.' It insists that human beings have rights, but religious institutions and commitments do not.

Blasphemy is currently *the* debating point over free speech. The French tradition of lampooning religious pomposity through caricature arches back to the Revolution (Weston Vauclair, 2015: 7; Trouillard, 2020). The problem is that clerics of every religious hue deem themselves superior, anointed, and above secular critique. The *Qu'ran* does not prescribe punishments for blasphemy or prohibit representation of its true believers' favorite prophet (Saiya, 2016). Rather non-specific, albeit vaguely threatening, fates await blasphemers, but there is no sign of this occurring in the material world.[25] The OIC's *Cairo Declaration on Human Rights in Islam*, however, avows that in the best of all possible worlds, 'knowledge is combined with faith' and Islam is its sole custodian (Nineteenth Islamic Conference, 1993). Article

16 guarantees moral rights to the creators of texts, provided they do not run counter to Shari'ah. Article 22 (c) reads:

> Information is a vital necessity to society. It may not be exploited or misused in such a way as may violate sanctities and the dignity of Prophets, undermine moral and ethical Values or disintegrate, corrupt or harm society or weaken its faith.

Article 22 (d) avows that: 'It is not permitted to excite nationalistic or doctrinal hatred or to do anything that may be an incitement to any form or [sic] racial discrimination.' The Organisation subordinates other international protocols to Shari'ah and describes 'Islamophobia' as 'the worst form of terrorism' (Wahab, 2007). Its members generally walk out of global gatherings that address queer rights (Evans, 2012).

Emanuel Todd argues that blasphemy should not be outlawed, but calls for sensitive self-regulation because of the offense and discord that anti-Islamic sentiment provokes among the socially disenfranchised (2015). Advocates for that position also note the ambivalence of existing international accords on the right of the press to mock religions:

> the International Covenant on Civil and Political Rights … and the European Convention on Human Rights … quite clearly do allow for the possibility of speech being restricted in the name of public morality, and if and when a religion is inextricably linked with a nation's public morality, then it is difficult to see why this justification for restricting speech could not apply, at least in theory, to irreligious speech.
> *(Cox, 2016: 203)*

Given that Islam is the official religion of a quarter of all nations, rejecting their state codes of blasphemy is akin to maintaining that international law protecting free speech need not be endorsed by vast numbers of people and polities to be sovereign.

That said, the 2013 Rabat Plan of Action, adopted by the United Nations High Commissioner for Human Rights and many other international authorities, insists that blasphemy laws should not subvert open expression.[26] Countries that prohibit negative representations of religion frequently restrict religious freedom themselves (Henne, 2013). Islamic states that prohibit blasphemy are generally authoritarian, which generates violent resistance:

> blasphemy laws encourage terrorism by creating a culture of vigilantism in which terrorists, claiming to be the defenders of Islam, attack those they believe are guilty of heresy … a time-series, cross[-]national negative binomial analysis of 51 Muslim-majority states from 1991–2013 … finds

that states that enforce blasphemy laws are indeed statistically more likely to experience Islamist terrorist attacks than countries where such laws do not exist.

(Saiya, 2016)

Cartooning in particular seems to rile anxious sacerdotes, notably *Charlie Hebdo*'s caricatures of all three monotheistic religions; it has been unsuccessfully sued many times for defaming Catholicism (Ali, 2015). This is equal-opportunity 'anticlericalism' (Ervine, 2019: 24). The OIC's logic argues that the *Charlie Hebdo* cartoons may be deemed both blasphemous, because they ridicule the historic leader of a religion, and defamatory, as they ridicule adherents of that religion. In addition, the way that supporters of the magazine expressed their sentiments is perceived by some as solidarity *against* Islam as much as *for* free speech (Cox, 2016).

Some critics argue that 'the anti-religious stance displayed in the cartoons reflects freedom of speech for one set of worldviews but not for others' (Watson, 2016). Pope Francis condemned both the 2015 killings *and* the images that gave rise to them: 'One cannot provoke, one cannot insult other people's faith, one cannot make fun of faith. There is a limit. … Every religion has its dignity' (quoted in McElwee, 2015). Since 2003, various French administrations had urged the magazine to stop antagonizing Islamic believers, for fear of assault (Eichler, 2003: 89). The Iranian government criticized both the cartoonists and the gunmen (Barry, 2016), as did the eminent Hegelian communitarian and *New Left Review* co-founder Charles Taylor. He distanced himself from the murders, but argued that such attacks should surprise no-one, given the magazine's additions to the social and governmental critique and marginalization already experienced by those it mocked. While opposing limits to free speech, Taylor pointed to the folly of exercising it in such ways (Swan, 2015). Former *Charlie doyen* Olivier Cyran had long criticized the magazine for what he regarded as its growing obsession with Islam (2013). Surviving cartoonist Luz reacted against the attempts to make the periodical a symbol of anything in the wake of the attacks, insisting that its *raison d'être* was iconoclasm ("Luz," 2023). Delfeil de Ton (the pen name of *Charlie* co-founder Henri Roussel) denounced his assassinated colleagues for recklessly exposing themselves and others to danger (M. C., 2015).

Responses to the attack on Twitter/X saw #JeSuisCharlie become 'a metaphor for organizing news flows, opinions, affects and participatory events in the digital media ecosystem.' Within an hour of the murders, a dedicated wiki page had emerged (updated and translated into 70 languages). Within a day, over 50 French and international cities featured tributes. A phone application soon emerged to connect supporters wherever they were (Salovaara, 2015).

[N]on-Arabs living in Arab countries … [used] #JeSuisAhmed ("I am Ahmed") five times more often when … embedded in a mixed Arab/

non-Arab … network. Among Arabs living in the West, we find a great variety of responses, not altogether associated with the size of their expatriate community.

(An et al., 2016)

The political postures underpinning various tags disclose that #CharlieHebdo is linked to sympathy for victims, #JeSuisCharlie with absolutist support for free speech, #JeNeSuisPasCharlie with a cross-sectarian rejection of free speech both *by* Muslims (as offensive) and *for* Muslims (as something they do not warrant), and #JeSuisAhmed with recognition that a Muslim policeman was among those whose life was taken, and the need for limitations on free speech. Use of these slogans maps closely onto regions of linguistic and religious sectarianism, apart from #JeNeSuisPasCharlie, which appealed to right-wing Islamists and Christians alike, for different reasons. #jesuiskouachi (one of the killers) appeared 49,000 times on the day of the attacks on *Charlie*. Its adherents relished using free speech to identify with/as a mass murderer of caricaturists and their co-workers (An et al., 2016; Badouard, 2016).

Not all Muslims are as vulnerable or sanctimonious as their *bien-pensants*. Then-*Charlie* columnist Zineb El Rhazoui, who was away at the time of the killings, wrote a moving account humanizing the victims of the slaughter (2015). L'Association de Manifeste des Libertés [The Association for the Manifesto of Freedoms] Islamic group of French and Arab intellectuals supported open, funny critique (Szerman, 2006). Muslim humorists around the world have routinely engaged in religious satire, mocking themselves and others. Their number includes cartoonists subject to *fatwas* and state harassment, such as Ali Ferzat, Ali Dilem, Zunar, and Musa Kart, and authors who specialize in Bakhtinian profanation. As blasphemy laws bite, Islamic cartoonists chafe against their governments' pious assaults. Malaysia and Indonesia spoke out against the attacks, even as they were oppressing local caricaturists for purported blasphemy (Hirzalla and van Zoonen, 2016; Salovaara, 2015; El Hissy, 2013; Crispin, 2015; Parameswaran, 2015).

Muslim satirists relish cartooning's capacity to cause offense. That is its very point—edgy, naughty, troubling humor. This is not news, research, or a polemic in favor of freedom; it seeks to be disruptively amusing to readers by mocking public figures, past and present. The murdered cartoonists did not see themselves as political actors, but pomposity-prickers, whose work became political through reactions to it by Islamic and free-speech absolutists alike (Horsman, 2020).

For Will Self, satire per cartoons presupposes a shared ethics and sense of justice, with the prospect of unsettling power and comforting weakness (2015). The genre draws on social and cultural specificity, not the breadth of interpretation or sense of justice that come with daily duels between religious and secular governance; it relies on accepting the right to criticize anyone and anything. Balance should not be expected of caricatures. They are part of the news, part of journalism, like editorials and op-eds, but *only* part. Must every sermon, political column, op-ed, editorial, billboard, or party-political manifesto include every position in a debate? There is no reason why cartoons should enunciate all sides to an issue or be impartial. They are not textbook chapters, mathematical proofs, kinship maps, daily news stories, or scientific documentaries, which claim to give unvarnished accounts of fact. But they *are* embedded in journalism that may draw on such genres.

Charlie Hebdo campaigns against sectarianism and for secularism and anarchistic republican values; not for violence or racism (Gamper, 2022). The magazine's contempt for all religious icons, figures, and beliefs was a crucial element in its defense when sued by the Grande Mosquée de Paris [the Grand Mosque of Paris] and l'Union des Organisations Islamiques de France [the Union of French Islamic Organisations] in 2007 for republishing the Danish cartoons. The plaintiffs did not initiate actions against *France Soir*, for example, because it 'était dans un role d'information' [was functioning as journalism], thereby ignoring the discussions about religions in general throughout *Charlie*'s pages (quoted in Ervine, 2019: 34). They also sought to make the issue one of racism, rather than blasphemy, the better to invoke France's secular laws in their favor; but this failed, because it was clear that all religions were treated summarily and critically by the magazine. Official Islam was seeking preferential assistance from the court; it failed, and on appeal, the final 2008 judgment found *Charlie* was engaging in journalistic free speech. Other means were chosen to defang the cartoonists—their offices were firebombed in 2011 on the day a special number was released, supposedly with Mohammed as guest editor. The magazine responded by warning that the right would use the attack to justify anti-Islamic sentiment (Ervine, 2019: 39–40, 44).

And yet. Because the illustrations appeared in a periodical, the caricaturists were also journalists, as are their colleagues in the daily news; and the magazine includes 'serious' articles on the topic of its caricatures (Ervine, 2019: 19–20). That raises a series of complex questions, such as whether cartoons should be categorized as 'coverage' and the responsibility of the *bourgeois* media in general to cover Islam in ways endorsed by the religion. Secular media representations of Islam continue to stereotype it, emphasizing violence and negativity (Ahmed and Matthes, 2017). Critics insist that *Charlie Hebdo*'s caricatures of Mohammed are 'ill[-]judged, uncontrolled and limitless freedom of speech and a risky action that may have future consequences that might cause moral harm' (Švaňa, 2016: 67). Meanwhile, satirical Muslim rappers are routinely denied the right to expression by the French state (Kleppinger, 2016).

As hundreds of noted writers put it, 'equal-opportunity offence' is *Charlie Hebdo*'s aspiration. But can such an aspiration be met when its 'targets' do not have equivalent social standing (Greenwald, 2015)? This is the argument in favor of free speech being rooted in respect for differences (Hietalahti et al., 2016). In addition, the 2015 attack and others have unleashed a state response unparalleled in the last 60 years, and not just per the libertarian left's *cliché* complaints about surveillance. It is much more important and strategic than that logic will admit:

> For the first time since the end of the Second World War, the assumption that France is experiencing a new form of territorial war is explicit in the public debate. It has reinforced the strong conviction among the French politicians and diplomats that security requires close cooperation with the USA and a renouncement of the Gaullist paradigm of exceptionalism.
>
> *(Lequesne, 2016)*

There is a clear correlation between France's domestic and international suppression of Islam and terrorist attacks at home, by contrast with approaches that eschew repression of the religion (Saiya, 2020).

It's suggestive that most Parisian marchers supporting the magazine were from the middle and ruling classes (Todd, 2015). Billionaire feminist critic Élisabeth Badinter called for a boycott of stores vending Islamic fashion; Laurence Rossignol, a socialist politician, likened Muslim women in headscarves to African Americans supporting slavery; and Education Minister Najat Vallaud-Belkacem proposed a program of re-education for pupils who failed to support the magazine.[27] Although the murderers were French natives, French international broadcasting assiduously attributed the attacks to foreigners (Hollis-Touré, 2016; Kiwan, 2016; Połońska-Kimunguyi and Gillespie, 2016).

Of a thousand front pages across the globe, a third didn't feature the event. Very few re-published the relevant cartoons, and only European dailies universally highlighted what had happened (Niemeyer, 2019). Spanish, UK, and Norwegian reporters largely adopted a moderate approach, propelled by the desire not to offend their own multicultural societies by speaking on behalf of an imagined—or self-consciously constructed and sustained—civic consensus (Luengo and Ihlebæk, 2019). When the former *Charlie* journalist Caroline Fourest held up the offending front cover during an interview on Britain's Sky News, she was immediately censored by the network (Weston Vauclair, 2015: 10). The *Wall Street Journal* and *New York Times* intensified associations between Islam and terrorism after the murders, but CNN and the networks refrained from showing the illustrations that had provoked the ruckus (Nora Politzer and Olmos Alcaraz, 2020; Wolska-Zogata, 2015: 356).

As the images and debates proliferated, the reprisals continued: reporters at *Cumhuriyet*[28] in Turkey were convicted for 'inciting hate and enmity' because they reproduced the cartoons; India and Senegal blocked the magazine;

and following *Charlie*'s announcement of a competition for caricatures of Iran's Supreme Leader علی خامنه‌ای [Ali Khamenei] in 2023, Teheran illegally obtained access to *Charlie Hebdo*'s subscriber list (Watts, 2023).[29] The Revolutionary Guard Corps warned that the French people and the magazine's employees 'take a look at the fate of Salman Rushdie,' who had been stabbed the year before in the abdomen, neck, eye, chest, and thigh by an assailant driven by Iranian orders (Corps quoted in Averre, 2023). After the Turkish elections that year, the magazine depicted President Recep Tayyip Erdoğan being electrocuted in a bathtub, suggesting this was the only way his time in power would end ("Erdogan," 2023).

The balance between the benefits of free expression and the right to 'human dignity, equality, freedom to live without harassment and intimidation, social harmony, mutual respect, and protection of one's good name and honour' remains unclear (Parekh, 2017: 932). That dilemma relates to democracy's capacity to undermine itself by granting freedom of speech to those who reject forms of knowledge and inquiry that transcend superstition (Gershberg and Illing, 2022). In addition, any notion that cartooning is not journalism is under potential erasure, because the genre is sustained within periodicals that report and comment; it has family resemblances to claims to the truth, albeit in exaggerated ways.

Conclusion

Three tendencies thrive across contemporary news. Methodological individualism assumes individual consciousness is the principal, determining force defining and satisfying needs (Youniss et al., 1997). Methodological nationalism favors an exclusive focus on the world of states, eschewing other actors or sites of political-economic struggle and the planet's survival as crucial *foci*. Methodological absolutism presents superstition or speech as absolutes. J-schools incarnate, embrace, and further these tendencies.

The lofty hopes and goals outlined in this book's Introduction grow complex when citizenship is broken down into its component parts and twinned with material experiences of state, economic, and cultural pressure, control, and sensitivity. This becomes especially intense when nationalism drives reporters to convey and obey the pronouncements of a military-industrial complex; when the news is dominated by stock-market emotion and manipulation; when consumption overdetermines public health; and when free-speech fundamentalists and opponents make severe claims.

Some instances examined here hold the lives of millions immediately in their hands, per war. Others touch on everyday norms, but important ones, like food coverage. For its part, *Charlie Hebdo* is clearly a limit case, but one that encapsulates wider tensions. All see different conceptions of citizenship invoked, compromise the cherished norms that Anglo journalism claims to abide by, and show that understanding the genealogy of the three citizenships helps disassemble a vast, singular norm so that its reach and effect can be inspected.

Notes

1. We're not looking at 'citizen journalism' here, but rather how the concept of citizenship animates and contextualizes what professional journalism does, and how key aspects of civic life are undermined by the prevailing political economy.
2. https://charliehebdo.fr/.
3. https://www.law.cornell.edu/constitution/first_amendment.
4. https://constitutionnet.org/sites/default/files/declaration_of_the_rights_of_man_1789.pdf.
5. http://www.gutenberg.org/files/608/608-h/608-h.htm.
6. https://constitutionnet.org/sites/default/files/declaration_of_the_rights_of_man_1789.pdf.
7. The Justice did not see fit to refer to the empire's foreign victims.
8. Defined as the nightly news on the major broadcast English-language networks.
9. https://www.youtube.com/watch?v=4bsZJOcUCx0.
10. https://liberalarts.tulane.edu/departments/history/people/walter-isaacson.
11. https://www.private-eye.co.uk/issue-1532/eyeplayer/play-189.
12. http://fair.org/extra-online-articles/fair%E2%80%88study-think-tank-spectrum-2012/.
13. In turn that reminds us of the 1960s slogan: 'Visit the United States before it visits you.'
14. https://www.youtube.com/watch?v=mt77GAFWQV0.
15. https://au.int/en/theme/2021/arts-culture-and-heritage.
16. https://www.youtube.com/watch?v=xWvXHXa51H8.
17. https://europaregina.eu/creative-industries/europe/.
18. https://europaregina.eu/wp-content/uploads/2022/05/creative-industry-4.0-towards-a-new-globalized-creative-economy-unctad.pdf.
19. There is no prize for guessing their identities: the US and China.
20. https://www.cdc.gov/foodborneburden/estimates-overview.html.
21. http://www.oic-oci.org/oicv3/page/?p_id=52&p_ref=26&lan=en.
22. https://web.archive.org/web/20150112190856/http://actu-societe.nouvelobs.com/france-soir-prophete-journal-monde-musulman.html.
23. http://www.un.org/en/universal-declaration-human-rights/.
24. https://www.article19.org/data/files/medialibrary/38231/'Hate-Speech'-Explained---A-Toolkit-(2015-Edition).pdf.
25. http://quran.com/search?q=blasphem.
26. http://www.ohchr.org/Documents/Issues/Opinion/SeminarRabat/Rabat_draft_outcome.pdf.
27. Of 64,000 French schools, pupils at 200 declined to observe a minute's silence to show respect for the deaths at *Charlie Hebdo* (i.e., have their own speech stilled) (Stille, 2015).
28. https://www.cumhuriyet.com.tr/.
29. https://www.article19.org/resources/turkey-charlie-hebdo-prison-sentences-for-two-journalists-violate-freedom-of-expression/;https://www.article19.org/resources/not-name-world-press-freedom-day-116-days-charlie-hebdo/s.

2
ENVIRONMENT (WITH RICHARD MAXWELL)

Many conversations about journalism and the environment question how to communicate scientific knowledge, problems of bias, and the roles of state and capital. Coverage of those topics is indeed crucial, given the misinformation that reporters receive from the extractive industries and their paid allies versus the capacity and the will to convey the truth produced by climatologists. And it's certainly right to say that journalists help determine what people know of the natural world and their impact on it, which frequently lacks scientific acuity or a political-economic ethic of care.

But beyond that, the media are materially complicit with our climate crisis—as are we, writing this on laptops and communicating via email. For the very tools of the news contribute to global boiling: reporters have an impact on the environment, not just on representations of it. So this chapter focuses on twin aspects: the crucial question of how the climate crisis is covered, and the less-noted matter of journalism as an environmental problem.

Early coverage

Research into the possibility of climate change goes back centuries, prior even to the Industrial Revolution (Fleming, 1998). We focus here on US history, because that country has been a massive contributor both to climate change and to climate science. Journalism reportage of that knowledge began promisingly. In 1912, *Popular Mechanics* headlined 'The Effect of the Combustion of Coal on the Climate' (Molena, 1912). By 1930, it asked 'Is Our Climate Changing?' (Talman, 1930). Twenty years later, climatologists writing in the *Saturday Evening Post* queried 'Is the World Getting Warmer?' (Abarbanel and McClusky, 1950) and *Scientific American* headlined 'The Changing

DOI: 10.4324/9781032701660-3

Climate' (Kimble, 1950). *The New York Times* said 'The Weather Is Really Changing' (Engel, 1953) and inquired 'How Industry May Change Climate' (W. K., 1953). *Time* magazine noted that 'the hungry fires of industry' were generating 'a great greenhouse' ("Science," 1953) and went on to warn that within 50 years, 'burning fossil fuel ... may have a violent effect on the earth's climate' ("Science," 1956). The *New York Times* attributed the previous half century of warming to the extractive industries (Kaempffert, 1956). NBC's 1958 documentary *The Unchained Goddess* gained a third of the audience share the night it was broadcast (LaFollette, 2002: 62). The film featured a warning that humanity may

> be unwittingly changing the world's climate through the waste products of its civilization. Due to our releases in factories and automobiles every year of more than six billion tons of CO_2, which helps the air absorb heat from the sun, our atmosphere may be getting warmer.[1]

In 1961, the *New York Times* acknowledged that increased carbon dioxide in the air had been caused by 'fumes from industry' (Sullivan, 1961). By 1964, *Popular Mechanics* discerned 'the first dirty straws in the wind that air pollution may be causing dangerous long-term effects in the Earth's climate, effects that may be irreversible' (Hicks, 1964: 82). Allen Ginsberg appeared on *The Merv Griffin Show* in the 1960s to avow that 'the current rate of air pollution brought about by the proliferation of automobiles' might generate 'the rapid build-up of heat on the earth' and 'melt the polar ice caps, causing a flooding of the greater part of the globe' (quoted in Oreskes, 2023: 1–2). In 1974, a CIA briefing predicted that climate change would lead to 'drought, famine, and political unrest in the western world' (1). Three years later, the *New York Times* obtained a copy and warned of the risks described (Sterba, 1977).

But such coverage became 'sparse and rather fragmented' (Boykoff and Luedecke, 2016), in keeping with the developing post-war assumption that nuclear power would soon be the globe's primary energy source. And something else. Per the binarism detailed in the Introduction, much of the media gave in to propaganda, affording at least equal time to environmental perspectives along a right-left continuum, despite the fraudulent nature of reactionary claims (Hart and Feldman, 2014). The outcome is a citizenry confused by 'false balance reporting' (Imundo and Rapp, 2022).

Since the late 1960s, US and Western European PR firms, think tanks, and their loving parents/paymasters in the extractive sector have distorted the story. That and the commercialization of news and disinvestment in investigative journalism have disabled the media from responding in a robust, consistent manner to anti-scientific lies (Boykoff and Yulsman, 2013; Dembicki, 2022). Within months of the 1969 oil spill off the Santa Barbara coast that alerted *bourgeois* America to the ugliness of pollution, the extractive sector was sponsoring culture on PBS, reassuring the white middle classes of its good intentions. Network TV viewers were soon treated to the now-notorious 'Crying Indian' [sic] commercial, created for the second Earth Day in 1971.[2] Espera De Corti, an Italian American who had renamed himself 'Iron Eyes Cody,' was depicted in what passed for Native garb, weeping in the face of pollution and littering (Aleiss, 1996). This putative public-service announcement gained 'one of the highest viewer recognition rates in television history' and won numerous advertising awards (Dunaway, 2015: 79).

The work of Keep America Beautiful on behalf of beer and other sugar-drink manufacturers, 'Crying Indian' was part of a sizable portfolio of propaganda created for corporate polluters. It was designed to interpellate audience members as individually and collectively responsible for over-consumption. By the 1970s, that trend had turned into vigorous opposition to any legislation or regulation that might point to or oppose the environmental criminality controlled from corporate suites. It drew on the slogan that accompanied De Corti's weeping: 'People Start Pollution. People Can Stop It' (Dunway, 2015: 82, 92–94). Corporations? The military? No, 'people.'

'Merchants of doubt'

In addition to making ordinary people shoulder the blame for pollution, anti-science chorines frequently deny there is a climate crisis or say state action to mitigate it won't work. Creatures of cynical PR firms and coin-operated think tanks, these 'merchants of doubt' (Oreskes and Conway, 2010) are financed to help the extractive industries fend off pro-environmental legislation, 'dissipate pressure for progress' (Miller and Dinan, 2015: 99), attack the character and expertise of environmentalists, and undermine the legitimacy of independent climate science. Their particular target is the Intergovernmental Panel on Climate Change (IPCC), 'the world's leading authority on climate issues' (Oreskes and Conway, 2010: 2).

There are four principal arms of the doubt business: 'conservative "free market" thinktanks, public relations groups, fossil-fuel organisations and ideologically aligned media.' For decades, they have circulated misinformation about climate change. Drawing on strategies from campaigns to silence the truth about the health effects of smoking—many denialists from tobacco campaigns moved on to the climate project—the aim has been to infect 'conventional wisdom among the public' with 'uncertainties.' Examples include a 1991 program funded by coal utilities to 'recruit scientists' to 'reposition global warming as theory (not fact)' (Readfearn, 2015a). Desmog, a site for activist journalism ironically engineered by public-relations veterans, offers a useful tool to uncover 'the PR pollution that clouds climate science.' Its 'Global Warming Disinformation Database' provides voluminous background on individuals and institutions around the world who peddle fake science.³

The story of PR's role in our climate crisis is as shocking as it is clear, as stunning an indictment of corporate capitalism and its use of ideology as one could find (Almiron and Xifra, 2020)—and a statement of how the labor process of journalism has become so compromised that reporters often recycle PR nonsense. Thousands of these agencies even combine work for climate criminals with shilling for universities and pro-capitalist environmental groups (Milman, 2023).⁴

Consider a notorious 2000 memo that US Republican Party apparatchik Frank Luntz directed to the energy industry: 'Should the public come to believe that the scientific issues are settled, their views about global warming will change accordingly. Therefore, you need to continue to make the lack of scientific certainty a primary issue in the debate.' Luntz managed to have the phrase 'global warming' replaced by 'climate change,' because it was 'less frightening' (Readfearn, 2015b; Lakoff, 2010). He claims to have replicated this success by displacing 'drilling for oil' with 'energy exploration' in press coverage (Luntz, 2008: xviii, 167–69). Luntz has since recanted these absurdities and admits the need for urgent remedial action by the state (Adragna, 2019).

As a case study, let's look under the cover of Edelman, one of the world's biggest PR corporations.⁵ Forty years ago, its founder proudly announced a mission for the 21st century: 'to prove by our performance that public relations is not a devious kind of work, a covering up, a cosmeticizing or distortion of reality' (Edelman, 1983). But Edelman has form in the world of obfuscation across many industries. In tobacco, it dedicated decades to combating medical science, encouraging simpleton smokers to continue their deluded indulgence.⁶ In pharmaceuticals, it spruiked spurious studies guaranteeing hair regrowth to gullible guys (Moynihan et al., 2002). And in the extractive sector, its collaboration with Trans Canada sought to discredit anyone questioning the Energy East pipeline (McDiarmid, 2014).

The company's work is predicated on gaining favorable, free press coverage by invoking apparently disinterested people and organizations. Edelman's *Grassroots Advocacy Vision Document* incarnates civil-society mimesis on behalf of corporate distortion.⁷ This 'third party technique' moves away from 'self-interested messengers,' instead paying seemingly independent experts/ ordinary folks and astroturf organizations (*faux* grassroots activists) to vocalize corporate lines (Burton and Rowell, 2003). Edelman runs campaigns riven with junk science that are designed to appeal to everyday experience, always opposing democratic regulation underpinned by scholarly advice (Levantesi, 2022; Schäfer, 2012; Schlichting, 2013). In chemicals, it set up supposedly grassroots campaigns for Monsanto *contra* critiques of genetically modified food (Beder, 1998). In retail, it paid operatives masquerading as cross-country campers to blog favorably about Wal-Mart carparks and store managers (Frazier, 2006). Such activities run counter to the US PR industry's code of ethics, which says 'improper conduct' includes '"grass roots" campaigns or letter-writing campaigns to legislators on behalf of undisclosed interest groups' and 'employing people to pose as volunteers to speak at public hearings and participate in "grass roots" campaigns.'[8]

Edelman was caught out in 2014 because other major PR concerns announced they would no longer enable climate-change deniers (Goldenberg, 2014). The company encountered further difficulties when word spread that it worked for the American Petroleum Institute (API) through a subsidiary, Blue Advertising. Tax filings disclosed that API paid Edelman US$327.4 million between 2008 and 2012 (Quinn and Young, 2015). In return for this largesse, it had schooled the Institute in award-winning campaigns designed to avoid the charge of climate-change denial.[9] When the facts emerged, one of its senior people resigned in disgust. Edelman claimed to be misunderstood, sacrificed executives, announced that it believed in the science of climate change, and divested from Blue Advertising (Arena, 2021; Gunther, 2014; Elliott, 2014; Sudhaman, 2015).

But since the 2015 announcement that it would cease denying climate change, Edelman has undertaken campaigns for American Fuel and Petrochemical Manufacturers, ExxonMobil, and Shell (Wright et al., 2021; Westervelt, 2022a). Meanwhile, the founding eponym's dutiful son describes the company as 'a house of trust through our mission, values, and actions,' notably via 'environmental stewardship' (Edelman, 2019). The rewards for that putative stewardship are immense: Edelman registered record revenues in 2021 of US$985 million, up 15.4% on the previous year (Sudhaman, 2022).[10]

And API? Edelman's lessons were well learnt. The Institute's website advises that:

> The world needs solutions that advance human and economic development, enable emerging economies to progress while also developing their own domestic resources and satisfy global energy needs in ways that are compatible with reducing greenhouse gas emissions and achieving environmental progress.[11]

Here's a tendentious translation: 'We keep you warm, cool, lit, connected, and mobile, and we care about the poor—so don't regulate us. Like you, we worry about the environment and will fix it before we ruin it.' In 2022, API's head, Mike Sommers, boasted on Fox News that 'the most important environmental movement in the world is the American oil and gas industry' ("US Oil," 2022). The Institute immodestly describes Sommers as a 'thought leader,'[12] while *Fortune* magazine anoints him as joint 12th in its list of the 'World's 50 Greatest Leaders' (2021).

Other key chorines of climate denial that inflect journalism include a vast array of think tanks populated by failed, failing, fallen, falling, but above all flailing academics. Consider Willie Soon, an aerospace engineer. He describes the IPCC as 'a pure bully' that manipulates facts (Rowland, 2013). Soon made headlines in 2015 when investigators found that his climate-science denials were bought with US$1.5 million from fossil-fuel companies, something he had failed to disclose (Readfearn, 2015a). A decade after exposure as a shill for big oil, Soon remains a featured speaker on the climate. He attracts news coverage (Wilson, 2023), as does the front organization with which he is affiliated, the Center for Environmental Research and Earth Sciences.[13]

The list of similar bodies (current and defunct) includes the Mercatur Center, the American Enterprise Institute, the Committee for a Constructive Tomorrow, the George C Marshall Institute, the Global Warming Policy Foundation (it funnels millions to UK political grandees), the Acton Institute, the Heartland Institute (which defends Soon against 'the generously funded environmental left's attacks on an honest climate scientist'[14] and has claimed climate scientists are 'murderers and madmen' akin to أسامة بن محمد بن عوض بن لادن [Osama Bin Laden], Charles Manson, and the Unabomber, Tad Kaczynski), the Claremont Institute, the Legatum Institute, the Science and Public Policy Institute, the Discovery Institute, the Manhattan Institute for Policy Research, the Hoover Institution, the Institute of Public Affairs, the Reason Foundation, the Institute of Economic Affairs, the Fraser Institute, the Business Environmental Leadership Council, the Europäisches Institut für Klima und Energie, the TaxPayers' Alliance, the Heritage Foundation, the American Enterprise Institute, the World Business Council on Sustainable Development, the Ludwig von Mises Institute, the Initiative for Free Trade, the E Foundation for Oklahoma, Open Europe, the Cobden Centre, the Charles Koch Foundation, the Adam Smith Institute, and the Competitive Enterprise Institute, *inter alia*. Many are part of a loose global formation known as the Atlas Network[15] (Banerjee, 2017; Stone, 2013; Lawrence et al., 2019). Leading US entities alone received more than half a billion dollars from the extractive sector between 2021 and mid-2023 (Whitehead, 2023). The norm is to create lies in the US then circulate them across the EU (Almiron et al., 2020).

These European and Gringo servants of climate devastation gain their coin and distribute their fantasies in a coordinated way (Almiron et al., 2022; Burton, 2007). Many are creatures of petrostates as well as the firms that pay hundreds of millions in return for column inches, interviews, and lobbying (Center for International Policy, 2020). Climate crises are only part of their game (Ruser, 2018) and they are as keen to fund gullible/avaricious politicians across the Atlantic to forward or block an array of policies and programs as they are to obtain media coverage (Horton and Bychawski, 2022; Bychawski, 2022; Horton, 2023; Bright, 2023).

When not seeking to prevent rational intervention in the climate crisis, these institutions hope to retard it. 'Climate delay' focuses on legitimizing inaction or proposing purely corporate responses to the disaster (Lamb et al., 2020), countering anything democratic and scientific rather than plutocratic and self-serving. A classic instance of the process can be seen via DC's Atlantic Council. It describes itself as 'a group of foreign policy change-makers committed to achieving real-world impact through world-class research paired with innovative methods and engagement with a wide range of stakeholders. Our mission has never been more urgent, our work has never been more crucial, and the global stakes have never been higher.'[16] The principal funders of that 'mission' include the Abu Dhabi National Oil Company. One of the world's largest oil producers, it handed over more than US$5 million to the Council between 2018 and 2023 (Goldstein, 2023). The Company's chief executive, سلطان أحمد الجابر [Sultan Al Jaber], is also a government minister. He was selected to run the UN's 2023 Climate Conference of the Parties (COP), an extraordinary choice given Al Jaber's corporate and state positions: working for a systematically polluting firm and an administration that rejects the concept of refugee rights, engages in arbitrary detention and torture, and obstructs free expression, queer love, and discussions of public opinion (Harvey, 2023).[17] With the COP underway, he was on hand to advise that there was 'no science' supporting an end to fossil fuels, which would 'take the world back into caves' (quoted in Carrington and Stockton, 2023). The Atlantic Council and NBC had delivered full-throated justifications of Al Jaber's appointment as 'ideal' because of Al Jaber's 'rich background' (Kempe, 2023). Presumably 'rich' did not signify 'wealthy' to the Council or the network. Or did it? Meanwhile, any dissonance was not tolerated: Al Jaber's associates clandestinely edited Wikipedia pages outing him as an oil oligarch who had authorized a pipeline contract of US$4 billion (Stockton, 2023).

PR firms and think tanks are aided by J-school students and graduates[18]: journalism both provides personnel to these concerns and reiterates their distortions (Moreno et al., 2022). Yanqui student collaborators receive prejudicial *largesse*, with dubious projects assiduously funded. Hundreds of thousands of dollars have been pocketed by the US Student Free Press Association. It publishes *The College Fix*, which offers tendentious stories about the climate (Readfearn, 2016).[19] The Young America's Foundation boasts having trained thousands of tyro reporters to promote climate obfuscation.[20]

Even as cautious a body as the IPCC acknowledged in 2022 that 'corporate agents have attempted to derail climate-change mitigation by targeted lobbying and doubt-inducing media strategies' (557). Climate deniers do not focus on the ball when the player is available to attack, so speaking out against willful distortion can come at significant cost for climate scientists, who also run that risk in their push for advertising and PR firms to refuse fossil-fuel work (Coan et al., 2021; Mann and Toles, 2016; Lewandowsky et al., 2015; "450+," 2023). Decades of lies have traduced scholarly careers via coordinated campaigns of malefaction. The strong correlation between productive, highly cited, public-intellectual climate researchers and their denunciation on so-called 'social media' suggests there are organized campaigns against them, populated by professional writers, i.e., communications and J-school grads (Global Witness, 2023). Concerted assaults on meteorologists have been brutal, violent, and international; it comes as no surprise that US TV forecasters daring to relate weather trends to climate change are subject to extraordinary abuse (Parry et al., 2023; Associated Press, 2023). And apostasy is unacceptable. When a former US chorine of conventional political science turned against his true love to acknowledge in an op-ed that pluralism was a nonsense and corporations kept winning policy scrapes (Lindblom, 1977), Mobil Oil took out a full-page advertisement in the *New York Times* denouncing him (Mobil Oil, 1978).

Those strategies are probably a factor in the declining trust in science exhibited by the US population, especially among reactionaries (Kennedy et al., 2022). For when charlatans are accepted by mainstream journalists as legitimate rivals to scientific research, calls for action to protect the environment are more easily thwarted.

Contemporary coverage

Nathaniel Rich (the writer) and George Steinmetz (the photographer) produced 'Losing Earth,' a 30,000-word 2018 *New York Times Magazine* feature. The editors presented it as a 'work of history' focused on the 1980s, when the US almost joined the vanguard to save the planet from global warming. Naomi Klein acknowledged her excitement at seeing the paper 'throw the full force of its editorial machine behind' the article, bearing in mind its 'dereliction of duty' to report consistently on the climate crisis (2018). Of course, the 1980s were the decade when the *New York Times* adopted a vacillating tone on the environment, reiterating Republican lies throughout Ronald Reagan's scandal-laden Administration (Shabecoff, 1983).

The 2018 feature was accompanied by links to educational materials and critical commentaries.[21] It set off a series of rejoinders and corrections in various media outlets, notably over the story's failure to mention women involved in the struggle for climate science or identify key institutional malefactors across right-wing politics and corporate capital (Meyer, 2018; Leder, 2018). Critics also noted that its claims about putatively decent conservatives and fossil-fuel companies were misleading.

A key point of contention was that the story blamed the failure of political will to act against climate disaster on allegedly universal human flaws (Meyer, 2018). In Rich's words:

> If human beings really were able to take the long view—to consider seriously the fate of civilization decades or centuries after our deaths—we

would be forced to grapple with the transience of all we know and love in the great sweep of time. So we have trained ourselves, whether culturally or evolutionarily, to obsess over the present, worry about the medium term and cast the long term out of our minds, as we might spit out a poison.

(Rich and Steinmetz, 2018)

Creating an environmentally sound international order was never on the authors' agenda:

We can trust the technology and the economics. It's harder to trust human nature. Keeping the planet to two degrees of warming, let alone 1.5 degrees, would require transformative action. It will take more than good works and voluntary commitments; it will take a revolution. But in order to become a revolutionary, you need first to suffer.

(Rich and Steinmetz, 2018)

This aligns with the individualistic, consumerist rhetoric that is the desired master discourse of polluters. The idea of a universal humanity (a 'we') assumes every one of 'us' is equally able to transform the political economy. But the tasks of daily survival 'make it virtually impossible for most people to care—and organize—around forces not affecting them in the immediate present' (Aronoff, 2018). Geopolitical inequalities exclude vulnerable nations from political and corporate influence. The same applies to the impoverished within wealthy societies.

Here's the actual story:

The enormous development of industry, technology, and modern cities rested upon an implicit, exploitative environmental settlement. It was embedded in the industrialism of the big factory and the overpowering modernism of the tower block, and in the pollution from cars, power stations and chemical plants.

(Campbell et al., 1990: 27)

A small group of powerful countries, their past and present leaders, vast military forces, and immense multinational corporations are the parties responsible for climate change and continued inaction to thwart it. Blueprints for a greener planet proliferate, but major political-economic actors depend on such plans remaining on the drawing board. The wealthy are well aware of the ecological crisis and have planned for it—narcissistically, via various forms of survivalism (Rushkoff, 2022). Readers of the *New York Times* may appreciate being told that the blame for climate change falls equally on us all—rich, poor, strong, weak—but the real lesson, *contra* Rich et al., is that dealing with climate change requires collective citizen action, not personal consumer choice (McKibben, 2008).

Apart from being entirely impractical, the notion of individual responsibility for the crisis has a murky background. The idea of establishing one's very own carbon footprint was invented by BP's PR servants to divert attention from its nefarious activities and make consumers feel culpable (Kaufman, 2020; Solnit, 2021) via a notorious 2005 advertising campaign with the tagline 'What on earth is a carbon footprint? Everybody in the world has one' (quoted in Doyle, 2011: 200).

Some members of the group that BP calls 'Everybody' leave a larger residue than others. Consider the deaths of 11 people, 160,000 sea turtles, 105,000 sea birds, 8 billion oysters, and half the dolphin population of the *golfo de México* following the explosion of the corporation's Deepwater Horizon oil rig in 2010, as the company propelled 134 million gallons of oil across the coastlines of five states. It took six years of litigation before BP and partners were fined over US$20 billion (National Oceanic and Atmospheric Administration, 2017).

Like the state and the media, the company repeatedly invoked metaphors of war and death to describe its struggle to manage the disaster it had made (McClintock, 2010). And per the last chapter, Yanqui reporters on such topics followed the norms of a lifetime, focusing on official voices and disregarding alternative sources of expert and popular knowledge (Watson, 2014). Initially, coverage focused on the horrifying impact of the event and the difficulty of containing it. As time went on, journalists highlighted the ameliorating work of scientific, governmental, and industrial expertise. The crimes were not explained as the spectacular expression of a wider extractive tendency, but as an isolable, treatable disaster (Humphreys and Thompson, 2014).

Corporate oil finances millions of words about protecting the climate, matched only by the torrent of material practices that endanger it (Lei et al., 2022). Climate-change nonsense, be it outright denial or anti-democratic capitalist band-aid 'policy,' continues to receive disproportionate coverage and room in the US media (Freudenberg and Muselli, 2013), for example, the *Washington Post* (Mufson, 2020; Thiessen, 2021) and *New York Times* (Wetts, 2020; Halstead, 2020). For decades, the *Wall Street Journal* has ignored or distorted the relevant science (Pielke, 2012; Bast and Spencer, 2014; Schultz and Baker III, 2017; Jenkins, 2021; Climate Nexus, 2016).[22]

This is not only a US issue: flawed climate coverage is a global problem, varying with countries' economic instability, experience of climate catastrophe, and ideological tenor (Sklair, 2021; Barkemeyer et al., 2017). Between 2005 and 2019, reactionary parts of the US, British, Canadian, New Zealand/Aotearoan, and Australian press printed lies about climate change (McAllister et al, 2021). German, Indian, and Swiss newspapers often promote distortions even amongst reportage weighted in favor of science (Brüggemann and Engesser, 2017). Mathias Döpfner, head of Germany's largest media conglomerate, Axel Springer, welcomes climate change and has pushed his position to the group's tabloid, *Bild* (Oltermann, 2023). France offers significant time to reactionary lies (Grundmann and Scott, 2014). The British press has allocated extraordinary space to such anti-knowledge (Gillings and Dayrell, 2023). In China, environmental journalists struggle against asinine paradigms of development and growth as well as their Leninist polity, but manage to eschew the *faux* even-handedness of Anglos, albeit situating matters largely in terms of the infallibility of their glorious leaders and the desire to rival the US as a superpower (Li, 2022; Song et al., 2022; Huan, 2023; Guo et al., 2023). Russia demonstrates strong correlations between economic crises, newspaper owners' energy interests, and the level of coverage (Boussalis et al., 2016). Japan has seen dramatic changes in the frequency and tenor of environmental journalism (Sampei and Aoyagi-Usui, 2009). Major Italian newspapers averaged just five stories a week on the climate crisis in 2022 ("Un anno," 2023). April 2023 saw international newspaper attention to climate change down 4% on the previous month; wire services 16%; radio 26% (Media and Climate Change Observatory, 2023a). As the northern summer heated up alarmingly, so did coverage—July 2023 world newspaper attention was up by 14% on June, wire services by 19% (Media and Climate Change Observatory, 2023b).

US English-language broadcast networks have a poor record: in 2022, the climate garnered 1.3% of news time (MacDonald, 2023). The following year, when California was deluged with extraordinary levels and rates of precipitation, they basically ignored the causes, which included climate change (Fisher and MacDonald, 2023). The right-wing US media stridently refuse the truth: angry swivel-head cable mavens feast on minor disagreements among experts (Dunlap and Jacques, 2013; Anshelm and Hultman, 2014; Hart and Feldman, 2014; Fisher et al., 2023). IPCC coverage in Sweden, Brazil, the US, Australia, and Britain sees continued lying by conservative TV networks and a serious failure to engage by others (Painter et al., 2023). The performance of network journalism in Italy is abject: 0.7% of news over the first quarter of 2022 ("The Climate," 2022). Favored new places for reactionaries to denounce science or extractive corporations to brandish their purportedly green credentials are news-oriented podcasts, influencers' sites, and video games (Westervelt, 2021; Dimitriadis et al., 2023; Berner, 2023).

In general, reporters in the Global South look more closely at the human implications of climate change (Hase et al., 2021) but often problematically. Consider Latin America. Its dominant media reflect a history of authoritarian regimes, usually under the direction of the US, that serve local oligarchs. Journalists frequently abjure reporting on the degradation caused by the extractive and manufacturing sectors, other than during dramatic disasters

(Takahashi et al., 2018). In Brazil, even the purportedly progressive media describe the science and policy implications of environmental catastrophe from the Global North's perspective, eschewing discussion of the colonial roots of climate devastation (Beiling Loose, 2022). Chile's liberals cover climate change twice as often as do reactionaries (Dotson et al., 2012). Colombia is marked by the brutal suppression of environmental defenders. In 2022, the conservative government was rewarded with major international prizes for environmental protection by an array of capitalist lackeys, from *National Geographic* to the Rainforest Coalition. It received adulatory local media coverage, apart from criticism in some alternative outlets ("*National Geographic*," 2022; "Gran noticia," 2022; "Duque posa," 2021).

Again and again, climate criminals are treated by many reporters as credible commentators and policy proponents, even though the record shows these institutions should not be trusted. For example, a third of the globe's largest 2,000 corporations avow that they are committed to net-zero emissions, claiming to be environmental 'leaders.' Based on their current policies and programs, 93% of them will not achieve their putative goal. In-depth analyses of the biggest are damning (Accenture, 2022; New Climate Institute, 2023). If challenged in court, tame journalists defend the lies think tanks and their funders tell as 'free speech,' claiming they are petitioning the public to adopt positions on policy matters (Westervelt, 2022b). This tactic was invented in the 1960s, when extractive firms and their think-tank pets learnt to paint themselves as champions of debate covered by the First Amendment (Kerr, 2013).[23]

The problems of the environment and journalism don't end with the extractive and manufacturing sectors. Sports have generally been regarded as ecologically sustainable, with residues of sweat, blood, mud, tears, tape, code, and joy rather than carbon and carcinogens. That myth is in real trouble now (Miller, 2018, 2019). Because of climate change, within six decades few world cities will be cool enough to host summer sports safely (Gaind, 2016). Competitors are already falling ill and dying. Distance races in particular are dramatically worsening runners' health (Nowak et al., 2022). Extreme heat kills college and professional 'football' players across the US in sizable numbers, as their artificially bloated, vulnerable bodies are 'tested' in the summer months of preparation for Fall fixtures (Nichols, 2014). Competitors in avowedly healthier sports frequently fall ill and die due to exerting themselves in extreme temperatures (Wallace et al., 2019; Bernard et al., 2021). The data on sickness brought about by exercise as temperatures increase are startling: 'Compared with 1991–2000, the hours of at least moderate risk of heat stress for light outdoor activity (eg, walking) increased by an average of 241 hours per person (20.1% increase) annually during 2013–22. For moderate-intensity activity (e.g., jogging or cycling), there was an increase of 253 hours (19.0% increase)' (*The Lancet*, 2023: 14).

Many sports embrace greenwashing, per the National Football League (NFL) green program, which dates back to 1993.[24] But these sports are not truly adjusting—as you would expect, since team owners donate millions of dollars to their pet Republican Party (Armour and Schad, 2020). Less than a third of US and Canadian pro stadia choose renewable energy; the NFL's Dallas Cowboys, for instance, require 750 MW on game day. The National Hockey League (NHL) sprays around 321 million gallons of water a year (McHale, 2019). 'NHL Green' promotes hydrofluorocarbon refrigerants, 'a potent greenhouse gas,' to freeze rinks (Environmental Investigation Agency, 2021). For all baseball's environmental claims, it gains sponsorship from major corporate polluters, such as automobile and airplane manufacturers and energy miscreants in natural gas, petroleum, and transportation (New Weather Institute, 2021).[25] In 2018, MLB teams together traveled 7.5 million km, emitting 122,000 tonnes of CO_2 (Wynes, 2021).

Association football is also affected by climate change, which produces unprecedented flooding, endangering pitches among other sporting venues (The Climate Coalition, 2018). And the impact is reciprocal, given where football equipment is made and transported for sale and use, the water and chemicals involved in ground maintenance, the food consumed at games, the electricity required to cover and watch fixtures, and the impact of travel and tourism (Malhado and Rothfuss, 2013). The sport is responsible for 0.3–0.4% of the world's annual emissions—equivalent to Denmark (Ashoo, 2021). English Premier League domestic team travel over the 2016–17 season generated approximately 1,134 tonnes of CO_2-eq (Tóffano Pereira et al., 2019). In 2022–23, there were 81 short-haul flights over a two-month period (Lockwood, 2023). Because England is a small place, most hops are of very short duration. Many involve flying empty planes to airports to pick up players. In the case of Arsenal, this travel has included a 14-minute executive-jet jaunt to Norwich; for Manchester United, a ten-minute plane ride to the mighty Leicester (de Menezes, 2015; Stanton et al., 2021). It goes without saying that the League and Arsenal boast green credentials[26] and United modestly announces that '[e]veryone at the club is committed to tackling environmental and social issues at regional, national and international levels, using the Manchester United brand to leverage support and create awareness of the issues facing the planet.'[27]

In France, Paris Saint-Germain drones on about how environmentally friendly it is.[28] Owned by Qatar, the team flies across the country on that nation's airline rather than taking sustainable options. When questioned about this in 2022, management mockingly replied that the team had considered a 'sand-yacht' as an alternative. Heaven forfend chaps travel by train. The club's most famous player, Lionel Messi, tootled around the world 52 times in two months that summer, accounting for thousands of tonnes of emissions ("PSG," 2022). He is part of the 1% of the world's population responsible for half of aviation emissions, via private jets (Murphy and Simon, 2021).

Estimating the environmental impact of the men's World Cup Finals is complex. But offset programs designed to minimize the bootprint of the 2014 Finals in Brazil were unsuccessful—2.72 million tonnes of carbon were emitted (Crabb, 2018; Sturrock, 2018). The Fédération Internationale de Football Association (FIFA) acknowledged that the 2018 event in Russia generated well over 2.1 million tonnes (FIFA, 2019: 68). The 2022 Finals were held in Qatar, for all its problematic vote-winning, grotesque labor abuses, notorious contempt for human rights—and wholesale unsustainability as a venue, given limited natural resources, vast importation of workers to construct venues, and abundant use of air-conditioning in stadia (Abusin et al., 2020). The vast Global South corporations involved—the Chinese property developer Wanda, cellphone merchant Vivo, cattle-torturer Mengniu, and electronics manufacturer Hisense, plus Qatar Airways and Qatar Energy—continued on their merry sponsorship way (Tweedale, 2018; Ronald, 2022).

The Fédération Internationale de l'Automobile is the governing body of world motor sport. Its Environment and Sustainability Commission is run by former Mexican President Felipe Calderón, notorious for environmental despoliation, rampant corruption, cosmic inefficiency, and grotesque militarization during his Sexenio. He has announced 'una nueva era que renuevaun fuerte compromiso con el medio ambiente' [a new era of strong commitment to the environment] (quoted in "Felipe Calderón," 2022). The Fédération's 2022 *Environmental Strategy 2020–2030* promises immediate carbon neutrality, through reduced emissions and carbon-credit capitalism, and net zero in 2030, by removing carbon waste. All of this is to be done while maintaining 'relevance and leadership.'

Corporate motor sport claims to be 'an environmental science lab,' passing on gains in efficiency to everyday motoring (Richards, 2021). That is the mantra across car racing. But its flagship, Formula One, is responsible for more than 250,000 tonnes of CO_2 emissions annually, the same as 55,000 automobiles: 0.3% from racing; 45% from air, sea, and road transport of cars; and 27.7% from the movement of workers, promoters, partners, and executive hangers-on (Scott, 2013; Black, 2010; Lim, 2022; McLaren Racing 2021: 10). The sport's annual electricity use would power 45,000 US homes (Zerrener, 2019). The industry's claims for reduced emissions are controversial (Reis Mourao, 2018): 'supposedly eco-friendly hybrid power units' are 'a life-support mechanism for the sport in its traditional guise' (Williams, 2019). Siting the event around the world makes it impossible to reduce such figures meaningfully, absent locating equipment and personnel permanently in each venue (Lim, 2022). The real nettle to be grasped is international travel; not just of people, but of heavy machinery across the globe, for a season that lasts almost ten months a year (Richards, 2023). Each team flies 160,000 km a year to test cars and compete (King, 2013). When Formula One merrily decamps to cities around the world, it has deleterious effects on birdlife, waterways, trees, noise, and trash (Tranter and Lowes, 2009). Spaces that were once commons are transformed into promotional sideboards for commerce; public havens from traffic become private heavens for automobiles (Lowes, 2004). And estimates of the sport's environmental impact often exclude construction of the roads and buildings it uses in these places; after the US and China, concrete is the world's largest emitter of carbon, at 8% of the global total (Lehne and Preston, 2018; Watts, 2019).

The Olympics are constitutively environmental: their very division between summer and winter contests is climatic, their environmental history dubious (Müller et al., 2021). In the run-up to the failed British empire's laughably self-celebratory 2012 summer Games in London, BP was in disgrace following its pollution of the *golfo*. Help was at hand. The US Olympic Committee brightly announced 'BP is in the middle of a crisis that everyone is interested in resolving as soon as possible' (quoted in Hersh, 2010). The Games represented a veritable coming-out party for that toxifying, terrorizing company as 'the BP board outlined how they had made a business case internally for their sponsorship of the Olympics, the costed returns for which included building and protecting their brand' (England, 2012). Company research after the event disclosed that 82% of the British public knew this convicted environmental criminal had sponsored London's absurdity, and well over a third of them believed the firm sought 'a cleaner planet' (Reynolds, 2012).

Many Olympic sports elect to avoid or alter geography. Swimmers and divers are sedulously sheltered from salt and river water and basketball players securely shielded from weather. Skateboarders and motocross riders rely on the evisceration of anything natural in their path. Our fellow-animals are largely absent, other than the enslaved horses of equestrianism and the pentathlon (one that stepped out of line in the 2020 Tokyo Olympiad was slapped into submission), skeet shooting's mimetic birds—and occasional mascots ("Tokyo Olympics: German," 2021; Sin, 2014).

Tokyo 2020 saw the organizers pillaging rainforests to build their stadium (Rainforest Action Network, 2018), razing public parks and housing, ruining iconic landmarks (Zirin and Boykoff, 2019), and re-imagining Fukushima: don't fear radiation (Boykoff and Gaffney, 2020), it's safer than smoking (Ware, 2021) (apropos, 1964 featured an Olympic cigarette, leading to massive increases in Japanese smoking then and lung cancer today [Tomizawa, 2016]). Officials estimated that 2.73 million tonnes of CO_2 would be emitted courtesy of the 2020 Games—more than many countries produce in a year ("A Greener," 2021), though banning foreign spectators because of the syndemic probably diminished that figure (Tokyo Organising Committee, 2021).

The 1964 Tokyo Olympics had been held in October. But a repeat of such a calendar was unacceptable to the key plutocratic broadcaster, NBC.

Ever since poor ratings for the September 2000 Sydney Games, NBC gets what NBC buys: US$7.75 billion worth of influence, ensuring a calendar that suits seasonal US holidays and hence advertisers (Rutenberg, 2000; Armour, 2014; Timms, 2021). No matter that a thousand fatalities during the 2018 Japanese summer were declared 'The First Undeniable Climate Change Deaths' (Merino, 2020), or that in 2019, the Games period saw Tokyo's daily maximum temperature average 92°F with 80% humidity, and 20,000 people were hospitalized nationwide as a consequence (Lee, 2019). During the event itself, host broadcaster NHK's meteorologist Sayaka Mori noted that the weather was 'torturing the Olympians and volunteers.'[29] Athlete testimony was equally damning.[30]

The *bourgeois* media sometimes draw attention to these matters but do not engage critically with sporting capitalism (Guest, 2022; Danjon, 2022; Richards, 2023). Journalistic coverage of major sports' risible commitments to a greener future embarrass rather than illuminate (The Climate Coalition, 2018),[31] and that multiple oxymoron 'corporate social responsibility' is used to greenwash a multitude of social harms, ecology notable among them (Fifka and Jäger, 2020). Needless to say, NBC covered the 2021 'heat wave' and typhoon at the time of the Games as 'another hit of nature's power' (Siemaszko, 2021; Associated Press, 2021). Meanwhile, its hegemons complained that a 'drumbeat of negativity' surrounding COVID-19 had dragged ratings down (Hsu, 2021). The natural world, its manipulation and avoidance, should be front and center in Games coverage. That doesn't happen. Most negative media coverage of Qatar's World Cup focused on human rights (Paché, 2020), such that journalists in the Global South tended to attack the supposed imposition of Western cultural norms visible in critiques of the Qataris ("World Cup 2022," 2022). And the sycophantic media greenwash Formula One. Reporters are logocentrically dependent on the sport's existence and jet about to cover it (Scott, 2013; Elliott, 2014). Conventional press reporting even argues that '[c]yclists are miles behind Formula 1 in the environmental race' (Pickford, 2014). True-believer journalists refer to it as 'The World's Most Sustainable Sport' (Sylt, 2015). As discussed in the next chapter, this is in keeping with the failure of sporting journalism to engage the clientelism that resides at its very heart.

Journalists as environmental actors

Beyond such malfeasance, reporters' own hands are responsible for our climate peril as part of a lengthy history of environmental despoliation by journalism that is rarely referenced in J-schools, textbooks, research, or newsrooms (López, 2011). From the development of print through to mobile telephony, technologies used by writers and publishers have drawn upon, created, and emitted dangerous substances, producing multi-generational risks for ecosystems and employees. Journalism has relied on the systematic deforestation, conflict mining, and unsustainable industrialization that characterize obtaining its raw materials—from paper, over the last two centuries, to cellphones, over the last two decades (Maxwell and Miller, 2012).

In the early 1800s, coal-burning, steam-powered presses multiplied the potential volume of printed pages three to four times and added synthetic elements to the environment. These new mechanical systems were soon accompanied by chlorine compounds, derived from manufacturing sodium carbonate and caustic soda used in textile, glass, and soap production. The chlorine allowed patterned and colored rags to be bleached prior to processing and pulping into paper. Soda alone emitted toxic byproducts and generated carbon dioxide. Women did most of the preparatory work in the US, removing buttons, cutting, and ripping seams (Maxwell and Miller, 2012).

We can see this labor process movingly dramatized in Herman Melville's story 'The Paradise of Bachelors and the Tartarus of Maids.' Its narrator finds himself in London 'in the smiling month of May' 1849,[32] carousing with affluent, unmarried lawyers who welcome him to their 'band of brothers.' Two years later, across the waters, the same narrator encounters women pulping, pressing, and folding rags in a chilly New England mill where recycled cotton and linen are used to make paper. Their faces are 'pale with work, and blue with cold,' their eyes seem 'supernatural with unrelated misery,' and verbal communication is 'banished from the spot.'[33] Melville juxtaposes the perilous labor of print technology's women workers with the luxurious cloisters of the male ruling class. The two groups are separated by time, space, gender, class, climate, labor, communication, and risk. The bachelors' fancy attire and healthy complexions are worlds away from the toxic rag room, where the 'air swam with the fine, poisonous particles, which from all sides darted … into the lungs.' The narrator connects the scenes and their actors. Realizing that London ragpickers had collected discarded clothing for export to US paper mills, he surmises that 'among these heaps of rags there may be some old shirts, gathered from the dormitories of the Paradise of Bachelors' (1855).

A century later, Martin Heidegger described a male forester cutting down trees:

> who measures the felled timber in the woods and who to all appearances walks the forest path in the same way his grandfather did [but] is today ordered by the industry that produces commercial woods, whether he knows it or not. He is made subordinate to the orderability of cellulose, which for its part is challenged forth by the need for paper, which is then delivered to newspapers and illustrated magazines. The latter, in their turn, set public opinion to swallowing what is printed, so that a set configuration of opinion becomes available on demand.
>
> *(1977: 299)*

The forester's physical actions replicate those of his ancestors doing the same work. The difference is that his pace and rhythm are set by the pulp and paper industries; he provides the raw materials from which magazines, newspapers, and books come to be made—the very things he may read on his nights off. And just as journalism relies on this man's invisible labor, he relies on *its* labor. The resultant texts both entertain him and take his engagement as evidence of customer satisfaction and public opinion. Together, they represent transformations in the labor process and technological change from Melville's time.[34]

These remarkable tales alert us to the media's two historic environmental roles: representation and materiality. The first story links consumption to labor, gender to class, and environment to paper. It provides the means for readers to consider the life of commodity signs across continents. The second ties one worker's primary-industry labor to the products of secondary and tertiary industries he later consumes.

In each case, connections between social and ecological categories and actors are disclosed through imaginative writing. The stories may or may not be based in empirical history, but they uncover and link the labor process, journalism's conditions of existence, and its environmental impact. Melville and Heidegger are unlikely paragraph-dwellers, but they blend the dual themes of this chapter, incarnating questions that point to the media's ongoing collusion with our current crisis.

Newspapers were one of the world's first commodities produced *en masse*. Impermanency, obsolescence, was a key (Anderson, 2006: 35). Even though 'news becomes history' when it is archived and consulted well after the fact, papers are the ultimate 'perishable commodity' (Park, 1940: 676). That ephemeral prominence but ongoing materiality has seen them become repositories for memory, fantasy, broken glass, and cat litter, as well as the experience of 'meanwhile.' Just a fifth of US newspapers are recycled. Most end up in landfills without being read (Sibley, 2009; Edwards et al., 2009; Paper Task Force, 1995: 4; Canonico et al., 2009). They may inhabit virtual as well as physical trash cans, returning as faulty recollection, perhaps a measure of confusion and psychosis—news stories recur in Freud's account of missteps and metaphors in parapraxes and dreams (2011).

Paper and pulp are the leading US commercial users of water, the fourth biggest emitters of toxins into waterways, and the third largest industrial consumers of energy, making them the third worst emitters of greenhouse gases; and we can add to this the toxic problems of paper waste in landfills, carbon emissions from transporting printed material, and monocultural forestry (Planet Ark, 2008). Globally, the pulp and paper industries emitted 190 Mt of CO_2 in 2021, a record high that represented 2% of the world's emissions (International Energy Agency, 2022). Print labor contends with poisonous solvents, inks, fumes, dust, and wastewater (Maxwell and Miller, 2012).

Per Melville and Heidegger, many of these risks are invisible to journalists, so separate are they from the labor processes that make their tools and disseminate their work. Such items seemingly appear in retail outlets fully formed, without any outward sign of their histories, but with a toxic pedigree most reporters never learn about (Merk, 2021; Laudati and Mertens, 2019).

New technologies of reading are often assumed to be greener than print, because they don't involve deforestation. But there is no accepted system for calculating the renewable virtues of paper versus the electrical vices of electronics, though the Confederation of European Paper Industries has a framework for determining carbon footprints.[35] Paper producers increased recycling from 5% of all fiber in 2004 to 24% in 2010 and reduced carbon emissions by 25% between 2006 and 2010. They save 5 million trees annually, arguing that youthful trees absorb carbon dioxide more readily than venerable ones and digital publishing does nothing to remove CO_2 from the atmosphere, though this is controversial (Book Environmental Council and Green Publishing Initiative, 2013; Hudiburg et al., 2019 Pugh, 2020). The average e-reader uses 33 pounds of minerals; a paper book, two-thirds of a pound. The respective corollary figures in related fields are 79 gallons of water versus two gallons and a 100 kW hours of fossil fuels versus two hours, with proportional emissions of CO_2. The amount of time per day that electricity is used for digital reading, especially via the power grid, must also be factored into determining environmental impacts (Maxwell and Miller, 2012; Delgado, 2022).

Manufacturing, distributing, and using communication devices account for 3.5% of global emissions—probably 14% by 2040 (Matyjaszek, 2021). The cellphone, a staple of the journalistic craft, relies on hazardous mining of metals by child slaves and indentured workers in locations where ores are exported for processing. They are exposed to respiratory hazards and radioactive elements, often in countries where the industry is unregulated or laws poorly enforced. Miners frequently work on unstable terrain or in vulnerable underground sites where they confront fire and structural collapse. Breathing ore dust can lead to lung diseases, including bronchitis, silicosis, and cancer. Gold-mining byproducts feature the poisonous neurotoxins lead, cyanide, and mercury (Grossman, 2016: 67–68; Ronsse, 2019).[36] Hong Kong's Students and Scholars Against Corporate Misbehaviour group and México's Centro de Reflexión y Acción Laboral [Center for Labor Research and Action] have published investigative reports on labor conditions in the production of communications devices.[37] But most journalists appear oblivious, both to the topic and their part in it. We are likelier to read stories extolling the opportunities and efficiencies of instantaneous communication.

The International Telecommunication Union (ITU) advises that two-thirds of the world's 8 billion people use the internet; it hopes to bring connectivity to everyone by 2030 (2022). But once the gadgets that begin their lives in dangerous mines have been manufactured, their environmental despoliation is far from complete. The ITU is wise enough to say that these technologies cause grave environmental problems, so it presses for 'climate neutrality' and more efficient energy use. The 2008 World Telecommunication Standardization Assembly urged members to reduce the carbon footprint of communication, in accordance with the UN Framework Convention on Climate Change (Touré, 2008).

Such a transformation requires evaluation of the electricity used in online searches and exchanges of information. Most of those transfers are probably coal-powered, though their energy sources are as hard to pin down as the packet system itself. We do know that Google's 2011 carbon footprint was almost equal to that of Laos or the UN, largely due to its search engines (Clark, 2011). The company is now committed to green energy, but that doesn't mean anything in terms of the power sources drawn on by users, or how its answers travel across the virtual ether.[38] And of course it has broken its commitment to ban climate-change denial videos from YouTube because of the revenue from distributing lies (Center for Countering Digital Hate, 2023).

Reporters' cellphones are often in use, but frequently left in semi-repose. The International Energy Agency calculates that US$80 billion was wasted on powering mobile devices in standby mode in 2014—beyond Canada's annual energy 'needs.' It estimates that 400 TW hours per year are wasted in this way. That figure is equivalent to 'the annual electricity generated by 133 mid-size coal-fired power plants (500 megawatts each), each requiring 1.4 million tonnes of coal per year' (2014). Data usage on smartphones grew from less than 1% of energy use in 2010 to ten times as much five years later (Malmodin and Lundén, 2018: 16). One hour of video streaming to a mobile device uses more electricity than two new refrigerators (Mills, 2013); each minute a person uses TikTok, 2.63 grams of carbon are emitted.[39]

And when journalists' communications technologies are discarded, they become electronic or e-waste, of which about 53.6 Mt was generated in 2019, a 21% jump in the five years since 2014. In 2021, the worldwide mountain of e-waste totaled an estimated 57.4 million tonnes—more than the Great Wall of China, Earth's heaviest artificial object. E-waste is predicted to amount to 74 Mt by 2030 ("International E-Waste," 2021). It generates serious threats to workers' and residents' health and safety wherever plastics and wires are burnt, monitors smashed and dismantled, and circuit boards grilled or leached with acid. The toxic chemicals, noxious gases, and heavy metals that flow from such practices have perilous implications for people, other animals, soil, and water, both locally and downstream. E-waste recyclers in the informal economy—known colloquially as ragpickers, drawing on coinage from Melville's day—suffer an historically unprecedented prevalence of low hemoglobin, high monocyte and eosinophil counts, gum disease, diarrhea, and dermatitis. Extraordinary levels of psychological distress are also reported (Reis de Oliveira et al., 2012; Premalatha et al., 2014; Devi et al., 2014; Andeobu et al., 2023). As noted above, much of the problem lies with the invisibility of these issues, secreted as they are behind the veil of the technological sublime, of computing power and high-concept design, marketing, and merchandising (explained in Chapter 4). But there is also a willful obfuscation.

Consider that seemingly benign metaphor, 'the cloud,' a euphemism for bricks-and-mortar data centers. It signifies the place where all good software goes for rest and recuperation, emerging on demand, refreshed and ready to spring into action. Here is a classic case of the sign (an invisible service) exceeding its referent (a physical building) while being hugely obscured. Compare the cloud to visible, concrete equivalents of an earlier era: telephone exchanges, post offices, and power stations—the materiality of a popular if implicit socialism. But the truth is out there. Seemingly ephemeral and natural—literal clouds are necessities of life that rain on us then go away—these server farms are often coal-fired. The US National Mining Association and the American Coalition for Clean Coal Electricity gleefully avow that the 'Cloud Begins with Coal.' They note that the world's communication technologies use 1,500 TW hours each year—equivalent to Japan and Germany's overall energy use combined, and 50% more than the aviation industry, amounting to a tenth of global electricity (Mills, 2013). While digital traffic increased thirtyfold in the decade to 2015, 'computing capacity per amount of energy' grew 100 times over the same period (Malmodin and Lundén, 2018: 11) and average data-center electricity consumption stabilized after 2010 (International Energy Agency, 2017: 105–06). But many 'clouds' don't operate sustainably, especially in nations with dirty electricity mixes that rely extensively on coal, which is the case in Anglo countries. In 2020, data storage and transmission emitted 330 Mt of CO_2, 0.6% of greenhouse-gas emissions.[40] Although energy efficiency is improving, that makes for reduced costs at the same time as additional 'needs' become manifest (Mytton, 2020)—William Jevons' paradox, that when prices fall, overall expenditure increases (1866). The US Government calculates that data centers consume '10 to 50 times the energy per floor space of a typical commercial office building,' with responsibility for 2% of the nation's electricity use.[41] By 2023, data centers were consuming as much electricity as Britain ("Can Computing," 2023). Cloud consumption is predicted to account for 4% of global energy in 2030. And these hidden buildings require a lot of water—the Google cloud used 21.198 million liters in 2022, an increase of 20% on 2021; Microsoft's 6.435 million, up 34% from the previous year (Google, 2023; Microsoft, 2022).

Clouds also have indirect environmental impacts: the extractive industries spent US$2.5 billion in 2020 searching for oil and gas via Microsoft and

Google (Greenpeace USA, 2020). By the end of the decade, oil and gas exploration will pay US$15 billion to use the cloud ("Can Computing," 2023; Greenpeace USA, 2020). One of Amazon's strategic money-making priorities is 'automating the climate crisis' (Merchant, 2019) as it proclaims a 'digital oilfield of the future' (Ramos, 2020). Small wonder the firm has been denounced by ecological watchdogs (White and Day, 2023).

Greenpeace International has pioneered a 'Click Clean' campaign (2014).[42] But barriers to a greener data future proliferate, thanks to the fossil-fuel lobby's plaything-politicians, the finance industry, and surveillance, where instantaneous data transmission is deemed critical (Shehabi et al., 2016; Lewis, 2014; Zook and Grote, 2017). And the cloud's blend of physical invisibility and virtual availability is controlled by corporate beneficiaries of public subvention: Alibaba, Amazon, Google, and Microsoft ("Do the Costs," 2021). Governments have given Amazon US$5.1 billion since 2012 to fund data centers, *inter alia*; in the four years to mid-2023, the state of Illinois alone handed over US$468 billion to Microsoft and Facebook to subsidize their clouds (Kaye, 2019; Tarczynska et al., 2022; Miller, 2023; Whiton, 2023).

These matters are generally ignored by the *bourgeois* media; but the story is not entirely bleak. The BBC has convened researchers and organized studies of its footprint to reform internal policies and programs (West and Crowther, 2013). The Corporation estimated its 2016 TV energy use at 0.6% and 2018 radio energy consumption at 0.1% of the nation's overall number. It committed to cut carbon emissions by a quarter and energy consumption by a tenth between 2015 and 2022 (Fletcher and Chandaria, 2020). The *Guardian* has opened itself up to environmental scrutiny, highlighting newsprint and airplane travel (the latter is generally accorded responsibility for about 7% of greenhouse-gas emissions and frequently undertaken by junketeering 'travel writers' who urge readers to add frequent-polluter miles, or by 'war correspondents') (Dodd, 2007; Wood et al., 2014; Weston et al., 2023).

And here's a surprise. In 2007, Rupert Murdoch told News Corp/Fox that

> [c]limate change poses clear, catastrophic threats. We may not agree on the extent, but we certainly can't afford the risk of inaction. ... News Corp is a global company. ... Our operations affect the environment all over the world. ... Printing and publishing newspapers, producing films, broadcasting television signals, operating 24-hour newsrooms. It all adds carbon to the atmosphere.

The corporation acknowledged a 2020 carbon footprint of 143,342 Mt, a significant reduction on previous years ("News Corp's," 2022).

When Toby lived in LA, he spent some time speaking to people at Fox about their efforts on this score, which run counter to the firm's deserved reputation for climate-change denial, but not to its internal acknowledgment of reality (blended with an oleaginous desire to diminish costs and avoid regulation). Units at News Corp and 21st Century Fox boasted an 'energy team leader,' and there was regular intervention from on high. Dedicated managers were paid for this work, while other participants received non-monetary recognition. The Fox lot in Hollywood bought renewable-energy certificates from facilities across the country to offset its carbon footprint, and broadcast studios in Turkey used natural cooling and heating (Carbon Disclosure Project, 2010). Anyone venturing to deepest Brentford in west London could see an otherwise grotesque light-industrial wasteland distinguished by the Sky satellite networks' micro wind farm. One of Murdoch's beneficiaries of filial piety, James Murdoch (2009), boasted in his *Washington Post* op-ed 'Clean Energy Conservatives Can Embrace' that: 'At News Corporation, we have saved millions by becoming more energy-efficient.' That's millions of dollars, not vegetables, fruit, or animals.

Fox News Channel does not cover its parent company's initiative. Climate-change policy may apply to the network in terms of industrial production, but does not suit its audience targeting; hence 86% of the network's climate-change stories in the first half of 2019 dismissing environmental science (Public Citizen, 2019). Who knows what Fox News employees made of the company's 'Green It, Mean It' campaign, or how many availed themselves of the bounty paid to workers who rode buses or purchased hybrid vehicles (Sheppard, 2010; Kurland and Sell, 2010)?

Meanwhile, in their homeland of Australia, the Murdochs have a near monopoly of newsprint and a far-right cable news station dedicated to misleading the public about the environment, including bizarre, concerted campaigns of harassment against the nation's Bureau of Meteorology (Bacon and Jegan, 2020; Readfearn, 2023). Despite announcing a conversion in 2021 to the reality disclosed by climate science, the Corporation's drive to spread environmental misinformation has shown few signs of slowing (Fielding, 2022; Readfearn, 2022). In Britain, its vanity news station, TalkTV, is littered with presenters denying climate science (Barnett, 2023).

Here's the rub—having selected Murdoch as the corporate executive most responsible for blocking efforts to stop global warming in 2010, *Rolling Stone* succinctly summarized his corporation's contradictory efforts: 'Murdoch may be striving to go green in his office buildings, but on the air, the only thing he's recycling are the lies of Big Coal and Big Oil' (Goodell, 2011: 39). For such people, there is no contradiction between green work policies and anti-green journalism. Both are designed to maximize profit. The Fox/News Corp confessional project is couched in terms of risk—of regulation, financial peril, reputation, 'lost viewership/readership,' and 'lost revenues from business partners and advertisers for companies that that [sic] have a poor reputation on environmental issues' (Carbon Disclosure Project, 2010). In effect, then, science and democracy are problems, not sources of truth and justice. The social and environmental duty to care for other living creatures is absent from the rhetoric.

And reporters' own organizations? The occupation is not very forthcoming on such subjects. The Society of Professional Journalists has made no discernible reference to its members' carbon footprint since 2007.[43] Britain's National Union of Journalists adopted a policy calling for greener workplaces that same year, but shows no taste for problematizing its complicity in the problem.[44] The International Federation of Journalists is silent on the topic.[45] That *lacuna* is even evident when associations unfurl their credentials as committed to reporting climate-change science[46]; the Project for Improved Environmental Coverage fails the test of reflexivity.[47] WWF India's otherwise excellent *Recommendations on Environmental Journalism* (WWF, 2009) do not address the necessity of knowing and publishing the carbon footprint of reportage.[48]

Such neglect is attributable to the state of professional training, both on and off the job. Ecological impact has not been a priority. One must turn to environmental studies and occupational health to find sizable and distinguished contributions to knowledge on the topic, largely coming from West Africa, East Asia, and Latin America (Mukherjee et al., 2003; Ray et al., 2004; da Silva et al., 2006; Nnorom and Osibanjo, 2009; Devi et al., 2014; Reis de Oliveira et al., 2012; for work within communication and media studies, see Maxwell et al., 2015; López et al., 2024).

Conclusion

This was an uncomfortable chapter to write. On the one hand, we are clearly calling for more investigative, critical environmental coverage that highlights scientific knowledge and discloses obfuscation by corporations, PR firms, and think tanks. On the other, we suggest a need for *less* discourse, because culture and communication are not endlessly renewable, inexhaustible resources, *contra* assumptions underpinning the potential and value of democracy (Maxwell and Miller, 2013). We appear to suggest that journalists should do less research, less travel, less recording, and less writing—even as they are being hemmed in and proletarianized as part of the *bourgeois* media's de-professionalizing project across the Global North. We don't wish to contribute to that.

We *are*, however, clear that there is no place in the media for climate denial and the production of doubt where there need be none. If we want to secure our ecosystems, something must be done about the hundreds of millions of dollars dedicated to anti-scientific propaganda that produce harm by opposing the actions needed to combat climate change, with particular implications for future generations and the Global South (Funk and Rainie, 2015; Lavik, 2016). No rational argument, no fact about atmospheric warming, and no majority opinion aligned with scientific consensus possess the inherent power to counter the misinformation wielded by fossil-fuel industrialists and their dutiful paid supporters and ideological fellow-travelers.

We are similarly clear in our call for an audit of the impact of journalistic research and a transparent declaration of reporters' and readers' carbon footprints as a new principle of the field. The profession's codes of ethics need amendment to address this failure. A circuit breaker is required to depart our era of unsustainability.

J-schoolers should be reading Melville and Heidegger's stories cited earlier, with ecology located at the heart of the profession via a horizontal and vertical history that looks at the entire material life of the commodity sign called journalism: mineral extraction and the manufacture, transport, consumption, disposal, and recycling of devices and texts.

As Bruno Latour explains:

> It is very difficult for most people used to the industrialised way of life, with its dream of infinite space and its insistence on emancipation and relentless growth and development, to suddenly sense that it is instead enveloped, confined, tucked inside a closed space where their concerns have to be shared with new entities: other people of course, but also viruses, soils, coal, oil, water, and, worst of all, this damned, constantly shifting climate.
> *(2021)*

Journalists must grasp this reality and explain it to the public. For climate change comes to us all as a cluster of historical and contemporary fact, prediction, projection, and public knowledge. Amelioration of our present and future circumstances depends on reporting that recognizes and deals with that frequently contradictory amalgam (Callison, 2014).

Rich and Steinmetz's essay was a provocative middle-class introduction to the challenges climate scientists have faced over the years. But like most Yanqui reportage, it sought refuge in psychological claims that failed to account for why many nations, social movements, and researchers think differently from powerful governments and corporations. Meanwhile, the *New York Times* continues to publish climate skeptics, often because of their cathectic market beliefs in opposition to democratic solutions to the crisis (Riggio, 2022). Environmental journalism remains marginal.

Notes

1 https://www.youtube.com/watch?v=lPPh_PWl4hg&t=2998s&ab_channel=VincentMignerot.
2 https://www.youtube.com/watch?v=8Suu84khNGY&ab_channel=JustinEngel.
3 http://www.desmogblog.com/global-warming-denier-database.
4 https://fminus.org/#conservation/1.

5 https://www.provokemedia.com/ranking-and-data/global-pr-agency-rankings/2021-pr-agency-rankings/top-250.
6 http://www.corporatewatch.org/company-profiles/edelman.
7 https://www.documentcloud.org/documents/21047455-tc-energy-east-grassroots-advocacy-vision-document.
8 https://www.prsa.org/about/ethics/prsa-code-of-ethics.
9 https://www.blueadvertising.com/#home-top.
10 When a prominent magazine invited one of us to write about Edelman and its tricksters, the column was rejected on legal advice. The same magazine rejected another commissioned piece on corruption in football, for the same reasons. It no longer invites Toby to do anything. Thank you, *The Conversation*.
11 https://www.api.org/climate.
12 https://www.api.org/about/president-and-ceo.
13 https://www.youtube.com/watch?v=oVQWaFLL0AU&ab_channel=CEREScience; https://www.ceres-science.com/about.
14 https://heartland.org/about-us/who-we-are/willie-soon/.
15 https://www.atlasnetwork.org/partners.
16 https://www.atlanticcouncil.org/.
17 https://www.amnesty.org/en/location/middle-east-and-north-africa/united-arab-emirates/report-united-arab-emirates/.
18 https://www.themuse.com/advice/journalism-major-degree-jobs-careers.
19 https://www.thecollegefix.com/subject/climate-change/.
20 https://www.yaf.org/?s=climate.
21 http://www.pulitzercenter.org/blog/losing-earth-sparks-broad-debate-climate-change-blame-and-gender.
22 https://cleancreatives.org/learn-2022.
23 https://www.documentcloud.org/app?q=%2Bproject%3Amobil---corporate-speech-207202%20; see Mobil Oil's tactics https://s3.documentcloud.org/documents/21398673/1971_commsproposaltoexecs_schmertz.pdf.
24 https://www.nfl.com/causes/nfl-green/.
25 https://www.mlb.com/mlb-together/green.
26 https://www.premierleague.com/news/2327983;https://www.arsenal.com/sustainability.
27 https://csr.manutd.com/.
28 https://en.psg.fr/teams/club/content/paris-saint-germain-team-up-with-the-un-to-protect-the-environment-club-psg.
29 https://twitter.com/sayakasofiamori?ref_src=twsrc%5Egoogle%7Ctwcamp%5Eserp%7Ctwgr%5Eauthor.
30 https://www.bbc.co.uk/news/av/world-asia-58110846.
31 You can read about environmentally sound construction practices or the seemingly altruistic planting of trees https://www.mancity.com/news/club-news/picture-special/2018/february/man-city-support-show-the-love-campaign. A serious ecological audit of power and water use, garbage creation, and travel is absent.
32 No surprise it was 'smiling.' April had seen one of southern England's heaviest snowstorms, which cut off telegraphy, *inter alia* (Plester, 2021; "Meteorological," 1849).
33 Melville's account has generated significant critical discourse, albeit only recently addressing environmental questions (Serlin, 1995; G Thompson, 2012; Senchyne, 2020).
34 It is irksome to cite Heidegger approvingly, given his collusion with National Socialism, but this apocryphal anecdote is illuminating.
35 http://www.cepi.org/system/files/public/documents/publications/transport/2009/TransportCarbonFootprintAssessment%20Guidelines.pdf.

36 https://www.youtube.com/watch?v=JcJ8me22NVs&ab_channel=SkyNews.
37 http://sacom.hk/media-type/investigative-reports/;http://www.cerealgdl.org/index.php/es/.
38 http://www.google.com/green/energy/use/#purchasing.
39 https://www.comparethemarket.com.au/energy/features/social-carbon-footprint-calculator/.
40 https://www.iea.org/energy-system/buildings/data-centres-and-data-transmission-networks.
41 https://www.energy.gov/eere/buildings/data-centers-and-servers.
42 http://www.greenpeace.org/usa/en/campaigns/global-warming-and-energy/A-Green-Internet/clickingclean/.
43 http://www.google.com/cse?cx=016561358561312553625:jrlnopll9n0&q=carbon%20footprint#gsc.tab=0&gsc.q=carbon%20footprint&gsc.page=1.
44 https://www.nuj.org.uk/news/nuj-signs-environmental-pledge/.
45 https://www.google.be/search?q=site%3Aifj.org+carbon%20footprint.
46 http://colombia.ifj.org/en/contents/climate-change-how-to-report-the-story-of-the-century-2.
47 http://greeningthemedia.org/.
48 For example, http://www.ifj.org/about-ifj/ifj-code-of-principles/.

3
SPORTS (WITH DAVID ROWE)

There is a problem stalking this chapter: the dramatic economic success and cultural importance of mainstream sports versus the image of the reporters who focus on them. Sports journalists cover events that stir extraordinary passions and produce material that many listeners, readers, and viewers devour. They are cathectically invested in their jobs—and have low social and professional standing.

Some of this relates to the notion that sports, like popular culture more generally, are not valuable or serious, but a distraction from more profound civic responsibilities and pastimes. In the first century, Juvenal wrote sorrowfully and mockingly that everyday Romans '[c]ouldn't care less' when it came to voting: 'Only two things really concern them: bread and the Games' (1998: 505). A millennium ago, John of Salisbury warned that juggling, mime, and acting had a negative impact on 'unoccupied minds … pampered by the solace of some pleasure' (quoted in Zyvatkauskas, 2007). A few centuries later, Edward Said was even more worried:

> consciousness of sports, with its scores and history and technique and all the rest of it, is at the level of sophistication that is almost terrifying, especially if you compare it with the lack of awareness of what's going on in the world. That's where you get the sense that the investment is being made in those things that distract you from realities that are too complicated.
>
> *(1993: 23)*

Fred Halliday longed for 'a time before public discourse was dominated by footballers' (2009). And Eco's concept of sports cubed is a warning: sports

DOI: 10.4324/9781032701660-4

are multiplied first by media coverage *per se* and then by the seemingly insatiable coverage *of* that coverage (sports journalists write and talk about themselves in a heroic and seemingly inexhaustible burst of largely male banter). This puts them, and their readers, at a progressively further remove from social and environmental issues (1987: 162–64). So why are sports part of 'news,' and why are we writing about them? Do they intrinsically, necessarily, fail the great tasks of journalism adumbrated in the Introduction?

The answer is that sports' popularity and universality mean there is something to be engaged. Journalism is both part of that thing and a potentially positive agent of change. The paradox at the heart of sports is their simultaneously transcendent and imprisoning qualities, and astonishing capacity to allegorize. Hence their fascination for the public and their place in journalism. In the US, 65% of newspaper readers focus on politics. In second place comes sports, with 59% (Schenk, n.d.). The *Guardian*'s most-read stories online from 2010 to 2014 saw football rank behind only world news and well ahead of British politics (Sedghi et al., 2014). TV and streaming ratings in the US Anglo world are dominated by sports (Gough, 2023). In 2021, private-equity corporations invested US$51 billion in them. The three biggest US pro sports each had 2022 revenues in excess of US$10 billion, while association football received over US$20 billion just from the sale of media rights internationally ("Saudi Arabia," 2023).

With the advent of consumer capitalism, the sporting body has become an increasingly visible *locus* of media desire. The manipulation of appearance through fashion codes and adornment, calculated nutrition, and physical conditioning has changed the daily terms of trade in the clothes we wear, the desires we feel, and the images we create and consume. It's not just women who are objects of the gaze, not just women who are physically damaged in the interests of social expectations, and not just men inspecting the bodies of others for foibles and follicles. In the past five decades, professional male sports have transformed themselves into an international capitalist project; female athletes are on the same path. New pressures accompany the spoils. Stars are soon shriveled up, their bodies broken on wheels of lies, distortions, and fantasies constructed and manipulated by complicit colleges, corporate owners, hypocritical rather than Hippocratic medical staff, mindless media, and their own tragic delusions of invulnerability and *bourgeois* individualism. Eco again: 'The athlete is already a being who has hypertrophized one organ, who turns his body into the seat and exclusive source of a continuous play. The athlete is a monster … dedicated to total instrumentalization' (1987: 161).

Such ephemerality encapsulates the disposability of consumer capitalism, and the process of displacing one star with another. For top-level pro male sports are big business, and are often said to be relatively immune to macroeconomic distress, thanks to long-term broadcast and now streaming deals that guarantee cash flow, although sponsorship contracts suffer when the greed and incompetence of highly geared entities compromise their wish for self-promotion ("Is it," 2009; Földesi, 2014). The COVID-19 syndemic briefly battered that *donnée* (Alam and Abdurraheem, 2023), but the big leagues swiftly recovered.

Dedicated sports media proliferate across all the major languages, inciting advertising and coverage as well as being formed by them (Horky and Nieland, 2013). Association football is their principal obsession, other than during the summer Olympics and the Indian Premier League of cricket, along with gambling on which whipped horse will obey its slave master most successfully. How did that happen?

Audiences to the world's most popular sports were built up over years by technicians, producers, reporters, and commentators working for state broadcasters, then exploited by capitalist companies too unimaginative, averse to newness, and indolent to innovate themselves. This predatory practice is evident in the history of US basketball, which was pioneered on television by San Francisco's public station; international cricket (developed as a spectator sport by public networks in Britain, Australasia, the Anglo Caribbean, South Asia, and South Africa); and football across Europe. Public culture bore the cost of developing sports that went on to be exploited commercially. Journalism was complicit in the articulation and exploitation of spectators in their transformation from publics to consumers, with a correspondingly detrimental impact on the link between sports and citizenship (Scherer and Rowe, 2014).

A quarter of a century ago, Jason Cowley asked 'is there anything better to write swiftly about to deadline than sport, with its inherent sense of an ending, secular grandeur and mass appeal?' (1999). But problems of legitimacy and professional and public repute have long troubled sports reporters. Their work appears at the back of the paper or the tail of the news bulletin, something of minor historical and political import. They occupy what is often called the newsroom's 'toy department,' a conceptual and physical area populated by fans rather than 'serious' journalists (Rowe, 2007; Steen et al., 2021). Their fanboy approach doesn't help. It has three components: vicarious pleasures that derive from projecting oneself into the scene, enjoying others' physical endeavor and aptitude, and developing formal and informal professional networks (Reed, 2018).

The key change to sports journalism over the past three decades has been democracies' deregulation of the electronic media, such that radio and television need not provide omnibus services, from drama to current affairs to weather. The emergence of channels and stations dedicated purely to sports has given greater prominence and power to many reporters—no longer must they share newsrooms with those allegedly embarked on a higher calling of greater prestige. Per the freedom enjoyed by Milanese journalists working for

La Gazzetta dello Sport[1] since the 1890s, Parisians celebrating the end of Occupation by founding *L'Équipe*,[2] or *Madridistas* faithfully incanting the word of the Bernabeu in *Marca*[3] from the 1940s, no-one dare suggest at ESPN in Buenos Aires that football doesn't matter by contrast with the rest of what goes on in the building. But issues of seriousness and legitimacy remain for sports desks within conventional omnibus newsrooms (Boyle et al., 2010). The sense of marginality can be even greater for online sports reporters for digital media, who work for the 'toy department within the toy department' (McEnnis, 2020).

Beyond such intra-professional legitimacy, four problems stalk contemporary sports journalism: nationalism, gender/race, technology, and clientelism. They form the core of this chapter.

Nationalism

A potent brew of collective narcissism routinely crossvalidates sports and nations via myths of representativeness, justice, and upward mobility that idealize existing political, economic, military, and social life—distorting conflict, then re-signifying it on the pitch and the page as part of martial masculinity. Instructions to broadcasters such as the following are not uncommon:

> Create a feeling that the competitors don't like each other. ... Studies have shown that fans react better, and are more emotionally involved, if aggressive hostility is present. ... Work the audience at the emotional level and get them involved in the game.
>
> *(Hitchcock, 1991: 75)*

TV coverage of the 2014 men's World Cup of football in Portugal, Ghana, the US, and Germany indicates how common extreme nationalism has become (Horky et al., 2020).

Nationalistic journalism in the US celebrates a putative 'American exceptionalism' that supposedly makes the country an exporting rather than an importing sports culture. The concept of exceptionalism began as an attempt to explain why socialism had not taken greater hold in the US per the conventions of Marxism (Zimmer, 2013). It has since turned into an excessive rhapsody to Yanqui world leadership, difference, and sanctimony. So we encounter claims made—in all seriousness—that 'foreignness' can render a sport unpopular in the US and the media will not accept practices coded as 'other' (Brown, 2005).

Away from association football, the US specializes in a profoundly nationalistic hyper-masculinity that has been coordinated by the military and the media since the American War in Việt Nam. The Armed Forces Bowl[4] is a college 'football' competition sponsored by Lockheed Martin, one of the corporations reliant on welfare via the private development and public-sector purchase of murderous technology. In this instance, promotional activities are not about selling products to fans, per most sports underwriting, but rather creating goodwill toward militaristic welfare through homologies that sports journalism draws between nationalism and *matériel* (Butterworth and Moskal, 2009).[5] Such coverage manufactures and interpellates ideological links between violence, masculinity, and sacrifice. The Pentagon under Obama paid millions to the NFL for celebrating militarism on television (Baxter, 2015). In hockey, owners associated with militarism are lauded for their nationalism, relations with Trump, and purported nous, per the fawning coverage of ESPN (Wyshynski, 2023). A glance at *Sports Illustrated* reveals a lengthy history of casually, uncritically reporting ties between the military and sports.[6] It can be no surprise that US TV sports fans, notably white men, are strong supporters of imperialist warmongering (Stempel, 2006).

One might regard US pro sports as akin to socialism by stealth: a draft for *faux* students who have been trained for free in directly and indirectly state-subsidized universities, limits on salaries, revenue-sharing, stadia paid for through taxation, exemptions from anti-trust legislation, no threat of relegation, and restrictions on competition (Ford, 2002). This is a planned, command economy by any other name, working with the recognition that sporting firms need viable opponents in order to survive. Competition differs from its role in other forms of capitalism—more an end than a means. But this is deeply managed competition; *gringo* billionaires cannot face the true market discipline known as relegation.

A seemingly endless supply of right-wing reporters and commentators rejoice in criticizing association football. Republican Jack Kemp derided actual football before Congress as a 'European socialist' sport by contrast with its 'democratic' US rival (quoted in Lexington, 2006), though the data show that the presumed liberal orientation of association football fans in the US is unstable, if it exists at all (Rewilak, 2023). The *Village Voice*[7] whined that '[e]very four years the World Cup comes around, and with it a swarm of soccer nerds and bullies reminding us how backward and provincial we are for not appreciating soccer enough' (Barra, 2002). During the 2010 men's Finals, this xenophobia saw Glenn Beck, one of the right's pitchmen in the *bourgeois* media, refer to Obama's policies as 'the World Cup' of 'political thought,' advising us that 'the rest of the world likes Barack Obama's policies, we do not' and 'we don't want the World Cup, we don't like the World Cup, we don't like soccer.' Convicted Watergate conspirator G Gordon Liddy decried the game on his talk show because it 'originated with the South American Indians' and asked 'Whatever happened to American exceptionalism?' His guests from the coin-operated Media Research Center called it 'a poor man or poor woman's sport' that 'the left is pushing … in schools across the country' ("As the World," 2010). Apropos, the Center says it seeks 'to defend and preserve

America's founding principles and Judeo-Christian values.'[8] Frustrated by football's prominence and popularity, these people are desperate to attack its 'European … death and despair' (Webb, 2009). They denounce it as 'un-American' in *Politico*, the *Seattle Times*, the *National Review*, *USA Today*, the *Denver Post*, and *Breitbart* (Webb, 2014; Esser, 2015; Schneider, 2022; Lee, 2014; Rosen, 2010; Flynn, 2014; Wright, 2014). These ethnocentric denunciations—predicated, of course, on letting Latin@s and migrants know they're not 'American'—largely flow from the intemperate keystrokes and irate penmanship of angry white men. Habte Selassie (2002) connects anti-football politics to Cold War scapegoating of immigrants, with the sport's refusal in the 1940s and 1950s a rejection of difference.

Time magazine's former European business correspondent notes the world-historical extent of cultural protectionism in the US (Ledbetter, 2002). Nativist prejudices against football are fast turning into death-throes against the tide of history; the clouds grow heavy and thick around elderly, inadequate ways of understanding the US sporting market.

From 2005, demographic change, audience desire, and corporate targeting began to speak: the US had English- and Spanish-language TV networks covering leagues in Europe, Asia, Africa, Australia, Latin America—and the US (men's and women's from 2009). In Los Angeles, 93,000 people turned up to watch a match in 2022. Many other fixtures drew upwards of 50,000 spectators (Dockery, 2023). English-language TV coverage of the 2022 Men's World Cup Finals drew 30% more viewers than the 2018 event (Gough, 2023). The sport is almost as popular as baseball and basketball and ahead of hockey, motorsport, and golf; among the young, it tops everything other than the NFL (Enten, 2022). Inter Miami had 9 million followers on Instagram in early 2023, fifth among all US pro sports teams (Burke, 2023). By the end of the year, that number had risen to over 15 million and the club was in fourth place behind some basketball franchises, but of course tens of millions of followers behind European giants ("Of the 20," 2023). The most marketable athletes in the US that year included three female and male footballers in the top five, with Messi number one ("Most Marketable," 2023). The remaining *macho* nationalists opposing the sport are effectively parodied by *The Onion*'s 'Soccer Officially Announces It Is Gay' satire.[9]

But what of nationalism within world football? Consider that bloodthirsty paean to racism and war, *La Marseillaise*. It includes the notorious lines '*Qu'un sang impur/Abreuve nos sillons*' [Let impure blood/Water our furrows] (Dubois, 2013). When Algeria played France in Paris for the first time in 2001, the host's national anthem was booed by a crowd mainly comprised of postcolonial survivors and the game called off after a pitch invasion. This followed a history of the Front National's leader calling footballers who declined to sing along 'fake Frenchmen' (Andress, 2018). When English and

French fans joined in *La Marseillaise* before their countries met in a football match at Wembley just days after the November 2015 terrorist killings at the Stade de France, the Bataclan, and street cafés in Paris, they did so in the presence of the British monarchy, the French presidency, the police, and the military.[10] The event was broadcast and celebrated on public television and radio (McKenzie, 2015). It incarnated nationalism meeting football, via state presence, lyrical content, uniformed imagery, armed environment, declaration of war, stadium setting, and journalistic rapture.[11]

Was this performance covered as a manifestation of nationalism through military values and symbols—a hymn to hierarchy, conduct, clothing, and propaganda? Did reporters discuss the politics of these bloodthirsty imperial nations and weapons exporters? The event was hailed quite differently in the *bourgeois* media, lauded as an uplifting occasion of loving solidarity and often likened to the tear-jerking sequence in *Casablanca* (Mihály Kertész [Michael Curtiz], 1942) when Paul Henreid, Corinna Mura, and Madeleine Lebeau led the crowd singing the same anthem in opposition to Nazism ("Wembley: La Marseillaise," 2015; Gibson and Quinn, 2015; De Freitas, 2022; "Wembley en bleu-blanc-rouge," 2022; Cockcroft and Tonkin, 2015).[12]

Critical football reporting alert to cultural politics went missing, as is generally the case when progressive possibilities are overdetermined by journalism's lust to stoke the fires of popular militarism through associations with sports (Kelly, 2023). For the majority tendency in the sporting media leans toward chauvinism, per the US. George Orwell famously described international sports as 'war minus the shooting' (1945). That pithy observation came from his report on a 1945 'goodwill' British tour by the Soviet football club, commando Дина́мо Москва́ [Dynamo Moscow] (Dmowski, 2015).[13] Orwell feared that such 'sporting contests lead to orgies of hatred' because of their inherent competitiveness. His colonial and militia experience of football in Burma, India, and Spain had been of uncontrolled and passionate derision expressed by one section of a crowd toward another. No surprise, then, that in *Nineteen Eighty-Four*, 'the proles' were fascinated by the sport; it 'filled up the horizons of their minds' (Orwell, 1949: 41).

Theodor Adorno and Max Horkheimer articulated a 'left-half at football, a black-shirt, a member of the Hitler Youth, and so on' (1979: 164). HG Wells drew a homology between football teams and armed divisions (1902: 184). For Herbert Marcuse, the game represented a

> [c]onspicuous social mobilization of aggressiveness, the militarization of the affluent society. This mobilization goes far beyond the actual draft of manpower ... no longer the "classical" heroizing of killing in the national interest, but rather its reduction to the level of natural events and contingencies of daily life.
>
> *(2009: 195)*

Consider the historical and ongoing relationship between nationalism, militarism, and football journalism in Colombia. Between the turn of the century and 1940, the sport emerged from being the pastime of governmental and commercial élites to a national obsession. Its stages shifted from polo, golf, and gun clubs to unpaved streets. That transformation was assisted by radio coverage of matches and a new counter-public sphere of followers. The spread of telex, telephone, and radio across the country saw football become a core segment of newspapers, popularly celebrated for its political neutrality amid the virtual civil war that raged from the 1940s to the 1960s (Quitián Roldán, 2013; Ruiz Patiño, 2017).

That helped install the sport as the principal source of a nation popular by the mid-1970s, a way of binding the nation together across social classes via nationalistic cultural myths circulated by the media that saw football gain adherents on the left and right throughout Latin America (Galeano, 1997). It was both the design of élites seeking to incorporate the population into their projects, and the joint creation of those very popular classes, via carnival, expressivity, and hopes for upward mobility—simultaneously the monetary property of the oligarchy and the symbolic property of the people. Reporters facilitate, incarnate, and fail to theorize that process (Quitián Roldán and Urrea Beltrán, 2016a and 2016b; Santos Molano, 2016; Jaramillo Racines, 2011). The great triumph of the national men's team, defeating Argentina 5-0 away in a 1993 qualifying match for the World Cup,[14] is commemorated by the *bourgeois* media as an epochal moment of collective pride. They tend to pass over the fact that 76 people died and over 900 were wounded in the aftermath (Watson, 2018).

By the 2010s, with political peace (of a sort) on the agenda, the state began to emerge into the narcissistic glow of football's floodlights as a means of regenerating the national popular. Its ironic exemplification was a new link to militarism, celebrated to the skies by journalists. The two national commercial TV networks, RCN and Caracol, shared coverage of the 2016 regional Copa América. RCN joined with the Colombian military to produce commercials of joy, nationalism, and militarism that doubled as implicit promotions for its billionaire owner, the late Carlos Ardila Lülle, baron of the sugar-drinks firm Postobón, proprietor of Medellín's Atlético Nacional club side (Pablo Escobar's favorite), and an honoree for services to the armed forces (Rodríguez Romero and Duque Oliva, 2007; López de la Roche, 2003; Luna Geller, 2016).

Thanks to dutiful journalism, RCN and the military merged with Radamel Falcao, James Rodríguez, and their compatriots ("El Batallón," 2016): the network's five promotional spots for the Copa featured the military under the rubric of the *Himno Copa América Centenario 2016 #YoCreo* [Copa América Centenary Anthem 2016 #IBelieve]. When viewed in combination, the various military versions comprise seven minutes of striking propaganda.[15] For a helicopter and parachute commercial, the setting was an airfield. Soldiers dropped to the ground draped in the slogan's flag and air force planes carried the slogan on their fuselage. The navy provided uniformed women and men to play instruments and sing, and a ship to carry a banner alongside the flag. The presidential guard was in 19th-century attire, part of Colombia's mimicry of Prussian uniforms.[16] Nationalism coursed through these ventures' veins. And RCN celebrated itself, the team, fans, and the armed forces as one, in seemingly endless paeans to these commercials and what they represented.[17] Conversely, when protests by players over the labor process and their remuneration in the Categoría Primera A saw them 'sitting' or only touching the ball lightly at the beginning of matches, that peaceful direct action was not screened ("WiN sports," 2019; "Hablan de veto," 2019).

Of course, Colombia has other Anglo associations apart from football. These were emblematized by the front page of *The Sun* on the day of England's match against the national team in the 2018 men's World Cup. Troping the drug cocaine and the partially homonymous name of England's captain, Harry Kane, *The Sun* depicted him with 'GO KANE' in the headline, to the righteous outrage of the Colombian embassy and media (Taylor, 2018). In response to their complaints, the next day's paper read:

> The front page of yesterday's Sun may have given the impression that Colombia is well known for its cocaine trade. This was unfair on the Colombian people, who are far more embarrassed by the way their cheating, fouling, play acting, mean-spirited national football team played last night.
> We are happy to set the record straight.
> *(Neville, 2018)*

El Tiempo characterizes *The Sun* as 'especializado en chismes, deportes y farándula' [specializing in gossip, sports, and show-business nosiness] (Arbeláez, 2018). Its cheekily adolescent xenophobia/tabloid imperialism is typical of the 'journalism' targeted at the UK's white, monolingual working class. That superciliousness conceals a pride in Britain's vicious slaving past that characterizes the paper—one more moment when nationalism overdetermines what journalism might otherwise be.

There is nothing new here; it represents continuity with a chauvinistic history that will simply not go away, suggesting regrettable links to the present that will probably prosper long into the future. That applies to occupational as well as textual inequalities among social identities. The British have no monopoly on it.

Gender and race

Sports reporting is often seen as the province of 'middle-aged men billowing smoke and swilling beer … star-struck sport wannabes playing at being serious scribes' (Rowe, 2013), a world in which, to quote Raymond Chandler, '[t]he smell of old dust hung in the air as flat and stale as a football interview' (1949). It is certainly true that across the globe, sporting journalism is dominated by male athletes and authors (Franks and Neill, 2018). Analysis in Britain, Australia, and the US discloses bias against covering sportswomen and hiring female reporters.

Traditional Yanqui commentary on basketball and tennis infantilizes women athletes and frames their achievements ambivalently (Messner et al., 1993). For marketers in the Global North, young, affluent men have long been deemed the most desirable media spectators. By contrast with other segments of the population, they have tended to watch little other television, demonstrated unsteady preferences for brands—and earnt sizable incomes. Sports were generally their thing, and their tastes became disproportionately influential on programming (Commission on the Future of Women's Sport, 2010: 7).

In 2019, women's sport was allocated 7% of space in UK broadsheets and 1% in tabloids (Tobitt, 2023). US English-language television remains fixated on men's college and pro fixtures, with 'a stark contrast between the exciting, amplified delivery of stories about men's sports, and the often dull, matter-of-fact delivery of women's sports stories' (Cooky et al., 2015: 261). In 2019, 5.1% of network TV sports news covered women (Cooky et al., 2021). In 2017, Maltese and Greek TV allocated them 2% of TV sports time; in Sweden, the numbers varied between 3 and 6%; in Britain, 4 to 10% (Women in Sport, 2018). Central and Eastern European Olympics coverage systematically excludes women (Antunovic and Bartoluci, 2023). Sometimes this defies capitalist logic: in 2009, the million people viewing England's Football Association Women's Cup Final out-rated numerous men's cricket, rugby, and football fixtures, and the British Women's Open Golf drew larger audiences than the men's Ryder Cup contest between the US and Europe (Commission on the Future of Women's Sport, 2010: 6–8). The Final of the 2022 Euro tournament drew three times the number watching in 2017, as 50 million tuned in ("Women's Euro," 2022). In Australia, the national women's team achieved larger audiences during the 2023 World Cup Finals than the principal men's 'football' events, the Australian Football League Grand Final and rugby league's State of Origin (Snape, 2023). The Cup saw 9 million Colombians tune in to their side's first match—a record (Worswick, 2023). It is clear that the barrier to adequate textual representation of women is patriarchal parthenogenesis and market illogic, not 'popularity.'

The same applies to occupational representation. Of nearly 9,000 accredited journalists at the 2022 men's World Cup finals, just 10% were women (Cairns, 2023). In 2021, *gringas* were just 16.7% of their country's sports editors, 17.8% of columnists, 14.4% of reporters, and 24.7% of copy editors. The following year, 15% of sports journalists were women (Lapchick, 2021; Tomasik and Gottfried, 2023). Survey research indicates that male reporters do not welcome changes to this imbalance (Schmidt, 2018). Women in Switzerland are assigned the least-prominent sports (Schoch, 2013). In 2021, men wrote 87% of Australian sports stories and provided 84% of quotations, representing greater marginalization of women than other areas of national journalism (Price with Williams, 2021: 7, 14–15). A UK Sky Sports maven acknowledged in 2018 that: 'At recent press conferences for the leading football clubs in the Premier League, Championship and Scottish Premiership we counted 310 reporters covering 25 clubs. Nearly 300 were men; fewer than 10 per cent were women' (Cairns, 2018). Prior to a 2023 men's cricket match between England and Australia, the assembled crowd of reporters included just one woman, one black man, and one South Asian.[18] Although there has been some progress in coverage and hiring, British women sports journalists are poorly paid next to their male counterparts (Bennett, 2022; Rowe and Boyle, 2022; Shalala, 2020).

Men account for 85% of French sports reporters (Biraud, 2023). In 2021, the documentary *Je ne suis pas une salope, je suis une journaliste* [*I'm Not a Slut, I'm a Journalist*] (Marie Portolano and Guillaume Priou), detailing the experiences of women sports journalists in France, was broadcast on Canal+. The network excised footage implicating one of its male stars, Pierre Ménès, in sexual assault (Dodman, 2021). A collective of 150 women reporters proceeded to publish an open letter in *Le Monde* announcing their determination to put an end to the low status of female sports and journalists, noting that 'les chiffres prouvent que les hommes embauchent des hommes, qui parlent des hommes' [the data show that men hire other men, who in turn focus on men] ("Femmes journalistes," 2021).

The problems go beyond hiring and into hysterical male audiences. When Pablo Armero, a member of the men's Colombian team, was arrested in 2016 for assaulting his wife, but selected for the side the following year, the prominent journalist Andrea Guerrero criticized his inclusion. She received numerous death threats (Salazar, 2018). The 2018 men's World Cup saw numerous cases of women reporters being verbally and physically assaulted (Roxborough and Mango, 2018; Dodman, 2021). UK women reporters experience serious abuse (Rowe and Boyle, 2022) and Just Not Sports launched #MoreThanMean in 2016, a video that highlighted online sexual harassment of US women sports journalists in which men read out abusive tweets from other guys targeting Sarah Spain and Julie DiCaro, who were sitting in front of them.[19] The result rapidly reached over 4 million viewers and attracted mainstream and sports media coverage (Antunovic, 2019).

The racial story is similarly lamentable in predominantly white countries. Consider these figures: white people form 82% of the British population.[20] Over half a century of BBC TV's flagship football show, *Match of the Day*,[21] there has never been a black host, despite the statistically disproportionate number of black players (43%, many of them immigrants) by contrast with the overall black UK population (4%) and the proliferation of black pundits among ex-pros. The Corporation's Radio 5 Live[22] (known colloquially as 'Radio Bloke') offers nearly 30 hours of football coverage a week; just 60 minutes had minority hosts at last count. The BBC's domestic sports presenters and correspondents are almost all white.[23] Minority women held eight of Britain's 456 media jobs in 2016 at Wimbledon, the Rio Olympic and Paralympic Games, and the men's football Euros.[24]

You'd better have been a straight white man if you wanted to report on football in the UK in 2018: of the 338 roles assigned to sports journalists, five went to black folks and seven to South Asians. And almost half the respondents to a survey by Sports Media LGBT said they had experienced or witnessed discrimination in newsrooms between 2016 and 2018 (Sports Journalists' Association, 2019). The percentage was higher in 2022 (Black Collective of Media in Sports, 2023). The 2018 men's World Cup saw British papers dispatch one black journalist out of more than 60, alongside three women from the entire UK media (Woozencroft, 2018; Sports Journalists' Association, 2019).[25] In 2022, the written media saw tiny proportions of black (2.6%) and female (3.8%) reporters assigned to the men's football Euros (Black Collective of Media in Sports, 2023). No national newspaper has had a black sports editor.[26] In the 2020–21 season, the four companies that shared UK screen rights to English football (Amazon, the BBC, BT Sport, and Sky) hired 37 play-by-play commentators. Two were black (Hughes, 2021). Data from 2022 indicate that more than two-thirds of the black people employed in sports TV were former athletes (Black Collective of Media in Sports, 2023).

Similar trends are clear in the US, where people of color are 40% of the US population: in 2017, 85% of sports editors, 76.4% of assistant sports editors, 80.3% of columnists, 82.1% of reporters, and 77.7% of copy editors/designers were white. In 2021, across all sports, minorities accounted for just 20.8% of sports editors, 27.7% of assistant sports editors, and 22.9% of columnists and reporters (Lapchick, 2018, 2021).

European radio and television commentary routinely praises white football stars for their acumen, industriousness, and intelligence, in stark contrast with the representation of their minority colleagues (RunRepeat, 2020). UK television fetishizes black footballers via animalistic metaphors (Campbell and Bebb, 2022). White commentators often use such descriptions as '"pace and power" or "athleticism" to describe a Black player—without also commenting on their tactical intelligence, skill, creativity or work ethic.' As a consequence, 'they are not only missing the mark in terms of their soccer critique, but also denying Black players' humanity' (Doyle, 2020). When 'alternative' forms of whiteness are afield, per Bosnian or Portuguese players, commentators grow confused about what would be apt descriptions (van Lienden and van Sterkenburg, 2023). These findings are met with predictable fear and arrogance by dominant journalists, who bleat about free speech and inform us that the problem lies with new arrivals on the job and ex-players (Samuel, 2020; PA, 2020).

There is more discourse today about this inequality and bigotry, and new organizations are dedicated to changing the situation (UNESCO, 2023a). That bodes well for change; but it would be charmingly naïve to imagine either the old guard or their progeny willingly giving up hegemonic hierarchies that have delivered affirmative action for them and their kind for so long. And all too often, what may appear to be advances are not just about successful militancy and justice, though those influences are significant. They are also to do with demography and class privilege, with 'various stakeholders participating in the networked media of the 2010s ... "serving" a particular version of liberal feminism that rendered gender equality in women's sports particularly visible' (Cooky and Antunovic, 2022: x) as fractions of capital now target female and minority audiences. For instance, in early 1990s Canada, the beer company that owned The Sports Network (TSN) sought an isomorphism of sports, audiences, and alcohol intake through its cable motto: 'We deliver the male' (quoted in Sparks, 1992: 330). In 1998, ESPN guaranteed 'More tackles, less tutus' ("There's," 1998). But two decades later, TSN promised 'Sponsorship programs on TSN.ca ... tailored to your target audience,'[27] and ESPN shared with potential advertisers 'a myth buster: Both men and women are watching women's sports.'[28]

Consider some transformations in one of the world's historically *macho* sports. A particular kind of daredevilry defined Formula One in its first decades. Incarnating the fantasy of the talented amateur, the *bourgeois* media built up the bravado of debonair posh-boy drivers, concentrating on the drunken and sexual 'off-track hijinks' of a Mike Hawthorn ('The Gay Cavalier') in the 1950s or a James Hunt ('Hunt the Shunt [crash]') in the 1970s; the very presence behind the wheel of such aristocratic names as Count Carel Godin deBeaufort, Alfonso, Marquis de Potago, and Prince Bira of Siam; and the 'romantically' fatal accidents of Piers Courage and Jim Clark (Williams, 2021).

This was a time when Enzo Ferrari claimed 'marriage slowed his drivers down' (Williams, 2021). In 2010, the renowned 1950s driver Stirling Moss compared the present with the past like this: 'When the race finishes, instead of chasing girls like they did in my day, now they go and say "thanks" to

Vodafone.' Male nostalgia valorizes a time 'When Sex Was Safe & Racing Dangerous.'[29] Although the sport may lack the racy scandals of yore, they continue to generate coverage: the fallen 1970s libertine Hunt was commemorated in a *Mail on Sunday* headline of 2013: 'To You, James Hunt Was an F1 Playboy Who Bedded 5,000 Women. To Me, He Was Dad—Who Doted on Me … and his 300 Budgies' (Graham, 2013). A decade later, its daily counterpart led with tales of 'how he slept with 33 … [BA] air hostesses during his two-week stay in Tokyo' (Nagle, 2023). And the past remains present—in 2023, a commentator was found to have engaged in 'inappropriate touching' of women involved in motorsport (Waterson, 2023) and the 2023 Spanish *Grand Prix* saw Italy's Sky Sport broadcast remarkable displays of sexism by its ex-driver commentators (Tondo, 2023).

The Netflix series *Formula 1: Drive to Survive*[30] (2018–) stimulated huge television ratings increases for Formula One's environmental despoliation (50%) (Lawrence, 2021). It attracted new female aficionados by chronicling what the *New Yorker* terms 'grand melodramas and intricate microdynamics … a new kind of broken fourth wall between the world of sports and entertainment' (Battan, 2022). But motorsport's 'emphasis on technological progress has always been accompanied by a deep cultural conservatism' (Williams, 2020). Formula One excludes women from most seats of power, perpetuates gendered wage disparities, and is more than 90% white (Sylt, 2019; Boxall-Legge, 2020). And it still sends cars 'snaking through the streets of Monaco past grandstands full of the world's most glamorous women,' with 'Naomi Campbell and Heidi Klum hanging off the arms of the team bosses' (Reid, 2008) (Campbell was 'speechless' over the 2018 decision to ban 'grid girls,' with *The Sun* on hand to provide the cover story 'Formula Dumb' [Tippet, 2019]).[31]

In short, the sport remains the creature of '[i]nternational playboys, Machiavellian billionaires, humble heroes, racing-world royalty, overachieving underdogs, aging has-beens, hotheaded bullies'—and tobacco firms, which staved off advertising bans for years by negotiating exemptions (Battan, 2022)—all of them surrounded by a huge band of complicit reporters. Once cigarette commercials were exiled from television, legal drug-peddlers turned to covert advertising as part of their restless search to manufacture addicts. The best-known company involved with Formula One has been Marlboro, part of Phillip Morris International. The company 'adorned' McLaren's livery for a quarter of a century and Ferrari's for a decade. A 1989 race saw it on view almost 6,000 times during television coverage (Irimia, 2022; Blum, 1991).

Overt sponsorship was not banned until 2006 (Reid, 2015). Philip Morris quickly shifted to subliminal product placement.[32] In place of brand names, it deployed barcodes and a campaign based on the search for transforming smoking into a 'safe' addiction, signaled with—hey presto—tropes of its usual logo.³³ For its part, British American Tobacco turned to a company slogan after being barred from naming itself (Dewhirst and Hunter, 2002).³⁴ McLaren's 2019 'global partnership' aims 'to deliver the world's tobacco and nicotine consumers a better tomorrow' (quoted in Mitchell, 2019). This is referred to in medical research as 'smokescreen' marketing (Barker et al., 2019). It handed Formula One a cool US$105 million in 2021, US$4.5 billion lifetime (STOP and FM, 2021). In 2022, the Australian Communications and Media Authority investigated broadcast breaches of tobacco advertising regulations at that year's Melbourne Grand Prix (ACMA, 2022).

Why is this not the object of investigative journalism? Why does one learn of such things from medical research or celebratory sports stories? And why so little attention to the disgraceful environmental record? An outlier, the nevertheless avowed petrol head Richard Williams, imagines a world without Formula One, when 'the curtains of history will have been drawn across the entire spectacle' (2019). There are few like him.

Technology

Sports journalism was once divided on a hierarchical basis. The well-remunerated male journalistic élite of the Anglo world working for 'quality' capital-city newspapers had license to cover major athletes, teams, and competitions and, occasionally, sports' historical and cultural dimensions. This quasi-aristocracy—in the US and Canada, elevated to the status of 'writers'—could ply its trade in relative isolation from the sports industry *per se*. Televised press conferences provided opportunities for famous sports journalists to assert their comparative eminence while local reporters discharged proletarian functions, loitering 'in febrile packs outside dressing rooms in the hope of entrapping a teenage millionaire player' (Cowley, 1999; also see "Sports Journalism," 2017).

Although such arrangements and their associated divisions of labor still exist, technology and the political economy have attenuated them, flattening occupational roles ("Sports Journalism," 2017). Few mainstream sports journalists retain the privilege of periodic, leisurely, long-form stories. Communications technology and ownership concentration have diversified the forms and accelerated the rhythms of a shrinking, busier workforce (Hutchins and Rowe, 2012). They have punctured the membranes separating professionally produced, securely copyrighted journalism from the freely generated and circulated work of amateurs bearing tablets and cellphones.

Given the current data fetish that is Taylorizing³⁵ sport—think of the 'expected goals' category in football, which almost trumps goals scored—it is no surprise to see software that writes stories grow in popularity among news executives and proprietors. The Associated Press (AP) has been using Automated Insights' Wordsmith program for years to cover fixtures where it would not otherwise have sent a journalist (Finley, 2015). Yahoo! Sports does so to generate millions of match reports aimed at Fantasy Football participants, egging on advertisers by boasting of 'over 100 years of incremental audience engagement.'[36] New technology also holds significant implications for visual reportage. Football photojournalists face dual, contradictory challenges: capitalist property lines are increasingly being drawn around events, thereby limiting their access, and cellphone cameras turn paying spectators into rivals (Haynes et al., 2017). This became a huge scandal in 2023 when it emerged that *Sports Illustrated* was running pieces by imaginary journalists, with fabricated names, biographies, and images (Harrison, 2023c); *Sports Illustrated*, whose authors had included some actual people, such as William Faulkner, Robert Frost, John Steinbeck, Jack Kerouac, and Don DeLillo (Graham, 2013). *USA Today* and numerous Gannett publications have been forced to rewrite artificial intelligence (AI) sports reports, so poor was the quality and frequent the self-plagiarism across stories and sites (Harrison, 2023a and 2023b). As usual, these mistakes flowed from political-economic decisions secreted behind consumerist propaganda: jobs were cut by new owners, inadequate technology was introduced, and phony explanations were given, claiming this was a response to audience desires (Landymore, 2023).

These developments in technological capacity and commercial distortion trouble the hitherto comfortable, self-enclosed world of sports journalism. When reporters had relative autonomy, it was possible to withstand the hostility of angry sports fans and the slights of journalistic peers from more prestigious beats. But with analogic technology giving way to digital, what sports journalists did, and who could claim to be one, came into question (Bradshaw and Minogue, 2019). In the digital age, why hire a sports reporter when almost anyone can 'do' sports journalism?

And as we shall see in the next chapter, it is rarely sufficient nowadays to be competent in one medium, such as print, radio, or television. Technological proliferation and miniaturization mean avowed print journalists are expected to appear on, and even make, radio and television programs. They must write multiple stories to feed voracious websites while blogging and attending to 'social' media platforms that take these texts far beyond the countries in which they are produced.

This crisis of professional legitimacy is exacerbated by sporting organizations and celebrities using 'social' media to communicate directly with fans through heavily managed encounters (Doyle et al., 2022). Access to athletes via scheduled interviews and press conferences now sees sports journalists increasingly criticized as lackeys of major clubs and superstar coaches and players. Always at risk of premature occupational demise because of being cut off by displeased sources/suspects, reporters increasingly ask banal 'how do you feel?' questions or provide gentle prompts to burnish official profiles. They perform promotional roles (English, 2016). For example, relationships between spokespeople for German Bundesliga football clubs and print journalists have seen reporters become more dependent on officials than *vice versa*, with growing pressure to write stories amenable to team interests (Grimmer, 2017). Reporters are now 'part of the sports service industry' (Perreault and Bell, 2022: 410).

A longitudinal investigation of football media outlets using the site-formerly-known-as-Twitter between 2010 and 2017 reveals that the drive to find content has augmented the number and velocity of messages, stimulated seemingly infinite duplication, and encouraged concentration on star clubs, players, and managers. Ironically, given cybertarian claims to the contrary, the research discloses that the platform is largely a 'one-directional broadcasting medium, where content is increasingly homogenized … search engine optimisation and attractive headlines trump journalistic content' (Cable and Mottershead, 2018). Far from there being necessary and positive relationships between technological change, textual abundance, and discursive diversity, the likes of MLB and the NFL deploy 'blockbuster' strategies that seek to roll over any journalists standing in their way (Elberse, 2013).

The intermeshing of professional and 'social' media was not initially countenanced by corporations and journalists (Sheffer and Schultz, 2010); they thought there would be competition for the attention of easily distracted viewers, listeners, and readers. Instead, reporters are frequently bypassed or spend their time staring at amateur digital offerings, mining fan sentiment and seeking *vox pops* that are magically licensed and legitimized as the word from the street or terrace. It is mind-boggling to hear supporters who run podcasts interviewed by the BBC as authorities on play, context, and, most bizarrely, public opinion, when 'their' audiences are not random samples.

Sports journalists still conduct set-piece descriptions, commentaries, analyses, in-depth interviews, and occasional research, with purportedly newsworthy items achieving viral status by circulating wildly across platforms, especially if there is a whiff of scandal. Sometimes reporters obtain exclusives or leaks because of their organizational status. But they routinely monitor official announcements, gossip columns, fan websites, and star web pages. Like many other areas of journalism, the result is frequently headlines and story descriptions designed to tease and shock—or regurgitate PR. Digital sports journalists receive major abuse from readers of 'social' media and frequently succumb to competitive pressure to retain and develop responses through self-censorship or by responding to gossip rather than reporting what can be verified (Bradshaw, 2021). That amplifies research regarding the dance of sports reporting in general (Kroon and Eriksson, 2019; Lambert, 2019; Oelrichs, 2022), including the struggle to pull rank by evoking much-mythologized traditions 'rooted in the same norms and practices their pre-digital, legacy media counterparts would have expected,' with 'the product' reflecting 'the pull of economic capital and perception of participants' (Perreault and Bell, 2022: 410).

These pressures further endow a powerful and unworthy tendency—clientelism—where journalism depends on its source to the point of being a mouthpiece. The mutual imbrication of sports and media ownership overdetermines reportage.

Clientelism: a story fit for a king

International sports represent the ultimate in commodification and governmentalization, as youthful technocrats and hegemonic greybeards commingle.[37] That tendency is evident in clubs: Western European football teams were once small, city-based businesses, drawing on athletes who had grown up close to their grounds. They were run rather like not-for-profits, representing and regenerating local cultures, albeit sometimes dominated by industrial combines (in Germany) or *petit-bourgeois machistas* (in Britain).

By the 1990s, many clubs had become creatures of exchange. In the course of this radical transformation, they fell prey to fictive capital, transmogrifying into sources of asset inflation used by rentiers to service other debts through cash flow from television and merchandising. This passage of European football from public to private goods is clearly a matter of great regret for Eduardo Galeano (2016) and Yanis Varoufakis (1998: 230) alike.

As noted earlier, a neoliberal shift in policymaking was crucial: the deregulation of European broadcast media across the 1980s and 1990s. With new communications technologies and consumer electronics proliferating, élite national leagues and transnational competitions maximized their worth for channels that were dedicated exclusively to sports and desperately needed material. In the decade from 1990, a period of minimal macroeconomic inflation, the cost of European football TV rights grew 800%. Despite that increase, the content was desirable when compared to the expense of producing drama or even news and current affairs, because football's development costs and star salaries were largely borne by clubs themselves rather than television stations. In addition, gaining the right to cover popular leagues became a route to securing cable, satellite, and broadband subscribers (Miller, 2010).

In 2015, telecommunications companies masquerading as TV networks, i.e., BT and Sky, paid US$7.9 billion between them for the right to screen English Premier League matches over the next three seasons—a 70% increase on the previous contract. International sales added US$4.3 billion to the figure (Bonesteel, 2015). For the period 2022–25, British rights went for a reduced figure of £5 billion, while international ones amounted to £5.05 billion (Mackey, 2023). The domestic rights for four years from 2025 were sold for £6.7 billion ("Premier League Agrees," 2023).

In the same week as the 2015 deal, sports' share of television viewing in the UK was just 6.23%—well behind hobbies, news, documentaries, and other genres ("Weekly Viewing by Genre," 2015). Sky Sports 1 had 0.99% of the TV audience. Together, the network's channels—drama, news, football, and so on—'commanded' 8.3% of all viewers. BT Sport secured 0.39% ("Weekly Viewing by Channel," 2015). In April 2023, a key moment in the football season, live sports were not in the top 50 programs ("Weekly Top 50 Shows," 2023). In the week of the gigantic 2023 domestic contract, two sports show snuck into the 50 most popular TV programs in Britain, at numbers 42 and 45.[38] So for all the nonsense peddled by reporters, sports don't matter terribly much to most people in the UK.

The real struggle clearly transcended football. It was between capitalists competing to obtain marginal consumer subscriptions for broadband and telephony, as wealthy corporations sought to decimate their rivals' core business. Football fandom was the field of contestation. The social cost was denying access to certain viewers. Sports reporters steered away from such realities—and what flowed from them.

Now the issue is the removal of coverage even from cable and satellite, with Apple TV purchasing the global rights to Major League Soccer for US $2.5 billion for a decade from 2023 to match its deals for MLB fixtures and Amazon's US$10 billion capture of certain Yankees home games and parts of the NFL (Kafka, 2021; Silverman and Ourand, 2022; Battaglio, 2022; Gregory with Zorthian, 2023). This time, rather than being a struggle for broadband, per the UK a decade earlier, the drive is toward 'direct-to-consumer' services and brands: a gradual displacement of television (Weprin, 2021). For commentators and other journalists, this means neither being part of a wider news organization, nor a specialized sports one—rather, it mandates the kind of contingent, isolated employment for which contemporary media firms are renowned. This reached such a scandalous point that Britain's Competition and Markets Authority (CMA) investigated a possible wage-fixing cartel of Sky, ITV, the Premier League, the BBC, Sunset & Vine, and BT Sport (later renamed TNT Sports after a merger with Discovery) to suppress freelance workers' remuneration.[39] There has been minimal press coverage of the case, despite the implications for journalists and their colleagues.

The rights paid for football, both locally and abroad, have attracted foreign proprietors to the English Premier League, from Russian oligarchs to indebted Gringos, from Thai politicos on the run to reactionary Republicans loving the gun (Fordham, 2020). For example, in 2020, Aston Villa was part-owned by the fourth-richest African in the world; Leicester City by Thai clientelists, of whom more below; Wolverhampton Wanderers by a Chinese multinational; Manchester City by an Emirati; and Sheffield United by a Saudi. Arsenal, Villa, Bournemouth, Liverpool, Crystal Palace, and

Manchester United were under full or partial US control. Southampton was 80% Chinese-owned and 20% Austrian (the latter the only female proprietor), Everton 77% Iranian. Watford was run by an Italian, and Russian oligarchs were majority or full owners of Chelsea and Bournemouth. Their wealth, and that of the few Britons involved, derived from an array of sources: pornography; publishing; daddies and daddies-in-law; state-owned/dubiously privatized energy firms; equity conglomerates/raiders; shopping malls; construction; gambling addiction; video games; theater; duty-free stores; US sports teams; corporatized food; healthcare; sporting apparel and equipment; manufacturing; (putative) match-fixing; and forex trading (Miller, 2020). The 2023–24 season began with 9 Gringos among the League's 20 club owners ("English Premier," 2023).

Those owners, largely drawn from beyond the orbit of traditional fandom, are accompanied by shadowy operatives who are forever fiddling with visa applications, tax avoidance and evasion, funky measurements of on-field performance, company-man 'social' media utterances attributed to players, and existing or prospective corporate welfare from governments. There is almost zero press coverage of that political economy.

When allied to the British public's monolingualism and xenophobia, this influx of otherness via the international proprietorship and management of putatively local clubs has produced ambivalent reactions. Fans like the infusions of cash to purchase players and fund spectators' creature comforts, but are wary of owners who are not what hacks call 'football men,' especially if they seek to rename clubs, refashion logos to suit imagined future audiences in other countries, or use cash flow to hypothecate (Hayton et al., 2015). There is some evidence that this attitude diminishes when foreign owners turn up to games, smile at the right moments, and appear to invest in, rather than borrow against, the value of teams they have bought (Ludvigsen, 2019).

There is rarely any serious interrogation of these folks by the media. Take, for example, the dubious business and political dealings of Leicester City's owners, family members of the Thai airport duty-free group King Power International. They are celebrated over and over in the *bourgeois* press and fan fora as ideal proprietors (Miller, 2016; Bi, 2015) and became globally famous because their middle-ranking, middle-England football club won the Premier League in 2016. This was against all the odds, beyond even 'finding Elvis alive'; such a triumph occurred once in every 70,000 simulations (Hood et al., 2018).

King Power grew to be loved by Leicester fans (Whitwell, 2016). When an emotional supporter broke down on the BBC following a victory, it became an international news story.[40] The manager cried on the field (Taylor and Hytner, 2016). And in what was perhaps the ultimate among a series of narcissistic male melodramas, a BBC journalist called his father on air to celebrate the Premiership triumph. Both men wept.⁴¹ All very moving, in the eyes of some; self-indulgent hegemonic masculinity for others.

Leicester's owners have questions to answer about 30 years of oligarchic tendencies and sharp business practices, dating from the group's 'opaque' origins in downtown Bangkok. Over that period, what began as a single duty-free store attained industry-wide dominance (Holmes, 2016). In 2006, the body responsible for Thailand's airports alleged that King Power had obtained its retail concession and duty-free license for Suvarnabhumi airport without an open bidding process (Phongpaichit and Baker, 2013). An article written by a Southeast Asia correspondent rather than a sports journalist noted that 'when a Korean competitor recently tried to enter the market, it was allowed to start building a duty-free store in Bangkok,' but 'blocked from opening pick-up counters at the capital's two major airports. Without the pick-up counters, customers cannot receive their tax-free purchases' (Holmes, 2016). As the *Bangkok Post* wryly put it, 'King Power's chief business acumen is in securing such monopolistic duty-free concessions in the first place and then to keep leveraging its myriad revenue streams. This is a murky area where business and politics intersect' (Pananond and Pongsudhirak, 2016). For example, in 2013 the company's then-owner, วิชัย รักศรีอักษร [Vichai Raksriaksorn], changed his last name by Royal assent to วิชัย ศรีวัฒนประภา [Khun Vichai Srivaddhanaprabha], which signifies 'light of progressive glory.' The following year, the company gained Air Asia's in-flight duty-free concession, culminating 25 years of business. In 2019, King Power was granted Bangkok's duty-free concession for another decade, despite counter-bids and evidence that sales were poor by contrast with regional airports that allowed competition (Yuda, 2019).

The dissident blog *Political Prisoners in Thailand*⁴² had this to say about King Power's late head: for 'the Chinese business class in the 1920s, getting a royal family name was a sign of inclusion and acceptance. Today, it must be a fitting reward for a very wealthy supporter of the wealthiest.' Such a story is in keeping with Vichai's status as someone who grew up with a cohort that grants favorable business conditions to those with the right political connections. It's a well-established form of clientelism that he parlayed excellently, as both beneficiary and donor (Hewison, 2015; Pananond and Pongsudhirak, 2016).

King Power works with the controversial provincial strongman, machine politician, and fellow team owner เนวิน ชิดชอบ [Newin Chidchob] and cultivates close ties with administrations and coup leaders (Hookway, 2012; Pananond and Pongsudhirak, 2016). At the same time, the company diligently, dutifully plays on the status of the Thai monarchy and its fealty: King Power's Foundation, which avowedly seeks to 'help underprivileged children and youth on the path toward a better life, through education and health services,' named no fewer than six of its seven initiatives after the last monarch, three of which said they loved him.⁴³

Prior to Leicester's improbable triumph, Vichai's singular sporting achievement had been to establish the Thailand Polo Association,⁴⁴ which connected him to global royalty and high society and local military and police. The light-of-progressive-glory and his relatives featured on the Association's management committee, and King Power linked its British team to Leicester (Gilmour, 2016). Vichai installed his son อัยยวัฒน์ ศรีวัฒนประภา [Aiyawatt Srivaddhanaprabha] to run City and play polo. Reading the son-of-the-light-of-progressive-glory's reflections on the sport and his family's part in it is like taking a brief guided tour around the international élite; Aiyawatt is pleased to count British princes among his teammates and chums. No wonder the *Financial Times* found 'Vichai does not lack financial muscle and plays the same league as any football-club owning Russian oligarch or Gulf investment fund' ("Free Beer," 2016).

King Power says its football goal is 'to develop Leicester City's fan base internationally and particularly in Asia, while boosting Thailand's global reputation and capabilities through the management of the Club.'⁴⁵ On winning the title, the company announced a new tool for scouting potential talent—its very own reality show for would-be stars.⁴⁶ Just six years after the family had bought the team for £39 million in 2010, it was said to be worth £436 million (Holmes, 2016). By 2022, the figure was £742 million.⁴⁷ That should have been enough time for UK journalists to serve the public interest by examining how King Power went about its business. Such an analysis would have focused on its clientelist role in Thai corporate life and the animal victims and survivors of the other 'sport' it endows, polo.⁴⁸

But there are self-imposed barriers in UK sports journalism to disclosing the dubious business and political dealings of Leicester's owners (Miller, 2016). Toby experienced difficulty publishing an *exposé* in the Anglo media, so frightened were they by King Power's long arm of Leicesterian litigation (further thanks to *The Conversation*'s timorous editors for refusing a piece they had invited). Instead, fans and reporters alike admire the free beer and pie for supporters and supercars for players provided by the firm—classic clientelism, gestated through ever-more hyperbolic effusions in the press (Haughton, 2018; Rathborn, 2016). Only when the club slid into relegation in 2022–23 was this love-in questioned, as ticket-holders and journalists alike sought explanations for a tarnished 'light of progressive glory.'⁴⁹ Meanwhile, the CMA's announcement in 2021 that it was investigating probable breaches of competition law by City and the retailer JD Sports over the sale of branded merchandise lay essentially unreported after two years of research, and received limited coverage when the Authority ultimately found the parties guilty and fined the team the maximum possible amount.⁵⁰ The media focused on the matter at hand, failing to contextualize the club's owners and their history of problematic conduct.

The Leicester story encapsulates numerous problems identified across this and the previous chapter. As the influence of global money intensifies, the public deserves greater journalistic acumen and coverage of football's political economy via investigative reporting of the corruption that is rife in ruling associations, the sport's environmental impact, the role of banner advertising and podcasts in supporting the animal slavery and human addiction of gambling, and systematic human-rights offenses by the owners of Paris Saint-Germain, Girona, Newcastle United, and Manchester City—topics that are almost entirely left to one side by the fanboys of the sporting press.[51] The profession's low status is merited, given its uncritical approach toward the political-economic realities of its objects of engagement.

Conclusion

Sports can be shown to embody the distinction between a world of domination, scientific management, and an artificially generated dislike of others; and a world of collaboration, spontaneity, and fellowship. AT&T's 1999 campaign to win the local US telephone market featured a blurred graphic of children sprinting, captioned 'Remember racing with your friends?' offset with 'Competition helped everyone run faster'[52]—pure metaphorization in the service of capital. But when tempted to express disdain for sport's banal competitiveness and disciplinary obsessions, we acknowledge the untrammeled ecstasy of catching a wave or seeing someone else do so—a perfect utopian alternative to this seemingly most capitalistic of metaphors. Imagine if those paradoxes/contradictions formed part of journalism.

Orwell understood the positive as well as the negative aspects of football for everyday life and politics. He referred admiringly to a miner who emerged from the pit covered head to toe in coal dust, then proudly washed and changed into his best clothes to attend a match, imagining a socialist future that would sparkle with the pleasure of watching football (Orwell, 1937: 3, 11). Jacques Attali argues that sports provide one of the few topics that can generate discussion in almost any venue, potentially leading to a common understanding where none had seemed possible (2001: 262). Durkheim maintained that sports could 'balance and relieve … serious life' (1961: 361). Bertolt Brecht noted: 'We have our eye on those huge concrete pans, filled with 15,000 men and women of every variety of class and physiognomy, the fairest and shrewdest audience in the world' (1964). He saw potential for vibrancy and even revolution, akin to the political pleasure that John Lennon experienced when football crowds chanted The Beatles' 'All Together Now' (1971). Situationists celebrated when the *soixante-huitards* took over the offices of the Fédération Française de Football (Solidarity, 2001). Lukács held that proletarian crowds interpreted football as a spectacular expression of industrial experience (1972). TH Marshall regarded attendance as a 'common right' (1950, p. 82). Stuart Hall discerned an 'overwhelming mirror of football' in the social world (1998: 191), and Althusser an oscillation between exuberant arrogance and passive conformity (1971: 162). Adorno reflected on this duality: 'On the one hand, … an anti-barbaric and anti-sadistic effect by means of fair play, a spirit of chivalry, and consideration for the weak. On the other … aggression, brutality, and sadism' (2010). Simmel saw sports as a motor and index of social life: 'the desire to gain advantage, trade, formation of parties and the desire to win from another, the movement between opposition and co-operation, outwitting and revenge' (1949: 258). Cabral thought teams modelled the unity of purpose and diversity of identity needed for revolutionary change (1979: 4). Ulrich Beck avowed that football could counter nationalism through its postcolonial/global capitalist ecumenism (2002).

But reporting? Cowley laments that 'sports writing has, like sport itself, never been more debased, a rancid world where journalists pay millionaires for interviews and sports editors salivate over hurried, quotes-driven copy, seldom redeemed by stylistic grace' (1999). Without the renewal and reinvention of its purpose and labor force, including a belated embrace of critical investigation and political economy, sports journalism will fail to achieve a long-coveted professional legitimacy and may see its public relevance further eroded.

Notes

1. https://www.gazzetta.it/.
2. https://www.lequipe.fr/.
3. https://www.marca.com/.
4. https://www.armedforcesbowl.com/.
5. https://www.armedforcesbowl.com/great-american-patriot-award.
6. https://www.si.com/search?query=Military.
7. https://www.villagevoice.com/.
8. https://www.mrc.org/.
9. https://www.theonion.com/soccer-officially-announces-it-is-gay-1819594939.
10. https://www.youtube.com/watch?v=o6O_8RohRrI.
11. https://www.youtube.com/watch?v=tWwkU-CWy9o.
12. https://www.youtube.com/watch?v=HM-E2H1ChJM.
13. https://www.youtube.com/watch?v=pYFTYanZXiE.
14. https://www.youtube.com/watch?v=mOO3hTaH5tw.
15. https://www.youtube.com/watch?v=2QpdtsP79w4.
16. https://www.youtube.com/watch?v=EqQxvthwia4&app=desktop.
17. https://www.youtube.com/watch?v=z7myTM35OLU.
18. Dean Wilson BBC Radio, June 28, 2023.
19. https://www.youtube.com/watch?v=9tU-D-m2JY8&ab_channel=JustNotSports.

20 https://www.statista.com/statistics/1327747/diversity-english-professional-football/; https://www.ethnicity-facts-figures.service.gov.uk/uk-population-by-ethnicity/national-and-regional-populations/population-of-england-and-wales/latest.
21 https://www.bbc.co.uk/programmes/b007t9y1.
22 https://www.bbc.co.uk/sounds/play/live:bbc_radio_five_live.
23 https://tvnewsroom.online/bbc-news/bbc-news-sports-presenters-reporters-199594/.
24 https://bcoms.co/.
25 The 2022 event saw the BBC do much more toward real diversity, though this did not extend to including scholarly experts, who might be heard elsewhere discussing art, politics, science, or weather, but are basically excluded from sports unless they teach at business schools https://www.fourfourtwo.com/features/world-cup-2022-bbc-presenters-pundits-commentators-tv-radio.
26 https://bcoms.co/.
27 https://www.tsn.ca/advertise-with-tsn-ca-1.80463.
28 https://www.disneyadvertising.com/our-brands/espn/.
29 https://www.youtube.com/watch?v=GGP5FEIMza4&ab_channel=PolePosition Motorsport
30 https://www.youtube.com/watch?v=PSLTXPefVGE&ab_channel=Netflix.
31 https://www.youtube.com/watch?v=hemNFwxxfyg&ab_channel=GoodMorning Britain.
32 https://www.youtube.com/watch?v=6j7bH9sPq38.
33 https://www.youtube.com/watch?v=ue3MThMYxZU.
34 https://www.youtube.com/watch?v=SPs0LlK3DRI&ab_channel=BAT.
35 Taylorization refers to the eponym derived from FW Taylor, whose methods of scientific management created modern factory capitalism. The equivalent in the Soviet Union was Stakhanovism (Börnfelt, 2023).
36 https://automatedinsights.com/customer-stories/yahoo/.
37 https://www.youtube.com/watch?v=_SPa4zpuC0Y; https://www.youtube.com/watch?v=S-HA7HKSD9I.
38 https://www.barb.co.uk/viewing-data/most-viewed-programmes/.
39 https://www.gov.uk/cma-cases/suspected-anti-competitive-behaviour-relating-to-the-purchase-of-freelance-services-in-the-production-and-broadcasting-of-sports-content.
40 http://www.bbc.co.uk/programmes/p03cl1cc.
41 https://www.bbc.co.uk/programmes/p03sx9j3.
42 https://thaipoliticalprisoners.wordpress.com/.
43 https://www.kingpower.com/en/corporate/social-events-activities/king-power-foundation.
44 http://www.thailandpolo.or.th/committee.
45 https://www.kingpower.com/en/business/sports/lcfc?lang=en.
46 https://www.kingpower.com/en/business/sports/lcfc?lang=en.
47 https://www.forbes.com/teams/leicester-city/?sh=477928a710fc.
48 https://www.peta.org.uk/blog/the-death-of-prince-harrys-polo-pony-is-not-an-isolated-incident/.
49 https://podcasts.apple.com/gb/podcast/when-youre-smiling-a-leicester-city-podcast/id323988539?i=1000614856165; https://www.youtube.com/watch?v=I6Ss0p2Oiro&t=201s&ab_channel=TifoFootball.
50 https://www.gov.uk/cma-cases/suspected-anti-competitive-behaviour-in-relation-to-the-sale-of-leicester-city-fc-branded-products-and-merchandise; https://www.gov.uk/government/news/leicester-city-fc-to-be-fined-up-to-880k-after-admitting-anti-competitive-arrangement-with-jd-sports.

51 But see https://www.addiction-ssa.org/commentary/football-and-gambling-an-unholy-matrimony; https://lavdn.lavoixdunord.fr/484416/article/2018-11-08/une-affaire-de-fichage-ethnique-revelee-au-psg; https://medium.com/@NcGeehan/the-men-behind-man-city-a-documentary-not-coming-soon-to-a-cinema-near-you-14bc8e393e06; https://www.abc.net.au/news/2019-12-08/why-paddy-power-pioneer-quit-betting-industry/11777058?pfmredir=sm; and https://www.abc.net.au/news/2019-12-05/bet365-whistleblower-says-winners-given-delays/11768486.
52 *New York Times*, June 3, 1999, p. A19.

4
TECHNOLOGY

For much of the world's population, 'technoscience frames … everyday life at all levels, down to our notion of the self' (Biagioli, 2009: 818). Consider these numbers: in 1965, fewer 'than 12 materials were in wide use: wood, brick, iron, copper, gold, silver, and a few plastics.' Today, there is a comprehensive 'materials basis to modern society' (Graedel et al., 2015). The computer chip that enabled me to type this chapter contains over 60 of them.

The technology that relies on these materials is both a key index of modernity and its doom-laden consequence and portent—a bravura blend of reason and magic, of confidence and hubris. As befits their genealogy of 'millenarianism, rationalism, and Christian redemption' channeled through 'monks, explorers, inventors, and … scientists,' technologies guarantee a present and future that appear at once perfect and monstrous: life, liberty, happiness; death, enslavement, misery. They amount to a secular religion, offering transcendence via machinery rather than political-economic activity; machinery that is always already obsolete and has a saturnine side (Dinerstein, 2006: 569; Nye, 2006: 598).

As Armand Mattelart explains, we are given 'an eternal promise symbolizing a world that is better because it is united. From road and rail to information highways, this belief has been revived with each technological generation' (2000: viii). Almost a century ago, Keynes suggested the near future would see a 15-hour work week, thanks to technology and compound interest (1963: 358–73). But technologized societies always produce 'unintended consequences' (Merton, 1936): good and bad, pacific and violent, democratic and capitalist, characterized by military, governmental, scholarly, and commercial desires and perversions. There's a moment in *Defence of the Realm* (David Drury, 1986) when the wizened hack Vernon Bayliss is unable to operate a miniature tape recorder he's bought. His younger colleague Nick Mullen shows him how to do so, joking that Vernon hasn't entered 'the Industrial Revolution,' let alone 'the age of technology.' They both end up murdered by the British state, but per the genre of heroic but personally flawed journalists seeking justice, the truth comes out, in part thanks to recording technology.

Whereas initial modernization by states was primarily concerned with establishing national power and accumulating and distributing wealth, developed modernity produces new, trans-territorial risks, beyond the scope of traditional governmental guarantees of collective security and affluence. As part of this, a shift occurred in the Global North from investments in chemical and electronic technologies and toward communications technologies. Michael Hardt and Antonio Negri graphically, romantically, describe the subsequent exchange of knowledge through computers as 'immaterial labor' (2000: 286, 290–92). How right they were, in terms of propaganda; how wrong in terms of environmental and social relations.

Unsurprisingly, a 'new practice of piety' emerges with each 'new communications technology' (Hunter, 1988: 220), in contradictory, competitive form: love letters/critiques, fantasies/anxieties, and annunciations/denunciations remorselessly, repetitively accompany media innovations (Wajcman, 2004: 1–9; Naughton, 2014: 74–84). Hence Baron [sic] Anthony Giddens advising that the 'digital revolution … has made the world one,' but 'is fracturing and dividing' the result (2018).

Seeming binary oppositions that are in fact logocentrically interdependent continue to characterize discussion of the 'new.' Communication technologies' credulous cheerleaders are as numerous as their redundant reporters, crotchety critics, and pullulating protestors—and more powerful. This chapter examines journalism's technological utopias and dystopias, foreshadowing consideration of big data/AI and the labor process.

Utopias

The Catholic Church invested in medieval printing as soon as the technology became available. By the 16th century, it ran the largest communication apparatus in the West, blasting briefs, bulls, confessions, indulgences and so around the globe. Reformation critics did the same (Meserve, 2021). Since the Industrial Revolution, the media's capacity to bind and unbind time and space through the visibility and audibility of signs from elsewhere has stimulated discussion of a new world order, predicated on the assumption that universally shared knowledge can transcend the chauvinism of sovereign states (Marvin, 1988: 192–93). This tendency is always twinned with desires to open the world up to commercial conquest, exploitation, and mercantilism. Sometimes the two wishes, for democracy and capitalism, have been in conflict; sometimes they have not (Mattelart, 2000: 1).

At the 1849 International Congress of Peace, Victor Hugo predicted that 'the electric wire of concord shall encircle the globe and embrace the world' (Peace Congress Committee, 1849: 12). Charles Knight, a key figure in 19th-century US publishing, referred to telegraphy and photography as 'victory over time and space' (quoted in Briggs and Burke, 2015: 104). When the International Telegraph Union was formed in 1865, its inaugural meeting was hailed by French foreign minister Édouard Drouyn de Lhuys as 'a genuine Congress of peace' thanks to the device's 'exchange of ideas' between 'scattered members of the human family' (quoted in Mattelart, 2000: 20). JS Mill's drive toward global capitalism saw him insist that there be no 'taxes on the communication of information' via advertising, newspapers, or the post (2004: 232).

Far from being unique to our era, the notion of 'instantaneous information' is a 19th-century one: some of the globe's principal news agencies were formed between the 1830s and 1850s to take advantage of the telegraph (Mattelart, 2000: 23). They were created in ways that permitted relative autonomy from trust-busting (Markoff, 1995; Silberstein-Loeb, 2014). In France, the telephone's appearance in the 1870s marked a dialogic moment in the country's communications history. Reciprocity and accessibility were available as never before; what had been exclusively governmental and scientific instruments became public property and crucial tools for reporters (Attali and Stourdzé, 1977: 97–98).

By the early 20th century, Jack London saw moving pictures as an antidote to violence: 'Gaze horror-struck on the war scenes, and you become an advocate of peace' (1915). DW Griffith defended his racist epic *The Birth of a Nation* (1915) by arguing that it was undermining previously restricted access to 'truths of history' that had hitherto been policed by universities (quoted in Gross et al., 1988: 31). Decades later, Jeffrey Katzenberg assured us that *Schindler's List* (Steven Spielberg, 1993) would 'bring peace on earth, good will to men' and 'set the course of world affairs' (quoted in Fogel, 1994: 315).

Guglielmo Marconi, radio's principal inventor, said broadcasting would 'make a material contribution towards greater understanding and amity between Nations, the cementing of home life and the happiness of the individual' (1924). In 1927, the BBC adopted 'nation shall speak peace unto nation' as its motto. The ether, a metaphysical expression of radio waves, was thought to offer contact with the dead and cure for the cancerous (Walker, 1973: 34). Henry Ford claimed: 'The airplane and radio know no boundary. They pass over the dotted lines on the map without heed or hindrance. They are binding the world together. … Thus may we envision a United States of the World' (1929: 9, 18–19). Australian Broadcasting Commission

Chair Richard Boyer celebrated the breakdown of patriarchal authority in the home brought about by counterfactual, permissively available information springing from the radio (Miller, 1949: 185–86).

Rudolf Arnheim's 1935 'Forecast of Television' imagined the next new device broadcasting simultaneous global experiences: train disasters, conference papers, public meetings, sports, concerts, carnivals, and aerial vistas. A common vision of the news would surpass linguistic competence and interpretation, with 'the wide world itself enter[ing] … our room' to bring global peace by showing spectators 'we are located as one among many' (1969: 160–63). Two years later, Barrett C Kiesling suggested TV would 'some day end war' (1937: 248), while RCA/NBC's David Sarnoff welcomed 'the greatest opportunity ever given us for creating close ties of understanding among the peoples of the world' (2004: 310). Pope Pius XII issued an encyclical letter admiring television's capacity to communicate 'the news, thoughts and usages of every nation,' providing 'food for the mind especially during the hours of recreation' and offering the Vatican a means of uniting 'the worldwide flock with its Supreme Pastor' (1957). All these claims assumed reporters would guide us in this glorious journey toward a pacific life.

Vannevar Bush, US Director of the Office of Scientific Research and Development during World War II, proclaimed computing as the release of humanity 'from the bondage of bare existence' (1945). When the Telstar satellite went into operation, President Kennedy welcomed 'an era of international communications' that could 'insure a greater understanding among peoples of the world' (1962). A year later, the UK's future Prime Minister Harold Wilson warned that 'Britain will become a stagnant backwater, pitied and condemned by the rest of the world' if it didn't keep up with new technology. He promised 'undreamed of living standards and the possibility of leisure on an unbelievable scale … a Britain that is going to be forged in the white heat of this revolution' (1963: 2–3, 7). The Organisation for Economic Co-operation and Development (OECD) decreed the coming of an 'information society' in 1975, IBM did the same two years later, and the European Communities (now Union) in 1979. A 1978 report to the French president predicted an imminent 'informational agora' (Nora and Minc, 1980: 140). This technological utopia was understood to be bring an end to ideological and social forces: class would cease to matter (Mattelart, 2002).

Bill Clinton's Presidential science advisor, John H Gibbons, announced that '[i]nformation superhighways will revolutionize the way Americans work, learn, shop, and live,' while Vice President Al Gore said the internet would 'educate, promote democracy, and save lives' (quoted in Gomery, 1994: 9). The *Magna Carta for the Information Age* proposed that political-economic transformations toward democracy since the 13th century had been eclipsed by technological change:

The central event of the 20th century is the overthrow of matter. In technology, economics, and the politics of nations, wealth—in the form of physical resources—has been losing value and significance. The powers of mind are everywhere ascendant over the brute force of things.

(Dyson et al., 1994)

Fellow-traveler Nicholas Negroponte predicted that by 2017 children were 'not going to know what nationalism is,' thanks to their ability to learn online about other countries (quoted in "Negroponte," 1997). Neoclassical economist Jagdish Bhagwati avowed that 'multinationals and their host governments cannot afford to alienate their constituencies' because of journalism's capacity for international communication (2002: 4, 6). The Papacy discerned 'an interconnected globe humming with electronic transmissions—a chattering planet nestled in the provident silence of space' (Pontifical Council for Social Communications, 2002).

Today, Facebook declares that it can 'decrease world conflict' through inter-cultural understanding. Twitter announced itself as 'a triumph of humanity' (quoted in "A Cyber-House," 2010: 61), ready 'to help increase the collective health, openness, and civility of public conversations' in the name of 'progress.'[1] When the corporation was renamed, Chief Executive Linda Yaccarino modestly announced that 'X will go further, transforming the global town square.'[2] TikTok 'wants to inspire and encourage a new generation to have a positive impact on the planet and those around them,' according to its 'ForGood' page.[3] Instagram seeks to 'bring the world closer together.'[4] Snapchat promises it can 'contribute to human progress by empowering people to express themselves, live in the moment, learn about the world, and have fun together.'[5] YouTube's 'mission is to give everyone a voice and show them the world.'[6] The distinction between producers and consumers is said to have eroded via the emergence of prosumers. WhatsApp wishes 'to let people communicate anywhere in the world without barriers.'[7] Reddit describes itself as 'home to thousands of communities, endless conversation, and authentic human connection.'[8] Headspace has 'one mission: to improve the health and happiness of the world.'[9] Its rival Calm undertakes 'to make the world happier and healthier.'[10]

The OECD says new technologies develop low-polluting economies in the Global South through energy efficiency, adaptation to climate change, mitigation of diminished biodiversity, and reduced pollution (Houghton, 2009). We are informed that cellphones streamline markets in countries where banking and economic information are scarce, thanks to the provision of market data connecting buyers and sellers and facilitating perfect competition. This purportedly ensures 'the complete elimination of waste' and massive reductions in poverty and corruption (Jensen, 2007). At the height of the 2008–09 Depression, the telecommunications industry claimed it would 'take the world out of financial crisis' by dynamizing developing markets (Hibberd, 2009). Schumpeterian celebrants insist that these developments rid us of decadent, incompetent media companies (Brock, 2013 is a stereotypical example) while earnest seekers after new business models and laughably named 'chief technology officers' engorge themselves in capitalist self-congratulation (Braiker, 2014; D'Vorkin, 2012).

The dominant discourse about journalism and technology is of a movement toward increased realism and decreased cost, driven by audience desire, professional dedication, and competitive motivation, the 'demands of the new media' supposedly 'imposed on the older media' (Innis, 2009: 47). Conventional accounts chart successive new media technologies appearing along relatively autonomous and benign paths that are as additive as they are competitive, as syntagmatic as they are paradigmatic (Winston, 1996). When the venerable variety cannot carry certain new content, it is supplemented or displaced (words and data fly via telegraph and telephone; words, data, and music through radio; words, data, music, and images on TV and the internet). Emergent media are said to cross-reference one another, serving distinct as well as overlapping peoples and interests in a putatively glorious journey toward 'peaceful co-existence' (Steinberg, 1955: 260). The mythology of a sometimes slow, sometimes rapid chain reaction of inventions makes the media appear agreeably, progressively genealogical. This history is rife with accounts from the media themselves, which often tell us that digitization derived from the laid-back musings of California dreamers transformed into corporate service, a contemporary Enlightenment magically delivering text, voice, data, video, and music to customers (Barbrook and Cameron, 1996; Turner, 2006; Leadbetter and Miller, 2004).

The argument runs that the deregulated, individuated world of the internet transforms consumers into producers, frees the disabled from confinement, encourages new subjectivities, rewards intellect and competitiveness, links people across cultures, and allows billions of flowers to bloom in a postpolitical cornucopia. Faith in devolved media-making amounts to a secular religion, offering transcendence in the here and now via a reporter's veritable 'literature of the eighth day, the day after Genesis' (Carey, 2005). It's a return to the mythology of the talented amateur, but this time without connotations of class and gender. Anyone can be a journalist.

Time magazine exemplified this love of a seemingly beneficent epoch when it chose 'You' as 2006's 'Person of the Year,' because 'You control the Information Age. Welcome to your world' (Grossman, 2006). The *Guardian* fell prey to the same touching magic: someone called 'You' headed its 2013 list of the hundred most important people in the media, displacing mogul after mogul.[11] Tom Englehardt, a notable progressive, says we are living in a golden age of journalism because of 'the rise of the reader' (2014).

He celebrates these times because they supposedly signal that the public has become a group of curators, splicing together news from sources that fly faster than the speed of thought across the globe.

There is great excitement within the profession over 'drone journalism'[12] and 'immersive journalism' (Nuwer, 2017). *Forbes* magazine says 'artificial intelligence gives our storytellers a bionic suit—providing real-time trending topics to cover, recommending ways to make headlines more compelling and suggesting relevant imagery' (Zalatimo, 2018). The *New York Times* and the BBC offer virtual-reality stories as part of their febrile search for an appealing new form (Baía Reis and Castro Coelho, 2018). None of this has amounted to anything significant apart from allocating resources.

In a putative age of big data, truth comes bundled in numbers that deskbound journalists turn into graphs, which are visual and hence seemingly superior to other forms of knowledge. Everybody's banging on about big data these days, from the *Guardian*'s 'Sustainable Business Podcast' (2015) to the *Financial Times* (Harford, 2014) to AT&T (Neff, 2014) to boosters on behalf of the Global South (Mutsvairo et al., 2019). *Le Monde* has declared this the moment 'Quand le mathématicien devient sexy' [When Mathematicians Became Sexy] (Durut, 2013).

Some assert that big data will entirely transform journalism by putting it into popular hands (Baack, 2015). These true believers see the potential for adding value to research and investigative journalism as a saving grace of technological change for those with the right skills to participate, thereby offsetting the negative impact of any job losses (Mair et al., 2013). Information-society chorines, many of them reporters, rejoice that a full 90% of currently existing data was created in the last few years (Ramanathan, 2013; SINTEF, 2013; Hsu, 2013). The late David Carr, a *New York Times* technology booster, wrote this to young journalists in 2013:

> Right now, being a reporter is a golden age. There may be a lack of business models to back it up, but having AKTOCA on—All Known Thought One Click Away—on my desktop, tablet or phone makes it an immensely deeper, richer exercise than it used to be.[13]

Dystopias

We can see Carr's assumption played out in J-school curricula that are devoid of multilingual, theoretical, or critical perspectives.[14] His *clichés* and those of cybertarian capitalists replicate rhetoric from the advent of telegraphy; only the names have changed. Eighty years ago, Brecht said, 'I stood on the hill, and there I saw the Old approaching, but it came as the New' (2018: 2229) and Orwell described media utopias in ways that resonate still:

Reading recently a batch of rather shallowly optimistic "progressive" books, I was struck by the automatic way in which people go on repeating certain phrases which were fashionable before 1914. Two great favourites are "the abolition of distance" and "the disappearance of frontiers". I do not know how often I have met with the statements that "the aeroplane and the radio have abolished distance" and "all parts of the world are now interdependent".

(1944)

Despite their tendency to repeat history, utopians have trouble dealing with it. For example, the League of Nations' 1936 *International Convention Concerning the Use of Broadcasting in the Cause of Peace*[15] succeeded in obtaining several signatories, but not Germany, China, the US, the USSR, Italy, or Japan. Broadcast propaganda spiraled within and across fascism, state socialism, and capitalist democracy ("Reich and Japan," 1936). The same shock of history applied 70 years later when California, the beating heart of information technology that was supposed to model a harmonious and profitable future for all, was the *fons et origo* of the world's greatest economic disaster since the Great Depression (Schiller, 2014).

Something very powerful is in play that fosters historical forgetfulness, wish-fulfillment, and technocentric policies. It comes at serious conceptual cost. For example, the idea that art, markets, realism, or innovation shape changes in media technologies cannot account for why filmstock long privileged white skin tones over black. That occurred because dye couplers that highlighted darker-toned skin were not a priority for the movie industry. Whiteness came cheaply and early, at the nexus of aesthetics, chemistry, commerce, and race—a nexus that should disturb causation myths of immanent realism, supply and demand, or apolitical progress (Winston, 1996: 40–43).

The noted physicist J Robert Oppenheimer, who led the group that developed the atomic bomb, talked about the instrumental rationality that animated the people who created this awesome technology. Once those scientists saw what was feasible, the device's impact lost intellectual and emotional significance for them. They had been overtaken by what he labeled its 'technically sweet' quality (United States Atomic Energy Commission, 1954: 81).

Today, a 'technological sublime' incarnates the quasi-sacred power bestowed on high-tech machinery, notably consumer electronics (Nye, 1994). The emergence of that sublime is attributable to Japanese, Western European, and US industrial achievements of the post-Second World War period, when the successful provision of food, power, communications, and water allied with the emergence of new consumer products to supplant nature's capacity to inspire astonishment. It mixes the sublime—the awesome, the ineffable, the uncontrollable, the powerful—and the beautiful—the approachable, the attractive, the pliant, the soothing. In philosophical aesthetics, the sublime and the beautiful are generally regarded as opposites (Eagleton, 1990). The unique quality of high-concept media machinery has been to combine them: thanks to seductive design and marketing, citizen workers like journalists are ineluctably drawn toward such gadgetry.

This technological sublime relies on an earlier process: the '[f]etishism which attaches itself to the products of labour' once these objects are in the hands of consumers, who lust after them as if they were 'independent beings' (Marx, 1987). Such commodities elicit desire by wooing customers, glancing at them sexually, and looking pretty in ways that borrow from romantic love, but reverse that relationship: people learn about romantic love from commodified humanity, hyperextended beyond the norm in a complex mix of marketing methods, social signs, and national emblems (Haug, 1986).

Adorno defined modernity as the 'technical domination of nature' (1975); in Eco's wry words, 'Disneyland tells us that technology can give us more reality than nature' (1987: 44). For Luxemburg, '[e]ach new step in the perfection of productive technology is at the same time a step in the subjugation of physical nature' (2014: 173). The hidden reality is that most communications innovations emerged from just such desires, via a mixture of militarism, imperialism, and scholarship, with the results subsequently handed over, often *gratis*, to corporate capital (Marx, 1996: 154; Virilio, 1989; Lankes, 2021; Hills, 2002, 2007).

The history connecting media technology to militarism is deep and widespread. International telegraphy depended on the British navy protecting sea lanes, and its growth was stimulated by the Crimean War (Gross et al., 1988: 3–4). Radio developed during the Boer and Russo-Japanese Wars. It spread not through JS Mill's precious open competition, but because of tightly drawn and secured lines of imperial and cartel control (Williams, 1989: 120; Mattelart, 2000: 13–14). In 1920s China, northern warlords monopolized the radio spectrum for military purposes. In the US, that privilege fell to the Navy, which invested in radio's invention, replication, and hardware from the turn of the century to the teens (Hazlett, 1990: 135; Douglas, 2020: 102–43). The proliferation of broadcast towers and loudspeakers across the country for military and police purposes created an effortless listening medium. World Wars I and II saw numerous advances in transmission and portability (Juniper, 2004; Dubenskij, 2014; Johnson, 2017).[16]

The Second World War stimulated the advent of transistors, which made it possible to develop genres and themes for radio stations to organize listeners, increase transmission and reproduction, and mobilize new spaces of reception, such as the beach, car, and workplace. Radio came to displace the newspaper's monopoly over time—but limited reach—by temporal continuity and an augmented dominion over space. This transformative history was clearly conditioned by both overlapping and successive iterations of the device via military, industrial, and consumer radio, each with their own imperatives and limits, notably reporting information and politics (Miller, 1992).

Transistor-driven computers, communications satellites, and the internet were all creatures of the Cold War, generated by academics financed by Pentagon money (Mattelart, 2000: 52–53). And the smartphone? Its click wheels, multi-touch screens, global positioning systems, lithium-ion batteries, signal compression, hyper-text markup language, liquid crystal displays, and numerous other innovations resulted from funding under the aegis of the US Defense Advanced Research Projects Agency, the European Organization for Nuclear Research, the US Department of Energy, the CIA, the National Science Foundation, the US Navy, the US Army Research Office, the National Institutes of Health, and the US Department of Defense—with the work undertaken by research universities (Mazzucato, 2015). Beyond communications, everything from solar to geothermal energy was understood and explored during the Second World War, dropped until the Global North's petrostates ran into trouble in the 1970s (Braudel, 1981: 435), then discarded again, once economies were de-democratized and income redistributed upward. That was that, until climate change was recognized and the forces of innovation unleashed once more.

As we saw in Chapter 2, laptops, tablets, and cellphones, adored by reporters, have past and future blood in their central processing units; blood already shed by youthful slave miners, blood soon to be spilled by infant recyclers. The principal media ratings company, Nielsen, rejoices that 'Africa is in the midst of a technological revolution, and nothing illustrates that fact [better] than the proliferation of mobile phones,' noting that 'more Africans have access to mobile phones than to clean drinking water' (Hutton, 2011). There were 629 million cellphone subscriptions in Africa in 2014, even as 260 million of its people lacked potable water (mobiThinking, 2014). When tens of millions cannot safely drink, the celebration of mobile communication at the expense of public health is appalling (Silver et al., 2019). The reality of cellphones' impact on the international economy is that gigantic corporations use instantaneous trading via such technologies to alter the lives of others without a skerrick of consultation (Zook and Grote, 2017). This is something one reads about rather more often in third-sector activist reports and scholarly studies than the press.

Against the *nostrum* a century ago of media technologies opening up a brand-new day of mutual understanding and world peace, the London *Times* was concerned that this fresh 'form of excitement … massacres, horrible catastrophes, motor-car smashes, [and] public hangings' would capture children's 'greedy eyes,' denaturing the true horror of violence (quoted in Barker, 1993: 11). Telegraphy enabled a massive increase in the velocity of information. Journalism became less deliberative and more instantaneous, which drew critiques of the shift from public affairs to popular minutiae

(Czitrom, 1982: 15, 19–21; Lever and Wheeler, 1993: 127). As newspaper readers began to express an 'avid impatience for fresh nourishment every day' (Benjamin, 1970: 87), reporters' capacity to transmit truth before breakfast was accused of exhausting emotional energy at the wrong time of day and facilitating working-class gambling (Commager, 1974: 419–20). The *Atlantic Monthly* argued that the new technology drove an 'eager wish of the journalist not to be a day behind his competitor, abolishes deliberation from judgment and sound digestion from our mental constitutions. We have no time to go below surfaces' (Stillman, 1891: 694).

Harold Innis connected journalistic sensationalism to the increasingly low cost of newsprint (1986: 4). Brecht was concerned that 'the radio should step out of the supply business and organize its listeners as suppliers,' or it would become '*one-sided* when it should be two-sided' (2000: 42). Sarnoff questioned his own faith in television. Its position 'in the intimate background of one's home' ensured 'a far more powerful force than anything we have yet known,' with the capacity to transmit 'propaganda intended to arouse racial animosities, religious hatreds, and destructive class struggles' (1942). While Pope Pius XII had high hopes for new forms of communication, he warned that unless 'subjected to the sweet yoke of Christ,' they would be a 'source of countless evils,' enslaving viewers' minds (1957). Freud counseled that the omniscience accorded to deities was rendered human through such new technologies as the telephone, making people into 'a kind of prosthetic God.' Because these artificial organs had not been fully integrated with bodies, they spelt trouble (1930: 43).

For such critics, the opulence of media technology is matched only by its barren civilization. Both left and right criticize a surfeit of signage and a deficit of understanding cheapening public culture (Martín-Barbero and Rey, 1999: 15–16, 22, 24). Those concerns recur in anxieties that 'the symbolic sphere of our existence … can be used to justify or legitimize direct or structural violence' (Galtung, 1990: 291). The development of the psy-function and communication studies has led to a century of attempts to correlate use of new media technologies with violent conduct (Comstock, 1989; Comstock and Scharrer, 1999). Today, even true believers worry that virtual reality and its kind will cultivate a propagandized rather than an informed citizenry (Bailenson, 2018: 330). In Isabelle Stengers' words:

> Faced with the fantastic promises coming, for example, from biotechnology, one is sometimes reminded of Neverland, where the pirates chase Peter Pan and the Lost Children, who are chased by the Indians [*sic*], who are themselves chased by the wild animals who are chased by the Lost Children. Who believes whom, follows whom, is captured by the dream of whom?
>
> *(2018: 55)*

Today's 'social' media are one more *cliché* dalliance with new technology's supposedly innate capacity to endow users with transcendence, concealing whose interests they serve and the cult of newness they embrace (Ogan et al., 2009). Even the editors of *Wired* magazine admit that the internet has been undone by the corporatization of knowledge and the sealed-set model of phone applications (Anderson and Wolff, 2010)—a return to Brecht's critique—while Pope Benedict XVI expressed anxiety that 'it is easy for heated and divisive voices to be raised and where sensationalism can at times prevail' (2013). Pope Francis avowed that the internet 'enables us to choose or eliminate relationships at whim, thus giving rise to a new type of contrived emotion which has more to do with devices and displays than with other people and with nature' (2015).

New knowledges, technologies, diseases, and warfare displace prior social, cultural, and economic life (Mosca, 1939: 21–23). As Marcuse explained 80 years ago, technological convergence always intensifies managerial coordination from above (1941). Prosumers are really 'consumers who do more and more of the work that producers used to pay employees for' (Ross, 2010), and the internet is 'the greatest noise that yields no information' (Eco, 2020: 52–53)—a noise made in part by journalists acclaiming new media, even as their increasingly contingent labor is subject to it.

Big data/artificial intelligence

Beyond the hum that emanates from utopic faith healing, snake-oil internet discourse, and moral panics over audiences, some critical questions are being posed of communications technology, such as whether big data and its artificial compilation and distribution will truly make governments and firms alert to the public interest, or undermine privacy, research, creativity, and 'good' jobs—including journalism.

I have strong feelings of *déjà vu* as I trudge through the stupefying claims made for big data and AI by reporters, academics, and corporate hucksters. First, I am transported to the 1970s and the touching credulity of cliometrics, when we were assured that data would reform history and historiography, freeing writers and readers from gossipy morganatic and anecdotal social history alike (Woodman, 1972). Then I am suddenly hurled into the early 1990s, a faithful, dutiful subscriber to *Wired* magazine in its heyday, signing up for a brave new world of liberty (memorably skewered by Streeter, 2005). Just when I think I am stably ensconced, the catapult throws me into the 21st century and 'evidence-based public policy' (better known as policy-based evidence), which seeks to transform political science into the *ur*-discourse of statecraft, displacing an allegedly warlock world of irrationality, extremism, and populism (Marmot, 2004).

Then I suddenly recall evaluating a very distinguished J-school a few years ago. Its success had rested on many things, one of which was a lucrative and rightly respected public opinion polling service. A member of our team insisted that such work was the past, a relic. It should end, with its current resources—and more—allocated toward the generation and sale of big data. The school already taught the topic, but that wasn't enough for this person. He wanted its entire public face dedicated to his fantasies of tomorrow. Luckily, he was one of four on our panel, so his loudness meant those desires were duly mentioned, but nothing beyond that.

Back to the 1970s: somewhere vaguely near cliometrics lurked the real master discourse emerging at that time—a heady mixture of Cold War futurism and *bourgeois* economics that incarnated technological determinism and neoliberalism. Its dread work is still with us. We saw in Chapter 1 how this neoclassical regression, with all its revanchist hostility to working people, took over journalism.

The ever-so-certain utopic discourse on journalism and numerical representation and composition duly performs various maneuvers: it lists websites that explain 'analytics' (once known as 'analysis,' now displaced by re-disposing an adjective as a noun); is careful to admire (while ignoring) forebears who did quaint things like speak to people and read documents in order to find stuff out; incarnates cybertarian ideology; does not value qualitative social science, such as ethnography; pays no attention to political economy; is dedicated to essentialist views (there really *are* cohorts such as Generation Z and they really *do* process, for example, pictures differently from their elders); doesn't read media scholarship; finds journalistic norms, traditions, and innovations outside the Global North to be of passing or no interest; and leaves spectacularly unattended changes in the labor process that are due to pressures exerted not by technology, but the stock-market bets of lizard-shoed financial advisors (Mair et al., 2013).

True believers would do well to consider the work of Justin Lewis. He proceeds from the fundamental understanding that the most quantoid of quantoids needs words, which have meaning at both denotative and connotative levels, and must translate them into numbers in order to add and subtract, then back into words in order to make a point. At the same time, the most qualtoid of qualtoids selects phenomena to discuss because they matter in some way—and numbers will always be part of what matters (Lewis, 1996, 2001, 2008). I suspect true believers in big data won't read Lewis, because their world is so tightly encased in certainty that being reduced to textuality might make it all end in tears.

What do readers glean from journalistic data, big or small, given our much-vaunted mixed-media, multi-platform style of sovereign consumption? The science available is largely educational. It shows that cellphones, for example, have a negative impact on learning. For 'low-achieving and at-risk students,' banning their use is 'equivalent to an additional hour a week in school, or to increasing the school year by five days' (Murphy and Beland, 2015). And J-school? Cornell's renowned 'Laptop and the Lecture' study, published in 2003, showed that attendees remembered lectures better if they did not use laptops during class. Subsequent research has confirmed the risks of technological multitasking with smartphones and the value of taking notes with pen and paper rather than digitally—and not only for those doing so; others get distracted by people typing in ways they do not when surrounded by old-style writing (Hembrooke and Gay, 2003; Sana et al., 2013). People who engage heavily in media multitasking are worse at completing multiple tasks than others. Sending texts and engaging with 'social' media seriously diminish those capacities, and learning more generally (David et al., 2015; Gingerich and Lineweaver, 2014; Lawson and Henderson, 2015; Ophir et al., 2009).

The fascination with big data leads us inevitably, inexorably, to the Next Big Thing—artificial intelligence. But there is nothing new about AI—it has been part of everything from credit checks to customer ordering to citizen surveillance for a long time. AI has had an impact on journalism for a decade and a half: it first 'wrote' a sports story in 2009, which became a model for the machinery's extension into other culture industries (Brambilla Hall, 2018). The *Los Angeles Times* has had a Quakebot since 2014. It connects instantly to the newsroom with stories when serious tremors in the Southland are sensed by the nation's Geological Survey. Following a quick check of this draft by the human on duty, the piece is published. Information on the system is catalogued under 'people' by the paper. One can email the bot.[17] It hasn't answered me.

Again, there are utopic and dystopic components to the discourse of artificial intelligence. It is seen as a force disrupting the *clientelismo* that has dogged much of the world. Large sets of machine-collated and -sifted data have exposed international ruling-class concealment of wealth and influence, sorting different forms of oligarchic malfeasance so reporters can make sense of them (Broussard, 2018: 44–46). There is a grand future for such work. Interlocking directorates and oligarchical tendencies mean that Colombia, for example, is normally run by politicians with significant media interests. The prospect of instant, unedited, online access to their activity has excited many (Montaña, 2014). In Brazil, *Aos Fatos* used the bot *Fátima* to counter fascist lies during the 2022 Presidential election,[18] and some journalists find automated fact-checking improves their work experience (Manfredi Sánchez and Ufarte-Ruiz, 2020; Johnson, 2023). It is also claimed that AI can prevent mass violence by alerting reporters in 'real time' to clashes and establishing whether the testimony of eyewitness journalism is part of a pattern (Yankoski et al., 2021). The World Economic Forum and Reuters even see AI as a key riposte to climate change (Neslen, 2021). UN agencies collude in these unsubstantiated claims via 'AI for the Planet.'[19] Needless to say, PR has been a major player in this mythology, planting stories around the globe (Bourne, 2019) per the mode we encountered in Chapter 2. Meanwhile, AI agents have untold negative impacts on the climate, thanks to their gigantic carbon footprints (Jones, 2018; Strubell et al., 2019; Lacoste et al., 2019; Heikkilä, 2022).

More prosaically than the idea of salvation from climate change, Bayerischer Rundfunk deploys the machinery to moderate online comments and AP generates shot lists to organize video holdings ("Artificial Intelligence Is Remixing," 2023). Such uses of the technology may appear quite mundane, but they have serious implications for the quality of work and the labor process alike. For example, Dataminr®'s 'AI for Modern Newsrooms' is favored by more than 650 news desks worldwide. It promises 'the earliest possible indications of breaking news,' ensuring journalists will 'gain an edge in covering the stories that matter most to their audiences.' Al Jazeera, CNN, DW, the *Daily Mail*, and the *Washington Post* are listed as satisfied customers.[20] The system works like this: the company investigates algorithmically the dark and deep webs, 'social' media, blogs, sensors attuned to the internet of things, and digital audio. Alerts from these sources provide virtually instantaneous information to subscribers, based on their thematic and geographical desires. This is called 'live journalism,' even though it dodges moving, breathing, listening, and speaking reporters. News organizations usually seek additional validation of stories prior to publishing them—but do so based on what search engines dictate.[21] Apropos, Dataminr® does more than 'report'—it also engages in surveillance of peaceful social movements on behalf of the state (Biddle, 2020).

NightCafé's 'AI Art Generator' promises visitors they will '[c]reate beautiful art in seconds with the help of Artificial Intelligence.' Its self-anointed task is typically immodest: NightCafé is on 'a mission to democratize art creation.' Far from an attempt 'to make artists redundant,' the firm wishes 'to make art creation accessible to the masses ... regardless of skill level.'[22] Such sites function by appropriating the work of photographers and artists via 'data training,' which is to say machine-generated collection and re-disposal (Thorpe, 2023). As a consequence, thousands of cultural producers are posting 'Do Not AI' slogans in web galleries and on 'social' media. They seek regulation to prevent 'algorithmic disgorgement'—artworks taken without consent (Volpicelli, 2023). Plagiarism without acknowledgment appears to be as rife as are obsessive attempts to detect and punish it. Meanwhile, AI aids the US blockade of Cuba, affecting journalism coming from the island (Gómez González, 2023).

The technology is certainly expanding its reach and monetary value. The World Economic Forum estimates AI will be 'worth' US$127 billion in 2025.

AP's reports on company balance sheets have expanded from 300 to 4,000 via AI, disseminated quickly through the wire service itself and its media subscribers in ways designed to facilitate faster, increased trading (Galily, 2018; Brambilla Hall, 2018; Blankenspoor et al., 2017). We are witnesses to:

> the wealthiest companies in history (Microsoft, Apple, Google, Meta, Amazon …) unilaterally seizing the sum total of human knowledge that exists in digital, scrapable form and walling it off inside proprietary products, many of which will take direct aim at the humans whose lifetime of labor trained the machines without giving permission or consent.
>
> *(Klein, 2023)*

Those firms mix oligopolistic power with oligarchic networking. Liberals throw their hands in the air and suggest such corporations be brought into the world of global governance—not as self-interested lobbyists, but as formal actors within civil society that can help forge a new multilateralism (Higgott, 2022: 107). I wonder. But most of all, I wonder about what is occurring in the world of work for reporters: the difference from the past is AI's mass availability and the desire of capital to displace all forms of work, not just the primarily physical and proletarian (Dyer-Witheford et al., 2019).

The labor process

In the 18th century, the first great theorist of the division of labor, Adam Smith, took this as his key example:

> One man draws out the wire, another straightens it, a third cuts it, a fourth points it, a fifth grinds it at the top for receiving the head; to make the head requires three distinct operations; to put it on is a peculiar business, to whiten the pins is another; it is even a trade by itself to put them into the paper …
>
> The division of labor … occasions, in every art, a proportionable increase of the productive powers of labor.
>
> *(1970: 110)*

The expression 'division of labor' is used by orthodox economists to describe sectoral differences in an economy, the occupations and skills of a workforce, and the organization of tasks within firms. Neoclassical economists suggest incomes increase with age, albeit at diminishing rates; unemployment and earnings relate to skills; highly educated people benefit from training; markets determine the division of labor; and human-capital investments are less predictably valuable than more material ones (Becker, 1983: 16). These neoliberals have come to blame workers, along with other factors, for what they call 'X-inefficiency,' i.e., elements within companies that limit their profitability (Leibenstein, 1978). Most labor-economics theory is based on such assumptions, generally derived from the US. There is minimal regard for empirical evidence from elsewhere, or theories based on labor as a *source* of value, rather than a *limitation* on it.

Marxism offers a different story from such supply-and-demand magic. For one thing, at their best, Marxist analysts talk to people, visit places, uncover the past, and add and subtract numbers that represent actually existing activity. This is what they find: objects and services obtain surplus value as commodities through exploitation of the labor that makes them. Once these commodities enter circulation at a price, they gain exchange value. The power gained by capitalism, through ever-widening exchange, includes both surplus value, realized as profit, and authority over the conditions and possibilities of labor, embodied as workplace power. The division of labor is the mechanism linking productivity, exploitation, and social control. As its subdivisions multiply and spread geographically, capital acquires a talent for hiding the cooperation of labor that constitutes it and expanding its reach when necessary to counter redistributive gains made by workers through political activity (Marx, 1906: 49, 83). The market is extended internationally to sustain this division of labor, in keeping with the desire for a worldwide factory and mercantile republic (Mattelart, 2002: 595).

Friedrich Engels argued that 'the limitless perfectibility of machinery under modern industry' becomes a 'law by which every individual industrial capitalist must perfect his [*sic*] machinery more and more, under penalty of ruin,' eventually 'making human labor superfluous' (2003: 71). As Marx and he maintained, the worker 'becomes a mere appendage of the machine,' even as labor is required to produce more and more rapidly (Marx, 1996: 7). The very idea of work as a job performed for people beyond one's immediate social unit, as something that can be sub-divided with individuals easily replaced, is crucial for modern capitalism. Labor is undertaken in visible ways, the better to surveil, measure, and remold it (Gorz, 2013: 67).

Since the 1970s, 'knowledge workers' such as journalists have gained in status among *bourgeois* economists, thanks to information-based industries that promise endless gains in productivity and putatively pure competitive markets (Bar with Simard, 2006: 351). This supposed 'aristocracy of talent,' elevated by the meritocratic discourse of progress, 'open' information, and the culture industries, luxuriates in ever-changing techniques, technologies, and networks (Kotkin, 2001: 22).

Business leeches love such talk, dreaming of 'virtual workers' (Webber and Wallace, 2009: 200–19). For the *Harvard Business Review*, the 'history of work ... is the history of people outsourcing their labor to machines' (De Cremer and Kasparov, 2021). That may have started with factory assembly, but it has moved on—and necessitates a translation from the *Review*'s words, *viz.* 'capitalists outsourcing others' labor to machines.' Even reactionaries worry that 'techno-feudalism' threatens their beloved middle class (Kotkin, 2020).

Four decades ago, Alvin Toffler invented the concept of 'the cognitariat' (1983) to describe workers with high levels of educational attainment and facility with cultural technologies and genres. They play key roles in the production and circulation of goods and services, through both creation and coordination. A *'culturalisation of production'* may *en*able these intellectuals, by placing them at the center of world economies, but also *dis*able them, because it does so under conditions of flexible production and ideologies of 'freedom.' This new proletariat is not defined in terms of factories, manufacturing, or opposition to ruling-class power and ideology. Indeed, it is comprised of those whose immediate forebears, with similar or less cultural capital, formed a salariat and were guaranteed healthcare and retirement income. By contrast, the cognitariat lacks both the organization of the traditional working class and the political *entrée* of the old middle class (Negri, 2007). The way that marginal cultural labor, from jazz musicians to street artists, has long survived *sans* regular compensation and security models the expectations we are *all* supposed to have, displacing our parents' or grandparents' assumptions about steady employment (Ehrenreich, 2006). Reporters are members of this rapidly expanding cognitariat (Miller, 2013).

AP maintains that robot journalism will create new jobs, with greater diversity of everything from skills to cultural backgrounds (Brambilla Hall, 2018; Blankenspoor et al., 2017). Conversely, the Open AI corporation/foundation predicts a '100%' impact on the journalism labor market (Eloundou et al., 2023). As a consequence, superannuated reporters now trading as scholars are part of a headlong rush into moral panic over misinformation, intellectual property, and the emergent tendency of search engines to answer queries with explanations rather than providing links that permit further verification (Bell, 2023; Stokel-Walker, 2023).

We are witnessing 'a more flexible specialised and decentralised form of labour process,' a 'hiving-off or a contracting-out of functions and services hitherto provided "in house"' (Hall, 1990: 118). When I migrated to Gotham in 1993, interviewers for broadcast stations' news shows would come to my apartment as a team: a full complement of sound recordist, camera operator, lighting technician, and journalist. Within a decade, they were rolled into one person, as a consequence of the process whereby 'machinery increasingly obliterates different types of labour' (Marx, 1996: 9), *'shortening the turnover time for capital'* (Luxemburg, 2014: 364).

More content must be produced from fewer resources, and more and more multi-skilling is required. In my example, journalists have taken over the other tasks. If they work for companies like NBC, they may be obliged to write copy for several web sites *and* provide different edited versions of the original story for MSNBC, CNBC, CNBC Africa, CNBC Europe, and CNBC Asia, in addition to the parent network and individual channels. Poor-quality sound and image are accepted nowadays as interviewees speak from their homes and offices via videotelephony. The division of journalists' labor is being transformed—and its costs lugged onto others. An interview I gave to BBC World News in 2023 relied on my paying for electricity, bandwidth, and Zoom. In order to improve connectivity, I was not permitted to see my interlocutors. No-one suggested a serious discussion conducted in a studio.

The conglomerates that have come to own much of the *bourgeois* media do not see what they do as a public trust, as business conducted in the collective interest. Rather, they view all their properties as designed for profit, with margins determined by stock markets. This has made for large-scale layoffs and proletarianization: splitting, combining, or destroying positions. Latin America is an instance—in Brazil, for example, public intellectuals routinely have to take more than one job, many journalists moonlight as PR writers, and legislation and political candidacy have been monitored by AI's *Opperação Serenata de Amor* since 2016 (Paiva et al., 2015; Monnerat, 2018).[23] Full-time opportunities are on the wane.

The US is similar. Gannett owns the biggest chain of newspapers in the country, across 43 states. The company posted a fourth-quarter 2022 profit of US$32.77 million. Many of its employees at the time were able to eat only thanks to public assistance and charities (Schulz, 2023; Darcy, 2023). Internationally, the BBC, CNN, and Thomson Reuters journalists use 'robo-writing software.' They are dubious about the technology's ability to sense the qualitative import of stories, but certain of its appeal to their employers (Thurman et al., 2017). *Bild*, Europe's best-selling newspaper, regards AI as the future and the replacement of journalists its great gift (Henley, 2023).

'Content farms' aplenty pose as news outlets populated by reporters, generally without providing information about their ownership or control and frequently using the latest form of automatic writing to edit stories published by 'conventional' media (Sadeghi and Arvanitis, 2023). These farms stand ready to collude in journalists' de-professionalization. Reporters And Data And Robots claims to blend the machinic and the human in a wondrous mix that 'breaks the content compromise which forces organisations to choose between high quality, reliable and bespoke content or mass-produced superficial output.' Its five reporters 'generated' 400,000 articles between them in the company's first five years of 'life.'[24] Canada's Postmedia Network has institutionalized round-the-clock digital reportage, targeting male readers.[25] It relies on outsourced labor, unoriginal analysis, and bloviation (Daum and Scherer, 2018). Consider also Mindworks Global Media, a company outside New Delhi that provides US and European newspapers with Indian-based journalists and copy editors working long distance. There are 35–40% cost savings on employing reporters in the Global North (Lakshman, 2008; Tady, 2008). It promises 'to drive higher revenue through lead generation and cost efficiency through productivity gains' via 'AI-powered news curation, content production and data products.'[26] Or perhaps your firm of choice is Local Labs, formerly Journatic, which has paid stringers US$10 an hour—without healthcare coverage—to write allegedly 'hyper-local' stories taken from internet sources and published under *noms de plume* (Tarkov, 2012).[27] Either way, we are seeing the New International Division of Cultural Labor, first discerned four decades ago, ineluctably making its way into journalism, such that reporters may not be anywhere near the sites of their stories or even their purported beats.

They may not even be people, per the *Sports Illustrated* fiasco mentioned in Chapter 3. The new coinage favors 'synthetic media' and 'automated journalism.' Examples of comprehensive services include Reuters News Tracer and JX Press (which has hired no reporters since its engineer-driven launch in 2008 and is well-funded by news giants because 'machines meet human expectations').[28] Hundreds of such entities have emerged in the last decade, generally without reference to their ethical, copyright, or labor-process implications (Ufarte-Ruiz et al., 2023). The tendency is clear: a 'standardization, decomposition, deskilling, automated management and human computation, algorithmic cooperation, digital measurement, and surveillance of labor' (Altenried, 2022: 159).

Job losses are not entirely to be lamented. It is high time that the Global South turned the tables, delivering stories to the Global North about the latter after a century that was mostly the other way round. That reorientation also destabilizes the narrative of decline centered on Europe and white-settler colonies, because it is truly a golden age of journalism in the Global South with the growth of alphabetic middle classes (Roper, 2023).

But we should also note the de-professionalization that accompanies the associated demise of participant observation and research. And journalism is a long way behind the times in terms of ethics covering the social relations of technology and work; fewer than 10% of countries address such questions (Díaz-Campo and Segado-Boj, 2015). For instance, medical education and communications companies provide ghostwriting services, paid for by corporations, that deliver 'research' to academics and bribe them to sign. One in ten papers in leading medical outlets have been the work of ghosts, and pharmacorps pressure medical journals to print favorable findings in return for lucrative advertising (Miller, 2008a; Fugh-Berman, 2010). Technology has been to the fore in enabling these activities, along with the J-schools and communication departments that provide the necessary reserve army of labor.

Conclusion

Alongside the comforting certitude of the diligently faithful, there is clearly a dystopic side to technology and contemporary journalism: the digital is said to have diminished workers' and readers' attention spans; de-professionalized reporters by proletarianizing and deskilling them; stimulated PR; generated churnalism; and jeopardized on-the-spot reportage (Jackson and Moloney, 2016 and Macnamara, 2015 are sweetly ambivalent about this). Bob Franklin summarizes these trends:

> the continuing innovations in communication technologies; the harshly competitive and fragmenting markets for audiences and advertising revenues; dramatic reductions in the entry costs of some online outlets for news; the collapse of the traditional business model to resource journalism; an expansive role for social media as sources and drivers of news; dynamic changes in government media policy; as well as shifting audience requirements for news, the ways in which it is presented and, given the expansive number of (increasingly mobile) devices on which it is received, even the places and spaces where news is produced and consumed.
>
> *(2012: 663)*

In this world, flexibility can be a mega-sign of affluence, and precariousness its flipside: one person's calculated risk is another's burden of labor; inequality is represented as the outcome of a moral test; and the young are supposed to regard insecurity as an opportunity, not a constraint. What used to be the fate of artists and musicians—where 'making cool stuff' and working with relative autonomy was meant to outweigh ongoing employment—has become a norm across virtually every sector of the economy. The outcome is contingent labor as a way of life. It's a rotten deal. There would be no culture, no media, without labor. It is not x-inefficiency. It is the beating heart of creativity and social justice.

Weber insisted we understand technology as nothing more than a '*mode of processing material goods*' (2005: 27) and Harvey Sacks explained 'the failures of technocratic dreams that if only we introduced some fantastic new communication machine the world will be transformed.' He noted the very banality of such introductions, when one more 'technical apparatus' is 'being made at home with the rest of our world' (1995 *Volume II*: 548).

It's obvious that whereas 'technological determinism' assumes technical advances derive from research and experimentation, then alter the societies into which they emerge, such things happen under 'already existing social relations and cultural forms' when innovations are 'selected for investment towards production' (Williams, 1989: 120; also see Curran, 2002). So the Great Depression 'led industry to shift from the production methods inherited from the 19th century, based on coal and steam, to the new technologies based on electricity, oil and petrol' (Campbell et al., 1990: 24). Most communications technologies arrive once the requisite social relations are in place— well after the technical means to make them, not the other way round. Lots of seemingly 19th- and 20th-century innovations could have been introduced before they were, but were delayed for market reasons: businesses bothered to invest once the urban proletariat had been made alphabetic and a middle class had grown (Winston, 2007).

Fernand Braudel's sweep of history discloses a binary akin to the oscillation between utopic and dystopic technological visions. He refers to an historical tendency: 'the accelerator, then the brake.' One tendency propels innovation. The other produces what can be longstanding equilibria. That stasis is not due to a failure of imagination or work by scientists, but rather to commerce, state, and education, which individually and collectively may 'encourage or restrain progress' (1981: 430–31). In journalistic terms, we can see a search for such an equilibrium in the use of the digital by reporters as a means of telling and sharing stories rapidly and directly (Martin-Neira et al., 2023). This is a repeat of what happens when a segment of labor underpinning certain social forces does well out of technological change. That workforce endorses the political-economic system that supports it and eschews fundamental change (Gallego and Kurer, 2022) until an equilibrium is displaced, along with the world as they had known it.

Seven decades ago, Stuart Hall wrote about the spread of consumer electronics among the poor as part of a legitimate materialism, born out of centuries of physical deprivation and want (1958: 26). But 50 years later, he discerned:

> an exponential rise in the marketing of "technological desire." The mobile phone, fast broadband connection and a Facebook entry are now "necessities of life", even in places where millions do not have them or actually know what they do. News, information, views, opinions and commentaries have been, as they say, "democratized"—i.e. flattened out—by the internet, in the illusion that, since internet space is unregulated, the net is "free"; and one person's view is as good as another's in the marketplace of opinion. We know more about the trivial and banal daily round of life of other people than we do about climate change or sustainability.
>
> *(2011: 722–23)*

And the more we veer as writers and audiences into the virtual world, the greater is our impact on the material one. We need to adopt a calm view of new technology, considering utopic and dystopic perspectives—but above all, understanding the history of once-new media technologies and their impact on journalism's labor process, when combined with changes in capitalist social relations.

Notes

1. https://about.twitter.com/en.
2. https://twitter.com/lindayacc/status/1683213798386147329?s=20.
3. https://www.tiktok.com/forgood.
4. https://about.instagram.com/.
5. https://values.snap.com/privacy/transparency/community-guidelines.
6. https://about.youtube/.
7. https://www.whatsapp.com/about/.
8. https://www.redditinc.com/.
9. https://www.headspace.com/about-us.
10. https://www.calm.com/blog/about.
11. http://www.theguardian.com/media/2013/sep/01/you-them-mediaguardian-100-2013.
12. http://www.dronejournalismlab.org/.
13. https://www.reddit.com/r/IAmA/comments/16k598/iama_columnist_and_reporter_on_media_and_culture/.
14. Consider https://journalism.nyu.edu/undergraduate/courses/; https://www.city.ac.uk/prospective-students/courses/undergraduate/journalism; https://journalism.stanford.edu/curriculum.
15. http://www.worldlii.org/int/other/treaties/LNTSer/1938/80.html.
16. https://dp.la/exhibitions/radio-golden-age/radio-frontlines.
17. https://www.latimes.com/people/quakebot.
18. https://www.aosfatos.org/.
19. https://www.aifortheplanet.org/en/content/about-us.
20. https://www.dataminr.com/news.
21. https://www.dataminr.com/hubfs/Case-Studies/deutsche-welle-uses-dataminr-to-stay-competitive-and-keep-pace-with-evolving-media-industry.pdf.
22. https://nightcafe.studio/; https://nightcafe.studio/pages/about-nightcafe.
23. https://www.serenatadeamor.org/.
24. https://pa.media/radar/.
25. https://www.postmedia.com/.
26. https://mindworksglobal.com/.
27. http://www.locallabs.com/.
28. https://www.reutersagency.com/en/reuters-community/reuters-news-tracer-filtering-through-the-noise-of-social-media/; https://www.cbinsights.com/company/jx-press.

CONCLUSION

The bulk of this book has been dedicated to very bad news: journalism's complicity with the powerful forces it is meant to interrogate, plus financial and technological tendencies that diminish the number and impact of reporters. We are remorselessly told that only online media attract audiences, who aren't interested in news; that journalism doesn't matter; and that a golden age has ended (Hirschorn, 2009; Rosenblum, 2017; Lepore, 2019; Chu, 2016 are typical examples). Against that bad-news story, this Conclusion looks at some different data and offers suggestions for journalism education and regulation.

Claims that the profession is doomed themselves stand under erasure. For here's the good news: interest in journalism around the world is greater than ever before, because alphabetization is rocketing upward. Everywhere. Two hundred years ago, 12% of the world's population was alphabetic; 45 years ago, 68%; now it's 86% (Roser and Ortiz-Ospina, 2018; UNESCO, 2023b). And people who can read, read journalism, be it about politics, war, food, the environment, or sports.

Worldwide newspaper revenue from print circulation and advertising exceeds US$90 billion; the digital figures add up to just US$22 billion. Over half a billion people pay for printed papers; fewer than 60 million for digital versions. The strongest revenue growth for news comes from the Global South (Roper, 2023). The old *Newspaper Death Watch* is itself moribund.[1]

Among wire services, Reuters is read and watched by over a billion people a day. AP claims 'half the world's population' views its reporting daily.[2] News websites see absolute BBC domination: well over a billion visits in January 2023, followed far behind by MSN and CNN. The *Guardian* is easily ahead of Fox News (BBC, 2023: 9). The BBC's weekly news audience is close to half a billion, and growing by millions every year ("BBC," 2021). The World Service alone has 364 million listeners a week, a third aged between 15 and 24.[3] Two hundred million go to CNN's web site and nearly three hundred million tune in to DW each week.[4] France 24's digital platforms are visited by over 45 million monthly and its network seen by 60 million.[5] Over 80% of Yanquis listen to terrestrial radio weekly; more than half tune in to news (Forman-Katz, 2023). NPR is heard by 46 million a week.[6] So the doom-and-gloom claims of public uninterest and disinterest in news are just that—claims.

And there is increased journalistic diversity; for instance, the black middle class in Colombia and Brazil is newly prominent in communications. Edna Liliana Valencia has anchored the Latin American edition of France 24,[7] Afro-descended journalists generate devoted followings (Orozco Cabrales, 2019), and the Fundación Color de Colombia supports black reportage, art, and politics.[8] Sweden's SVT has a 50-50 gender split and 22% migrant representation in its newsroom, close to parity with the nation's demography (Lück et al., 2020; "Allt fler," 2021). In Spain, Lucía Mbomío has regularly reported for Antena 3 and Televisión Española (Romero, 2016).[9] Audrey Pulvar was the first black news anchor on French TV and continues to be a prominent commentator.[10]

So among the pessimistic accounts of journalism's demise and failure lie positive signs. But there are three problems. One is ideological, a toxic blend of neoclassical economics' fetishization of selfishness with an often-virulent nationalism in the work of columnists and reporters. The second problem is that rich economies have developed in the direction of fictive capital. Investments in the media are made by people and firms that lack any attachment to the industries where they are putatively involved, with assets stripped and traded based on opportunity cost rather than social value. The third problem is that there remains insufficient journalistic diversity in wealthy nations, at both presentational and executive levels. Transformation is therefore needed in two domains, the philosophical and the institutional.

Good journalism requires research, interpretation, dissemination, and mobilization (Cassidy, 2005). To protect and develop those capacities, we must transcend conventional political-economic space and time in search of globally sustainable work that counters the elemental risks created by capitalist growth. Such changes can be accommodated by conservative as well as radical thinkers: Burke acknowledged each generation as 'temporary possessors and life-renters' of the natural and social world. People must maintain 'chain and continuity,' rather than acting ephemerally, as if they were 'flies of a summer.' He called for 'a partnership not only between those who are living, but between those who are living, those who are dead, and those who are to be born' (1986: 192–95). This can be achieved by a cross between critical theory, participant observation, and political economy.

Critical theory calls for self-reflexivity on the part of writers, readers, artists, and spectators. Participant observation tries to break down barriers between everyday life and macro-sociological influences. Political economy seeks diverse ownership and control of industries. They share a desire to understand the world as it is experienced not only by policy, corporate, and military élites, but by those 'lost in the great anonymous sludge of history' (Snow, 1987: 26–27), who live in 'continual fear and danger of violent death,' their existence 'solitary, poor, nasty, brutish, and short' (Hobbes, n.d., Chapter XIII). We need journalism that appreciates their realities and can express and help produce an *'empirical and practical consciousness'* enriched through 'theoretical understanding' to generate 'a *specifically global* consciousness' (Mandel, 1994: 85).

We should regard journalists not just as professionals but also as intellectuals. Each social group creates 'organically, one or more strata of intellectuals which give it homogeneity and an awareness of its own function not only in the economic but also in the social and political fields': the industrial technology, law, economy, and culture of such groups. The '"organic" intellectuals that every new class creates alongside itself and elaborates in the course of its development' assist in the emergence of that class. Reporters operate in '[c]ivil society … the ensemble of organisms commonly called "private," that of "political society" or "the State",' comprising the '"hegemony" which the dominant group exercises throughout society' alongside the '"direct domination" or command exercised through the State and "juridical" government' (Gramsci, 1978: 5–7, 12).[11]

So how might reporters become both more open and more reflexive about their work, acknowledging openly in whose interests they write and speak? Adding a new layer of ethical self-awareness and public disclosure can improve journalism's standing and its informative role.

In that spirit, I have two proposals. One is an education for journalists in semiotics as applied to truth, which will enable an appreciation of how reality is understood and communicated. So instead of objectivity as a goal, fetishistically desired but rarely obtained—a desirable but unattainable end, best approximated by seeking two dueling points of view and relying on mommy state, daddy corporation, or aunt-uncle think tank—let's get real. Signs, society, and reality can never be disentangled, other than analytically. Each applies its own pressure to understanding and conveying the truth. Journalists must allocate equal and semi-autonomous significance to natural phenomena, social forces, and cultural meaning in order to understand contemporary life.

Just as objects of scientific knowledge come to us in hybrid forms that are coevally subject to social power and textual meaning, so the latter two domains are affected by the natural world. Science relies on more science to claim and sustain its truthfulness, along with the force of phenomena

(Carey, 2009: 36, 61). Per journalism, its systems of verification depend on 'repetitive, even stylized narratives' (Schiller, 1981: 1) in which the '"world of text" ... [is] a world of objects and performances' (Chartier, 2005: 38–39).

Latour rejects discussion of things, populations, or discourses in themselves, exemplifying his preferred alternatives by looking at how truth is established as a blend of those elements: missile guidance systems are technologies of killing, manufacturing, and logic; articles in science journals illustrate capitalist industry and academic method as much as molecular truth; the history of inventors covers the space between thinking, publishing, and investing; and 'the domestication of microbes' has political significance for society, meaning, and biology. In other words, '[r]hetoric, textual strategies, writing, staging, semiotics—all these are really at stake, but in a new form that has a simultaneous impact on the nature of things and on the social context' (1993: 3–5).

Unraveling such forces requires participant observation at multiple levels and in varied places if we are to record, understand, and explain what is going on—a 'multi-sited ethnography' undertaken 'to examine the circulation of cultural meanings, objects, and identities in diffuse time-space' (Marcus, 1998: 79). Understanding society requires investigating it up, down, and sideways, in accordance with Laura Nader's call for studies of the powerful and the oppressed alike (1972). In turn, that necessitates appreciating the operation of semiosis. Horst Ruthrof argues that 'what we call reality is the product of the interaction of at least two different sign systems' (1992: 102), a mixture of correspondence and coherence forms of creating meaning. I'll explain his theories and indicate their relevance to journalism.

Ruthrof maintains that the overarching interpretative authority of language makes it 'our dominant sign system.' Language can adjudicate—or at least account for the differences between—sign systems that contradict one another. As he puts it, '[l]inguistic construals of reality gather meaning according to the rate of corroboration by non-linguistic signs' (1992: 103). This does not mean these systems are subservient to language, but they are less capable of abstraction. Such forms of corroboration achieve a complex intermingling of individuality and sociability in establishing and contesting meaning. Interpretation is a function of membership of a variety of semiotic communities rather than an overarching truth (1992: 119).

Ruthrof offers a 'ladder of discourses,' commencing at the highest rung with the most 'saturated social discourse' and descending to more technical ones (1992: 134). He places 'literary discourse' at the top because it can activate all the processes at work in different forms of language, through referentiality in other systems and an awareness of internal presentational norms. Put another way, this is about establishing a diegetic world, the extratextual domain to which it refers, and the production of meaning (1992: 134–35); a form of journalistic reflexivity acknowledging its conditions of existence that one can find in feminist and New Journalism and *crónicas*.

The second rung is 'mythical language.' By this Ruthrof means the erasure of process and the highlighting of enunciation, thereby favoring an 'authoritative-authoritarian' world of singular accounts that brook no interrogation (1992: 134, 143); we have seen that in complicit US-UK coverage of imperial adventurism. The next category is 'historiography,' the extent to which historical narrative is determined by evidence. He finds a double world, per literary discourse: a picture of the past and a speaking subject, a simulacrum and a point of enunciation (1992: 134, 143, 145). Both become apparent to the reader when critical researchers and self-reflexive reporters disclose the who/what/when/where/how/why/*cui bono* of journalism.

The following rung is 'juridical language.' It divides 'the letter and the spirit of the law'—court and congressional reporting and exegetical versus socio-cultural judicial interpretation. It mingles interpretations of the past with prescriptions for the future in a complex mixture of constitutions, case law, and contemporary values (1992: 134, 147). Ruthrof's next stage is 'everyday speech,' with modality rather than formal propositionality critical to understanding the workings of power (1992: 134, 149); examples would be *vox pop* segments of a story. His sixth rung is 'technical language,' instructional signs such as labeling on cans or the classification of museum exhibits. This supposedly non-ideological form of address is necessarily connected to obsolescence, waste disposal, and public health (1992: 134, 154, 156); its corollary is the jargon of newsrooms. The final category is 'scientific statements' (1992: 134, 156), which attempt to establish agreed systems of falsification and verification; here we have the *nostra* of J-schools and editorial suites.

Journalism clearly borrows from these rungs of meaning, but often unconsciously. It should do so more straightforwardly and self-reflexively to avoid the binarism-balance dilemma. That doesn't necessitate lengthy footnotes or theoretical expositions prior to reporting on a sudden catastrophe, social concern, or scientific finding; it means ensuring theoretical depth underpinning explanations or positions proffered by the great and the good, rather than their reiteration as seemingly authoritative remarks.

The second transformation needed is institutional. The prevailing orthodoxy sees reporters produce stories by obeying generic rules of topic, prose, and structure, as if the world came to them in unvarnished form. They follow what is known as the 'Inverted Pyramid' (Walker et al., 2009). It prioritizes what is deemed to be 'most newsworthy' in terms of those involved and what happened when, where, why, and how; sloping down to 'important details'; and concluding with background information.

This model has been criticized by feminist practitioners and other analysts who are concerned that it seeks the approval of fellow-journalists rather than interesting readers and audiences and should be replaced by linear narrative (Walker et al., 2009; Kulkarni et al., 2022). In addition, the urgent tasks of movement journalism do not fit the pyramidal model (Simonton, 2017).

We need a radical shift in pedagogy and professional action. Students and editors must appreciate and practice affirmative action based on demography and knowledge and learn the history of media technologies and their impact on the labor process of journalism, in combination with changes in capitalist social relations. Students must learn that objectivity generally draws on binaristic accounts of the truth, excluding definitive findings, multiperspectivalism, and profound uncertainty, and gives cover to parthenogenetic corporate and managerial policies and preferences. Sources must be enriched to include more voices from social movements and radical scholarship. No-one should be interviewed as a regional expert who doesn't speak the relevant languages or qua climate expert absent appropriate qualifications. Outlets must audit the environmental impact of journalistic research and make transparent declarations of reporters' and readers' carbon footprints.

Then there is the question of regulation. The world sees minimal legislation requiring media proprietors to disinvest from other business interests and create serious boundaries between themselves and 'their' editors and between journalism and advertising. We need a mandated separation of news organizations from other capitalist interests—as a bare minimum. There must be statutory independence between the editorial, opinion, reporting, and advertising elements of journalism. When proprietors and editors shelve stories, they should publish explanations and all those involved make their monetary and political interests and affiliations generally known, with specific disclosure when they impinge on coverage. Media corporations must be required by law to undertake ecological and militarism audits of everything they do. Other than when informants' identities are protected in the public interest, all meetings between state officials, oligarchs, owners, and journalists should be published. PR needs to be overseen statutorily, just as broadcasting has been for over a century.

The formidable forces arrayed against journalism are unsatisfactory education and training, state and corporate censorship, discrimination, and finance. To those who throw anxious hands in the air at the very notion of regulation: we already have it in truckloads, much of it private, much of it public. The flow of information is conditioned by the policies of corporations, proprietors, editors, unions, religions, and universities as much as states. The mainstream press has shown that self-regulation in the service of democracy is no longer credible. Regulation should be undertaken by practitioners and experts unrelated to the party-political system and capitalist investments, so retired and independent journalists along with academics.

Efforts to improve journalism today focus too little on such matters and too much on furphies like 'disinformation.' Consider the 2016 Brexit plebiscite and US General Election. The lies told by campaigners for Brexit were relevant to that outcome, of course. But so was the fact that the initiative was not wholeheartedly opposed by the left and the government, which added to successive administrations' failure to appreciate the international division of labor's impact on the working class or grasp the necessity to revise prevalent monarchical and imperial fantasies across the population. In the US, a poor electoral campaign by the Democrats, misogyny, and a similar incapacity to appreciate working-class skepticism over globalization produced a notorious outcome. In media terms, impoverished coverage of Brexit added to decades of invented and repeated absurdities 'about' the European Union, while US network and cable news' obsession with Trump tweets and bloviation amplified his words beyond other voices (Cushion and Lewis, 2017; Pickard, 2020). Hence Leslie Moonves, the head of CBS prior to his disgrace over numerous instances of alleged sexual assault and harassment, announcing during the 2016 Presidential campaign that Trump's candidacy 'may not be good for America, but it's damn good for CBS ... The money's rolling in and this is fun' (quoted in Bond, 2016).

In each case, journalism was a culprit, a crucial adjunct to wider social forces. Misinformation? Disinformation?—reporters specialized in it. Forget about nerdy boys with nascent mustaches crouched over desktop computers in their fetid basements, sending out lies paid for by the Kremlin or the Republican Party. Economic policy founded on corporate power—accepted and legitimized by reporter after reporter—is a bit more influential than those likely lads ("AI Will," 2023).

To counter the longstanding tendencies I have identified, we need cohorts of young people dedicated to transcending the methodological individualism and nationalism on which they have been reared. They must learn to track the lives of commodity and propaganda signs—seeing how science, cellphones, images, the political economy, exploitation of human and other animals, consumer activism, militarism, imperial historiography, and front organizations are theorized, formed, funded, and circulated—and to whose benefit and cost. Working with the third sector and governments, they should protect locals who work full-time in conflict zones as a matter of priority (Larsen et al., 2021). Reporters from the Global North must theorize and address the state, spend time in the Global South working with journalists, and demand compensation for the damage done by wealthy countries there, standing for 'participative democracy, horizontality, inclusiveness, and direct action' (Fians, 2022). We must confront the challenges of neoliberalism, warfare, and the Anthropocene, confident in our ability at least to engage them with a transparent reflexivity that is unafraid of holding ourselves accountable. That should be journalism's reflexive lodestar.

This book began with the suggestion that journalism tells contemporary stories purportedly based in fact and operating within certain values of open information blended with ideas of privacy, the public interest, and what interests the public. It should embrace knowledge produced by social movements, academia, business, unions, and so on that can transcend binaries, sometimes give absolute answers and sometimes absolute uncertainty, and adopt perspectives inimical to major parties and the fractions of capital they represent.

That is a complex road to hoe, especially in the light of corporate domination. But there are already some exemplars of good practice. Press On, for instance, favors 'collaboration between journalists and grassroots movements, and supporting journalism created by oppressed and marginalized people.'[12] Brazilian reporters from the *favelas* [informal housing] call for decolonizing the profession, in both senses of representation: textual and occupational (Ferreira, 2021). *Mediapart* is an independent, participatory paper, financed by readers, who also write for it.[13]

Writing in 1909 for the *American Journal of Sociology*, 'An Independent Journalist' suggested the following:

> only generous endowment could "emancipate" a great newspaper and enable it to be true to its highest ideals—to be honest in all things, to tell the truth boldly, to eschew sensationalism and vulgarity. And wealthy philanthropists have been urged to establish an "exemplary," a model newspaper, just as model libraries, model tenements, model orchestras are established by endowment.
>
> *(1909: 322)*

Contemporary endowments provide some useful monitoring and critique of reportage,[14] but the public interest has not been met over the past century in the way imagined above. The news needs to be funded from a levy on for-profit television and radio networks, financial newspapers and magazines, and purely online platforms, most notably aggregators such as Google, Reddit, and Apple. We have some foundation examples: in the US, the decline in local news slowed down thanks to US$500 million provided by philanthropists in 2023 (Abernathy, 2023).

Peace journalism and environmental materialism offer alternatives to what is currently taught and practiced. They pose *cui bono?* questions of public and private investment in militarism and the economy, examining state and capital's murderous and ecological impact. Both activist logics and scholarly methods, they oppose 'any political system that sees nature only through the lens of demands for unlimited economic growth' (Light, 1998: 345, 348). Measuring survival separately from monetary exchange, they prioritize peace and sustainability over profit and seek degrowth and democratic control of business (Perez de Fransius, 2014; Nohrstedt and Ottosen, 2022; Barber et al., 2018; Bertrand, 2019; Benton, 1996; Goldman and Schurman, 2000; Martínez-Alier, 2012; Maxwell et al., 2015; O'Connor, 1998; Latouche, 2009).

Although few reporters undertake significant investigations of the bodies that administer sports, some scholars and hacks do speak out (Jennings,

1996, 2006; Sugden and Tomlinson, 2003; Miller, 2015; Rowe, 2017; Conn, 2017; Maguire, 2020) and long-form writing is making a significant contribution to critical journalism. It can blend interpretation, background, and data to create something of value for more leisurely and in-depth reading than the 24-cycle of news allows. *L'Équipe* has specialized in 'slow journalism,' challenging cybertarian orthodoxy (Tulloch and Xavier Ramon, 2017; Le Masurier, 2016). In Brazil, the *crônica* [chronicle] and short story provide interesting alternatives to established norms. García Márquez drew on football to lend his explorations both color and comprehensiveness. In *Noticia de un secuestro* [*News of a Kidnapping*], a fictionalized report-cum-ethnography of cartel lawlessness, prisoners and their guards connect with one another through football, transcending the haze and violence that otherwise characterized their lives together (García Márquez, 1996). In the Anglo world, *The Athletic* has sought to break away from fast and furious 'file now, ask questions, fix later' routines and to criticize (up to a point) what it loves (Conway et al., 2020; Ferrucci, 2022). When FIFA claimed that offsets would mitigate all World Cup Finals emissions in 2022, *Le Monde* exposed that as a 'mirage' (Mandard, 2022) and *Scientific American* described the event as a 'Climate Catastrophe' (Boykoff, 2022). The Swiss Fairness Commission subsequently ruled that FIFA (which is based in Zürich) had lied in claiming the Finals were the first 'fully carbon neutral' such event.[15] The past few years have seen the emergence of the *Microcontos de Futebol* [*Football's Little Stories*] series (McEnnis, 2017); the web documentary *Triângulo do Futebol*, on the history of the sport in the Triângulo Mineiro and Alto Paranaíba (Oliveira Venancio, 2018)[16]; and the *Dibradoras* [*Breakers*] website, weekly podcast, and blog (Caselli, 2018), a prominent instance of women establishing their own sports media.[17] Australia has a Siren Sport collective and the US *Just Women's Sports*.[18] UK newspaper coverage of the 2019 FIFA Women's World Cup was six times greater than in 2015 (Pope et al, 2023). In 2022, women's sport was allocated 35% of space in British broadsheets and 25% in tabloids (Tobitt, 2023). For the first time in US history, Telemundo's 2023 World Cup commentaries were all female, while a large cohort of Brazilian women reported (Cauich, 2023; Dissat, 2023). And a small cohort of investigative journalists unveils the truth to sports fans—examples include Roberto Fuentes Vivar (2019), Jean-Luc Ferré (2020), Sergi López-Egea (2019), and Dave Zirin, who rightly blew the whistle on Australian Open tennis as 'the Tip of a Melting Iceberg' (2020)—plus veterans like Brian Glanville, who presciently renamed English football 30 years ago 'the Greed Is Good League' (2018).

Let's revisit Tönnies' words from the Introduction: '[j]ournalism is the small change of literature, which penetrates every corner of the home, multiplies knowledge, stimulates thought, repeatedly communicates truth and untruth, authenticity and inauthenticity, evokes passionate feelings, confirms attitudes, forms opinions, and supports conversation' (2000: 146). Its goal should be to achieve something of what Marx strove for:

> The free press is the ubiquitous vigilant eye of a people's soul, the embodiment of a people's faith in itself, the eloquent link that connects the individual with the state and the world, the embodied culture that transforms material struggles into intellectual struggles and idealises their crude material form. It is a people's frank confession to itself, and the redeeming power of confession is well known. It is the spiritual mirror in which a people can see itself, and self-examination is the first condition of wisdom. It is the spirit of the state, which can be delivered into every cottage, cheaper than coal gas. It is all-sided, ubiquitous, omniscient. It is the ideal world which always wells up out of the real world and flows back into it with ever greater spiritual riches and renews its soul.
>
> *(1842)*

That answers the query, why journalism? What we need now is a journalism worthy of the name.

Notes

1. https://newspaperdeathwatch.com/.
2. https://www.reutersagency.com/en/about/about-us/; https://www.ap.org/about/.
3. https://www.bbc.com/aboutthebbc/whatwedo/worldservice.
4. https://cnnpressroom.blogs.cnn.com/cnn-fact-sheet/; https://dwadsales.com/.
5. The data come from 67 of the 183 countries where it is broadcast https://www.france24.com/en/about-us.
6. https://www.nationalpublicmedia.com/audience/.
7. See https://www.youtube.com/watch?v=Xr4WvxIVGIQ&ab_channel=ZOLFM.
8. See https://www.facebook.com/fundacioncolordecolombia/.
9. https://www.rtve.es/television/20140522/lucia-mbomio/939827.shtml.
10. https://www.paris.fr/pages/audrey-pulvar-7962.
11. Extensive use has been made of hegemony theory beyond the Global North. In Latin America, Gramsci's notion of the national popular harnessing class interests is common sense for both left and right (Massardo, 1999). The same applies in South Asia and segments of the Middle East and Africa (Patnaik, 2004; Dabashi, 2013; Marks and Engels, 1994).
12. https://www.presson.media/.
13. https://www.mediapart.fr/qui-sommes-nous?userid=ff1ceb71-e66f-4e91-b4ce-3f6546e67d52.
14. Consider the Pew Charitable Trusts https://www.pewtrusts.org/en/about/how-we-work/investment-philosophy.
15. http://climatecasechart.com/wp-content/uploads/sites/16/non-us-case-documents/2023/20230607_19052_decision.pdf.
16. https://www.facebook.com/triangulodofutebol/.
17. https://dibradoras.com.br/.
18. https://sirensport.com.au/what-is-siren/; https://justwomenssports.com/.

REFERENCES

"450+ Scientists' Letter to Agencies: Drop Fossil Fuel Clients." (2023). *Clean Creatives* https://cleancreatives.org/scientists.

"A Cyber-House Divided." (2010, September 4). *Economist*: 61–62.

"A Greener Games? Tokyo's Environmental Impact." (2021, July 17). *Voice of America* https://www.voanews.com/a/east-asia-pacificgreener-games-tokyos-environmental-impact/6208269.html.

"AI Will Change American Elections, But Not in the Obvious Way." (2023, August 31). *Economist* https://www.economist.com/united-states/2023/08/31/ai-will-change-american-elections-but-not-in-the-obvious-way.

"Allt fler beviljhade medborgarskap." (2021, March 18). *Statistikmyndigheten* https://www.scb.se/hitta-statistik/statistik-efter-amne/befolkning/befolkningens-sammansattning/befolkningsstatistik/pong/statistiknyhet/befolkningsstatistik-helaret-20202/.

"Artificial Intelligence is Remixing Journalism into a Soup of Language." (2023, May 4). *Economist* https://www.economist.com/business/2023/05/04/artificial-intelligence-is-remixing-journalism-into-a-soup-of-language.

"As the World Cup Starts, Conservative Media Declare War on Soccer." (2010, June 11). *Media Matters for America* https://www.mediamatters.org/research/201006110040.

"Banking's Problem is Bigger Than NatWest." (2023, July 26). *Telegraph* https://www.telegraph.co.uk/opinion/2023/07/26/bankings-problem-is-bigger-than-natwest/.

"BBC on Track to Reach Half a Billion People Globally Ahead of its Centenary in 2022." (2021, November 26). *BBC Media Centre* https://www.bbc.co.uk/mediacentre/2021/bbc-reaches-record-global-audience/.

"Can Computing Clean Up its Act?" (2023, August 16). *Economist* https://www.economist.com/science-and-technology/2023/08/16/can-computing-clean-up-its-act.

"Caricaturistas latinoamericanos condenan atentado contra *Charlie Hebdo*." (2015, January 8). *El Universo* https://www.eluniverso.com/noticias/2015/01/08/nota/4409776/caricaturistas-latinoamericanos-condenan-atentado-contra-charlie/.

"Declaration of Frank A. Pometti in Support of the Debtors' Chapter 11 Petitions and First Day Relief." (2023, May 15). United States Bankruptcy Court Southern District of New York 23-10738 Doc 3.

"Do the Costs of the Cloud Outweigh the Benefits?" (2021, July 3). *Economist* https://www.economist.com/business/2021/07/03/do-the-costs-of-the-cloud-outweigh-the-benefits.

"Duque posa de ambientalista, recibe premio, pero no convence." (2021, September 21). *Confidencial Colombia* https://confidencialcolombia.com/lo-mas-confidencial/duque-posa-de-ambientalista-recibe-premio-pero-no-convece/2021/09/21/.

"Dyke: BBC is 'Hideously White'." (2001, January 6). *BBC News* http://news.bbc.co.uk/1/hi/scotland/1104305.stm.

"El Batallón Guardia Presidencia cree en la selección Colombia." (2016, June 3). *Noticias RCN* http://www.noticiasrcn.com/videos/tc-dangond-el-batallon-guardia-presidencial-cree-seleccion-colombia.

"English Premier League Club Owners in Season 2023-24—Full List." (2023, June 26). *Tribuna* https://tribuna.com/en/news/football-2023-06-26-english-premier-league-club-owners-in-season-202324-full-list/.

"Erdogan, seule la fatalité nous en débarrassera!" (2023, May 17). *Charlie Hebdo* https://charliehebdo.fr/editions/1608/.

"Felipe Calderón dio su primer informe como miembro de la FIA, máximo órgano de automovilismo." (2022, March 11). *Infobae* https://www.infobae.com/america/deportes/2022/03/11/felipe-calderon-dio-su-primer-informe-como-miembro-de-la-fia-maximo-organo-de-automovilismo/.

"«Femmes journalistes de sport, nous occupons le terrain!»" (2021, March 22). *Le Monde* https://www.lemonde.fr/idees/article/2021/03/21/femmes-journalistes-de-sport-nous-occupons-le-terrain60739233232.html.

"Free beer and prawns for Leicester City's Thai fans." (2016, May 1). *Financial Times* https://www.ft.com/content/aeda22be-0fbc-11e6-91da-096d89bd2173.

"Gran noticia para Colombia: Le otorgan poderoso premio ambiental internacional al presidente Iván Duque por ser un protector de los océanos." (2022, June 27). *Semana* https://www.semana.com/nacion/articulo/gran-noticia-para-colombia-le-otorgan-poderoso-premio-ambiental-internacional-al-presidente-ivan-duque-por-ser-un-protector-de-los-oceanos/202237/.

"Hablan de veto o censura para transmitir protestas de jugadores del fpc." (2019, October 7). *Comutricolor* https://comutricolor.com/futbol-colombiano/hablan-de-veto-o-censura-para-transmitir-protestas-de-jugadores-del-fpc/.

"How Objectivity in Journalism Became a Matter of Opinion." (2020, July 16). *The Economist* https://www.economist.com/books-and-arts/2020/07/16/how-objectivity-in-journalism-became-a-matter-of-opinion.

"In Iraq Crisis, Networks are Megaphones for Official Views." (2003, March 18). *FAIR* https://fair.org/take-action/action-alerts/in-iraq-crisis-networks-are-megaphones-for-official-views/.

"International E-Waste Day: 57.4 mm Tonnes Expected in 2021." (2021). WEEE Forum https://weee-forum.org/wsnews/international-e-waste-day-2021/.

"Is it Recession-Proof?" (2009, February 12). *The Economist* https://www.economist.com/international/2009/02/12/is-it-recession-proof.

"Journalist Casualties in the Israel-Gaza War." (2023, December 5). Committee to Protect Journalists https://cpj.org/2023/12/journalist-casualties-in-the-israel-gaza-conflict/.

"Los derechos laborales de un periodismo latinoamericano en crisis." (2022, December 5). *Rebelión* https://rebelion.org/los-derechos-laborales-de-un-periodismo-latinoamericano-en-crisis/.

"Luz: Le soutien à *Charlie Hebdo* est à "contre-sens" de ses dessins." (2015, January 10). *Le Point* https://www.lepoint.fr/culture/luz-le-soutien-a-charlie-hebdo-est-a-contre-sens-de-ses-dessins-10-01-2015-18954373.php.

"Meteorological Observations for April 1849." (1849). *The London, Edinburgh, and Dublin Philosophical Magazine and Journal of Science* 34, no. 231: 479.

"Most Marketable Athletes of 2023." (2023). *SportsPro* https://50mm.sportspromedia.com/athletes/.

"*National Geographic* Honors Two World Leaders for Their Outstanding Commitment and Action Toward Protecting Our Ocean." (2022, June 27). *National Geographic* https://blog.nationalgeographic.org/2022/06/27/national-geographic-honors-two-world-leaders-for-their-outstanding-commitment-and-action-toward-protecting-our-ocean/.

"Negroponte: Internet is Way to World Peace." (1997, November 25). *CNN* http://edition.cnn.com/TECH/9711/25/internet.peace.reut/.

"News Corp's Carbon Footprint—Fiscal 2020." (2022, February). *News Corp* https://www.news.co.uk/app/uploads/2022/02/NewsCorpCarbonFootprintFY20-2.pdf.

"*New York Times* Company, Petitioner, v. United States. United States, Petitioner, v. The *Washington Post* Company et al." (1971). *403 U.S. 713* https://www.law.cornell.edu/supremecourt/text/403/713.

"Of the 20 Most Followed Sports Teams on Instagram, European Soccer Leads the Way With 15 Clubs, Led by Real Madrid and Barcelona." (2023, November 23). *Boadroom* https://boardroom.tv/most-followed-sports-teams-instagram/.

"Play On." (2009, May 30). *The Economist*: 79.

"Premier League Agrees Record £6.7bn Domestic TV Rights Deal." (2023, December 4). *BBC* https://www.bbc.co.uk/sport/football/67619756.

"PSG Face Backlash for Mocking Eco-Friendly Travel Plea." (2022, September 6). *France 24* https://www.france24.com/en/france/20220906-psg-face-backlash-for-mocking-eco-friendly-travel-plea.

"Reich and Japan Shun Radio Treaty." (1936, March 27). *New York Times*: 17.

"Saudi Arabia is Spending a Fortune on Sport." (2023, August 10). *Economist* https://www.economist.com/briefing/2023/08/10/saudi-arabia-is-spending-a-fortune-on-sport.

"Science: Invisible Blanket." (1953, May 25). *Time*: 82–85.

"Science: One Big Greenhouse." (1956, May 28). *Time* https://content.time.com/time/subscriber/article/0,33009,937403,00.html.

"Sports Journalism: Changing Journalism Practice and Digital Media." (2017). *Digital Journalism* 5, no. 5: 493–672.

"Sustainable Business Podcast." (2015). *Guardian* http://www.theguardian.com/sustainable-business/big-data-sustainability-podcast.

"The Climate Crisis in Television Information in the First Four-Month Period of 2022." (2022, August 1). *Osservatorio di Pavia* https://www.osservatorio.it/en/la-crisi-climatica-nellinformazione-televisiva-nel-primo-quadrimestre-del-2022/.

"The Great US Baking Craze Continues with 42% Increase in Baking Cookbook Sales, NPD Says." *NPD* https://www.npd.com/news/press-releases/2021/the-great-us-baking-craze-continues-with-42-increase-in-baking-cookbook-sales-npd-says/.

"There's Life Outside Sports. There's Also Ballet." (1998, May 11). *Broadcasting and Cable*: 24–25.

"Tokyo Olympics: German Pentathlon Coach Thrown Out for Punching Horse." (2021, August 7). *BBC* https://www.bbc.co.uk/sport/olympics/58127366.

"Un anno di informazione sulla crisi climatica." (2023, April 20). *Osservatorio di Pavia* https://www.osservatorio.it/en/un-anno-di-informazione-sulla-crisi-climatica/.

"U.S. Food Imports Rarely Inspected." (2007, April 16). *NBC News* https://www.nbcnews.com/health/health-news/u-s-food-imports-rarely-inspected-flna1C9474489.

"US Oil and Gas Industry the World's 'Most Important Environmental Movement,' Energy Exec Says." (2022, May 27). *Fox Business News* https://www.foxbusiness.com/energy/us-oil-gas-industry-worlds-most-important-environmental-movement-energy-exec.

"Weekly Top 50 Shows." (2023, April). *BARB* https://www.barb.co.uk/viewing-data/most-viewed-programmes/.

"Weekly Viewing by Channel." (2015, December). *BARB* http://www.barb.co.uk/whats-new/monthly-viewing-by-channel-group?s=4.

"Weekly Viewing by Genre." (2015, December). *BARB* http://www.barb.co.uk/whats-new/weekly-viewing-by-genre?s=4.

"Wembley en bleu-blanc-rouge, frissonnante Marseillaise." (2022, November 17). *L'Avenir* https://www.lavenir.net/sports/football/2015/11/17/wembley-en-bleu-blanc-rouge-frissonnante-marseillaise-photos-et-video-SOM57ZNJBVDLHK7YTDSEZH-6SAE/.

"Wembley: La Marseillaise as an Act of Defiance." (2015, November 16). *BBC News* https://www.bbc.com/news/magazine-34832114.

"WiN sports dimayor censuran protesta futbolistas acolfutpro." (2019, October 6). *Pulzo* https://www.pulzo.com/deportes/win-sports-dimayor-censuran-protesta-futbolistas-acolfutpro-PP779513.

"Women's Euro 2022: Record Global Audience Watched Tournament in England." (2022, August 31). *BBC* https://www.bbc.com/sport/football/62735293.

"World Cup 2022: How Media Around World Judged Qatar Tournament." (2022, December 20). *BBC* https://www.bbc.co.uk/sport/football/64038338.

"World's 50 Greatest Leaders." (2021). *Fortune* https://fortune.com/ranking/worlds-greatest-leaders/.

Aalberg, Toril, Stylianos Papathanassopoulos, Stuart Soroka, James Curran, Kaori Hayashi, Shanto Iyengar, Paul K. Jones, Gianpietro Mazzoleni, Hernando Rojas, David Rowe, and Rodney Tiffen. (2013). "International TV News, Foreign Affairs Interest and Public Knowledge: A Comparative Study of Foreign News Coverage and Public Opinion in 11 Countries." *Journalism Studies* 14, no. 3: 387–406.

Abarbanel, Albert and Thorp McClusky. (1950, July 1). "Is the World Getting Warmer?" *Saturday Evening Post*: 22–23, 57, 60–63.

Abernathy, Penelope Muse. (2023). *The State of Local News 2023* https://localnews-initiative.northwestern.edu/projects/state-of-local-news/2023/report/.

Abrahamian, Ervand. (2003). "The US Media, Huntington and September 11." *Third World Quarterly* 24, no. 3: 529–44.

Abusin, Sana, Noora Lari, Salma Khaled, and Noor Al Emadi. (2020). "Effective Policies to Mitigate Food Waste in Qatar." *African Journal of Agricultural Research* 15, no. 3: 343–50.

Accenture. (2022). *Accelerating Global Companies Toward Net Zero by 2050* https://www.accenture.com/content/dam/accenture/final/capabilities/strategy-

and-consulting/strategy/document/Accenture-Net-Zero-By-2050-Global-Report-2022.pdf#zoom=40.

Aday, Sean. (2005). "The Real War Will Never Get on Television: An Analysis of Casualty Imagery in American Television Coverage of the Iraq War." *Media and Conflict in the Twenty-First Century*. Ed. Philip Seib. New York: Palgrave Macmillan. 141–56.

Aday, Sean. (2010). "Chasing the Bad News: An Analysis of 2005 Iraq and Afghanistan War Coverage on NBC and Fox News Channel." *Journal of Communication* 60, no. 1: 144–64.

Aday, Sean, Steven Livingston, and Maeve Herbert. (2005). "Embedding the Truth: A Cross-Cultural Analysis of Objectivity and Television Coverage of the Iraq War." *International Journal of Press/Politics* 10, no. 1: 3–21.

Adorno, Theodor W. (1975). "Culture Industry Reconsidered." Trans. Anson G. Rabinbach. *New German Critique* 7: 12–19.

Adorno, Theodor W. (2010). "Education After Auschwitz." https://sites.evergreen.edu/arunchandra/wp-content/uploads/sites/395/2018/07/AdornoEducation.pdf.

Adorno, Theodor W. and Max Horkheimer. (1977). "The Culture Industry: Enlightenment as Mass Deception." *Mass Communication and Society*. Eds. James Curran, Michael Gurevitch, and Janet Woollacott. London: Edward Arnold. 349–83.

Adorno, Theodor and Max Horkheimer. (1979). *Dialectic of the Enlightenment*. Trans. John Cumming. London: Verso.

Adragna, Anthony. (2019, August 21). "Luntz: 'I Was Wrong' on Climate Change." *Politico* https://www.politico.com/story/2019/08/21/frank-luntz-wrong-climate-change-1470653.

Ahmed, Saifuddin and Jörg Matthes. (2017). "Media Representation of Muslims and Islam from 2000 to 2015: A Meta-Analysis." *International Communication Gazette* 79, no. 3: 219–44.

Alam, Md. Mahmudul and Ibraheem Ishola Abdurraheem. (2023). "COVID-19 and the Financial Crisis in the Sports Sector Around the World." *Sport in Society* 26, no. 1: 154–67.

Aleiss, Angela. (1996, May 26). "Native Son." *Times-Picayune*: D1.

Alicino, Francesco. (2015). "Freedom of Expression, *Laïcité* and Islam in France: The Tension between Two Different (Universal) Perspectives." *Islam and Christian-Muslim Relations* 27, no. 1: 51–75.

Ali, Rashad. (2015). "Blasphemy, Charlie Hebdo, and the Freedom of Belief and Expression: The Paris Attacks and the Reactions." *Institute for Strategic Dialogue* http://www.strategicdialogue.org/wp-content/uploads/2016/02/Freedomofexpression0215WEBFINALVS3-FINAL.pdf.

Ali, Tariq. (2015, January 22). "Short Cuts." *London Review of Books* http://www.lrb.co.uk/v37/n02/tariq-ali/short-cuts.

Al-Kaisy, Aida. (2023). "Structural Racism in UK Newsrooms." *Ethical Journalism Network* https://ethicaljournalismnetwork.org/structural-racism-in-uk-newsrooms-research-and-fieldwork-conducted-by-the-ejn-jan-jul-2022.

Almiron, Núria and Jordi Xifra, eds. (2020). *Climate Change Denial and Public Relations: Strategic Communication and Interest Groups in Climate Inaction*. London: Routledge.

Almiron, Núria, Jose A. Moreno, and Justin Farrell. (2022). "Climate Change Contrarian Think Tanks in Europe: A Network Analysis." *Public Understanding of Science* 32, no. 3: 268–83.

Almiron, Núria, Maxwell Boykoff, Marta Narberhaus, and Paco Heras. (2020). "Dominant Counter-Frames in Influential Climate Contrarian European Think Tanks." *Climatic Change* 162, no. 4: 2003–020.Altenried, Moriz. (2022). *The Digital Factory: The Human Labor of Automation*. Chicago: University of Chicago Press.

Althusser, Louis. (1971). *Lenin and Philosophy and Other Essays*. Trans. Ben Brewster. New York: Monthly Review Press.

Ambrey, Christopher L., Christopher M. Fleming, Matthew Manning, and Christine Smith. (2016). "On the Confluence of Freedom of the Press, Control of Corruption and Societal Welfare." *Social Indicators Research* 128: 859–80.

American Press Institute. (2021, April). *A New Way of Looking at Trust in Media: Do Americans Share Journalism's Core Values?* https://www.americanpressinstitute.org/publications/reports/survey-research/trust-journalism-values/.

An, Jisun, Haewoon Kwak, Yelena Mejova, Sonia Alonso Saenz de Oger, and Braulio Gomez Fortes. (2016). "Are You Charlie or Ahmed? Cultural Pluralism in Charlie Hebdo Response on Twitter." *International AAAI Conference on Web and Social Media* http://arxiv.org/abs/1603.00646.

An Independent Journalist. (1909). "Is an Honest and Sane Newspaper Press Possible?" *American Journal of Sociology* 15, no. 3: 321–34.

Andeobu, Lynda, Santoso Wibowo, and Srimannarayana Grandhi. (2023). "Informal E-Waste Recycling Practices and Environmental Pollution in Africa: What is the Way Forward?" *International Journal of Hygiene and Environmental Health* 252 https://doi.org/10.1016/j.ijheh.2023.114192.

Anderson, Benedict. (2006). *Imagined Communities: Reflections on the Origin and Spread of Nationalism*, rev. ed. London: Verso.

Anderson, Hephzibah. (2023, August 6). "The BBC's Fergal Keane: 'The Breakdowns Get Harder to Recover from Each Time'." *Guardian* https://www.theguardian.com/books/2023/aug/06/fergal-keane-bbc-war-correspondent-memoir-the-madness-ptsd?CMP=ShareiOSAppOther.

Anderson, Chris and Michael Wolff. (2010, August 17). "The Web is Dead: Long Live the Internet." *Wired* https://www.wired.com/2010/08/ff-webrip/.

Andress, David. (2018, July 3). "The Song that Once Unified France is Tearing it Apart." *Quartz* https://qz.com/1320059/la-marseillaise-frances-national-anthem-is-causing-tension-once-again/.

Anon. (1882). *The Alternative: A Study in Psychology*. London: Macmillan.

Anshelm, Jonas and Martin Hultman. (2014). "A Green Fatwā? Climate Change as a Threat to the Masculinity of Industrial Modernity." *NORMA: International Journal of Masculinity Studies* 9, no. 2: 84–96.

Antunovic, Dunja. (2019). ""We Wouldn't Say It to Their Faces": Online Harassment, Women Sports Journalists, and Feminism." *Feminist Media Studies* 19, no. 3: 428–42.

Antunovic, Dunja and Bartoluci Sunčica. (2023). "Sport, Gender, and National Interest During the Olympics: A Comparative Analysis of Media Representations in Central and Eastern Europe." *International Review for the Sociology of Sport* 58, no. 1: 167–87.

Arbeláez, María Fernanda. (2018, July 4). "El polémico titular de 'The Sun' antes del partido Colombia-Inglaterra." *El Tiempo* https://www.eltiempo.com/mundo/europa/la-polemica-portada-de-the-sun-previo-a-colombia-vs-inglaterra-238592.

Arena, Christine. (2021, December 1). "I Left a Major Agency Because of Its Stance on Climate Change." *AdWeek* https://www.adweek.com/agencies/i-left-a-major-agency-because-of-its-stance-on-climate-change/.

Armour, Nancy. (2014, May 7). "NBC Universal Pays $7.75 billion for Olympics Through 2032." *USA Today* https://eu.usatoday.com/story/sports/olympics/2014/05/07/nbc-olympics-broadcast-rights-2032/8805989/.

Armour, Nancy and Tom Schad. (2020, October 2). "Sports Team Owners Listen to Players, but Support Republicans to the Tune of Millions of Dollars." *USA Today* https://eu.usatoday.com/in-depth/sports/2020/10/01/election-2020-sports-team-owners-support-republicans-millions/3562973001/.

Arnheim, Rudolf. (1969). *Film as Art*. London: Faber and Faber.

Aronoff, Kate. (2018, August 2). "What the 'New York Times' Climate Blockbuster Missed." *The Nation* https://www.thenation.com/article/archive/new-york-times-climate-blockbuster-misses/.

Artemas, Katie, Tim P. Vos, and Margaret Duffy. (2018). "Journalism Hits a Wall." *Journalism Studies* 19, no. 7: 1004–120.

Asad, Talal. (2005). "Reflections on Laïcité & the Public Sphere." *Items and Issues* 5, no. 3: 1–11.

Ashoo, Sam. (2021, December 3). "Climate Crisis: How Can Football Make a Difference?" *Euronews* https://www.euronews.com/2021/10/28/the-climate-crisis-why-football-can-no-longer-hide.

Associated Press. (2021, July 26). "Pandemic Olympics Endured Heat, and Now a Typhoon's en Route." *NBC News* https://www.nbcnews.com/news/world/pandemic-olympics-endured-heat-now-typhoon-s-en-route-n1274796.

Associated Press. (2023, July 9). "'You Should Have Seen This Note': US Meteorologists Harassed for Reporting on Climate Crisis." *Guardian* https://www.theguardian.com/environment/2023/jul/09/meterologists-harassment-climate-crisis.

Atkins, Peter and Ian Bowler. (2001). *Food in Society: Economy, Culture, Geography*. London: Arnold.

Attali, Jacques. (2001). *Bruits: Essais sur l'économie politique de la musique*, 2nd ed. Paris: Librairie Arthème Fayard/Presses Universitaires de France.

Attali, Jacques and Yves Stourdzé. (1977). "The Birth of the Telephone and Economic Crisis: The Slow Death of Monologue in French Society." *The Social Impact of the Telephone*. Ed. Ithiel de Sola Pool. Cambridge, MA: MIT Press. 97–111.

Austin, J. L. (1962). *How to Do Things with Words: The William James Lectures Delivered at Harvard University in 1955*. Oxford: Clarendon Press.

Australian Communications and Media Authority. (2022, February 11). "ACMA Investigates Tobacco Advertising on Grand Prix Broadcasts." https://www.acma.gov.au/articles/2022-02/acma-investigates-tobacco-advertising-grand-prix-broadcasts.

Averre, David. (2023, January 11). "'Do Not Play with Muslims': Iran Warns the French they Could Face the Same Fate as Salman Rushdie After *Charlie Hebdo* Magazine Mocks Ayatollah Khamenei with Spoof Cartoons." *Daily Mail* https://www.dailymail.co.uk/news/article-11623703/Iran-delivers-stark-warning-Charlie-Hebdo-magazine-mocks-Ayatollah-Khamenei.html?ico=topics_pagination_desktop.

Baack, Stefan. (2015). "Datafication and Empowerment: How the Open Data Movement Re-Articulates Notions of Democracy, Participation, and Journalism." *Big Data & Society* 2, no. 2 doi: 10.1177/2053951715594634.

Bacon, Wendy and Arunn Jegan. (2020, December). "Lies, Debates, and Silences: How News Corp Produces Climate Scepticism in Australia." *GetUp!* https://climate-report.wendybacon.com/2020-12LiesDebatesandSilences.pdf.
Badouard, Romain. (2016). ""Je ne suis pas Charlie". Pluralité des prises de parole sur le web et les réseaux sociaux." *Le Défi **Charlie**. Les medias à l'épreuve des attentats*. Ed. Pierre Lefébure and Claire Sécail. Paris: Lemieux.
Bærug, Jan Richard and Halliki Harro-Loit. (2012). "Journalism Embracing Advertising as Traditional Journalism Discourse Becomes Marginal." *Journalism Practice* 6, no. 2: 172–86.
Baía Reis, António and António Fernando Vasconcelos Cunha Castro Coelho. (2018). "Virtual Reality and Journalism." *Digital Journalism* 6, no. 8: 1090–100.
Bailenson, Jeremy. (2018). *Experience on Demand: What Virtual Reality Is, How It Works, and What It Can Do*. New York: WW Norton.
Ballard, Janette. (2021, June 11). "Cookbooks are Selling Like Hotcakes." *University of Denver Magazine* https://magazine.du.edu/cookbooks-are-selling-like-hotcakes/.
Banerjee, Neela. (2017, December 22). "How Big Oil Lost Control of its Climate Misinformation Machine." *Inside Climate News* https://insideclimatenews.org/news/22122017/big-oil-heartland-climate-science-misinformation-campaign-koch-api-trump-infographic/.
Bar, François with Caroline Simard. (2006). "From Hierarchies to Network Firms." *The Handbook of New Media: Updated Students Edition*. Eds. Leah Lievrouw and Sonia Livingstone. Thousand Oaks, CA: Sage. 350–63.
Barber, Daniel A., Lee Stickells, Daniel J. Ryan, Maren Koehler, Andrew Leach, Philip Goad, Deborah van der Plaat, Cathy Keys, Farhan Karim, and William M. Taylor. (2018). "Architecture, Environment, History: Questions and Consequences." *Architectural History Review* 22, no. 2: 249–86.
Barbrook, Richard and Andy Cameron. (1996). "The Californian Ideology." *Science as Culture* 6, no. 1: 44–72.
Barclay, Donald A. (2018). *Fake News, Propaganda, and Plain Old Lies: How to Find Trustworthy Information in the Digital Age*. Lanham, MD: Rowman & Littlefield.
Barkemeyer, Ralf, Frank Figge, Andreas Hoepner, Diane Holt, Johannes Kraak, and Pei-Shan Yu. (2017). "Media Coverage of Climate Change: An International Comparison." *Environment and Planning C: Politics and Space* 35, no. 6: 1029–054.
Barker, Alexander B., Magdalena Opazo Breton, Rachael L. Murray, Bruce Grant-Braham, and John Britton. (2019). "Exposure to 'Smokescreen' Marketing During the 2018 Formula 1 Championship." *Tobacco Control* 28: e154–55.
Barker, Martin. (1993). "Sex, Violence, and Videotape." *Sight and Sound* 3, no. 5: 10–12.
Barkin, Steve M. (2003). *American Television News: The Media Marketplace and the Public Interest*. Armonk: ME Sharpe.
Barlow, William. (1988). "Community Radio in the US: The Struggle for a Democratic Medium." *Media, Culture & Society* 10, no. 1: 81–105.
Barnes, Bart. (2004, August 14). "Giving Americans Entrée to Cuisine." *Washington Post*: A1.
Barnett, Adam. (2023, August 2). "'CO2 is Life': Talk TV Presenter Andre Walker Hosts YouTube Show That Spreads Climate Science Denial." *DeSmog* https://www.desmog.com/2023/08/02/co2-is-life-talktv-presenter-andre-walker-hosts-youtube-show-lois-perry-climate-science-denial/.
Barra, Allen. (2002, July 2). "Nil and Void." *Village Voice* https://www.villagevoice.com/2002/07/02/nil-and-void/.

Barry, James. (2016). "Pragmatic Dogma: Understanding the Ideological Continuities in Iran's Response to the *Charlie Hebdo* Attacks." *Islam and Christian-Muslim Relations* 27, no. 1: 77–93.

Bast, Joseph and Roy Spencer. (2014, May 26). "The Myth of the Climate Change '97%'." *Wall Street Journal* https://www.wsj.com/articles/SB10001424052702303480304579578462813553136.

Basu, Laura. (2018). *Media Amnesia: Rewriting the Economic Crisis*. London: Pluto.

Battaglio, Stephen. (2022, June 14). "Why Apple TV Has Become the Exclusive Streaming Home for Major League Soccer." *Los Angeles Times* https://www.latimes.com/entertainment-arts/business/story/2022-06-14/apple-tv-will-become-the-exclusive-streaming-home-for-major-league-soccer.

Battan, Carrie. (2022, March 11). "How 'Drive to Survive' Remade Formula 1." *New Yorker* https://www.newyorker.com/culture/culture-desk/how-drive-to-survive-remade-formula-1.

Baudrillard, Jacques. (1988). *Selected Writings*. Ed. Mark Poster. Stanford: Stanford University Press.

Baxter, Christopher. (2015, May 7). "Which NFL Teams Got Your Federal Tax Dollars?" *NJ* https://www.nj.com/politics/2015/05/whichnflteamsaregettingyourfederaltaxdolla.html.

BBC. (2023). *BBC Annual Plan 2023/24* https://www.bbc.co.uk/mediacentre/documents/bbc-annual-plan-2023-2024.pdf.

Bebel, August. (1971). *Society of the Future*. Trans. Don Danemanis. Ed. K. Villiers. Moscow: Progress Publishers.

Beck, Ulrich. (2002). "The Cosmopolitan Society and its Enemies." *Theory, Culture & Society* 19, nos. 1-2: 17–44.

Becker, Gary S. (1983). *Human Capital: A Theoretical, and Empirical Analysis, with Special Reference to Education*, 2nd ed. Chicago: University of Chicago Press.

Becker, Gary. (1993). "Nobel Lecture: The Economic Way of Looking at Behavior." *Journal of Political Economy* 101, no. 3: 385–409.

Beder, Sharon. (1998). "Public Relations' Role in Manufacturing Artificial Grass Roots Coalitions." *Public Relations Quarterly* 43, no. 2: 20.

Beiling Loose, Eloisa. (2022). "Cobertura climática desde o Sul: Análise crítica de discusros jornalísticos não hegemônicos." *Estudos em Jornalismo e Mídia* 19, no. 1: 219–32.

Bell, Emily. (2023, March 3). "A Fake News Frenzy: Why ChatGPT Could be Disastrous for Truth in Journalism." *Guardian* https://www.theguardian.com/commentisfree/2023/mar/03/fake-news-chatgpt-truth-journalism-disinformation?ref=newsletter.14watts.com.

Benjamin, Walter. (1970). "The Author as Producer." Trans. John Heckman. *New Left Review* 62: 83–96.

Bennett, Gabriella. (2022, May 14). "Sports Journalism is Less Sexist Than it Was—But There's Still a Long Way to Go." *Guardian* https://www.theguardian.com/football/blog/2022/may/14/sports-journalism-is-less-sexist-than-it-was-but-theres-still-a-long-way-to-go.

Bentham, Jeremy. (2012). *The Collected Works of Jeremy Bentham: On the Liberty of the Press, and Public Discussion, and Other Legal and Political Writings for Spain and Portugal*. Eds. Philip Schofield and Catherine Pease-Watkin. Oxford: Oxford University Press.

Benton, Ted, ed. (1996). *The Greening of Marxism*. New York: Guilford.

Bernard, Paquito, Guillaume Chevance, Celia Kingsbury, Aurélie Baillot, Ahmed-Jérôme Romain, Virginie Molinier, Tegwen Gadais, and Kelsey N. Dancause. (2021). "Climate Change, Physical Activity and Sport: A Systematic Review." *Sports Medicine* 51: 1041–059.

Berner, Ilana. (2023, October 2). "After Decades of Climate Deception, Shell Uses Forntite to Court Demographic Most Concerned About Climate Change." *Media Matters for America* https://www.mediamatters.org/climate-deniers/after-decades-climate-deception-shell-uses-fortnite-court-demographic-most.

Bernstein, Carl. (1977, October 20). "The CIA and the Media." *Rolling Stone* https://www.carlbernstein.com/the-cia-and-the-media-rolling-stone-10-20-1977.

Berry, Mike. (2013a). "The *Today* Programme and the Banking Crisis." *Journalism* 14, no. 2: 253–70.

Berry, Mike. (2013b, August 23). "Hard Evidence: How Biased is the BBC?" *The Conversation* https://theconversation.com/hard-evidence-how-biased-is-the-bbc-17028.

Berry, Mike, Karin Wahl-Jorgensen, Iñaki Garcia-Blanco, Lucy Bennett, and Joe Cable. (2021). "British Public Service Broadcasting, the EU and Brexit." *Journalism Studies* 22, no. 15: 2082–102.

Bertrand, Aliénor. (2019). "A Rupture Between Human Beings and Earth: A Philosophical Critical Approach to Coviability." *Coviability of Social and Ecological Systems: Reconnecting Mankind to the Biosphere in an Era of Global Change.* Vol. 1: The Foundations of a New Paradigm. Eds. Olivier Barrière, Mohammed Behnassi, Gilbert David, Vincent Douzal, Mireille Fargette, Thérèse Libourel, Maud Loireau, Laurence Pascal, Catherine Prost, Voyner Ravena-Cañete, Frédérique Seyler, and Serge Morand. Cham: Springer. 269–84.

Bhagwati, Jagdish. (2002). "Coping with Antiglobalization: A Trilogy of Discontents." *Foreign Affairs* 81, no. 1: 2–7.

Bi, Yuan. (2015). "Integration or Resistance: The Influx of Foreign Capital in British Football in the Transnational Age." *Soccer & Society* 16, no. 1: 17–41.

Biagioli, Mario. (2009). "Postdisciplinary Liaisons: Science Studies and the Humanities." *Critical Inquiry* 35, no. 4: 816–33.

Bickes, Hans, Tina Otten, and Laura Chelsea Weymann. (2014). "The *Financial Crisis* in the German and English Press: Metaphorical Structures in the Media Coverage on Greece, Spain and Italy." *Discourse & Society* 25, no. 4: 424–45.

Biddle, Sam. (2020, October 21). "Twitter Surveillance Startup Targets Communities of Color for Police." *The Intercept* https://theintercept.com/2020/10/21/dataminr-twitter-surveillance-racial-profiling/.

Biraud, Gael. (2023, March 21). "Une charte pour plus de mixité dans le journalisme de sport." *La Marseillaise* https://www.lamarseillaise.fr/sports/une-charte-pour-plus-de-mixite-dans-le-journalisme-de-sport-OG13401816.

Black Collective of Media in Sports. (2023). *The D Word*[4]: *A Guide on Diversity in the Sports Media* https://drive.google.com/file/d/1qgWp-3-w1JhFq6fDXA8SPtI-zn24jvm8/view?fbclid=PAAaaUQ8M-dyD3OkDWXcklZN5ZQSh4MEs-fNkjmqU0YKTAQ9yIBmkx3Z08HZc.

Black, Richard. (2010, June 30). "Formula One Embarks on Carbon-Cutting Drive." *BBC* http://www.bbc.com/news/10456984.

Blankenspoor, Elizabeth, Ed deHaan, and Christina Zhu. (2017, May 10). *Robo-Journalism and Capital Markets Stanford Business Working Paper 3490* https://www.gsb.stanford.edu/faculty-research/working-papers/robo-journalism-capital-markets.

Blázquez, Niceto. (2016, September 22). "¿Por qué es importante el periodismo?" *Consultorio Ético* https://fundaciongabo.org/es/consultorio-etico/consulta/850.

Blum, Alan. (1991). "The Marlboro Grand Prix—Circumvention of the Television Ban on Tobacco Advertising." *New England Journal of Medicine* 324: 913–17.

Boland-Rudder, Hamish. (2019, December 11). "HSBC to Pay $192m Penalty for Helping Americans Evade Taxes." *International Consortium of Investigative Journalists* https://www.icij.org/investigations/swiss-leaks/hsbc-to-pay-192m-penalty-for-helping-americans-evade-taxes/.

Bolívar, Simón. (2003). *El Libertador: Writings of Simón Bolívar*. Trans. Frederick H. Fornoff. Ed. David Bushnell. Oxford: Oxford University Press.

Bond, Paul. (2016, February 29). "Leslie Moonves on Donald Trump: "It May Not Be Good for America, But It's Damn Good for CBS"." *Hollywood Reporter* https://www.hollywoodreporter.com/news/general-news/leslie-moonves-donald-trump-may-871464/.

Bonesteel, Matt. (2015, February 13). "Massive New English Premier League TV Deal Has the Rest of European Soccer Worried." *Washington Post* http://www.washingtonpost.com/blogs/earlylead/wp/2015/02/13/massive-new-english-premier-league-tv-deal-has-the-rest-ofeuropean-soccer-worried/.

Bonfiglioli, Catriona. (2020). "Analysing the Ethics of Weight-Related News Through the Lens of Journalism Codes." *Australian Journalism Review* 42, no. 2: 313–20.

Bonfiglioli, Catriona, Ben J. Smith, Lesley A. King, Simon F. Chapman, and Simon J. Holding. (2007). "Choice and Voice: Obesity Debates in Television News." *Medical Journal of Australia* 187, no. 8: 442–45.

Book Environmental Council and Green Publishing Initiative. (2013, January). *Book Industry Environmental Trends* http://www.greenpressinitiative.org/documents/TrendsReport2013.pdf.

Borjesson, Kristina, ed. (2002). *Into the Buzzsaw: Leading Journalists Expose the Myth of a Free Press*. Amherst: Prometheus Books.

Börnfelt, P-O. (2023). *Work Organisation in Practice: From Taylorism to Sustainable Work Organisations*. Cham: Palgrave Macmillan.

Bourne, Clea. (2019). "AI Cheerleaders: Public Relations, Neoliberalism and Artificial Intelligence." *Public Relations Inquiry* 8, no. 2: 109–25.

Boussalis, Constantine, Travis G. Coan, and Marianna Pobrezhskaya. (2016). "Measuring and Modeling Russian Newspaper Coverage of Climate Change." *Global Environmental Change* 41: 99–110.

Bowers, Simon. (2015, February 19). "Telegraph Owners' £250m HSBC Loan Raises Fresh Questions Over Coverage." *Guardian* https://www.theguardian.com/media/2015/feb/19/telegraph-250m-loan-hsbc-editorial-changes-yodel.

Boxall-Legge, Jake. (2020, June 30). "How Mercedes Can Address the Lack of Minority Representation." *Motorsport* https://www.motorsport.com/f1/news/how-mercedes-can-address-the-lack-of-minority-representation-in-f1/4816804/.

Boykoff, Jules. (2022, November 23). "The World Cup in Qatar is a Climate Catastrophe." *Scientific American* https://www.scientificamerican.com/article/the-world-cup-in-qatar-is-a-climate-catastrophe/.

Boykoff, Jules and Christopher Gaffney. (2020). "The Tokyo 2020 Games and the End of Olympic History." *Capitalism Nature Socialism* 31, no. 2: 1–19.

Boykoff, Maxwell and Gesa Luedecke. (2016). "Elite News Coverage of Climate Change." *Oxford Research Encyclopedia of Climate Science* https://

www.oxfordreference.com/display/10.1093/acref/9780190498986.001.0001/acref-9780190498986-e-357;jsessionid=307E8E755BCCAD24A46724D354CAB579.

Boykoff, Maxwell T. and Tom Yulsman. (2013). "Political Economy, Media, and Climate Change: Sinews of Modern Life." *WIREs Climate Change* http://sciencepolicy.colorado.edu/admin/publicationfiles/2013.19.pdf.

Boyle, Raymond, David Rowe, and Garry Whannel. (2010). "'Delight in Trivial Controversy?' Questions for Sports Journalism." *Routledge Companion to News and Journalism*. Ed. Stuart Allan. London: Routledge. 245–55.

Bradley, Peri, ed. (2016). *Food, Media and Contemporary Culture: The Edible Image*. Houndmills: Palgrave Macmillan.

Bradshaw, Tom and Daragh Minogue. (2019). *Sports Journalism: The State of Play*. London: Routledge.

Bradshaw, Tom. (2021). "Benefit or Burden?: Social Media and Moral Complexities Confronting Sports Journalists." *Insights on Reporting Sports in the Digital Age*. Ed. Roger Domenghetti. London: Routledge. 17–30.

Braiker, Brian. (2014, March 12). "Inside the *Texas Tribune* Model of Sustainable Journalism." *Digiday* http://digiday.com/publishers/texas-tribune-publisher-tim-griggs/.

Brambilla Hall, Stefan. (2018, January 15). "Can You Tell if This Was Written by a Robot? 7 Challenges for AI in Journalism." *World Economic Forum* https://www.weforum.org/agenda/2018/01/can-you-tell-if-this-article-was-written-by-a-robot-7-challenges-for-ai-in-journalism/.

Braudel, Fernand. (1981). *Civilization and Capitalism 15th-18th Century. Volume I. The Structures of Everyday Life: The Limits of the Possible*. Trans. Siân Reynolds. London: William Collins.

Brecht, Bertolt. (1964). "Emphasis on Sport." *Brecht on Theatre*. Ed. John Willett. London: Macmillan. 6–9.

Brecht, Bertolt. (2000). *Brecht on Film and Radio*. Trans. and Ed. Marc Silberman. London: Bloomsbury.

Brecht, Bertolt. (2018). *The Collected Poems of Bertolt Brecht*. Trans. and Ed. Tom Kuhn and David Constantine with Charlotte Ryland. New York: Liveright Publishing.

Brenan, Megan. (2020, September 30). "Americans Remain Distrustful of Mass Media." *Gallup Poll* https://news.gallup.com/poll/321116/americans-remain-distrustful-mass-media.aspx.

Brewin, Mark W. (2013). "A Short History of the History of Objectivity." *The Communication Review* 16, no. 4: 211–29.

Briggs, Asa and Peter Burke. (2015). *A Social History of the Media: From Gutenberg to the Internet*, 3rd ed. Cambridge: Polity.

Bright, Sam. (2023, March 30). "Conservatives Received £3.5 Million from Polluters, Fossil Fuel Interests and Climate Deniers in 2022." *DeSmog* https://www.desmog.com/2023/03/30/conservatives-received-3-5-million-from-polluters-fossil-fuel-interests-and-climate-deniers-in-2022/.

Brock, George. (2013, September 27). "Journalism is Going to Survive This Era of Creative Destruction." *New Statesman* http://www.newstatesman.com/business/2013/09/journalism-going-survive-era-creative-destruction.

Brondizio, Eduardo S., Stacey A. Giroux, Julia C. D. Valliant, Jordan Blekking, Stephanie Dickinson, and Beate Henschel. (2023, August 3). "Change Mindsets to Stop Millions of Food-Production Jobs from Disappearing." *Nature* 620: 33–36.

Brookes, Gavin and Paul Baker. (2021). *Obesity in the News: Language and Representation in the Press*. Cambridge: Cambridge University Press.
Broussard, Meredith. (2018). *Artificial Unintelligence: How Computers Misunderstand the World*. Cambridge, MA: MIT Press.
Brown, Sean Fredrick. (2005). "Exceptionalist America: American Sports Fans' Reaction to Internationalization." *International Journal of the History of Sport* 22, no. 6: 1106–135.
Brüggemann, Michael and Sven Engesser. (2017). "Beyond False Balance: How Interpretive Journalism Shapes Media Coverage of Climate Change." *Global Environmental Change* 42: 58–67.
Brüggemann, Michael, Jessica Kunert, and Louise Sprengelmeyer. (2022). "Framing Food in the News: Still Keeping the Politics Out of the Broccoli." *Journalism Practice* doi: 10.1080/17512786.2022.2153074.
Brunsdon, Charlotte. (2021). "History of the Present." *Writings on Media: History of the Present*. Stuart Hall. Ed. Charlotte Brunsdon. Durham, NC: Duke University Press. 11–28.
Bureau of Labor Statistics, U.S. Department of Labor. (2023a). *Occupational Outlook Handbook*, Public Relations Specialists https://www.bls.gov/ooh/media-and-communication/public-relations-specialists.htm.
Bureau of Labor Statistics, U.S. Department of Labor. (2023b). *Occupational Outlook Handbook*, News Analysts Reporters, and Journalists https://www.bls.gov/ooh/media-and-communication/reporters-correspondents-and-broadcast-news-analysts.htm.
Burke, Edmund. (1986). *Reflections on the Revolution in France and on the Proceedings in Certain Societies in London Relative to That Event*. Ed. Conor Cruise O'Brien. Harmondsworth: Penguin.
Burke, Edmund. (1994). "The Restraints on Men are Among Their Rights." *Citizenship*. Ed. Paul A. B. Clarke. London: Pluto. 121–23.
Burke, Elias. (2023, July 13). "Messi Has Made Miami the Fifth-Most Followed Team in the U.S—And He's Not Even Played Yet." *The Athletic* https://theathletic.com/4687173/2023/07/13/messi-miami-instagram-lionel/.
Burns, Catherine and Hannah Morrison. (2021, September 21). "UK-US Special Relationship: A Short History." *BBC News* https://www.bbc.co.uk/news/newsbeat-35783309.
Burton, Bob. (2007). *Inside Spin: The Dark Underbelly of the PR Industry*. Sydney: Allen & Unwin.
Burton, Bob and Andy Rowell. (2003). "Unhealthy Spin." *British Medical Journal* 326: 1205.Bush, Vannevar. (1945, July). "As We May Think." *Atlantic Monthly*: 101–08.
Butterworth, Michael L. and Stormi D. Moskal. (2009). "American Football, Flags, and "Fun": The Bell Helicopter Armed Forces Bowl and the Rhetorical Production of Militarism." *Communication, Culture & Critique* 2, no. 4: 411–33.
Bychawski, Adam. (2022, June 16). "Exclusive: US Climate Deniers Pump Millions into Tory-Linked Think Tanks." *openDemocracy* https://www.opendemocracy.net/en/dark-money-investigations/think-tanks-adam-smith-policy-exchange-legatum-iea-taxpayers-alliance-climate-denial/.
Byerly, Caroline M., ed. (2013). *The Palgrave International Handbook of Women and Journalism*. Houndmills: Palgrave.

Cable, Jonathan and Glyn Mottershead. (2018). ""Can I Click It? Yes You Can": Football Journalism, Twitter and Clickbait." *Ethical Space: The International Journal of Communication Ethics* 15, nos. 1–2: 69–80.
Cabral, Amílcar. (1979). *Unity and Struggle: Speeches and Writings: Texts Selected by the PAIGC.* Trans. Michael Wolfers. New York: Monthly Review Press.
Cairns, Andy. (2018). "A New Chapter in Sporting History." *British Journalism Review* 29, no. 2: 28–32.
Cairns, Andy. (2023). "It's Still All to Play For." *British Journalism Review* 34, no. 1: 45–48.
Calcutt, Andrew and Philip Hammond. (2011). *Journalism Studies: A Critical Introduction.* London: Routledge.
Callison, Candis. (2014). *How Climate Change Comes to Matter: The Communal Life of Facts.* Durham, NC: Duke University Press.
Campbell, Beatrix, Marian Darke, Tricia Davis, David Green, Joanna de Groot, Ron Halverson, Steve Hart, Martin Jacques, Charlie Leadbeater, Bert Pearce, Jeff Rodrigues, Mhairi Stewart, Nina Temple, and Communist Party Executive Committee. (1990). "The New Times." *New Times: The Changing Face of Politics in the 1990s.* Ed. Stuart Hall and Martin Jacques. London: Verso. 23–37.
Campbell, Paul Ian and Louis Bebb. (2022). "'He is Like a Gazelle (When He Runs)': (Re)constructing Race and Nation in Match-Day Commentary at the Men's 2018 FIFA World Cup." *Sport in Society* 25, no. 1: 144–62.
Camus, Albert. (1991). *Between Hell and Reason: Essays from the Resistance Newspaper Combat, 1944-1947.* Trans. Alexandre de Gramont. Hanover: Wesleyan University Press.
Camus, Renaud. (2012). *The Great Replacement Part 1.* Trans. /pol/'s/RWTS/ https://www.docdroid.net/8tGi9Vx/camus-r-2012-the-great-replacement-pdf#page=3.
Canonico, Scott, Royston Sellman, and Chris Preist. (2009). "Reducing the Greenhouse Gas Emissions of Commercial Print with Digital Technologies." *Proceedings of the 2009 IEEE International Symposium on Sustainable Systems and Technology* http://www.hp.com/hpinfo/newsroom/presskits/2009/ecosolutions/reduceimpact/ReducingGreenhouseGasEmissions.pdf.
Carbon Disclosure Project. (2010). *CDP Investor CDP 2010 Information Request: News Corporation* https://www.cdp.net/en-US/Pages/HomePage.aspx.
Carey, James W. (1993). "The Mass Media and Democracy: Between the Modern and the Postmodern." *Journal of International Affairs* 47, no. 1: 1–21.
Carey, James W. (1997). *James Carey: A Critical Reader.* Eds. Eve Stryker Munson and Catherine A. Warren. Minneapolis: University of Minnesota Press.
Carey, James W. (2005). "Historical Pragmatism and the Internet." *New Media & Society* 7, no. 4: 443–55.
Carey, James W. (2007). "A Short History of Journalism for Journalists: A Proposal and Essay." *Harvard International Journal of Press/Politics* 12, no. 1: 3–16.
Carey, James W. (2009). *Communication as Culture: Essays on Media and Society*, rev. ed. New York: Routledge.
Carlyle, Thomas. (1908). *On Heroes, Hero-Worship and the Heroic in History.* London: JM Dent.
Carlyle, Thomas. (1930). *The French Revolution: A History.* New York: The Modern Library.
Carr, David. (2003, March 25). "Reporting Reflects Anxiety." *New York Times* https://www.nytimes.com/2003/03/25/us/a-nation-at-war-reporting-reflects-anxiety.html.

Carr, David. (2013). "Reddit: I Am a Columnist and Reporter on Media and Culture for *The New York Times*." *Reddit* https://www.reddit.com/r/IAmA/comments/16k598/iamacolumnistandreporteronmediaandculture.
Carrington, Damian and Ben Stockton. (2023, December 3). "Cop28 President Says There is 'No Science' Behind Demands for Phase-Out of Fossil Fuels." *Guardian* https://www.theguardian.com/environment/2023/dec/03/back-into-caves-cop28-president-dismisses-phase-out-of-fossil-fuels.
Caselli, Irene. (2018, December 18). "Fighting for an Equal Playing Field in Brazilian Sports Reporting." *International Journalists' Network* https://ijnet.org/en/story/fighting-equal-playing-field-brazilian-sports-reporting.
Cassidy, William P. (2005). "Variations on a Theme: Professional Role Conceptions of Print and Online Newspaper Journalists." *Journalism & Mass Communication Quarterly* 82, no. 2: 264–80.
Cauich, Eduard. (2023, August 16). "Telemundo's All-Female TV Crew Makes U.S. History." *Los Angeles Times* https://www.latimes.com/delos/story/2023-08-16/telemundo-all-women-tv-crew-makes-u-s-history.
Center for Countering Digital Hate. (2023, April). *YouTube's Climate Denial Dollars* https://foe.org/wp-content/uploads/2023/04/YouTubes-Climate-Denial-Dollars.pdf.
Center for International Policy. (2020, January). *Foreign Funding of Think Tanks in America* https://static.wixstatic.com/ugd/3ba8a14f06e99f35d4485b801f8dbfe33b6a3f.pdf.
Chan, J. Clara. (2022, November 18). "How Food Influencers Sharpen Their Brands: Print Cookbooks." *Hollywood Reporter* https://www.hollywoodreporter.com/business/digital/how-food-influencers-sharpening-their-brands-print-cookbooks-1235264296/.
Chandler, Raymond. (1949). *The Little Sister*. New York: Houghton Mifflin.
Charon, Jean-Marie. (2018, March 15). "Les journalistes en France en 2018: Moins nombreux, plus de femmes et plus précaires." *The Conversation* https://theconversation.com/les-journalistes-en-france-en-2018-moins-nombreux-plus-de-femmes-et-plus-precaires-93167.
Chartier, Roger. (1989). "Texts, Printings, Readings." *The New Cultural History*. Ed. Lynn Hunt. Berkeley: University of California Press. 154–75.
Chartier, Roger. (2004). "Languages, Books and Reading from the Printed Word to the Digital Text." Trans. Teresa Lavender Fagan. *Critical Inquiry* 31, no. 1: 133–52.
Chartier, Roger. (2005). "Crossing Borders in Early Modern Europe: Sociology of Texts and Literature." Trans. Maurice Elton. *Book History* 8: 37–50.
Chatignoux, Edouard, Amélie Gabet, Elodie Moutengou, Philippe Pirad, Yvon Motreff, Christophe Bonaldi, and Valérie Olié. (2018). "The 2015 and 2016 Terrorist Attacks in France: Was There a Short-Term Impact on Hospitalizations for Cardiovascular Disease?" *Clinical Epidemiology* 10: 413–19.
Chatterjee, Sumeet and Lawrence White. (2020, June 3). "HSBC and StanChart Back China Security Law for Hong Kong." *Reuters* https://www.reuters.com/article/us-hongkong-protests-hsbc-hldg-idUSKBN23A1ZO.
Cheruiyot, David. (2021). "The (Other) Anglophone Problem: Charting the Development of a Journalism Subfield." *African Journalism Studies* 42, no. 2: 94–105.
Chidester, Phillip J. (2009) ""The Toy Store of Life": Myth, Sport and the Mediated Reconstruction of the American Hero in the Shadow of the September 11th Terrorist Attacks." *Southern Communication Journal* 74, no. 4: 352–72.

Chu, Hyon S. (2016, November 19). "Clickbait, the Attention Economy, and the End of Journalism." *Medium* https://medium.com/@hyonschu/clickbait-the-attention-economy-and-the-end-of-journalism-c4f16d2c447d.

Churchill, Winston. (1920, February 8). "Zionism versus Bolshevism: A Struggle for the Soul of the Jewish People." *Illustrated Sunday Herald*: 5.

Churchill, Winston. (1946, March 5). "The Sinews of Peace ('Iron Curtain Speech')." https://winstonchurchill.org/resources/speeches/1946-1963-elder-statesman/the-sinews-of-peace/.

CIA. (1974). *A Study of Climatological Research as it Pertains to Intelligence Problems* http://www.climatechangefacts.info/ClimateChangeDocuments/CIA%20ClimateCoolingReport1974.pdf.

Clark, Alan. (1999, September 8). "Why Journalists Disgust Me." *Independent* https://www.independent.co.uk/arts-entertainment/why-journalists-disgust-me-1117267.html.

Clark, Duncan. (2011, September 8). "Google Discloses Carbon Footprint for First Time." *Guardian* http://www.guardian.co.uk/environment/2011/sep/08/google-carbon-footprint.

Clark, Jessica and Bob McChesney. (2001, September 24). "Nattering Networks: How Mass Media Fails Democracy." *lip*.

Climate Nexus. (2016). *How The Wall Street Journal Opinion Section Presents Climate Change* https://static1.squarespace.com/static/534ec657e4b03c887dde2641/t/575f6edd20c647ff95c170a0/1465872094069/FINALCNWSJwhitepaper-0613.pdf.

Coan, Travis G., Constantine Boussalis, John Cook, and Mirjam O. Nanko. (2021). "Computer-Assisted Classification of Contrarian Claims About Climate Change." *Scientific Reports/Nature Portfolio* 11: 2230.

Cockroft, Steph and Sam Tonkin. (2015, November 18). "'Aux armes, citoyens!'." *Daily Mail* https://www.dailymail.co.uk/news/article-3323408/Aux-armes-citoyens-Fan-s-video-shows-incredibly-emotional-Wembley-moment-English-French-supporters-joined-sing-La-Marseillaise-tribute-victims-Paris-attacks.html.

Coddington, Mark. (2015). "The Wall Became a Curtain: Revisiting Journalism's News-Business Boundary." *Boundaries of Journalism: Professionalism, Practices and Participation*. Eds. Matt Carlson and Seth C. Lewis. London: Routledge. 67–82.

Coffee-man. (2016). "The Case of the Coffee-men of London and Westminster. Or, an Account of the Impositions and Abuses, put upon Them and the whole Town, by the present set of News-writers. With the Scheme of the Coffee-men for setting up News-Papers of their own; and some account of their Proceedings thereupon. By a coffee-man." *Eighteenth-Century Coffee-House Culture Volume 2: The Eighteenth-Century Satire*. Ed. Markman Ellis. Abingdon: Routledge. 169–232.

Cohen, Lizabeth. (1989). "Encountering Mass Culture at the Grassroots: The Experience of Chicago Workers in the 1920s." *American Quarterly* 41, no. 1: 6–33.

Collins, Luke. (2008). "YouTube Generation No Match for the Man." *Engineering & Technology* 3, no. 9: 40–41.

Commager, Henry Steele. (1974). *The American Mind: An Interpretation of American Thought and Character since the 1880's*. New Haven, CT: Yale University Press.

Commission on the Future of Women's Sport. (2010). *Prime Time: The Case for Commercial Investment in Women's Sport*. London: Women's Sport and Fitness Foundation.

Comstock, George. (1989). "Violence." *International Encyclopedia of Communications Vol. 4*. Eds. Erik Barnouw, George Gerbner, Larry Gross, Wilbur Schramm, and Tobia L. Worth. New York: Oxford University Press. 289–94.
Comstock, George and Erica Scharrer. (1999). *Television: What's On, Who's Watching, and What It Means*. San Diego, CA: Academic Press.
Conn, David. (2017). *The Fall of the House of FIFA: The Multimillion-Dollar Corruption at the Heart of Global Soccer*. New York: Nation Books.
Conway, Ryan and Carl Anka with Roshane Thomas. (2020, June 28). "Why are Football Crowds so White?" *The Athletic* https://theathletic.com/1876499/2020/06/28/football-crowds-supportersdiversity-fans-ethnicity/.
Cook, Chris. (2015, February 19). "More *Telegraph* Writers Voice Concern." *BBC News* https://www.bbc.co.uk/news/health-31529682.
Cook, Philip and Conrad Heilmann. (2013). "Two Types of Self-Censorship: Public and Private." *Political Studies* 61, no. 1: 178–96.
Cooky, Cheryl and Dunja Antunovic. (2022). *Serving Equality: Feminism, Media, and Women's Sports*. New York: Peter Lang.
Cooky, Cheryl, LaToya D. Council, Maria A. Mears, and Michael A. Messner. (2021). "One and Done: The Long Eclipse of Women's Televised Sports, 1989-2019." *Communication and Sport* 9, no. 3: 347–71.
Cooky, Cheryl, Michael A. Messner, and Michela Musto. (2015). ""It's Dude Time!": A Quarter Century of Excluding Women's Sports in Televised News and Highlight Shows." *Communication & Sport* 3, no. 3: 261–87.
Council of Europe. (2019). *Democracy at Risk: Threats and Attacks Against Media Freedom in Europe* https://rm.coe.int/annual-report-2018-democracy-in-danger-threats-and-attacks-media-freed/1680926453.
Council of Europe. (2020, July). *Gender Equality in Media* https://rm.coe.int/prems-064620-gbr-2573-gender-equality-in-media/16809f0342.
Council of Europe. (2022, April). *Freedom of Expression in 2021* https://rm.coe.int/freedom-of-expression-2021-en/1680a6525e.
Cowley, Jason. (1999, March 5). "Kicked into Touch." *New Statesman* https://web.archive.org/web/20110605233504/http://www.newstatesman.com/199903050048.
Cox, Neville. (2016). "The Freedom to Publish 'Irreligious' Cartoons." *Human Rights Law Review* 16: 195–221.
Crabb, Lauren A. H. (2018). "Debating the Success of Carbon-Offsetting Projects at Sports Mega-Events. A Case from the 2014 FIFA World Cup." *Journal of Sustainable Forestry* 3, no. 2: 178–96.
Crispin, Shawn W. (2015). "Drawing the Line: Cartoonists Under Threat." *Committee to Protect Journalists* https://cpj.org/reports/2015/05/drawing-the-line-cartoonists-under-threat-free-expression-zunar-charlie-hebdo.php.
Cruz López, Julieta. (2021). "Estudios sobre periodismo y periodistas gastronómicos: Cuando las miradas académicas se sientan a la mesa." *Revista Iberoamericana de Comunicación* 41: 117–61.
Curran, James. (2002). "Media and the Making of British Society, c. 1700-2000." *Media History* 8, no. 2: 135–54.
Cushion, Stephen and Justin Lewis. (2017). "Impartiality, Statistical Tit-for-Tats and the Construction of Balance: UK Television News Reporting of the 2016 EU Referendum Campaign." *European Journal of Communication* 32, no. 3: 208–23.
Cyran, Olivier. (2013, December 5). ""«CHARLIE HEBDO», PAS RACISTE ? SI VOUS LE DITES…" *Article 11* https://www.article11.info/?Charlie-Hebdo-pas-raciste-Si-vous.

Czitrom, Daniel. (1982). *Media and the American Mind: From Morse to McLuhan.* Chapel Hill: University of North Carolina Press.

D'Vorkin, Lewis. (2012, May 2). "Sustainable Journalism." *Forbes* http://www.forbes.com/forbes/2012/0521/brief-word-entrepreneur-digital-sustainable-journalism-lewis-dvorkin.html.

Daley, Janet. (2023, December 2). "The *Telegraph*'s Proposed Takeover by a Foreign State Must Not be Allowed to Happen." *Telegraph* https://www.msn.com/en-us/money/companies/the-telegraph-s-proposed-takeover-by-a-foreign-state-must-not-be-allowed-to-happen/ar-AA1kTlSG.

da Silva, Marcelo Cozzensa, Anaclaudia Gastal Fassa, and David Kriebel. (2006). "Minor Psychiatric Disorders Among Brazilian Ragpickers: A Cross-Sectional Study." *Environmental Health* 5, no. 17 http://www.ncbi.nlm.nih.gov/pmc/articles/PMC1482695/.

Dabashi, Hamid. (2013, January 15). "Can Non-Europeans Think?" *Al Jazeera* http://www.aljazeera.com/indepth/opinion/2013/01/2013114142638797542.html.

Dabhoiwala, Fara. (2022). "Inventing Free Speech: Politics, Liberty and Print in Eighteenth-Century England." *Past & Present* 257, no. Supplement 16: 39–74.

Dabhoiwala, Fara. (2023). "Liberty, Slavery, and Biography: The Hidden Shapes of Free Speech." *Journal of British Studies* 62, no. 1: 104–31.

Danford, Natalie. (2005, March 21). "Video Made the Cookbook Star." *Publishers Weekly*: 24–26.

Danjon, Alexis. (2022, September 29). "L'amour immodéré des footballeurs pour les jets privés, dévastateur pour le climat." *L'Équipe* https://www.lequipe.fr/Football/Article/L-amour-immodere-des-footballeurs-pour-les-jets-prives-devastateur-pour-le-climat/1356653.

Darcy, Oliver. (2023, June 2). "Journalists at the Nation's Largest Newspaper Chain Are Walking Off the Job in a Showdown with its CEO." *CNN* https://edition.cnn.com/2023/06/01/media/gannett-strike-reliable-sources/index.html.

Daston, Lorraine and Peter Galison. (2007). *Objectivity.* New York: Zone Books.

Daum, Evan and Jay Scherer. (2018). "Changing Work Routines and Labour Practices of Sports Journalists in the Digital Era: A Case Study of Postmedia." *Media, Culture & Society* 40, no. 4: 551–66.

David, Prabu, Jung-Hyun Kim, Jared S. Brickman, Weina Ran, and Christine M. Curtis. (2015). "Mobile Phone Distraction While Studying." *New Media & Society* 17, no. 10: 1661–679.

Davidson, Cathy N. (1989). "Introduction: Toward a History of Books and Readers." *Reading in America: Literature and Social History.* Ed. Cathy N. Davidson. Baltimore, MD: Johns Hopkins University Press. 1–26.

Davidson, Donald. (1996). "The Folly of Trying to Define Truth." *Journal of Philosophy* 93, no. 6: 263–78.

De Cremer, David and Garry Kasparov. (2021, March 18). "AI Should Augment Human Intelligence, Not Replace It." *Harvard Business Review* https://hbr.org/2021/03/ai-should-augment-human-intelligence-not-replace-it.

De Freitas, Delphine. (2022, December 5). "Angelterre-France: Le jour où Wembley a etonné une émouvante "Marseillaise"." *TF1* https://techg.afphila.com/sport/football-coupe-du-monde-angleterre-france-le-jour-ou-le-stade-de-wembley-a-entonne-une-emouvante-hymne-marseillaise-2240862.html.

Delgado, Carla. (2022, February 17). "You May Need to Read Dozens of Books Each Year to Offset That New E-Reader." *Popular Science* https://www.popsci.com/environment/books-ereader-sustainability/.

del Palacio Montiel, Celia, ed. (2015). *Violencia y periodismo regional*. Mexico City: Juan Pablos.

Dembicki, Geoff. (2022). *The Petroleum Papers: Inside the Far-Right Conspiracy to Cover Up Climate Change*. Vancouver: Greystone Books.

de Nebrija, Antonio. (2016). "On Language and Empire: The Prologue to *Grammar of the Castilian Language* (1492)." Trans. Magalí Armillas-Tiseyra. *PMLA* 131, no. 1: 197–208.

de Pedro, Juan Pedro. (1999). "Democracy and Cultural Difference in the Spanish Constitution of 1978." *Democracy and Ethnography: Constructing Identities in Multicultural Liberal States*. Ed. Carol J. Greenhouse with Roshanak Kheshti. Albany: State University of New York Press. 61–80.

Della Rosa, Francesco, Brubo Dongay, Jérôme Van Rothem, Bruno Farah, and Atul Pathak. (2016). "We Are Charlie: Emotional Stress from "Charlie Hebdo Attack" Extensively Relayed by Media Increases the Risk of Cardiac Events." *Archives of Cardiovascular Diseases Supplements* 8: 2.

de Menezes, Jack. (2015, November 28). "Arsenal Criticized for Taking 'Ridiculous, Ludicrous and Farcical' 14-Minute Plane Flight to Norwich." *Independent* https://www.independent.co.uk/sport/football/premier-league/arsenal-criticised-for-taking-ridiculous-14-minute-plane-flight-to-norwich-a6752486.html.

Demopoulos, Alaina. (2023, April 24). "The Digital Graveyard: *BuzzFeed News* Joins Sites Hanging on in Eerie Afterlife." *Guardian* https://www.theguardian.com/media/2023/apr/24/buzzfeed-news-digital-graveyard-gawker-toast.

de Tocqueville, Alexis. (2000). *Democracy in America*. New York: Harper Perennial Modern Classics.

Devi, Kuruva Syamala, Arza V. V. S. Swamy, and Ravuri Hema Krishna. (2014). "Studies on the Solid Waste Collection by Rag Pickers at Greater Hyderabad Municipal Corporation, India." *International Research Journal of Environment Sciences* 3, no. 1: 13–22.

Dewhirst, Timothy and Amy Hunter. (2002). "Tobacco Sponsorship of Formula One and CART Auto Racing: Tobacco Brand Exposure and Enhanced Symbolic Imagery Through Co-Sponsors' Third Party Advertising." *Tobacco Control* 11: 146–50.

Díaz-Campo, Jesús and Francisco Segado-Boj. (2015). "Journalism Ethics in a Digital Environment: How Journalistic Codes of Ethics Have Been Adapted to the Internet and ICTs in Countries Around the World." *Telematics and Informatics* 32, no. 4: 735–44.

Dickler, Jessica. (2022, November 12). "The Top 10 Most-Regretted College Majors—And the Degrees Graduates Wished They Had Pursued Instead." *CNBC* https://www.cnbc.com/2022/11/12/the-top-10-most-regretted-college-majors.html.

Dimitriadis, Dimitris, Joey Grostern, and Sam Bright. (2023, August 16). "How Shell Used a 'Granfluencer' to Promote its Brand." *Desmog* https://www.desmog.com/2023/08/15/shell-granfluencer-promote-fossil-fuels-greenwash/.

Dinerstein, Joel. (2006). "Technology and Its Discontents: On the Verge of the Posthuman." *American Quarterly* 58, no. 3: 569–95.

Dissat, Cristina. (2023, July 21). "The Women's World Cup and the Rise of Women Sports Journalists in Brazil." Trans. Priscila Brito. *International Journalists' Network* https://ijnet.org/en/story/womens-world-cup-and-rise-women-sports-journalists-brazil.

Dmowski, Seweryn. (2015). "Football Sites of Memory in the Eastern Bloc 1945-1991." *European Football and Collective Memory*. Eds. Wolfram Pyta and Nils Havermann. Basingstoke: Palgrave Macmillan. 171–84.

Dockery, Lawrence. (2023, January 1). "Top 20 Biggest Soccer Attendances in USA During 2022." *World Soccer Talk* https://worldsoccertalk.com/news/top-20-biggest-soccer-attendances-in-usa-during-2022-20221231-WST-413598.html.

Dodd, Claire. (2007, April 9). "Carbon Copy." *Guardian* http://www.theguardian.com/environment/2007/apr/09/travelsenvironmentalimpact.mondaymediasection.

Dodman, Benjamin. (2021, March 26). "Harassed and Belittled, France's Female Sports Journalists Take on Bastion of Sexism." *France 24* https://www.france24.com/en/sport/20210326-harassed-and-belittled-france-s-female-sports-journalists-take-on-bastion-of-sexism.

Doherty, Carroll and Jocelyn Kiley. (2023, March 14). *A Look Back at How Fear and False Beliefs Bolstered U.S. Public Support for War in Iraq.* Pew Research Center https://www.pewresearch.org/politics/2023/03/14/a-look-back-at-how-fear-and-false-beliefs-bolstered-u-s-public-support-for-war-in-iraq/.

Dotson, Devin M., Susan K. Jacobson, Lynda Lee Kaid, and J. Stuart Carlton. (2012). "Media Coverage of Climate Change in Chile: A Content Analysis of Conservative and Liberal Newspapers." *Environmental Communication* 6, no. 1: 64–81.

Douglas, Omega. (2022). "The Media Diversity and Inclusion Paradox: Experiences of Black and Brown Journalists in Mainstream British News Institutions." *Journalism: Theory, Practice and Criticism* 23, no. 10: 2096–113.

Douglas, Susan J. (2020). *Inventing American Broadcasting 1899-1922*. Baltimore, MD: The Johns Hopkins University Press.

Downie, Leonard, Jr. (2023, January 30). "Newsrooms That Move Beyond 'Objectivity' Can Build Trust." *Washington Post* https://www.washingtonpost.com/opinions/2023/01/30/newsrooms-news-reporting-objectivity-diversity/.

Downie, Leonard, Jr. and Andrew Heyward with Rian Bosse, Stephen Kilar, Kristina Vera-Phillips, and Autriya Maneshni. (2023). *Beyond Objectivity: Producing Trustworthy News in Today's Newsrooms*. Stanton Foundation/Walter Cronkite School of Journalism https://cronkitenewslab.com/wp-content/uploads/2023/01/Beyond-Objectivity-Report-3.pdf.

Doyle, Jason P., Yiran Su, and Thilo Kunkel. (2022). "Athlete Branding via Social Media: Examining the Factors Influencing Consumer Engagement on Instagram." *European Sport Management Quarterly* 22, no. 4: 506–26.

Doyle, Julie. (2011). "Where Has All the Oil Gone? BP Branding and the Discursive Elimination of Climate Change Risk." *Culture, Environment and Eco-Politics*. Eds. Nick Heffernan and David A. Wragg. Newcastle upon Tyne: Cambridge Scholars Press. 200–25.

Doyle, Terrence. (2020, June 30). "Soccer Commentary is Full of Coded Racism." *FiveThirtyEight* https://fivethirtyeight.com/features/soccer-commentary-is-full-of-coded-racism/.

Dragomir, Marius. (2018). "Control the Money, Control the Media: How Government Uses Funding to Keep Media in Line." *Journalism: Theory, Practice and Criticism* 19, no. 8: 1131–148.

Dubenskij, Charlotte. (2014, June 18). "World War One: How Radio Crackled into Life in Conflict." *BBC News* https://www.bbc.com/news/uk-wales-27894944.

Dubois, Laurent. (2013, March). "The Blood of the Impure." *Africa is a Country* https://africasacountry.com/2013/03/the-blood-of-the-impure.

Duffy, Andrew and Yang Yuhong Ashley. (2012). "Bread and Circuses: Food Meets Politics in the Singapore Media." *Journalism Practice* 6, no. 1: 59–74.

Dunaway, Finis. (2015). *Seeing Green: The Use and Abuse of American Environmental Images*. Chicago: University of Chicago Press.
Dunlap, Riley E. and Peter J. Jacques. (2013). "Climate Change Denial Books and Conservative Think Tanks: Exploring the Connection." *American Behavioral Scientist* 57, no. 6: 699–731.
Durkheim, Émile. (1961). "The Solidarity of Occupational Groups." *Theories of Society: Foundations of Modern Sociological Theory. Volume I*. Ed. Talcott Parsons, Edward Shils, Kaspar D. Naegle, and Jesse R. Pitts. New York: Free Press of Glencoe. 356–63.
Durut, Matthieu. (2013, May 20). "Big data: Quand le mathématicien devient sexy." *Le Monde* http://archives.lesclesdedemain.lemonde.fr/organisations/big-data-quand-le-statisticien-devient-sexya-12-1769.html.
Duzán, Maria Jimena. (1994). Death Beat: A Colombian Journalist's Life Inside the Cocaine Trade. Trans. Peter Eisner. New York: Harper Collins.
Dyer-Witheford, Nick, Atle Mikkola Kjøsen, and James Steinhoff. (2019). *Inhuman Power: Artificial Intelligence and the Future of Capitalism*. London: Pluto.
Dyson, Esther, George Gilder, George Keyworth, and Alvin Toffler. (1994). *Cyberspace and the American Dream: A Magna Carta for the Knowledge Age*. Version 1.2. Progress and Freedom Foundation pff.org/issues-pubs/futureinsights/fi1.2magnacarta.html.
Eagleton, Terry. (1990). *The Ideology of the Aesthetic*. Oxford: Blackwell.
Eagleton, Terry. (2005). *The Function of Criticism*. London: Verso.
Eagleton, Terry. (2006). "On Telling the Truth." *Socialist Register* 42: 269–85.
Eagleton, Terry. (2011, November 28). "Leveson Inquiry: The Frontiers of Privacy." *Guardian* https://www.theguardian.com/commentisfree/2011/nov/28/leveson-inquiry-frontiers-of-privacy.
Earns-Branaman, Jesse Owen. (2016). *Journalism and the Philosophy of Truth: Beyond Objectivity and Balance*. London: Routledge.
Eco, Umberto. (1987). *Travels in Hyperreality*. Trans. William Weaver. London: Picador.
Eco, Umberto. (1995). "Crítica el periodismo." Trans. Adriana Guadarrama. *L'Unitá* https://studylib.es/doc/4795117/eco--umberto--1995-.-%E2%80%9Ccr%C3%ADtica-al-periodismo%E2%80%9D--roma.
Eco, Umberto. (2020). *How to Spot a Fascist*. Trans. Richard Dixon and Alastair McEwen. New York: Vintage.
Edelman, Daniel J. (1983). "Managing the Public Relations Firm in the 21st Century." *Public Relations Review* 9, no. 3: 3–10.
Edelman, Richard. (2019, August 2). "PR in the Public Interest." *Edelman* https://www.edelman.com/insights/pr-in-the-public-interest.
Edwards, Julia B., Alan C. McKinnon, and Sharon L. Cullinane. (2009). *Comparing CO_2 Emissions for Conventional and Online Book Retailing Channels in the UK*. Edinburgh: Heriot-Watt University.
Ehrenreich, Barbara. (2006). *Bait and Switch: The (Futile) Pursuit of the American Dream*. New York: Henry Holt.
Eichler, Jan. (2023). *Terrorism in Contemporary France: A Vicious Circle of Violence*. Cham: Springer.
Eide, Elisabeth. (2010). "Conflicting Readings: The Cartoon Crisis Seen from Pakistan." *Freedom of the Press: On Censorship, Self-Censorship, and Press Ethics*. Ed. Søren Dosenrode. Baden-Baden: Nomos. 126–48.

Eisenstein, Elizabeth L. (2005). *The Printing Revolution in Early Modern Europe*, 2nd ed. Cambridge: Cambridge University Press.

Eko, Lyombe. (2019). *The Charlie Hebdo Affair and Comparative Journalistic Cultures: Human Rights Versus Religious Rights*. Cham: Palgrave Macmillan.

Elberse, Anita. (2013). *Blockbusters: Hit-Making, Risk-Taking, and the Big Business of Entertainment*. New York: Henry Holt.

El Hissy, Maha. (2013). "Veiled Bodies, Vile Speech: Islam, the Carnivalesque and the Politics of Profanation." *Islam and the Politics of Culture in Europe: Memory, Aesthetics, Art*. Eds. Frank Peter, Sarah Dornhof, and Elena Argita. Bielefeld: Transcript. 127–42.

Eller, Claudia. (2020, June 3). "Reflecting Diverse Voices Starts in the Newsroom." *Variety* https://variety.com/2020/voices/opinion/diversity-in-the-newsroom-column-1234623583/.

Elliott, Larry. (2014, March 23). "How F1 and Champagne Might Help Us to Solve Global Warming." *Guardian* http://www.theguardian.com/business/2014/mar/23/solve-global-warming-pension-champagne-formula-1.

Elliott, Stuart. (2014, August 17). "Edelman P. R. Firm Acts to Correct Faux Pas." *New York Times* http://www.nytimes.com/2014/08/18/business/media/edelman-pr-firm-is-taking-steps-to-address-faux-pas-.html?r=1.

Eloundou, Tyna, Sam Manning, Pamela Mishkin, and Daniel Rock. (2023). *GPTs are GPTs: An Early Look at the Labor Market Impact Potential of Large Language Models*. Working Paper https://arxiv.org/pdf/2303.10130.pdf.

El Rhazoui, Zineb. (2015, January 9). "Zineb de «Charlie Hebdo»: «Il arrivait que l'on dise aux collègues: "Je vous aime"»." *Le Monde* https://www.lemonde.fr/societe/article/2015/01/09/zineb-el-rhazoui-de-charlie-hebdo-il-arrivait-que-l-on-dise-aux-collegues-je-vous-aime45525543224.html.

Emmison, Mike. (1983). "'The Economy': Its Emergence in Media Discourse." *Language, Image, Media*. Eds. Howard Davis and Paul Walton. Oxford: Basil Blackwell. 139–55.

Emmison, Mike and Alec McHoul. (1987). "Drawing on the Economy: Cartoon Discourse and the Production of a Category." *Cultural Studies* 1, no. 1: 93–111.

Engel, Leonard. (1953, July 12). "The Weather is Really Changing." *New York Times*: SM7.

Engels, Frederick. (2003). *Socialism: Utopian and Scientific*. Trans. Edward Aveling. Marxists Internet Archive http://www.marxists.org/archive/marx/works/1880/soc-utop/index.html.

England, Phil. (2012, April 25). "#London2012: An Olympian Exercise in Corporate Greenwashing." *Ceasefire* https://ceasefiremagazine.co.uk/london2012-olympian-exercise-corporate-greenwashing/.

Englehardt, Tom. (2014, January 21). "The Rise of the Reader." *TomDispatch* http://www.tomdispatch.com/blog/175796/tomgram%3Aengelhardt,theriseofthereader/.

English, Peter. (2016). "Twitter's Diffusion in Sports Journalism: Role Models, Laggards and Followers of the Social Media Innovation." *New Media & Society* 18, no. 3: 484–501.

Enten, Harry. (2022, December 12). "The US May Have Lost in the World Cup, But Soccer is More Popular Than Ever in America." *CNN* https://edition.cnn.com/2022/12/12/football/soccer-popularity-us-world-cup-spt-intl/index.html.

Environmental Investigation Agency. (2021). *On Thin Ice: How the NHL is Cheating the Climate* https://www.exposingclimatepollution.org/on-thin-ice.

Epstein, Edward J. (1974). *News from Nowhere: Television and the News.* New York: Vintage Books.

Ervine, Jonathan. (2019). *Humour in Contemporary France: Controversy, Consensus, and Contradictions.* Liverpool: Liverpool University Press.

Esser, Doug. (2015, July 15). "Why Soccer is Un-American and 10 Ways to Fix It." *Seattle Times* https://www.seattletimes.com/sports/sounders/take-2-why-soccer-is-un-american-and-10-ways-to-fix-it/.

Evans, Robert. (2012, March 8). "Islamic States, Africans Walk Out on UN Gay Panel." *Reuters Africa* http://af.reuters.com/article/topNews/idAFJOE82702T20120308?sp=true.

Eyck, Toby A. Ten. (2000). "The Marginalization of Food Safety Issues: An Interpretative Approach to Mass Media Coverage." *Journal of Applied Communications* 84, no. 2: 29–47.

Fakazis, Elizabeth and Elfriede Fürsich, eds. (2023). *The Political Relevance of Food Media: Beyond Reviews and Recipes.* London: Routledge.

Fattorini, Joseph. (1994). "Food Journalism: A Medium for Conflict?" *British Food Journal* 96, no. 10: 24–28.

Fears, Robin, Claudia Canales, Volker ter Meulen, and Joachim von Braun. (2019). "Transforming Food Systems to Deliver Healthy, Sustainable Diets—The View from the World's Science Academies." *The Lancet Planetary Health* 3, no. 4: E163–65.

Fédération Internationale de l'Automobile. (2022). *FIA Environmental Strategy 2020–2030*, 4th ed. https://www.fia.com/sites/default/files/fia_environmental_strategy_v4_web.pdf.

Ferré, Jean-Luc. (2020, January 16). "Les contraintes climatiques obligent le monde du sport à se repenser." *La Croix* https://www.la-croix.com/Sport/contraintes-climatiques-obligent-monde-sport-repenser-2020-01-16-1201072242.

Ferreira, Lenne. (2021, December 9). "Em 2022, descolonizar o jornalismo será o caminho para fortalecer narrativas atentas aos direitos humanos." *Medium* https://medium.com/o-jornalismo-no-brasil-em-2022/em-2022-descolonizar-o-jornalismo-ser%C3%A1-o-caminho-para-fortalecer-narrativas-atentas-aos-direitos-f96a065e5d3.

Ferrier, Michelle. (2019). "Attacks and Harassment: The Impact on Female Journalists and Their Reporting." *Troll-Busters and International Women's Media Foundation* https://16dayscampaign.org/wp-content/uploads/2019/03/Attacks-and-Harassment-PDF.pdf.

Ferrucci, Patrick. (2022). "Joining the Team: Metajournalistic Discourse, Paradigm Repair, the *Athletic* and Sports Journalism Practice." *Journalism Practice*, 16, no. 10: 2064–082.

Fians, Guilherme. (2022, March 18). "Prefigurative Politics." *Open Encyclopedia of Anthropology* https://www.anthroencyclopedia.com/entry/prefigurative-politics.

Fielding, Victoria. (2022, March 24). "Is News Corp Following Through on its Climate Change Backflip? Analysis of its Flood Coverage." *The Conversation* https://theconversation.com/is-news-corp-following-through-on-its-climate-change-backflip-my-analysis-of-its-flood-coverage-suggests-not-179468.

FIFA. (2019). *2018 FIFA World Cup Russia™ Sustainability Report* https://img.fifa.com/image/upload/ya7pgcyslxpzlqmjkykg.pdf.

Fifka, Matthias S. and Johannes Jäger. (2020). "CSR in Professional European Football: An Integrative Framework." *Soccer & Society* 21, no. 1: 61–78.

Fine, Ben and Ellen Leopold. (1993). *The World of Consumption.* London: Routledge.

Finkelstein, Joanne. (1989). *Dining Out: A Sociology of Modern Manners.* New York: New York University Press.

Finley, Klint. (2015, March 6). "In the Future, Robots Will Write News That's All About You." *Wired* https://www.wired.com/2015/03/future-news-robots-writing-audiences-one/.

Fish, Stanley. (1994). *There's No Such Thing as Free Speech, and It's a Good Thing, Too.* New York: Oxford University Press.

Fisher, Allison and Ted MacDonald. (2023, January 5). "National TV News Largely Ignores the Link Between Climate Change and the Deluge Devastating California." *Media Matters for America* https://www.mediamatters.org/broadcast-networks/national-tv-news-largely-ignores-link-between-climate-change-and-deluge.

Fisher, Allison, Evlondo Cooper, and Ilana Berger. (2023, July 20). "Right-Wing Media Deny Climate Change in Face of Deadly and Record-Breaking Extreme Weather Events." *Media Matters for America* https://www.mediamatters.org/climate-deniers/right-wing-media-deny-climate-change-face-deadly-and-record-breaking-extreme.

Fleming, James Rodger. (1998). *Historical Perspectives on Climate Change.* New York: Oxford University Press.

Fletcher, Chloe and Jigna Chandaria. (2020, October). *The Energy Footprint of BBC Radio Services: Now and in the Future.* Research and Development White Paper WHP 393 https://downloads.bbc.co.uk/rd/pubs/whp/whp-pdf-files/WHP393.pdf.

Flynn, Daniel J. (2014, June 12). "We Aren't the World: Why America Resists Soccer Imperialism." *Breitbart* https://www.breitbart.com/sports/2014/06/12/why-america-thwarts-the-soccer-imperialists/.

Flynn, Kerry. (2020, June 5). "Journalists of Color Are Fed Up and Speaking Out." *CNN* https://edition.cnn.com/2020/06/05/media/journalists-diversity/index.html.

Fogel, Danil Mark. (1994). "'Schindler's List' in Novel and Film: Exponential Conversion." *Historical Journal of Film, Radio and Television* 14, no. 3: 315–20.

Földesi, Gyöngyi Szabó. (2014). "The Impact of the Global Economic Crisis on Sport." *Physical Culture and Sport* 53: 22–30.

Food and Agriculture Organization of the United Nations, International Fund for Agricultural Development, UNICEF, World Food Programme, and World Health Organization. (2020). *The State of Food Security and Nutrition in the World* https://www.unicef.org/media/72676/file/SOFI-2020-full-report.pdf.

Ford, Henry. (1929). *My Philosophy of Industry: An Authorized Interview by Ray Leone Faurote.* New York: Coward-McCann.

Ford, Peter. (2002, June 19). "In Business of Sport, US One of Less-Free Markets." *Christian Science Monitor* https://www.csmonitor.com/2002/0619/p01s03-wogn.html.

Fordham, Josh. (2020, February 8). "Ranking Premier League Owners by Their Wealth—How Much are Liverpool, Chelsea and Manchester United's Shareholders are [*sic.*] Worth?" *talkSPORT* https://talksport.com/football/666456/ranking-premier-league-owners-wealth-liverpoolchelsea-manchester-united/.

Forman-Katz, Naomi and Mark Jurkowitz. (2022, July 13). *U.S. Journalists Differ from the Public in Their Views of 'Bothsidesism' in Journalism.* Pew Research Center https://www.pewresearch.org/short-reads/2022/07/13/u-s-journalists-differ-from-the-public-in-their-views-of-bothsidesism-in-journalism/.

Forman-Katz, Naomi. (2023, February 13). *For World Radio Day, Key Facts About Radio Listeners and the Radio Industry in the U.S.* Pew Research Center https://www.pewresearch.org/fact-tank/2023/02/13/for-world-radio-day-key-facts-about-radio-listeners-and-the-radio-industry-in-the-u-s/.

Forsskåll, Peter. (n.d.). "Thoughts on Civil Liberty." Trans. Theresa McGrane-Langvik, Maria Lindstedt, Agnes Jansson, Gunilla Jonsson, Thomas von Vegesack, Helena Jäderblom, and Gunnar Persson. *Peter Forsskåll* http://www.peterforsskal.com/thetext.html.

Foucault, Michel. (2007). The Politics of Truth. Trans. Lysa Hochroth and Catherine Porter. Ed. Sylvère Lotringer. Los Angeles, CA: Semiotext(e).

Foucault, Michel. (2008). *The Birth of Biopolitics: Lectures at the Collège de France, 1978-79*. Trans. Graham Burchell. Ed. Michel Senellart. Houndmills: Palgrave Macmillan.

Fourest, Caroline. (2015). *In Praise of Blasphemy: Why Charlie Hebdo is Not "Islamophobic"*. Paris: Bernard Grasset.

Foy, Simon. (2023, June 30). "HSBC Accused of Persecuting Hong Kongers Who Flee Territory." *Telegraph* https://www.telegraph.co.uk/business/2023/06/30/hsbc-accused-persecuting-dissidents-hong-kong-who-flee/.

Franklin, Bob. (2012). "The Future of Journalism: Developments and Debates." *Journalism Studies* 13, nos. 5–6: 663–81.

Franks, Suzanne and Deidre Neill. (2018). "This Sporting Life: Why so Few Women Sports Writers." *Journalism Education* 6, no. 3: 42–52.

Frazier, Mya. (2006, October 19). "Edelman Eats Humble Pie." *AdAge* http://adage.com/article/news/edelman-eats-humble-pie/112588/.

Freedman, Des. (2021). "Introduction: 'Just the Establishment'?" *Capitalism's Conscience: 200 Years of the Guardian*. Ed. Des Freedman. London: Pluto. 14–36.

French, Howard W. (2016, May 25). "The Enduring Whiteness of the American Media." *Guardian* https://www.theguardian.com/world/2016/may/25/enduring-whiteness-of-american-journalism.

Freud, Sigmund. (1930). *Civilization and Its Discontents*. Trans and Ed. Julian Strachey. London: Hogarth Press.

Freud, Sigmund. (2011). *Complete Works* https://www.holybooks.com/sigmund-freud-the-complete-works/.

Freudenberg, William R. and Violetta Muselli. (2013). "Reexamining Climate Change Debates: Scientific Disagreement or Scientific Certainty Argumentation Methods (SCAMs)?" *American Behavioral Scientist* 57, no. 6: 777–95.

Fugh-Berman, Adriane J. (2010). "The Haunting of Medical Journals: How Ghostwriting Sold "HRT"." *PLoS Medicine* 7, no. 9: e1000335.

Funk, Cary and Lee Rainie. (2015, January 29). *Public and Scientists' Views on Science and Society*. Pew Research Center http://www.pewinternet.org/2015/01/29/public-and-scientists-views-on-science-and-society/.

Fusté-Forné, Francesc and Pere Masip. (2018). "Food in Journalistic Narratives: A Methodological Design for the Study of Food-Based Contents in Daily Newspapers." International Journal of Gastronomy and Food Science 14: 14–19.

Fusté-Forné, Francesc and Pere Masip. (2020). "Food and Journalism: Storytelling About Gastronomy in Newspapers from the U.S. and Spain." Lifestyle Journalism: Social Media, Consumption and Experience. Ed. Lucía Vodanovic. London: Routledge. 129–40.

Gabler, Neal. (2013, November 1). "A Journalistic Revolution." Reuters https://www.reuters.com/article/gabler-journalism-idUKL1N0IM0ZX20131101.

Gaind, Nisha. (2016). "Most Cities Too Hot to Host 2088 Summer Olympics." Nature https://doi.org/10.1038/nature.2016.20503.

Galeano, Eduardo. (1997). *Open Veins of Latin America: Five Centuries of the Pillage of a Continent*. Trans. Cedric Belfrage. New York: Monthly Review Press.
Galeano, Eduardo. (2016, September 16). "Fútbol a sol y a sombra." *Don Patadon* http://www.don-patadon.com/2015/02/futbol-sol-y-sombra-de-eduardo-galeano.html.
Galily, Yair. (2018). "Artificial Intelligence and Sports Journalism: Is it a Sweeping Change?" *Technology in Society* 54: 47–51.
Gallego, Aina and Thomas Kurer. (2022). "Automation, Digitalization, and Artificial Intelligence in the Workplace: Implications for Political Behavior." *Annual Review of Political Science* 25: 463–84.
Gallup and Knight Foundation. (2023, January). *American Views 2022: Part 2: Trust, Media and Democracy* https://knightfoundation.org/reports/american-views-2023-part-2/.
Galtung, Johan. (1990). "Cultural Violence." *Journal of Peace Research* 27, no. 3: 291–305.
Galtung, Johan. (1995). "Prospects for Media Monitoring: Much Overdue, but Never Too Late." *Javnost—The Public* 2, no. 4: 99–105.
Gamper, Daniel. (2022). "Cartoons Go Global: Provocation, Condemnation and the Possibility of Laughter." *Philosophy and Social Criticism* 48, no. 4: 530–43.
Gans, Herbert J. (2003). *Democracy and the News*. Oxford: Oxford University Press.
Garbes, Laura. (2020, August 18). "'I Just Don't Hear It': How Hiteness Dilutes Voices of Color at Public Radio Stations." *American Prospect* https://prospect.org/culture/i-just-dont-hear-it-voices-of-color-npr-public-radio/.
Garcés Prettel, Miguel E. and Jesús Arroyave Cabrera. (2017). "Autonomía profesional y riesgos de seguridad de los periodistas en Colombia." Perfiles Latinoamericanos 49: 1–19.
García Márquez, Gabriel. (1996). *Noticia de un secuestro*. Mexico City: Editorial Diana.
Gaston, Sophia with Joseph E. Uscinski. (2018). *Out of the Shadows: Conspiracy Thinking on Immigration*. London: Henry Jackson Society/Center for Social & Political Risk.
Gaukroger, Stephen. (2012). *Objectivity: A Very Short Introduction*. New York: Oxford University Press.
Gauthier, Gilles. (1993). "In Defence of a Supposedly Outdated Notion: The Range of Application of Journalistic Objectivity." *Canadian Journal of Communication* 18, no. 4 https://cjc.utpjournals.press/doi/full/10.22230/cjc.1993v18n4a778?role=tab.
Gautney, Heather. (2022). *The New Power Elite*. New York: Oxford University Press.
Gellner, Ernest. (1988). *Plough, Sword and Book: The Structure of Human History*. Chicago: University of Chicago Press.
Gerges, Fawaz A. (2003). "Islam and Muslims in the Mind of America." *Annals of the American Academy of Political and Social Science* 588: 73–89.
Gershberg, Zac and Sean Illing. (2022). *The Paradox of Democracy: Free Speech, Open Media, and Perilous Persuasion*. Chicago: University of Chicago Press.
Gibson, Owen and Ben Quinn. (2015, November 17). "France and England Fans Sing La Marseillaise at Wembley Stadium." *Guardian* https://www.theguardian.com/world/2015/nov/17/france-england-fans-sing-la-marseillaise-wembley-stadium-paris-terror-attacks.

Giddens, Anthony. (2018, May 2). "A Magna Carta for the Digital Age." *Washington Post* https://www.washingtonpost.com/news/theworldpost/wp/2018/05/02/artificial-intelligence/.
Gillings, Mathew and Carmen Dayrell. (2023). "Climate Change in the UK Press: Examining Discourse Fluctuation Over Time." *Applied Linguistics* https://academic.oup.com/applij/advance-article/doi/10.1093/applin/amad007/7083268.
Gilmour, Rod. (2016, April 5). "Leicester City-Backed Polo Team King Power Foxes Set for Double Tilt." *Telegraph* https://www.telegraph.co.uk/polo/2016/04/05/leicester-city-backed-poloteam-king-power-foxes-set-for-double/.
Gingerich, Amanda C. and Tara T. Lineweaver. (2014). "OMG! Texting in Class = U Fail: Empirical Evidence That Text Messaging During Class Disrupts Comprehension." *Teaching of Psychology* 41, no. 1: 44–51.
Glanville, Brian. (2018, November 8). ""Infantino is as Rotten as Blatter"." *World Soccer* https://www.worldsoccer.com/world-soccer-latest/infantino-rotten-blatter-407740.
Global Witness. (2023, April). *Global Hating: How Abuse of Climate Scientists Harms Climate Action* https://www.globalwitness.org/en/campaigns/digital-threats/global-hating/.
Goddard, Peter, Piers Robinson, and Katy Parry. (2008). "Patriotism Meets Plurality: Reporting the 2003 Iraq War in the British Press." *Media, War & Conflict* 1, no. 1: 9–30.
Gohdes, Anita R. and Sabine C. Carey. (2017). "Canaries in a Gold Mine? What the Killings of Journalists Tell Us About Future Repression." *Journal of Peace Research* 54, no. 2: 157–74.
Golan, Guy. (2008). "Where is Africa?: Predicting Coverage of Africa by US Television Networks." *International Communication Gazette* 70, no. 1: 41–57.
Goldenberg, Suzanne. (2014, August 7). "Edelman Formally Declares it Will not Accept Climate Denial Campaigns." *Guardian* http://www.theguardian.com/environment/2014/aug/07/edelman-pr-climate-change-denial-campaigns.
Goldman, Michael and Rachel A. Schurman. (2000). "Closing the "Great Divide": New Social Theory on Society and Nature." *Annual Review of Sociology* 26: 563–84.
Goldstein, Luke. (2023, February 24). "Corruption at the Fifth Estate." *American Prospect* https://prospect.org/power/2023-02-24-based-corruption-fifth-estate-think-tanks/.
Gomery, Douglas. (1994). "In Search of the Cybermarket." *Wilson Quarterly* 18, no. 3: 9–17.
Gómez González, Gretchen. (2023, March 11). "AI: La nueva revolución del periodismo." *Cubaperiodistas* https://www.cubaperiodistas.cu/index.php/2023/03/ai-la-nueva-revolucion-del-periodismo/.
González de Bustamante, Celeste and Jeannine E. Relly. (2016). "Professionalism Under Threat of Violence: Journalism, Reflexivity, and the Potential for Collective Professional Autonomy in Northern Mexico." *Journalism Studies* 17, no. 6: 684–702.
Goodell, Jeff. (2011, February 3). "Who's to Blame—The 12 Politicians and Corporate Executives Most Responsible for Blocking Efforts to Halt Global Warming." *Rolling Stone*: 39–42.
Goodwin-Hill, Guy S. (2022, April 13). "Introductory Note to Memorandum of Understanding Between the Government of the United Kingdom of Great Britain and

Northern Ireland and the Government of the Republic of Rwanda." *International Legal Materials* 62: 166–70.
Google. (2023). *Environmental Report 2023* https://www.gstatic.com/gumdrop/sustainability/google-2023-environmental-report.pdf.
Gordon, Avery F. (2014). "On 'Lived Theory': An Interview with A. Sivanandan." *Race & Class* 55, no. 4: 1–7.
Gorz, André. (2013). *Capitalism, Socialism, Ecology*. Trans. Martin Chalmers. London: Verso.
Gottfried, Jeffrey, Amy Mitchell, Mark Jurkowitz, and Jacob Liedke. (2022). *Journalists Sense Turmoil in Their Industry Amid Continued Passion for Their Work* https://www.pewresearch.org/journalism/2022/06/14/journalists-give-industry-mixed-reviews-on-newsroom-diversity-lowest-marks-in-racial-and-ethnic-diversity/.
Gough, Christina. (2023, March 10). "Sports on U.S. TV—Statistics & Facts." *Statista* https://www.statista.com/topics/2113/sports-on-tv/#topicOverview.
Graber, Doris A. (2017). "Freedom of the Press: Theories and Realities." *The Oxford Handbook of Political Communication*. Eds. Kate Kenski and Kathleen Hall Jamieson. New York: Oxford University Press. 237–48.
Graedel, Thomas E., E. M. Harper, N. T. Nassar, and Barbara K. Reck. (2015). "On the Materials Basis of Modern Society." *Proceedings of the National Academy of Sciences of the United States of America* 112, no. 20: 6295–300.
Graham, Bryan Armen. (2013, February 18). "The 15 Coolest Writers You Never Knew Wrote for *Sports Illustrated*." *Sports Illustrated* https://www.si.com/extra-mustard/2013/02/18/the-15-coolest-writers-you-never-knew-wrote-for-sports-illustrated.
Graham, Caroline. (2013, May 26). "To You, James Hunt Was an F1 Playboy Who Bedded 5,000 Women. To Me, He Was Dad—Who Doted on Me…and His 300 Budgies." *Mail on Sunday* https://www.dailymail.co.uk/femail/article-2331043/James-Hunt-F1-playboy-bedded-5-000-women-To-Tom-Hunt-Dad--doted--300-budgies.html.
Gramsci, Antonio. (1978). Selections from the Prison Notebooks of Antonio Gramsci. Trans. Quentin Hoare and Geoffrey Nowell-Smith. New York: International Publishers.
Grand Rapids Institute for Information Democracy. (2005). *Violence, Soldier Deaths and Omissions*.
Greenpeace International. (2014). *Green Gadgets: Designing the Future—The Path to Greener Electronics* http://www.greenpeace.org/international/Global/international/publications/toxics/2014/Green%20Gadgets.pdf.
Greenpeace USA. (2020, May 19). *Oil in the Cloud: How Tech Companies are Helping Big Oil Profit from Climate Destruction* https://www.greenpeace.org/usa/reports/oil-in-the-cloud/.
Greenslade, Roy. (2003, February 17). "Their Master's Voice." *Guardian* https://www.theguardian.com/media/2003/feb/17/mondaymediasection.iraq.
Greenwald, Glenn. (2015, April 27). "Read the Letters and Comments of PEN Writers Protesting the *Charlie Hebdo* Award." *The Intercept* https://theintercept.com/2015/04/27/read-letters-comments-pen-writers-protesting-charlie-hebdo-award/.
Gregory, Sean with Julia Zorthian. (2023, December 5). "2023 Athlete of the Year Lionel Messi." *Time* https://time.com/6342417/athlete-of-the-year-2023-lionel-messi/.

Grimmer, Christoph G. (2017). "Pressure on Printed Press." *Digital Journalism* 5, no. 5: 607–35.
Gross, Larry, John Stuart Katz, and Jay Ruby. (1988). "Introduction: A Moral Pause." *Image Ethics: The Moral Rights of Subjects in Photographs, Film, and Television.* Eds. Larry Gross, John Stuart Katz, and Jay Ruby. New York: Oxford University Press. 3–33.
Grossman, Elizabeth. (2016) "The Body Burden: Toxics, Stresses and Biophysical Health." *The Routledge Companion to Labor and Media.* Ed. Richard Maxwell. New York: Routledge. 65–77.
Grossman, Lev. (2006, December 13). "*Time*'s Person of the Year: You." *Time* http://content.time.com/time/magazine/article/0,9171,1570810,00.html.
Grundmann, Reiner and Mike Scott. (2014). "Disputed Climate Science in the Media: Do Countries Matter?" *Public Understanding of Science* 23, no. 2: 220–35.
Guest, Peter. (2022, June 17). "How Much Environmental Damage Are Top Footballers Causing?" *Football Predictions* https://footballpredictions.net/blog/eco-friendly-footballers.
Gulyas, Agnes and David Baines, eds. (2020). *The Routledge Companion to Local Media and Journalism.* Abingdon: Routledge.
Gunther, Marc. (2014, August 19). "Climate Changeable: Waffling Lands PR Firm Edelman in Hot Water." *Guardian* http://www.theguardian.com/sustainable-business/2014/aug/19/climate-change-denial-flip-flop-public-relations-firm-edelman.
Guo, Jing, Xiaoyun Huang, and Kecheng Fang. (2023). "Authoritarian Environmentalism as Reflected in the Journalistic Sourcing of Climate Change Reporting in China." *Environmental Communication* doi/full/10.1080/17524032.2023.2223774.
Guo, Lei, Yi-Ning Katherine Chen, Hong Vu, Qian Wang, Radoslaw Aksamit, Damian Guzek, Marek Jachimowski, and Maxwell McCombs. (2015). "Coverage of the Iraq War in the United States, Mainland China, Taiwan and Poland." *Journalism Studies* 16, no. 3: 343–62.
Häberlein, Mark and Michaela Schmölz-Häberlein. (2020). "Georg Wilhelm Friedrich Hegel's Network in Bamberg." Trans. Andrew Godfrey and Ellen Yutzy Glebe. *Bavarian Studies in History and Culture* https://www.bavarian-studies.org/2020-haeberlein-schmoelz/.
Habermas, Jürgen. (2006). "Religion in the Public Sphere." *European Journal of Philosophy* 14, no. 1: 1–25.
Habermas, Jürgen. (2011). *The Structural Transformation of the Public Sphere: An Inquiry into a Category of Bourgeois Society.* Trans. Thomas Burger with Frederick Lawrence. Cambridge: Polity.
Hall, Stuart. (1958). "A Sense of Classlessness." *Universities and Left Review* 5: 26–31.
Hall, Stuart. (1974). "Media Power: The Double Bind." *Journal of Communication* 24, no. 4: 19–26.
Hall, Stuart. (1990). "The Meaning of New Times." *New Times: The Changing Face of Politics in the 1990s.* Eds. Stuart Hall and Martin Jacques. London: Verso. 116–34.
Hall, Stuart. (1995). "Parties on the Verge of a Nervous Breakdown." *Soundings* 1: 19–33.
Hall, Stuart. (1998). "The Windrush Issue: Postscript." *Soundings* 10: 188–92.
Hall, Stuart. (2011). "The Neo-Liberal Revolution." *Cultural Studies* 25, no. 6: 705–28.
Hall, Stuart. (2013). "Stuart Hall Interview—2 June 2011." *Cultural Studies* 27, no. 5: 757–77.

Hall, Stuart. (2021). *Writings on Media: History of the Present*. Ed. Charlotte Brunsdon. Durham, NC: Duke University Press.

Hall, Stuart and David Held. (1989, June). "Left and Rights." *Marxism Today*: 16–23.

Hall, Stuart and Doreen Massey. (2010). "Interpreting the Crisis." After the Crash: Reinventing the Left in Britain. Eds. Richard S. Grayson and Jonathan Rutherford. London: Soundings/Social Liberal Forum/Compass. 37–46.

Halliday, Fred. (2001). *The World at 2000: Perils and Promises*. Basingstoke: Palgrave.

Halliday, Fred. (2009). "International Relations in a Post-Hegemonic Age." *International Affairs* 85, no. 1: 50.

Halstead, Ted. (2020, January 9). "We Can't Slow Climate Change Without the Energy Companies." *New York Times* https://www.nytimes.com/2020/01/09/opinion/renewable-energy-oilcompanies.html.

Hanania, Richard and Max Abrams. (2023). "What Do Think Tanks Think? Proximity to Power and Foreign Policy Preferences." *Foreign Policy Analysis* 19, no. 1: orac031.

Hanitzsch, Thomas, Maria Anikina, Rosa Berganza, Incilay Cangoz, Mihai Coman, Basyouni Hamada, Folker Hanusch, Christopher D. Karadjov, Claudia Mellado, Sonia Virginia Moreira, Peter G. Mwesige, Patrick Lee Plaisance, Zvi Reich, Josef Seethaller, Elizabeth A. Skewes, Dani Vardiansyah Noor, and Kee Wang Yuen. (2010). "Modeling Perceived Influences on Journalism: Evidence from a Cross-National Survey of Journalists." *Journalism & Mass Communication Quarterly* 87, no. 1: 5–22.

Hanke, Robert. (1989). "Mass Media and Lifestyle Differentiation: An Analysis of the Public Discourse about Food." *Communication* 11, no. 3: 221–38.

Hardt, Michael and Antonio Negri. (2000). *Empire*. Cambridge, MA: Harvard University Press.

Harford, Tim. (2014, March 28). "Big Data: Are We Making a Terrible Mistake?" *Financial Times* http://www.ft.com/cms/s/2/21a6e7d8-b479-11e3-a09a-00144feabdc0.html#axzz2xXga2LUN.

Hargreaves, Ian. (2014). *Journalism: A Very Short Introduction*, 2nd ed. Oxford: Oxford University Press.

Harris, Lis. (2003). "The Seductions of Food." *Wilson Quarterly* 27, no. 3: 52–60.

Harrison, Maggie. (2023a). "*USA Today* and Many Other Newspapers Are Chruning Out Terrible AI-Generated Sports Stories." *Futurism* https://futurism.com/usa-today-newspapers-ai-generated-sports-stories.

Harrison, Maggie. (2023b). "*USA Today* Updates Every AI-Generated Sports Article to Correct "Errors"." *Futurism* https://futurism.com/usa-today-updates-ai-generated-sports.

Harrison, Maggie. (2023c). "*Sports Illustrated* Published Articles by Fake, AI-Generated Writers." *Futurism* https://futurism.com/sports-illustrated-ai-generated-writers.

Hart, P. Sol and Lauren Feldman. (2014). "Threat Without Efficacy? Climate Change on U.S. Network News." Science Communication 36, no. 3: 325–51.

Hartley, John. (1992). *The Politics of Pictures: The Creation of the Public in the Age of Popular Media*. London: Routledge.

Harvey, Fiona. (2023, January 11). "UAE to Launch Cop28 Presidency with Oil Boss Tipped for Leading Role." *Guardian* https://www.theguardian.com/world/2023/jan/11/uae-to-launch-cop28-presidency-with-oil-boss-tipped-for-leading-role.

Hase, Valerie, Daniela Mahl, Mike S. Schäfer, and Tobias R. Keller. (2021). "Climate Change in News Media Across the Globe: An Automated Analysis of Issue Attention and Themes in Climate Change Coverage in 10 Countries (2006-2018)." *Global Environmental Change* 70: 102353.

Hassell, Hans J. G., John B. Holbein, and Matthew R. Miles. (2020). "There is no Liberal Bias in Which News Stories Political Journalists Choose to Cover." *Science Advances* 6: eaay9344.

Hastings, Michael. (2003, February 26). "Billboard Ban." *Newsweek* https://www.newsweek.com/billboard-ban-139813.

Haug, W. F. (1986). *Critique of Commodity Aesthetics: Appearance, Sexuality and Advertising in Capitalist Society*. Trans. Robert Bock. Cambridge: Polity.

Haughton, Warren. (2018, December 26). "Leicester Give Out Free Mince Pies and Beer to Fans Before Game vs Man City on Boxing Day." *Sun* https://www.thesun.co.uk/sport/football/8054738/leicester-christmas-fans-free-beermince-pies-man-city/.

Hayes, Danny and Jennifer L. Lawless. (2021). *News Hole: The Demise of Local Journalism and Political Engagement*. Cambridge: Cambridge University Press.

Haynes, Richard, Adrian Hadland, and Paul Lambert. (2017). "The State of Sport Photojournalism." *Digital Journalism* 5, no. 5: 636–51.

Hayton, John William, Peter Millward, and Renan Petersen-Wagner. (2015). "Chasing a Tiger in a Network Society? Hull City's Proposed Name Change in the Pursuit of China and East Asia's New Middle Class Consumers." *International Review for the Sociology of Sport* 52, no. 3: 279–98.

Hazlett, Thomas W. (1990). "The Rationality of U.S. Regulation of the Broadcast Spectrum." *Journal of Law and Economics* 33, no. 1: 133–75.

Hegel, G. W. F. (2002). *Miscellaneous Writings of GWF Hegel*. Ed. Jon Stewart. Evanston: Northwestern University Press.

Heidegger, Martin. (1977). *Basic Writings from Being and Time (1927) to The Task of Thinking (1964)*. Ed. David Farrell Krell. Trans. Joan Stambaugh, J. Glenn Gray, David Farrell Krell, John Sallis, Frank A. Capuzzi, Albert Hofstadter, W. B. Barton, Jr., Vera Deutsch, William Lovitt, and Fred D. Wieck. New York: Harper & Row.

Heikkilä, Melissa. (2022, November 14). "We're Getting a Better Idea of AI's True Carbon Footprint." *MIT Technology Review* https://www.technologyreview.com/2022/11/14/1063192/were-getting-a-better-idea-of-ais-true-carbon-footprint/.

Helmore, Edward. (2021, June 21). "Fears for Future of American Journalism as Hedge Funds Flex Power." *Guardian* https://www.theguardian.com/media/2021/jun/21/us-newspapers-journalism-industry-hedge-funds.

Hembrooke, Helene and Geri Gay. (2003). "The Laptop and the Lecture: The Effects of Multitasking in Learning Environments." *Journal of Computing in Higher Education* 15, no. 1: 46–64.

Henley, Jon. (2023, June 20). "German Tabloid *Bild* Cuts 200 Jobs and Says Some Roles Will be Replaced by AI." *Guardian* https://www.theguardian.com/world/2023/jun/20/german-tabloid-bild-to-replace-range-of-editorial-jobs-with-ai.

Henne, Peter S. (2013). "The Domestic Politics of International Religious Defamation." *Politics and Religion* 6, no. 3: 512–37.

Herder, Johann Gottfried von. (2002). *Philosophical Writings*. Trans. and Ed. Michael N. Forster. Cambridge: Cambridge University Press.Herman, Edward S. (1999). *The Myth of the Liberal Media: An Edward Herman Reader*. New York: Peter Lang.

Herman, Edward S. and Noam Chomsky. (2008). *Manufacturing Consent: The Political Economy of the Mass Media*. London: Bodley Head.
Hersh, Philip. (2010, June 4). "Can USOC Avoid Stain from New Deal with BP?" *Los Angeles Times* http://latimesblogs.latimes.com/olympicsblog/2010/06/ca.html.
Hewison, Kevin. (2015). "Inequality and Politics in Thailand." *Kyoto Review of Southeast Asia* 17 https://kyotoreview.org/issue-17/inequality-and-politics-in-thailand-2/.
Hibberd, Mike. (2009, September 15). "Public Private Partnership." *Telecoms* http://www.telecoms.com/14505/public-private-partnership/.
Hicks, Clifford B. (1964, August). "The Air Around Us: How It is Changing." *Popular Mechanics*: 81–85, 178.
Hietalahti, Jarno, Onni Hirvonen, Juhana Toivanen, and Tero Vaaja. (2016). "Insults, Humour and Freedom of Speech." *French Cultural Studies* 27, no. 3: 245–55.
Higgott, Richard. (2022). *States, Civilisations and the Reset of World Order*. London: Routledge.
Hills, Jill. (2002). *The Struggle for Control of Global Communication: The Formative Century*. Urbana: University of Illinois Press.
Hills, Jill. (2007). *Telecommunications and Empire*. Urbana: University of Illinois Press.
Himelboim, Itai, Tsan-Kuo Chang, and Stephen P. McCreery. (2010). "International Network of Foreign News Coverage: Old Global Hierarchies in a New Online World." *Journalism & Mass Communication Quarterly* 87, no. 2: 297–314.
Hirschorn, Michael. (2009, January/February). "End Times." *The Atlantic* https://www.theatlantic.com/magazine/archive/2009/01/end-times/307220/.
Hirzalla, Fadi and Liesbet van Zoonen. (2016). ""The Muslims are Coming": The Enactment of Morality in Activist Muslim Comedy." *Humor* 29, no. 2: 261–78.
Hitchcock, John R. (1991). *Sportscasting*. Boston, MA: Focal Press.
Hix, Simon. (2015, November 27). "Brits Know Less About the EU Than Anyone Else." *LSE Blog Admin* https://blogs.lse.ac.uk/europpblog/2015/11/27/brits-know-less-about-the-eu-than-anyone-else/.
Hobbes, Thomas. (n.d.). *Of Man, Being the First Part of Leviathan* http://www.bartleby.com/34/5/13.html.
Hobbes, Thomas. (2017). *Three-Text Edition of Thomas Hobbes's Political Theory: The Elements of Law, De Cive, and Leviathan*. Eds. Deborah Baumgold. Cambridge: Cambridge University Press.
Hobsbawm, Eric and Terence Ranger, eds. (2002). *La invención de la tradición*. Trans. Omar Rodríguez. Barcelona: Editorial Crítica.
Hohendahl, Peter Uwe. (2016). *The Institution of Criticism*. Ithaca, NY: Cornell University Press.
Høiby, Marte and Rune Ottosen, eds. (2015). Journalism Under Pressure: A Mapping of Editorial Policies for Journalists Covering Conflict. Oslo: Høgskolen i Oslo og Akershus.
Hollande, François. (2015, January 8). "Charlie Hebdo—Statements by President Hollande." *France in the United States* http://www.franceintheus.org/spip.php?article6408.
Hollis-Touré, Isabel. (2016). "Introduction: Risk Assessing *Charlie Hebdo*." *French Cultural Studies* 27, no. 3: 219–22.
Holmes, Oliver. (2016, May 4). "The Thai Billionaire Whose Gamble on Leicester Just Paid Off." *Guardian* https://www.theguardian.com/football/2016/may/04/thai-billionaire-leicester-cityvichai-srivaddhanaprabha.

Hood, Matthew, William Chittenden, and Todd Jewell. (2018). "Never Tell Me the Odds: The Stingy Odds for Leicester City to Win the English Premier League." *Journal of Prediction Markets* 12, no. 1: 1–19.
Hookway, James. (2012, March 9). "Thai Politico in Hot Water Over Porn Star Party Plans." *Wall Street Journal* https://blogs.wsj.com/indonesiarealtime/2012/03/09/thai-politico-in-hot-waterover-porn-star-party-plans/tab/print/.
Horky, Thomas, Galen Clavio, and Christopher Grimmer. (2020). "Broadcasting the World Cup: A Multinational Comparative Analysis Broadcast Quality in the 2014 World Cup." *Soccer & Society* 21, no. 1: 15–28.
Horky, Thomas and Jörg-Uwe Nieland, eds. (2013). *International Sports Press Survey 2011 (Sport & Communication Volume 5)*. Hamburg: Horky Sport & Communication.
Horsman, Yasco. (2020). "What Was *Charlie Hebdo*? Blasphemy, Laughter, Politics." *Patterns of Prejudice* 54, nos. 1–2: 168–81.
Horton, Helena and Adam Bychawski. (2022, May 4). "Climate Sceptic Thinktank Received Funding from Fossil Fuel Interests." *Guardian* https://www.theguardian.com/environment/2022/may/04/climate-sceptic-thinktank-received-funding-from-fossil-fuel-interests.
Horton, Helena. (2023, March 30). "£3.5m of Tory Donations Linked to Pollution and Climate Denial, Says Report." *Guardian* https://www.theguardian.com/environment/2023/mar/30/tory-partys-35m-dirty-donations-revealed-by-desmog-analysis.
Hossain, Naomi. (2018). "How the International Media Framed 'Food Riots' During the Global Food Crises of 2007-12." *Food Security* 10: 677–88.
Houghton, John. (2009). "ICT and the Environment in Developing Countries: Opportunities and Developments." *Organization for Economic Cooperation and Development* http://www.oecd.org/ict/4d/44005687.pdf.
House of Commons Digital, Culture, Media and Sport Committee. (2019). *Disinformation and 'Fake News': Final Report Eighth Report of Session 2017-19*. London: House of Commons.
Howden, Daniel, David Hardaker, and Stephen Castle. (2006, February 10). "How a Meeting of Leaders in Mecca Set Off the Cartoon Wars Around the World." *Independent* http://www.independent.co.uk/news/world/middle-east/how-a-meeting-of-leaders-in-mecca-set-off-the-cartoon-wars-around-the-world-6109473.html.
Hsu, John. (2013, October 31). "Big Business, Big Data, Big Sustainability." *Carbon Trust* http://www.carbontrust.com/news/2013/10/big-business-big-data-big-sustainability.
Hsu, Tiffany. (2021, August 5). "NBC Tries to Salvage a Difficult Olympics." *New York Times* https://www.nytimes.com/2021/08/05/business/media/nbc-olympics-tv-ratings.html.
Huan, Changpeng. (2023). "Politicized or Popularized? News Values and News Voices in China's and Australia's Media Discourse of Climate Change." *Critical Discourse Studies* doi/abs/10.1080/17405904.2023.2200194.
Hudiburg, Tara W., Beverly E. Law, William R. Moomaw, Mark E. Harmon, and Jeffrey E. Stenzel. (2019). "Meeting GHG Reduction Targets Requires Accounting for all Forest Sector Emissions." *Environmental Research Letters* 14, no. 9 https://iopscience.iop.org/article/10.1088/1748-9326/ab28bb.
Huff, Richard. (2003, March 24). "Blitz of War Coverage on Nightly News." *Daily News*.

Hughes, Helen MacGill. (1981). *News and the Human Interest Story*. New Brunswick: Transaction Books.
Hughes, Matt. (2021, March 25). "Only TWO of 37 Used by Premier League Rights Holders are BAME." *Daily Mail* https://www.dailymail.co.uk/sport/football/article-9404157/SPECIAL-REPORT-black-TV-commentators.html.
Humphreys, Ashlee and Craig J. Thompson. (2014). "Branding Disaster: Reestablishing Trust Through the Ideological Containment of Systemic Risk Anxieties." *Journal of Consumer Research* 41, no. 4: 877–910.
Hunt, Leigh. (2003). *Selected Writings*. Ed. David Jesson-Dibley. London: Routledge.
Hunter, Ian. (1988). "Providence and Profit: Speculations in the Genre Market." *Southern Review* 22, no. 3: 211–23.
Hutchins, Brett and David Rowe. (2012). *Sport Beyond Television: The Internet, Digital Media and the Rise of Networked Media Sport*. New York: Routledge.
Hutton, Jan. (2011, September). "Mobile Phones Dominate in South Africa." *Nielsen Wire* https://www.nielsen.com/insights/2011/mobile-phones-dominate-in-south-africa/.
Imundo, Megan N. and David N. Rapp. (2022). "When Fairness is Flawed: Effects of False Balance Reporting and Weight-of-Evidence Statements on Beliefs and Perceptions of Climate Change." *Journal of Applied Research in Memory and Cognition* 11, no. 2: 258–71.
Innis, Harold A. (1986). *Empire and Communications*. Victoria: Press Porcépic.
Innis, Harold A. (2009). "A Plea for Time." *Canadian Cultural Studies: A Reader*. Eds. Sourayan Mookerjea, Imre Szeman, and Gail Faurschou. Durham, NC: Duke University Press. 37–53.
Instituto Interamericano de Derechos Humanos. (2007). *Estudios sobre la participación política de la población afrodescendiente: La experiencia en Colombia* https://www.corteidh.or.cr/tablas/24812.pdf.
Intergovernmental Panel on Climate Change. (2022). *Climate Change 2022: Mitigation of Climate Change* https://www.ipcc.ch/report/ar6/wg3/downloads/report/IPCCAR6WGIIIFullReport.pdf.
International Energy Agency. (2014). *More Data, Less Energy: Making Network Standby More Efficient in Billions of Connected Devices* http://www.iea.org/publications/freepublications/publication/MoreDataLessEnergy.pdf.
International Energy Agency. (2017). *Digitalization and Energy* https://www.iea.org/digital/.
International Energy Agency. (2022, September). *Pulp and Paper* https://www.iea.org/reports/pulp-and-paper.
International Federation of Journalists. (2019). *In the Shadow of Violence: Journalists and Media Staff Killed in 2018* https://www.ifj.org/fileadmin/userupload/IFJ2018KilledReportFINALpages.pdf.
International Telecommunication Union. (2022). *Measuring Digital Development: Facts and Figures 2022* https://www.itu.int/en/ITU-D/Statistics/Pages/facts/default.aspx.
Irimia, Silvian. (2022, March 11). "Best Sponsors in Formula One History." *Autoevolution* https://www.autoevolution.com/news/best-sponsors-in-formula-one-history-183650.html.
Jackson, Daniel and Kevin Moloney. (2016). "Inside Churnalism: PR, Journalism and Power Relationships in Flux." *Journalism Studies* 17, no. 6: 763–80.
Jackson, Janine. (2023, March 29). "'Media and Government Excuses are Basically Intertwined': *CounterSpin* Interview with Norman Solomon on Iraq Invasion." *FAIR* https://fair.org/home/media-and-government-excuses-are-basically-intertwined/.

Janssen, Esther. (2015). *Faith in Public Debate. On Freedom of Expression, Hate Speech and Religion in France and the Netherlands*. School of Human Rights Research Series 68 Intersentia http://www.faithinpublicdebate.com/.

Jaramillo Racines, R. (2011). "El fútbol de el Dorado: El punto de inflexión que marcó la rápida evolución del 'amateurismo' al 'profesionalismo'." *Curitiba: Revista de Asociación Latinoamericana de Estudios Socioculturales del Deporte* 1, no. 1: 111–28.

Jefferson, Thomas. (1787, January 16). "To Edward Carrington." *Founders* https://founders.archives.gov/documents/Jefferson/01-11-02-0047.

Jenkins, Holman W., Jr. (2021, April 16). "How a Physicist Became a Climate Truth Teller." *Wall Street Journal* https://www.wsj.com/articles/how-a-physicist-became-a-climate-truth-teller-11618597216.

Jennings, Andrew. (1996). *The New Lords of the Rings: Olympic Corruption and How to Buy Gold Medals*. London: PocketBooks.

Jennings, Andrew. (2006). Foul! The Secret World of FIFA: Bribes, Vote Rigging and Ticket Scandals. New York: HarperSport.

Jensen, Elizabeth. (2019, December 17). "New On-Air Source Diversity Data for NPR Show Much Work Ahead." *NPR* https://www.npr.org/sections/publiceditor/2019/12/17/787959805/new-on-air-source-diversity-data-for-npr-shows-much-work-ahead.

Jensen, Robert. (2007). "The Digital Provide: Information Technology, Market Performance, and Welfare in the South Indian Fisheries Sector." *Quarterly Journal of Economics* 122, no. 3: 879–924.

Jevons, William Stanley. (1866). *The Coal Question: An Inquiry Concerning the Progress of the Nation, and the Probable Exhaustion of Our Coal-Mines*, 2nd ed. London: Macmillan.

Johnson, Lesley. (2017). *The Unseen Voice: A Cultural Study of Early Australian Radio*. Abingdon: Routledge.

Johnson, Patrick R. (2023). "A Case of Claims and Facts: Automated Fact-Checking the Future of Journalism's Authority." *Digital Journalism* doi: 10.1080/21670811.2023.2174564.

Jolly, James and Agencies. (2021, December 17). "HSBC Fined £64m for Failures in Anti-Laundering Processes." *Guardian* https://www.theguardian.com/business/2021/dec/17/hsbc-fined-64m-failures-anti-laundering-fca.

Jones, Nicola. (2018, September 13). "How to Stop Data Centres from Gobbling Up the World's Electricity." *Nature* 561: 163–66.

Jones, Richard. (2003). "The New Look—and Taste—of British Cuisine." *Virginia Quarterly Review* 79, no. 2: 209–31.

Jones, Steve and Ben Taylor. (2013). "Food Journalism." *Specialist Journalism*. Eds. Barry Turner and Richard Orange. Abingdon: Routledge. 96–106.

Jornalistas & Cia. (2021, November). *Perfil Racial de imprensa brasileira* https://www.jornalistasecia.com.br/files/perfilracialdaimprensabrasileira.pdf.

Jungblut, Marc and Abit Hoxha. (2016). "Conceptualizing Journalistic Self-Censorship in Post-Conflict Societies: A Qualitative Perspective on the Journalistic Perception of News Production in Serbia, Kosovo, and Macedonia." Media, War and Conflict 10, no. 2: 222–38.

Juniper, Dean. (2004). "The First World War and Radio Development." History Today 54, no. 5 https://www.historytoday.com/archive/first-world-war-and-radio-development.

Juvenal. (1998). *The Sixteen Satires*, 3rd ed. Trans, and Ed. Peter Green. Harmondsworth: Penguin.

Kaempffert, Waldemar. (1956, October 28). "Science in Review: Warmer Climate on Earth May be Due to More Carbon Dioxide in the Air." *New York Times*: 191.

Kafka, Peter. (2021, March 18). "Amazon's $10 Billion NFL Deal is Huge—And a Sign That Sports is Staying on TV for a While Longer." *Vox* https://www.vox.com/recode/22338794/amazon-nfl-10-billion-tv-analysis.

Kant, Immanuel. (1987). *Critique of Judgment*. Trans. Werner S. Pluhar. New York: Hackett Publishing.

Kant, Immanuel. (1991). *Groundworks of the Metaphysics of Morals*. Trans. Mary J. Gregor. Cambridge: Cambridge University Press.

Kant, Immanuel. (1996). "An Answer to the Question: What is Enlightenment?" Trans. James Schmidt. What is Enlightenment? Eighteenth-Century Answers and Twentieth-Century Questions. Ed. James Schmidt. Berkeley: University of California Press. 58–64.

Kartz, Serge. (2019, November 19). "Porque o "doisladismo" é um totalitarismo." Le Monde Diplomatique Brasil https://diplomatique.org.br/porque-o-doisladismo-e-um-totalitarismo/.

Kassova, Luba. (2020, November). The Missing Perspective of Women in News https://www.iwmf.org/wp-content/uploads/2020/11/2020.11.19-The-Missing-Perspectives-of-Women-in-News-FINAL-REPORT.pdf.

Kaufman, Mark. (2020, July 13). "The Carbon Footprint Sham." Mashable https://mashable.com/feature/carbon-footprint-pr-campaign-sham.

Kaye, Kate. (2019, October 22). "Data Centers: Big Subsidies, Few Jobs." *Investigative Post* https://www.investigativepost.org/2019/10/22/data-centers-big-subsidies-few-jobs/.

Keay, Douglas. (1987, October 31). "Aids, Education and the Year 2000! Interview with Margaret Thatcher." *Woman's Own*: 8–10.

Kellner, Douglas. (2003). *From 9/11 to Terror War: The Dangers of the Bush Legacy*. Lanham, MD: Rowman & Littlefield.

Kelly, John. (2023). "A Critical Discourse Analysis of Military-Related Remembrance Rhetoric in UK Sport: Communicating Consent for British Militarism." *Communication & Sport* 11, no. 1: 192–212.

Kempe, Frederick. (2023, January 17). "Making the Case for Oil CEO Sultan Al Jaber to Lead the UN Climate Conference This Year." CNBC https://www.cnbc.com/2023/01/14/climate-change-oil-ceo-sultan-al-jaber-is-ideal-person-to-lead-cop-28.html.

Kennedy, Brian, Alec Tyson, and Cary Funk. (2022, February 15). Americans' Trust in Scientists, Other Groups Declines. Pew Research Center https://www.pewresearch.org/science/2022/02/15/americans-trust-in-scientists-other-groups-declines/.

Kennedy, John F. (1962, July 11). "Statement by the President on the Telstar Communications Satellite." https://www.presidency.ucsb.edu/documents/statement-the-president-the-telstar-communications-satellite.

Kerr, Robert L. (2013). "Creating the Corporate Citizen: Mobil Oil's Editorial Advocacy Campaign in *The New York Times* to Advance the Right and Practice of Corporate Political Speech, 1970-80." *American Journalism* 21, no. 4: 39–62.

Keynes, John Maynard. (1963). *Essays in Persuasion*. New York: WW Norton.

Kiesling, Barrett C. (1937). *Talking Pictures: How They are Made How to Appreciate Them*. Richmond: Johnson Publishing.

Kimble, George H. T. (1950, April 1). "The Changing Climate." *Scientific American* https://www.scientificamerican.com/article/the-changing-climate-1950-04/.

King, Ed. (2013, March 11). "Formula One: The Petrol Heads Driving the Green Economy." *Responding to Climate Change* http://www.rtcc.org/2013/03/11/formula-one-the-petrolheads-driving-the-green-economy/.

Kiwan, Nadia. (2016). "Freedom of Thought in the Aftermath of the *Charlie Hebdo* Attacks." *French Cultural Studies* 27, no. 3: 233–44.

Klausen, Jytte. (2009). *The Cartoons That Shook the World*. New Haven, CT: Yale University Press.

Klein, Naomi. (2018, August 3). "Capitalism Killed Our Climate Momentum, not "Human Nature"." *The Intercept* https://theintercept.com/2018/08/03/climate-change-new-york-times-magazine/.

Klein, Naomi. (2023, May 8). "AI Machines Aren't 'Hallucinating'. But Their Makers Are." *Guardian* https://www.theguardian.com/commentisfree/2023/may/08/ai-machines-hallucinating-naomi-klein.

Kleppinger, Kathryn. (2016). "When Parallels Collide: Social Commentary and Satire in French Rap Before and After *Charlie Hebdo*." *Contemporary French Civilization* 41, no. 2 http://dx.doi.org/10.3828/cfc.2016.10.

Kluge, Alexander. (1981–82). "On Film and the Public Sphere." Trans. Thomas Y. Levin and Miriam B. Hansen. *New German Critique* 24–25: 221–37.

Knowles, Sophie, Gail Phillips, and Johan Lidberg. (2017). "Reporting the Global Financial Crisis: A Longitudinal Tri-Nation Study of Mainstream Financial Journalism." *Journalism Studies* 18, no. 3: 322–40.

Kolmer, Christian and Holli A. Semetko. (2009). "Framing the Iraq War: Perspectives from American, U.K., Czech, German, South Africa, and Al-Jazeera News." *American Behavioral Scientist* 52, no. 5: 643–56.

Kotkin, Joel. (2001). *The New Geography: How the Digital Revolution is Reshaping the American Landscape*. New York: Random House.

Kotkin, Joel. (2020). *The Coming of Neo-Feudalism: A Warning to the Global Middle Class*. New York: Encounter Books.

Kreiss, Daniel. (2019). "The Social Identity of Journalists." *Journalism* 20, no. 1: 27–31.

Kroon, Åsa and Göran Eriksson. (2019). "The Impact of the Digital Transformation on Sports Journalism Talk Online." *Journalism Practice* 13, no. 7: 834–52.

Kulkarni, Shirish, Richard Thomas, Marlen Komorowski, and Justin Lewis. (2022). "Innovating Online Journalism: New Ways of Storytelling." *Journalism Practice* https://www.tandfonline.com/doi/full/10.1080/17512786.2021.2020675.

Kurland, Nancy B. and Deonne Zell. (2010). "The Green in Entertainment: A Conversation." *Journal of Management Inquiry* 19, no. 3: 209–18.

Lacoste, Alexandre, Alexandra Luccioni, Victor Schmidt, and Thomas Dandres. (2019). "Quantifying the Carbon Emissions of Machine Learning." *arXiv* https://arxiv.org/abs/1910.09700.

LaFollette, Marcel C. (2002). "A Survey of Science Content in U. S. Television Broadcasting, 1940s Through 1950s: The Exploratory Years." *Science Communications* 24, no. 1: 34–71.

Lakoff, George. (2010). "Why it Matters How We Frame the Environment." *Environmental Communication* 4, no. 1: 70–81.

Lakshman, Nandini. (2008, July 8). "Copyediting? Ship the Work Out to India." *Business Week* http://www.bloomberg.com/news/articles/2008-07-08/copyediting-ship-the-work-out-to-indiabusinessweek-business-news-stock-market-and-financial-advice.

Lamb, William F., Giulio Mattioli, Sebastian Levi, J. Timmons Roberts, Stuart Capstick, Felix Creutzig, Jan C. Minx, Finn Müller-Hansen, Trevor Culhane, and Julia K. Steinberger. (2020). "Discourses of Climate Delay." *Global Sustainability* 3, no. e17: 1–5.

Lambert, Charles M. (2019). *Digital Sports Journalism*. London and New York: Routledge.

Landymore, Frank. (2023, February 18). "*Sports Illustrated* Lays Off Journalists After Announcing Pivot to AI Content." *The_Byte* https://futurism.com/the-byte/sports-illustrated-lays-off-journalists-ai-content.

Lankes, R. David. (2021). *Forged in War: How a Century of War Created Today's Information Society*. Lanham, MD: Rowman & Littlefield.

Lansdall-Welfare, Thomas, Saatviga Sudhadar, James Thompson, Justin Lewis, FindMyPast Newspaper Team, and Nello Cristianini. (2017). "Content Analysis of 150 Years of British Periodicals." *PNAS* 114, no. 4: E457–65.

Lapchick, Richard. (2018, May 2). *Making Waves of Change: The 2018 Associated Press Sports Editors Racial and Gender Report Card*. The Institute for Diversity and Ethics in Sport https://www.scribd.com/document/510096226/7d86e5-9dca4bc2067241cdba67aa2f1b09fd1b.

Lapchick, Richard E. (2021). *Making Waves of Change: The 2021 Sports Media Racial and Gender Report Card™: Associated Press Sports Editors (APSE)* https://43530132-36e9-4f52-811a-182c7a91933b.filesusr.com/ugd/8af738b1530694d56142cc8a684649497f4746.pdf.

Larsen, Ana Grøndahl, Ingrid Fadnes, and Roy Krøvel, eds. (2021). *Journalist Safety and Self-Censorship*. London: Routledge.

Latouche, Serge. (2009). *Farewell to Growth*. Cambridge: Polity.

Latour, Bruno. (1993). *We Have Never Been Modern*. Trans. Catherine Porter. Cambridge: Harvard University Press.

Latour, Bruno. (2021, December 24). "The Pandemic is a Warning: We Must Take Care of the Earth, Our Only Home." *Guardian* https://www.theguardian.com/commentisfree/2021/dec/24/pandemic-earth-lockdowns-climate-crisis-environment.

Laudati, Ann and Charlotte Mertens. (2019). "Resources and Rape: Congo's (Toxic) Discursive Complex." *African Studies Review* 62, no. 4: 57–82.

Lavik, Trygve. (2016). "Climate Change Denial, Freedom of Speech and Global Justice." *Etikk i Praksis: Nordic Journal of Applied Ethics* 10, no. 2: 75–90.

Lawrence, Andrew. (2021, December 17). "'Big Egos, Power Struggles, Stunning Betrayals': How Netflix's *Drive to Survive* Turned Americans into F1 Fans." *Guardian* https://www.theguardian.com/media/2021/dec/17/netflixs-drive-to-survive-americans-f1-fans.

Lawrence, D. H. (2004). *Late Essays and Articles*. Ed. James T. Boulton. Cambridge: Cambridge University Press.

Lawrence, Felicity, Rob Evans, David Pegg, Caelainn Barr, and Pamela Duncan. (2019, November 29). "How the Right's Radical Thinktanks Reshaped the Conservative Party." *Guardian* https://www.theguardian.com/politics/2019/nov/29/rightwing-thinktank-conservative-boris-johnson-brexit-atlas-network.

Lawrence, Regina G. (2004). "Framing Obesity: The Evolution of News Discourse on a Public Health Issue." *Harvard Journal of Press/Politics* 9, no. 3: 56–75.

Lawson, Dakota and Bruce B. Henderson. (2015). "The Costs of Texting in the Classroom." *College Teaching* 63, no. 3: 119–24.

Leadbetter, Charles and Paul Miller. (2004). *The Pro-Am Revolution: How Enthusiasts are Changing Our Economy and Society*. London: Demos.

Leaños, John Jota. (2009). "Intellectual Freedom and Pat Tillman." *Handbook of Public Pedagogy: Education and Learning Beyond Schooling*. Eds. Jennifer A. Sandlin, Brian D. Schultz, and Jake Burdick. New York: Routledge. 313–18.

Lears, T. J. Jackson. (1983). "From Salvation to Self-Realization: Advertising and the Therapeutic Roots of the Consumer Culture, 1880-1930." *The Culture of Consumption: Critical Essays in American History, 1880-1980*. Eds. Richard Wightman Fox and T. J. Jackson Lears. New York: Pantheon. 1–38.

Leavis, Q. D. (1939). *Fiction and the Reading Public*. London: Chatto & Windus.

Leber, Rebecca. (2018, August 1). "*The New York Times* Fails to Name and Shame Climate Villains." *Mother Jones* https://www.motherjones.com/politics/2018/08/the-times-fails-to-name-and-shame-climate-villains/.

Ledbetter, James. (2002, October). "The Culture Blockade." *The Nation* https://www.thenation.com/article/archive/culture-blockade/.

Lee, Chang W. (2019, October 10). "Tokyo Braces for the Hottest Olympics Ever." *New York Times* https://www.nytimes.com/2019/10/10/sports/tokyo-braces-for-the-hottest-olympics-ever.html.

Lee, Jolie. (2014, June 26). "Huh? Soccer Un-American? Ann Coulter Thinks So." *USA Today* https://eu.usatoday.com/story/news/nation-now/2014/06/26/ann-coulter-soccer-column/11394947/.

Lehne, Johanna and Felix Preston. (2018). *Making Concrete Change: Innovation in Low-Carbon Cement and Concrete*. Chatham House https://www.chathamhouse.org/sites/default/files/publications/2018-06-13-making-concrete-change-cement-lehne-preston-final.pdf.

Lei, Mei, Gregory Trencher, and Jusen Asuka. (2022). "The Clean Energy Claims of BP, Chevron, ExxonMobil and Shell: A Mismatch Between Discourse, Actions and Investments." *PLoS One* 17, no. 2: e0263596.

Leibenstein, Harvey. (1978). *General X-Efficiency Theory & Economic Development*. New York: Oxford University Press.

Le Masurier, Megan. (2016). "Slow Journalism." *Journalism Practice* 10, no. 4: 439–47.

Lenin, Vladimir Il'ich. (1975). *The Lenin Anthology*. Ed. Robert C. Tucker. New York: WW Norton.

Lennon, John. (1971, January 21). "Interview with Tariq Ali and Robin Blackburn." Red Mole.

Lepore, Jill. (2019, January 28). "Does Journalism Have a Future?" *New Yorker* https://www.newyorker.com/magazine/2019/01/28/does-journalism-have-a-future.

Lequesne, Christian. (2016). "French Foreign and Security Challenges After the Paris Terrorist Attacks." *Contemporary Security Policy* 37, no. 2: 306–18.

Levantesi, Stella. (2022, June 16). "Climate Deniers and the Language of Climate Obstruction." *DeSmog* https://www.desmog.com/2022/06/16/climate-deniers-fossil-fuel-language-obstruction/.

Lever, Janet and Stanton Wheeler. (1993). "Mass Media and the Experience of Sport." *Communication Research* 20, no. 1: 125–43.

Lewandowsky, Stephan, Naomi Oreskes, James S. Risbey, Ben R. Newell, and Michael Smithson. (2015). "Seepage: Climate Change Denial and its Effect on the Scientific Community." *Global Environmental Change* 33: 1–13.

Lewis, Justin. (1996). "What Counts in Cultural Studies." *Media, Culture & Society* 19, no. 1: 83–98.
Lewis, Justin. (2001). *Constructing Public Opinion*. New York: Columbia University Press.
Lewis, Justin. (2004). "Television, Public Opinion and the War in Iraq: The Case of Britain." *International Journal of Public Opinion Research* 16, no. 3: 295–310.
Lewis, Justin. (2008). "Thinking by Numbers: Cultural Analysis and the Use of Data." *The SAGE Handbook of Cultural Analysis*. Eds. Tony Bennett and John Frow. Los Angeles: Sage Publications. 654–73.
Lewis, Justin. (2014, February 28). "How the BBC Leans to the Right." *The Independent* https://www.independent.co.uk/news/media/opinion/extract-how-the-bbc-leans-to-the-right-9129608.html.
Lewis, Justin. (2015, May 15). "Newspapers, not the BBC, Led the Way in Biased Election Coverage." *The Conversation* https://theconversation.com/newspapers-not-bbc-led-the-way-in-biased-election-coverage-41807.
Lewis, Justin, Andrew Williams, and Bob Franklin. (2008). "A Compromised Fourth Estate?" *Journalism Studies* 9, no. 1: 1–20.
Lewis, Michael. (2014). *Flash Boys*. New York: WW Norton & Company.
Lexington. (2006, June 10). "The Odd Man Out." *Economist*: 32.
Li, Haoyue Cecilia. (2022). "Smog and Air Pollution: Journalistic Criticism and Environmental Accountability in China." *Journal of Rural Studies* 92, no. 2: 510–18.
Li, You. (2022). "The Integration of Native Advertising in Journalism and its Impact on the News-Advertising Boundary." *The Institutions Changing Journalism: Barbarians Inside the Gate*. Ed. Patrick Ferrucci and Scott A. Eldridge II. Abingdon: Routledge. 31–45.
Liebling, A. J. (1964). *The Press*, rev. ed. New York: Ballantine Books.
Light, Andrew. (1998). "Reconsidering Bookchin and Marcuse as Environmental Materialists: Toward an Evolving Social Ecology." *Social Ecology After Bookchin*. Ed. Andrew Light. New York: Guilford Press. 343–84.
Lim, Vanessa. (2022, February 10). "Race to Reduce Singapore's F1's Carbon Footprint a Good Start, But Experts Are Mixed on Its Impact." *Channel News Asia* https://www.channelnewsasia.com/singapore/f1-singapore-formula-one-carbon-footprint-environment-2487536.
Lindblom, Charles E. (1977). *Politics and Markets: The World's Political-Economic Systems*. New York: Basic Books.
Lippmann, Walter. (1998). *Public Opinion*. New Brunswick: Transaction Books.
Livingston, Steven, W. Lance Bennett, and W. Lucas Robinson. (2005). "International News and Advanced Information Technology: Changing the Institutional Domination Paradigm?" *Media and Conflict in the Twenty-First Century*. Ed. Philip Seib. New York: Palgrave Macmillan. 33–55.
Lockie, Stewart. (2017). "Post-Truth Politics and the Social Sciences." *Environmental Sociology* 3, no. 1: 1–5.
Lockwood, David. (2023, March 23). "Premier League Domestic Flights: BBC Sport Research Shows 81 Flights from 100 Games." *BBC* https://www.bbc.co.uk/sport/football/65017565.
Löfgren Nilsson, Monica and Henrik Örnebring. (2016). "Journalism Under Threat." Journalism Practice 10, no. 7: 880–90.
London, Jack. (1915, February). "The Message of Motion Pictures." Paramount Magazine: 1–2.

London, Jack. (2010). *Revolution and Other Essays*. London: Mills & Boon.
Loo, Eric. (2019). "Reading "Asian Values" into Journalism Practices in Asia." *Oxford Research Encyclopedia of Communication* https://oxfordre.com/communication/display/10.1093/acrefore/9780190228613.001.0001/acrefore-9780190228613-e-781;jsessionid=63EF2B5CCD20E300F0F3175A4A3CEF02.
López, Antonio. (2011, May 5). "Greening a Digital Media Course." *New Media Literacies* http://www.newmedialiteracies.org/2011/05/greeningadigitalmediacours/#more-1195.
López, Antonio, Adrian Ivahkiv, Stephen Rust, Miriam Tola, Alendra Y. Chang, and Kiu-wai Chu, eds. (2024). *The Routledge Handbook of Ecomedia Studies*. New York: Routledge.
López de la Roche, Fabio. (2003). "Debate público, guerra y desregulación informativa en Colombia." *Íconos: Revista de FLACSO-Ecuador* 16: 54–64.
López-Egea, Sergi. (2019, December 13). "El reto climático en los grandes deportes." *elPeriódico* https://www.elperiodico.com/es/deportes/20191213/deporte-alerta-cambio-climatico-7773643.
Love, Maryann Cusimano. (2003). "Global Media and Foreign Policy." *Media Power, Media Politics*. Ed. Mark J. Rozell. Lanham, MD: Rowman & Littlefield. 235–64.
Lowes, Mark. (2004). "Neoliberal Power Politics and the Controversial Siting of the Australian Grand Prix Motorsport Event in an Urban Park." *Loisir et société/Society and Leisure* 27, no. 1: 69–88.
Lück, Julia, Tanjev Schultz, Felix Simon, Alexandra Borchardt, and Sabine Kieslich. (2020). "Diversity in British, Swedish, and German Newsrooms: Problem Awareness, Measures, and Achievements." *Journalism Practice* 16, no. 4: 561–81.
Ludvigsen, Jan Andre Lee. (2019). "Foreign Ownerships in the Premier League: Examining Local Liverpool Fans' Perceptions of Fenway Sports Group." *Soccer and Society* 20, no. 4: 602–25.
Luengo, María and Karoline Andrea Ihlebæk. (2019). "Journalism, Solidarity and the Civil Sphere: The Case of *Charlie Hebdo*." *European Journal of Communication* 34, no. 3: 286–99.
Lukács, Georg. (1972). History and Class Consciousness: Studies in Marxist Dialectics. Trans. Rodney Livingstone. Cambridge, Mass.: MIT Press.
Luna Geller, Alfonso José. (2016, June 3). "Armada Nacional al servicio de intereses de Ardila Lülle en la Copa América?" *Las 2 Orillas* http://www.las2orillas.co/armada-nacional-al-servicio-deintereses-de-ardila-lulle-en-la-copa-america/.
Lünenborg, Margreth and Débora Medeiros. (2023). "Under Pressure: Journalism as an Affective Institution." *Affect, Power, and Institutions*. Eds. Millicent Churcher, Sandra Calkins, Jandra Böger, and Jan Slaby. Abingdon: Routledge. 80–101.
Luntz, Dr. [sic] Frank. (2008). *Words That Worked: It's Not What You Say, It's What People Hear*. New York: Hyperion Books.
Luxemburg, Rosa. (2014). *The Complete Works of Rosa Luxemburg. Volume I: Economic Writings*. London: Verso.
Lyotard, Jean-François. (1988). *The Differend: Phrases in Dispute*. Trans. Georges Van Den Abbeele. Minneapolis: University of Minnesota Press.
M. C. (2015, January 15). "Delfeil de Ton, ancien de «Charlie», accuse Charb d'avoir entrainé l'équipe dan las «surenchère»." *20 Minutes* http://www.20minutes.fr/medias/1517631-20150115-delfeil-ancien-charlie-accuse-charb-avoir-entraine-equipe-surenchere.

Macaulay, Thomas Babington. (1848). *Critical and Historical Essays Contributed to The Edinburgh Review Vol. 1*, 5th ed. London: Longman, Brown, Green, and Longmans.

MacDonald, Ted. (2023, April 10). "35% of Climate Segments on Corporate Broadcast TV News in 2022 Featured Climate Solutions." *Media Matters* https://www.mediamatters.org/broadcast-networks/35-climate-segments-corporate-broadcast-tv-news-2022-featured-climate-solutions.

Mackey, Ed. (2023, March 8). "How Premier League TV Rights Work and How They Impact Your Costs and Subscriptions." *The Athletic* https://theathletic.com/4240951/2023/03/08/premier-league-tv-rights-how-work-cost/.

Macnamara, Jim. (2015). "The Continuing Convergence of Journalism and PR: New Insights for Ethical Practice from a Three-Country Study of Senior Practitioners." *Journalism & Mass Communication Quarterly* 93, no. 1: 118–41.

Maguire, Kieran. (2020). *The Price of Football: Understanding Football Club Finance*. Newcastle: Agenda Publishing.

Mair, John and Richard Lance Keeble with Paul Bradshaw and Teodora Beleaga. (2013). *Data Journalism: Mapping the Future*. Bury St Edmunds: Abramis.

Makala, Jeffrey. (2005, February 18). "The Joys of Cooking." *Chronicle of Higher Education*: B19.

Malhado, Acacía Cristina Mendes and Rainer Rothfuss. (2013). "Transporting 2014 FIFA World Cup to Sustainability: Exploring Residents' and Tourists' Attitudes and Behaviours." *Journal of Policy Research in Tourism, Leisure and Events* 5, no. 3: 252–69.

Malmodin, Jens and Dag Lundén. (2018). "The Energy and Carbon Footprint of the Global ICT and E&M Sectors 2010-2015." *Sustainability* 10, no. 9: 3027.

Malpas, Jeff. (1992). "Retrieving Truth: Modernism, Post-Modernism and the Problem of Truth." *Soundings* 75, nos. 2–3: 288–306.

Mamdani, Mahmood. (1996). *Citizen and Subject: Contemporary Africa and the Legacy of Late Colonialism*. Princeton: Princeton University Press.

Mandard, Stéphane. (2022, November 18). "Coupe du monde 2022: Le mirage de la compensation carbone pour atteindre la «neutralité» promise par la FIFA." *Le Monde* https://www.lemonde.fr/football/article/2022/11/18/coupe-du-monde-2022-le-mirage-de-la-compensation-carbone-pour-atteindre-la-neutralite-promise-par-la-fifa61504041616938.html.

Mandel, Ernest. (1994). Revolutionary Marxism and Social Reality in the 20th Century. Ed. Steve Bloom. Atlantic Highlands, NJ: Humanities Press.

Manfredi Sánchez, Juan Luis and María José Ufarte Ruiz. (2020). "Inteligencia artificial y periodismo: Una herramienta contra la desinformación." *Revista CIDOB d'Afers Internacionals* 124: 49–72.

Mann, Michael and Tom Toles. (2016). *The Madhouse Effect: How Climate Change Denial is Threatening Our Planet, Destroying Our Politics, and Driving Us Crazy*. New York: Columbia University Press.

Manning, Paul. (2013). "Financial Journalism, News Sources and the Banking Crisis." *Journalism: Theory, Practice and Criticism* 14, no. 2: 173–89.

Maras, Steven. (2013). *Objectivity in Journalism*. Cambridge: Polity.

Marconi, Guglielmo. (1924). "Foreword." *The Story of Broadcasting*. Ed. A. R. Burrows. London: Cassell. vii.

Marcos Recio, Juan Carlos, Juan Miguel Sánchez Vigil, and María Olivera Zaldua. (2017). "La enorme mentira y la gran verdad de la información en tiempos de la

postverdad." *Scire: Representación y organización del conocimiento* 23, no. 2: 13–23.
Marcotte, Amanda. (2023, February 21). "Fox News Texts Reveal the Truth: The Big Lie was a Con—That the Viewers Were in On." *Salon* https://www.salon.com/2023/02/21/fox-news-texts-reveal-the-truth-the-big-lie-was-a-con--that-the-viewers-were-in-on/.
Marcus, George E. (1998). *Ethnography Through Thick and Thin*. Princeton: Princeton University Press.
Marcuse, Herbert. (1941). "Some Social Implications of Modern Technology." *Studies in Philosophy and Social Sciences* 9, no. 3: 414–39.
Marcuse, Herbert. (2009). *Negations: Essays in Critical Theory*. Trans. and Ed. Jeremy J. Shapiro. London: MayFlyBooks.
Markoff, John. (1995, November 20). "If Medium Is the Message, the Message Is the Web." *New York Times*: A1, D5.
Marks, Shula and Dagmar Engels, eds. (1994). *Contesting Colonial Hegemony: State and Society in Africa and India*. New York: IB Tauris.
Marmot, Michael G. (2004). "Evidence Based Policy or Policy Based Evidence?" *British Medical Journal* 328, no. 7445: 906–07.
Marron, Maria B., ed. (2021). *Misogyny Across Global Media*. Lanham, MD: Lexington Books.
Marshall, T. H. (1950). Citizenship and Social Class and Other Essays. Cambridge: Cambridge University Press.
Martin, Christopher R. (2004). *Framed! Labor and the Corporate Media*. Ithaca, NY: ILR Press/Cornell University Press.
Martin, Randy. (2002). *Financialization of Daily Life*. Philadelphia, PA: Temple University Press.
Martín-Barbero, Jesús and Germán Rey. (1999). *Los ejercicios del ver: Hegemonía audiovisual y ficción televisiva*. Barcelona: Gedisa Editorial.
Martin-Neira, Juan Ignacio, Magdalena Trillo-Domínguez, and María Dolores Olvera-Lobo. (2023). "El periodismo científico ante la desinformación: Decálogo de buenas prácticas en el entorno digital y transmedia." *ICONO 14: Revista Científica De Comunicación y Tecnologías Emergentes* 21, no. 1 https://doi.org/10.7195/ri14.v21i1.194.
Martínez-Alier, Joan. (2012). "Environmental Justice and Economic Degrowth: An Alliance Between Two Movements." *Capitalism Nature Socialism* 23, no. 1: 51–73.
Marvin, Carolyn. (1988). *When Old Technologies Were New: Thinking About Electronic Communication in the Late Nineteenth Century*. New York: Oxford University Press.
Marx, Karl and Frederick Engels. (1995). *The German Ideology: Part One*. Ed. C. J. Arthur. New York: International Publishers.
Marx, Karl. (1842). *On Freedom of the Press* https://marxists.architexturez.net/archive/marx/works/1842/free-press/ch05.htm.
Marx, Karl. (1906). *Capital: A Critique of Political Economy*. Trans. Samuel Moore and Edward Aveling. Ed. Frederick Engels. New York: Modern Library.
Marx, Karl. (1987). *Capital: Vol. 1: A Critical Analysis of Capitalist Production*, 3rd ed. Ed. Friedrich Engels. Trans. Samuel Moore and Edward Aveling. New York: International Publishers.
Marx, Karl. (1996). *Later Political Writings*. Ed. Terrell Carver. Cambridge: Cambridge University Press.

Massardo, Jaime. (1999). "La recepción de Gramsci en America Latina: Cuestiones de orden teórico y político." *International Gramsci Society Newsletter* 9: electronic supplement 3 http://www.internationalgramscisociety.org/igsn/articles/a09s3.shtml.
Mattelart, Armand. (2000). *Networking the World, 1794-2000*. Trans. Liz Carey-Libbrecht and James A. Cohen. Minneapolis: University of Minnesota Press.
Mattelart, Armand. (2002). "An Archaeology of the Global Era: Constructing a Belief." Trans. Susan Taponier with Philip Schlesinger. *Media Culture & Society* 24, no. 5: 591–612.
Mattelart, Tristan and Leen d'Haenens. (2014). "Cultural Diversity Policies in Europe: Between Integration and Security." *Global Media and Communication* 10, no. 3: 231–45.
Matyjaszek, Harry. (2021, June 3). "The Energy Impact of Mobile Phones." *Energy Live News* https://www.energylivenews.com/2021/06/03/the-energy-impact-of-mobile-phones/.
Maxwell, Richard and Toby Miller. (2012). *Greening the Media*. New York: Oxford University Press.
Maxwell, Richard and Toby Miller. (2013). "Life Without Democracy, Life Without Citizenship, Life Without Media." *Life Without Media*. Eds. Eva Comas, Joan Cuenca, and Klaus Zilles. New York: Peter Lang. 43–61.
Maxwell, Richard, Jon Raundalen, and Nina Lager Vestberg, eds. (2015). *Media and the Ecological Crisis*. New York: Routledge.
Mazzoni, Marco and Giovanni Barbieri. (2014). "Grasshoppers Against Ants or Malfunctions of Capitalism? The Representation of the European Economic Crisis in the Main Italian Newspapers." *Perspectives on European Politics and Society* 15, no. 2: 238–53.
Mazzucato, Mariana. (2015). *The Entrepreneurial State: Debunking Public vs. Private Sector Myths*. New York: Public Affairs.
McAllister, Lucy, Meaghan Daly, Patrick Chandler, Marissa McNatt, Andrew Benham, and Maxwell Boykoff. (2021). "Balance as Bias, Resolute on the Retreat? Updates & Analyses of Newspaper Coverage in the United States, United Kingdom, New Zealand, Australia and Canada Over the Past 15 Years." *Environmental Research Letters* 16, no. 9: 094008.
McCarthy, Michael. (2004, May 18). "Violence in Iraq Puts Advertisers on Edge." *USA Today*: 2B.
McChesney, Robert W. (2003). "The Problem of Journalism: A Political Economic Contribution to an Explanation of the Crisis in Contemporary US Journalism." *Journalism Studies* 4, no. 3: 299–329.
McChesney, Robert W. (2013). *Digital Disconnect: How Capitalism is Turning the Internet Against Democracy*. New York: The New Press.
McClintock, Anne. (2010, June 24). "Militarizing the Gulf Oil Crisis." *CounterPunch* https://www.counterpunch.org/2010/06/24/militarizing-the-gulf-oil-crisis/.
McDiarmid, Margo. (2014, November 18). "Energy East Pipeline 'Advocates' Targeted in TransCanada PR Move." *CBC News* https://www.cbc.ca/news/politics/energy-east-pipeline-advocates-targeted-in-transcanada-pr-move-1.2838383.
McDonald, Ian R. and Regina G. Lawrence. (2004). "Filling the 24 x 7 News Hole." *American Behavioral Scientist* 48, no. 3: 327–40.
McElwee, Joshua J. (2015, January 15). "About Paris Attacks, Francis Says Freedom of Expression Has Certain Limits." *National Catholic Reporter* https://www.

ncronline.org/news/global/about-paris-attacks-francis-says-freedom-expression-has-certain-limits.

McEnnis, Simon. (2017). "Playing on the Same Pitch." *Digital Journalism* 5, no. 5: 549–66.

McEnnis, Simon. (2020). "Toy Department Within the Toy Department? Online Sports Journalists and Professional Legitimacy." *Journalism* 21, no. 10: 1415–431.

McHale, Kevin. (2019). "Give the Fans What They Really Want: How Professional Sports Stadiums Across the World can Positively Impact the Environment." *Texas Environmental Law Journal* 49, no. 1: 127–58.

McKenzie, Sheena. (2015, November 17). "England vs. France: How Singing "La Marseillaise" Became a Different War Chant." *CNN* http://edition.cnn.com/2015/11/17/sport/paris-attacks-french-national-anthem-football-wembley/.

McKibben, Bill. (2008). "Multiplication Saves the Day." *Orion* https://orionmagazine.org/article/multiplication-saves-the-day/.

McLaren Racing. (2021, April 14). *Sustainability at McLaren Racing* https://static-cdn.mclaren.com/static/pdf/SustainabilityatMcLarenRacing14April2021.pdf.

McMichael, Philip. (2017). *Development and Social Change: A Global Perspective.* Los Angeles, CA: Sage.

Media and Climate Change Observatory. (2023a, April). *MeCCO Monthly Summaries* 76 https://sciencepolicy.colorado.edu/icecaps/research/mediacoverage/summaries/issue76.html.

Media and Climate Change Observatory. (2023b, July). "A Foretaste of the Future." *MeCCO Monthly Summaries* 79 https://sciencepolicy.colorado.edu/icecaps/research/mediacoverage/summaries/issue79.pdf.

Melville, Herman. (1855). "The Paradise of Bachelors and the Tartarus of Maids." *Harper's New Monthly Magazine* 10: 670–78.

Mennell, Stephen. (2003). "Eating in the Public Sphere in the Nineteenth and Twentieth Centuries." *Eating Out in Europe*. Eds. Marc Jacobs and Peter Schollier. New York: Berg. 245–60.

Merchant, Brian. (2019, February 21). "How Google, Microsoft, and Big Tech Are Automating the Climate Crisis." *Gizmodo*.

Mergerson, Christoph. (2023, March 31). "Objectivity for What?" *The Nation* https://www.thenation.com/article/society/objectivity-for-what/.

Merino, Daniel. (2020, July 23). "The First Undeniable Climate Change Deaths." *Slate* https://slate.com/technology/2020/07/climate-change-deaths-japan-2018-heatwave.html.

Merk, Jeroen, ed. (2021) *Human Rights Risks in the ICT Supply Chain*. Edinburgh: Make ICT Fair. https://www.ed.ac. uk/files/atoms/files/humanrightsrisksintheictsupplychain0.pdf.

Merton, Robert K. (1936). "The Unanticipated Consequences of Purposive Social Action." *American Sociological Review* 1, no. 6: 894–904.

Meserve, Margaret. (2021). "The Papacy, Power, and Print: The Publication of Papal Decrees in the First Fifty Years of Printing." *Print and Power in Early Modern Europe (1500–1800*. Ed. Nina Lamal, Jamie Cumby, and Helmer J. Helmers. Leiden: Brill. 259–99.

Messner, Michael A., Margaret Carlisle Duncan, and Kerry Jensen. (1993). "Separating the Men from the Girls: The Gendered Language of Televised Sports." *Gender and Society* 7, no. 1: 121–37.

Meyer, Robinson. (2018, August 1). "The Problem with *The New York Times*' Big Story on Climate Change." *The Atlantic* https://www.theatlantic.com/science/archive/2018/08/nyt-mag-nathaniel-rich-climate-change/566525/.

Mhamdi, Chaker. (2017). "Framing "the Other" in Times of Conflicts: CNN's Coverage of the 2003 Iraq War." *Mediterranean Journal of Social Sciences* 8, no. 2: 147–53.

Microsoft. (2022). *2022 Environmental Sustainability Report* https://query.prod.cms.rt.microsoft.com/cms/api/am/binary/RW15mgm.

Mill, James. (n.d.). *Commonplace Book vol. 1* https://intellectualhistory.net/cpb1#cpb1ch2.

Mill, John Stuart. (1859). *On Liberty* http://www.econlib.org/library/Mill/mlLbty3.html.

Mill, John Stuart. (2004). *Principles of Political Economy with Some of Their Applications to Social Philosophy*, abridged. Ed. Stephen Nathanson. Indianapolis: Hackett Publishing.

Miller, Chris. (2023, February 2). "Are Virginia Ratepayers and Residents Subsidizing the Data Center Industry?" *Virginia Mercury* https://www.virginiamercury.com/2023/02/02/are-virginia-ratepayers-and-residents-subsidizing-the-data-center-industry/.

Miller, David and William Dinan. (2015). "Resisting Meaningful Action on Climate Change: Think Tanks, 'Merchants of Doubt' and the 'Corporate Capture' of Sustainable Development." *The Routledge* Handbook of Environment and Communication. Eds. Anders Hansen and Robert Cox. London: Routledge. 96–110.

Miller, J. D. B. (1949). "Radio in Our Lives." *Current Affairs Bulletin* 3: 183–99.

Miller, Michael E. (2015, June 3). "Andrew Jennings: Meet the Man That Exposed the FIFA Scandal that Toppled Sepp Blatter." *Independent* https://www.independent.co.uk/sport/football/international/andrew-jennings-meet-theman-that-exposed-the-fifa-scandal-that-toppled-sepp-blatter-10294970.html.

Miller, Toby. (1992). "An Editorial Introduction for Radio." *Continuum* 6, no. 1: 5–13.

Miller, Toby. (2006). "US Journalism: Servant of the Nation, Scourge of the Truth?" *Conflict, Terrorism and the Media in Asia*. Ed. Benjamin Cole. London: Routledge. 5–22.

Miller, Toby. (2007). *Cultural Citizenship: Cosmopolitanism, Consumerism, and Television in a Neoliberal Age*. Philadelphia, PA: Temple University Press.

Miller, Toby. (2008). *Makeover Nation: The United States of Reinvention*. Columbus: Ohio State University Press.

Miller, Toby. (2009). "Can Natural Luddites Make Things Explode or Travel Faster? The New Humanities, Cultural Policy Studies, and Creative Industries." *Media Industries: History, Theory, and Method*. Eds. Jennifer Holt and Alisa Perren. Malden: Wiley/Blackwell. 184–98.

Miller, Toby. (2010). *Television Studies: The Basics*. London: Routledge.

Miller, Toby. (2013). "The Cognitariat." *Cognitariat: Journal of Contingent Labor* 1 http://oaworld.org/index.php/cognitariat/article/view/4/4.

Miller, Toby. (2016, May 18). "Leicester City Cinderella story Authored by Thai Oligarch." *Asia Sentinel* http://www.asiasentinel.com/econ-business/leicester-city-little-cluboligarch/#frameId=appnextwidget&height=84.

Miller, Toby. (2018). *Greenwashing Sport*. London: Routledge.

Miller, Toby. (2019). "Sports, Politics, and Consumption: Olympic Ceremonies." *The Business and Culture of Sports: Society, Politics, Economy, Environment*, Vol. 3. Eds. Joseph Maguire, Mark Falcous, and Katie Liston. Detroit: Gale Virtual Reference. 67–84.

Miller, Toby. (2020, July 3). "Football, Television, Race—And Ownership." *CST Online* https://cstonline.net/football-television-race-and-ownership-by-toby-miller/.

Mills, Mark P. (2013). *The Cloud Begins with Coal: Big Data, Big Networks, Big Infrastructure, and Big Power*. National Mining Association and American Coalition for Clean Coal Electricity http://www.tech-pundit.com/wpcontent/uploads/2013/07/CloudBeginsWithCoal.pdf?c761ac.

Milman, Oliver. (2023, July 5). "'Double Agents': Fossil-Fuel Lobbyists Work for US Groups Trying to Fight Climate Crisis." *Guardian* https://www.theguardian.com/us-news/2023/jul/05/double-agent-fossil-fuel-lobbyists.

Milne, Seumas. (2015, February 27). "*Pinkoes and Traitors* by Jean Seaton Review—My Father, the BBC and a Very British Coup." *Guardian* https://www.theguardian.com/books/2015/feb/27/seumas-milne-on-pinkoes-and-traitors-by-jean-seaton-review-my-father-the-bbc-and-a-very-british-coup.

Milton, John. (1909–14). *Areopagitica: A Speech for the Liberty of Unlicensed Printing*. Cambridge, MA: Harvard University Press.

Mitchell, Greg. (2004, August 18). "Why the "Washington Post" Inside Story on Iraq Pre-War Coverage Falls Short." *Editor & Publisher*.

Mitchell, Scott. (2019, February 11). "Former BAR Team Owner BAT Back into Formula 1 with McLaren Deal." *Autosport* https://www.autosport.com/f1/news/former-bar-team-owner-bat-back-into-formula-1-with-mclaren-deal-5283606/5283606/.

Mitchell, Timothy. (1998). "Fixing the Economy." *Cultural Studies* 12, no. 1: 82–101.

Mobil Oil. (1978, February 9). "Business and Pluralism." *New York Times*: A21.

mobiThinking. (2014, May 16). "Global Mobile Statistics 2014 Part A: Mobile Subscribers; Handset Market Share; Mobile Operators." *mobiForge* http://mobiforge.com/research-analysis/global-mobile-statistics-2014-part-a-mobile-subscribers-handset-market-share-mobile-operators#subscribers.

Moeller, Susan D. (2004). *Media Coverage of Weapons of Mass Destruction*. Center for International and Security Studies at Maryland https://drum.lib.umd.edu/bitstream/handle/1903/7884/wmdstudyfull.pdf?sequence=1&isAllowed=y.

Molena, Francis. (1912, March). "Remarkable Weather of 1911: The Effect of the Combustion of Coal on the Climate—What Scientists Predict for the Future." *Popular Mechanics*: 339–42.

Monnerat, Alessandra. (2018, January 13). "Científicos de datos trabajan en el primer robot-periodista de Brasil para reportar sobre proyectos de ley de la Cámara." *LatAm Journalism Review* https://latamjournalismreview.org/es/articles/cientificos-de-datos-trabajan-en-el-primer-robot-periodista-de-brasil-para-reportar-sobre-proyectos-de-ley-de-la-camara/.

Montaña, Silvia. (2014). "*Case 2*: Colombia—An Ethnographic Study of Digital Journalistic Practices." *Global Journalism Practice and New Media Performance*. Eds. Yusuf Kalyango, Jr. and David H. Mould. London: Palgrave. 146–60.

Montañola, Sandy, Béatrice Damian-Gaillard, Eugénie Saitta, and Jeanne Wetzels. (2022, June 13). "Violences sexuelles: Quand les femmes journalists se taisent." *The Conversation* https://theconversation.com/violences-sexuelles-quand-les-femmes-journalistes-se-taisent-184665.

Moreno, J. Edward. (2020, July 24). "WSJ Editorial Board Calls Employee Concerns About Opinion Page 'Cancel Culture'." *The Hill* https://thehill.com/homenews/media/508870-wsj-editorial-board-calls-employee-concerns-about-opinion-page-cancel-culture/.

Moreno, Jose A., Mira Kinn, and Marta Narberhaus. (2022). "A Stronghold of Climate Change Denialism in Germany: Case Study of the Output and Press Representation of the Think Tank EIKE." *International Journal of Communication* 16: 267–88.

Mosca, Gaetano. (1939). *The Ruling Class*. Trans. Hanna D. Kahn, rev. and ed. Arthur Livingston. New York: McGraw-Hill.

Moynihan, Ray, Iona Heath, and David Henry. (2002). "Selling Sickness: The Pharmaceutical Industry and Disease Mongering." *British Medical Journal* 324: 886.

Mueller, Lisa and Lukas Matthews. (2016). "The National Elections in Niger, February-March 2016." *Electoral Studies* 43: 203–06.

Mufson, Steven. (2020, February 13). "The Fastest Way to Cut Carbon Emissions is a 'Fee' and a Dividend, Top Leaders Say." *Washington Post* https://www.washingtonpost.com/climate-environment/the-fastest-way-to-cut-carbon-emissions-is-a-fee-and-a-rebate-top-leaders-say/2020/02/13/b63b766c-4cfc-11ea-bf44-f5043eb3918astory.html.

Mukherjee, Sanjukta with Central Department for Development Studies, Tribhuvan University. (2003). *Child Ragpickers in Nepal: A Report on the 2002-2003 Baseline Survey*. Bangkok: International Labour Organization.

Müller, Martin, Sven Daniel Wolfe, Christopher Gaffney, David Gogishvili, Miriam Hug, and Annick Leick. (2021). "An Evaluation of the Sustainability of the Olympic Games." *Nature Sustainability* 4: 340–48.

Murdoch, James. (2009, December 4). "Clean Energy Conservatives Can Embrace." *Washington Post* http://www.washingtonpost.com/wp-dyn/content/article/2009/12/03/AR2009120303698.html.

Murdoch, Rupert. (2007, May 9). "Remarks." https://web.archive.org/web/20130509133621/http://gei.newscorp.com/what/2007/05/global-energy-initiative-launc.html#more.

Murphy, Andrew and Valentin Simon. (2021, April). *Private Jets: Can the Super-Rich Supercharge Zero-Emission Aviation?* Transport & Environment https://www.transportenvironment.org/wp-content/uploads/2021/05/202209_private_jets_FINAL_with_addendum.pdf.

Murphy, Richard and Louis-Philippe Beland. (2015, May 12). "How Smart is it to Allow Students to Use Mobile Phones at School?" *The Conversation* https://theconversation.com/how-smart-is-it-to-allow-students-to-use-mobile-phones-at-school-40621.

Mutsvairo, Bruce, Eddy Borges-Rey, Saba Bebawi, Mireya MárquezRamírez, Claudia Mellado, Hayes Mawindi Mabweazara, Marton Demeter, Michal Głowacki, Hanan Badr, and Daya Thussu. (2021). "Different, But the Same: How the Global South is Challenging the Hegemonic Epistemologies and Ontologies of Westernized/Western-Centric Journalism Studies." *Journalism & Mass Communication Quarterly* 98, no. 4: 996–1016.

Mutsvairo, Bruce, Eddy Borges-Rey, and Saba Bebawi, eds. (2019). *Data Journalism in the Global South*. Cham: Springer.

Mylonas, Yiannis. (2015). "Austerity Discourses in 'Der Spiegel' Journal, 2009-2014." *Triple C* 13, no. 1: 248–69.

Mytton, David. (2020). "Hiding Greenhouse Gas Emissions in the Cloud." *Nature Climate Change* 10: 700–01.

Nader, Laura. (1972). "Up the Anthropologist—Perspectives Gained from Studying Up." *Reinventing Anthropology*. Ed. Dell H. Hymes. New York: Pantheon Books. 284–311.

Nagle, Ben. (2023, November 22). "Gen Z, *Drive to Survive*, and the Rise of Alcohol-Free Booze…Why the Next Generation of F1 Fans Couldn't be Further Away from the Drink and Drug-Fueled Days of James Hunt and the 70s." *Daily Mail* https://www.dailymail.co.uk/sport/formulaone/article-12780721/Gen-Z-Drive-Survive-rise-alcohol-free-booze-generation-F1-fans-away-drink-drug-fueled-days-James-Hunt-70s.html.

National Geographic, Gallup, and Council on Foreign Relations. (2019). *U.S. Adults' Knowledge About the World* https://cdn.cfr.org/sites/default/files/reportpdf/NatGeoCFRUS%20Knoweldge.pdf.

National Oceanic and Atmospheric Administration. (2017, April 20). "Deepwater Horizon Oil Spill Settlements: Where the Money Went." https://www.noaa.gov/explainers/deepwater-horizon-oil-spill-settlements-where-money-went.

Naughton, John. (2014). *From Gutenberg to Zuckerberg: Disruptive Innovation in the Age of the Internet*. New York: Quercus.

Neff, Jack. (2014, March 25). "How Big Data Shapes AT&T's Advertising Creative." *AdAge* http://adage.com/article/cmo-strategy/t-big-data-shape-tv-creative/292313/.

Negri, Antonio. (2007). *Goodbye Mister Socialism*. Paris: Seuil.

Neslen, Arthur. (2021, August 11). "Here's How AI Can Help Fight Climate Change." *World Economic Forum* https://www.weforum.org/agenda/2021/08/how-ai-can-fight-climate-change/.

Neville, Steve. (2018, July 4). "*The Sun* Newspaper Issues "Apology"—of Sorts—for Controversial Colombia Headline." *Irish Examiner* https://www.irishexaminer.com/breakingnews/sport/soccer/the-sun-newspaper-issues-apology--of-sorts--for-controversial-colombia-headline-853035.html.

New Climate Institute. (2023, February). *Corporate Climate Responsibility Monitor 2023: Assessing the Transparency and Integrity of Companies' Emission Reduction and Net-Zero Targets* https://newclimate.org/sites/default/files/2023-04/NewClimateCorporateClimateResponsibilityMonitor2023Feb23.pdf.

Newman, Nic with Richard Fletcher, Antonis Kalogeropoulos, and Rasmus Kleis Nielsen. (2019). *Reuters Institute Digital News Report 2019* https://reutersinstitute.politics.ox.ac.uk/sites/default/files/inline-files/DNR2019FINAL.pdf.

New Weather Institute. (2021). *Sweat Not Oil: Why Sports Should Drop Advertising and Sponsorship from High-Carbon Polluters* https://static1.squarespace.com/static/5ebd0080238e863d04911b51/t/605b60b09a957c1b05f433e2/1616601271774/Sweat+Not+Oil+-+why+Sports+should+drop+advertising+from+high+carbon+polluters+-+March+2021v3.pdf.

New York Times. (2014, March 24). Innovation https://www.presscouncil.org.au/uploads/52321/ufiles/TheNewYorkTimesInnovationReport-March2014.pdf.

Nichols, Andrew W. (2014). "Heat-Related Illness in Sports and Exercise." *Current Reviews in Muscoloskeletal Medicine* 7: 355–65.

Niemeyer, Katharina. (2019). "The Front Page as a Time Freezer: An Analysis of the International Newspaper Coverage After the *Charlie Hebdo* Attacks." *Media, War & Conflict* 12, no. 2: 187–201.

Nietzsche, Friedrich. (2006). *On the Genealogy of Morality*. Trans. Carol Diethe. Ed. Keith Ansell-Pearson. Cambridge: Cambridge University Press.

Nineteenth Islamic Conference of Foreign Ministers (Session of Peace, Interdependence and Development). (1993). Cairo Declaration on Human Rights in Islam, Aug. 5, 1990, U.N. GAOR (1993). World Conf. on Hum. Rts., 4th Sess., Agenda Item 5, U.N. Doc. A/CONF.157/PC/62/Add.18 (1993) http://hrlibrary.umn.edu/instree/cairodeclaration.html.

Nkrumah, Kwame. (1964). *Africa Must Unite*. New York: Frederick A. Praeger.

Nkrumah, Kwame. (1970). *Consciencism: Philosophy and Ideology for De-Colonization*. New York: Modern Reader.

Nnorom, Innocent Chidi and Oladele Osibanjo. (2009). "Toxicity Characterization of Waste Mobile Phone Plastics." *Journal of Hazardous Materials* 161, no. 1: 183–88.

Nohrstedt, Stig A. and Rune Ottosen. (2022). "Obstacles for Critical Journalism in the Security Policy Sector: Revisiting Peace Journalism." *Insights on Peace and Conflict Reporting*. Ed. Kristin Skare Orgeret. Abingdon: Routledge. 32–49.

Nora, Simon and Alain Minc. (1980). *The Computerization of Society: A Report to the President of France*. Cambridge, MA: MIT Press.

Nora Politzer, Malia and Antonia Olmos Alcaraz. (2020). "Covert Islamophobia: An Analysis of *The New York Times* and *The Wall Street Journal* Before and After Charlie Hebdo." *Comunicación y Sopciedad* e7601: 1–24.

Norton-Taylor, Richard. (2020). *The State of Secrecy: Spies and the Media in Britain*. London: IB Tauris.

Nowak, Andrew S., Gabrielle E. Kennelley, Brian J. Krabak, William O. Roberts, Kate M. Tenforde, and Adam S. Tenforde. (2022). "Endurance Athletes and Climate Change." *Journal of Climate Change and Health* 6: 100118.

Nurisso, George C. and Edward Simpson Prescott. (2017, October 18). "The 1970s Origins of Too Big to Fail." *Economic Commentary* 17 https://www.clevelandfed.org/publications/economic-commentary/2017/ec-201717-origins-of-too-big-to-fail#D2.

Nuwer, Rachel. (2017, June 14). "Journalism's New Reality." *Pacific Standard* http://www.psmag.com/nature-and-technology/journalisms-new-reality.

Nye, David E. (1994). *American Technological Sublime*. Cambridge, MA: MIT Press.

Nye, David E. (2006). "Technology and the Production of Difference." *American Quarterly* 58, no. 3: 597–618.

Obama, Barack. (2008). *The Audacity of Hope: Thoughts on Reclaiming the American Dream*. New York: Crown Publishing.

Oborne, Peter. (2015, February 17). "Why I Have Resigned from the *Telegraph*." *openDemocracy* https://www.opendemocracy.net/en/opendemocracyuk/why-i-have-resigned-from-telegraph/.

Oborne, Peter. (2019, October 22). "British Journalists Have Become Part of Johnson's Fake News Machine." *openDemocracy* https://www.opendemocracy.net/en/opendemocracyuk/british-journalists-have-become-part-of-johnsons-fake-news-machine/.

Oborne, Peter. (2021). *The Assault on Truth: Boris Johnson, Donald Trump and the Emergence of a New Moral Barbarism*. London: Simon & Schuster.

Oborne, Peter. (2023, July 5). "Nigel Farage Row: When Muslims Have Their Bank Accounts Closed, Nobody Cares." *Middle East Eye* https://www.middleeasteye.net/opinion/uk-islamophobia-nigel-farage-muslims-bank-accounts-closed-nobody-cares.

O'Connell, Mikey. (2019, July 19). "Welcome to Peak Food TV: Inside Hollywood's Growing Hunger for Culinary Shows." Hollywood Reporter https://www.hollywoodreporter.com/movies/movie-features/gordon-ramsay-more-hollywoods-growing-hunger-food-tv-shows-1225214/.

O'Connor, James. (1998). *Natural Causes: Essays in Ecological Marxism*. New York: Guilford.

OECD. (2021, July). *Economic and Social Impact of Cultural and Creative Sectors* https://www.oecd.org/cfe/leed/OECD-G20-Culture-July-2021.pdf.

Oelrichs, Inga. (2022). "Just Copy and Paste? Usage and Patterns of Social Media Sources in Online Articles on Sport." *International Journal of Sport Communication* 15, no. 4: 325–35.

Ogan, Christine L., Manaf Bashir, Lindita Camaj, Yunjuan Luo, Brian Gaddie, Rosemary Pennington, Sonia Rana, and Mohammed Salih. (2009). "Development Communication: The State of Research in an Era of ICTs and Globalization." *Gazette* 71, no. 8: 655–70.

O'Hehir, Andrew. (2022, February 1). "Legendary Reporter Carl Bernstein on Journalism, Trump and History: 'The Truth is Not Neutral'." *Salon* https://www.salon.com/2022/02/01/legendary-newsman-carl-bernstein-on-journalism-and-history-the-truth-is-not-neutral/.

Oliveira Venancio, Rafael Duarte. (2018). "Performance no gramado, poética no texto: A crônica E O Conto de futebol como jornalismo esportivo alternativo." *Revista ALTERJOR Grupo De Estudos Alterjor: Jornalismo Popular e Alternativo* 18, no. 2: 2–27.

Olson, Mancur. (1971). *The Logic of Collective Action: Public Goods and the Theory of Groups*, 2nd ed. Cambridge, MA: Harvard University Press.

Olson, Mancur. (2000). *Power and Prosperity: Outgrowing Communist and Capitalist Dictatorships*. New York: Basic Books.

Oltermann, Philip. (2020, August 27). "Germany Finds it Hard to Love Hegel 250 Years After His Birth." *Guardian* https://www.theguardian.com/world/2020/aug/27/germany-finds-it-hard-to-love-hegel-250-years-after-his-birth.

Oltermann, Philip. (2023, April 13). "'I'm All for Climate Change': Axel Springer CEO Faces Heat Over Leaked Messages." *Guardian* https://www.theguardian.com/world/2023/apr/13/axel-springer-ceo-mathias-dopfner-leaked-messages-reported.

O'Neill, Molly. (2003). "Food Porn." *Columbia Journalism Review* 42, no. 5: 38–45.

O'Neill, Onora. (2002). *A Question of Trust: The BBC Reith Lectures 2002*. Cambridge: Cambridge University Press.

Ophir, Eyal, Clifford Nass, and Anthony D. Wagner. (2009). "Cognitive Control in Media Multitaskers." *Proceedings of the National Academy of Sciences of the United States of America* 106, no. 37: 15583–587.

Oreskes, Naomi. (2023, June 21). "Written Testimony Submitted to the US Senate Committee on the Budget Hearing on Dollars and Degrees: Investigating Fossil Fuel Dark Money's Systematic Threats to Climate and the Federal Budget: The Causes and Costs of Climate Delay." https://www.budget.senate.gov/imo/media/doc/Dr.%20Naomi%20Oreskes%20-%20Testimony%20-%20Senate%20Budget%20Committee1.pdf.

Oreskes, Naomi and Erik M. Conway. (2010). *Merchants of Doubt*. New York: Bloomsbury Press.

Organisation of Islamic Cooperation. (2015). *Eight OIC Observatory Report on Islamophobia May 2014-April 2015* http://www.oic-oci.org/oicv3/upload/islamophobia/2015/en/reports/8thObRepIslamophobiaFinal.pdf.

Orozco Cabrales, Sulena. (2019, July 8). "Top 10 de periodistas afrocolombianos más seguidos en redes sociales 2019." *El Tiempo* https://blogs.eltiempo.com/afrocolombianidad/2019/07/08/top-10-de-periodistas-afrocolombianos-mas-seguidos-redes/.
Orwell, George. (1937). *The Road to Wigan Pier*. London: Victor Gollancz.
Orwell, George. (1944, May 12). "As I Please." *Tribune* telelib.com/authors/O/OrwellGeorge/essay/tribune/AsIPlease19440512.html.
Orwell, George. (1945, December). "The Sporting Spirit." *Tribune* http://www.orwell.ru/library/articles/spirit/english/espirit.
Orwell, George. (1949). *Nineteen Eighty-Four* https://files.libcom.org/files/1984.pdf.
PA. (2020, June 30). "Clive Tyldesley Calls for Commentators to Receive Training on Racial Stereotyping." *Guardian* https://www.theguardian.com/football/2020/jun/30/clive-tyldesleycalls-for-commentators-to-receive-training-on-racial-stereotyping.
Paché, Gilles. (2020). "Sustainability Challenges in Professional Football: The Destructive Effects of the Society of the Spectacle." *Journal of Sustainable Development* 13, no. 1: 85–96.
Painter, James, Joshua Ettinger, David Holmes, Loredana Loy, Janaina Pinto, Lucy Richardson, Laura Thomas-Walters, Kjell Vowles, and Rachel Wetts. (2023). "Climate Delay Discourses Present in Global Mainstream Television Coverage of the IPCC's 2021 Report." *Communications Earth & Environment* 4 https://www.nature.com/articles/s43247-023-00760-2.
Paiva, Raquel, Márcio Guerra, and Leonardo Custódio. (2015). "Professional, Social and Regulatory Characteristics of Journalism in Online and Traditional Media in Brazil." *African Journalism Studies* 36, no. 3: 8–32.
Palmer, Michael, Oliver Boyd-Barrett, and Terhi Rantanen. (1998). "Global Financial News." *The Globalisation of News*. Ed. Oliver Boyd-Barrett and Terhi Rantanen. London: Sage Publications. 61–78.
Pananond, Pavida and Thinitan Pongsudhirak. (2016, May 6). "A Thai Monopoly and Leicester's Triumph." *Bangkok Post* https://www.bangkokpost.com/opinion/opinion/960953/a-thai-monopolyand-leicesters-triumph.
Paper Task Force. (1995). *Paper Task Force Recommendations for Purchasing and Using Environmentally Preferable Paper: Project Synopsis*. New York: Environmental Defense Fund.
Parameswaran, Prashanth. (2015, January 13). "*Charlie Hebdo* Exposes Southeast Asia's Hypocrisy." *The Diplomat* https://thediplomat.com/2015/01/charlie-hebdo-exposes-southeast-asias-hypocrisy/.
Parekh, Lord Bhikhu. (2017). "Limits of Free Speech." *Philosophia* 45: 931–35.
Park, Robert E. (1922). *The Immigrant Press and Its Control*. New York: Harper & Brothers Publishers.
Park, Robert E. (1940). "News as a Form of Knowledge: A Chapter in the Sociology of Knowledge." *American Journal of Sociology* 45, no. 5: 669–86.
Parry, Roland Lloyd and Benedicte Rey with Adria Laborda and Kate Tan. (2023, May 12). "Meteorologists Targeted in Climate Misinfo Surge." *Barron's* https://www.barrons.com/news/meteorologists-targeted-in-climate-misinfo-surge-276b0eee.
Patel, Ian Sanjay. (2021). *We're Here Because You Were There: Immigration and the End of Empire*. London: Verso.
Patnaik, Arun Kumar. (2004, March 13–19). "Gramsci Today." *Economic & Political Weekly*: 1120–123.

Peace Congress Committee. (1849). *Report of the Proceedings of the Second General Peace Congress, Held in Paris*. London: Charles Gilpin.
Perez de Fransius, Marianne. (2014). "Peace Journalism Case Study: US Media Coverage of the Iraq War." *Journalism* 15, no. 1: 72–88.
Perreault, Gregory and Travis R. Bell. (2022). "Towards a 'Digital' Sports Journalism: Field Theory, Changing Boundaries and Evolving Technologies." *Communication & Sport* 10, no. 3: 398–416.
Pettegree, Andrew. (2014). *The Invention of News: How the World Came to Know About Itself*. New Haven, CT: Yale University Press.
Pettegree, Andrew. (2015). *Brand Luther: 1517, Printing, and the Making of the Reformation*. New York: Penguin.
Pew Research Center. (2015). *How Scientists Engage the Public* http://www.pewinternet.org/2015/02/15/how-scientists-engage-public/.
Pew Research Center. (2018, May 18). *In Western Europe, Public Attitudes Toward News Media More Divided by Populist Views Than Left-Right Ideology* file:///Users/btamiller/Desktop/PERIODISMO/PARALEER/INTROD/PJ2018.05.14WesternEuropeFINAL.pdf.
Phillips, Peter. (2008, February 8). "Big Media Interlocks with Corporate America." *Project Censored* https://www.projectcensored.org/big-media-interlocks-with-corporate-america/?doingwpcron=1690873277.9379589557647705078125.
Phongpaichit, Pasuk and Chris Baker. (2013). "Reviving Democracy at Thailand's 2011 election." *Asian Survey* 53, no. 4: 607–28.
Pian Chan, Sharon, *rapporteur*. (2017, May). *The Future of Journalism: A Report on the Aspen Institute Dialogue on the Future of Journalism* https://www.aspeninstitute.org/wp-content/uploads/2017/05/2017-Future-of-Journalism-FINAL.pdf.
Pickard, Victor. (2020). *Democracy Without Journalism: Confronting the Misinformation Society*. New York: Oxford University Press.
Pickford, N. (2014, July 14). "Cyclists Are Miles Behind Formula 1 in the Environmental Race." *Hull Daily Mail* http://www.hulldailymail.co.uk/Cyclists-miles-Formula-1-environmental-race/story-21460343-detail/story.html.
Pielke, Roger, Jr. (2012, October 31). "Hurricanes and Human Choice." *Wall Street Journal* https://www.wsj.com/articles/SB10001424052970204840504578089413659452702.
Planet Ark. (2008, January 24). *The Role of E-Billing in Reducing the Environmental Impacts of Paper Consumption* http://papercutz.planetark.org/paper/impact.cfm.
Plester, Jeremy. (2021, April 22). "Weatherwatch: The Great Snowstorm that Engulfed Britain in April 1849." *Guardian* https://www.theguardian.com/uk-news/2021/apr/22/weatherwatch-the-great-snowstorm-that-engulfed-britain-in-april-1849.
Polanyi, Karl. (2001). *The Great Transformation: The Political and Economic Origins of Our Time*. Boston, MA: Beacon Press.
Połońska-Kimunguyi, Eva and Marie Gillespie. (2016). "Terrorism Discourse on French International Broadcasting: *France 24* and the Case of *Charlie Hebdo* Attacks in Paris." *European Journal of Communication* 31, no. 5: 568–83.
Ponce De Leon, Charles L. (2015, May 23). ""Perilously Close to Propaganda": How Fox News Shilled for Iraq War, and Jon Stewart Returned Sanity." *Salon* https://www.salon.com/2015/05/23/perilouslyclosetopropagandahowfoxnewsshilledforiraqwarandjonstewartreturnedsanity/.

Pontifical Council for Social Communications. (2002). *Ethics in Internet* https://www.vatican.va/roman_curia/pontifical_councils/pccs/documents/rc_pc_pccs_doc_20020228_ethics-internet_en.html.

Pope Benedict XVI. (2013, May 12). "Social Networks: Portals of Truth and Faith; New Spaces for Evangelization." https://www.vatican.va/content/benedict-xvi/en/messages/communications/documents/hf_ben-xvi_mes_20130124_47th-world-communications-day.html.

Pope Francis. (2015). *Laudato Si'* https://www.vatican.va/content/francesco/en/encyclicals/documents/papa-francesco_20150524_enciclica-laudato-si.html

Pope Pius XII. (1957). *Miranda Prorsus: Encyclical Letter of His Holiness Pius XII by Divine Providence Pope* https://www.vatican.va/content/pius-xii/en/encyclicals/documents/hfp-xiienc08091957miranda-prorsus.html.

Pope, Stacey, Rachel Allison, and Kate Petty. (2023). "Gender Equality In the "Next Stage" of the "New Age?" Content and Fan Perceptions of English Media Coverage of the 2019 FIFA Women's World Cup." *Sociology of Sport Journal* https://journals.humankinetics.com/view/journals/ssj/aop/article-10.1123-ssj.2022-0195/article-10.1123-ssj.2022-0195.xml.

Posetti, Julie and Nabeelah Shabbir, eds. (2022). *The Chilling: A Global Study of Online Violence Against Women Journalists*. International Center for Journalists/UNESCO https://www.icfj.org/sites/default/files/2023-02/ICFJ%20Unesco-TheChillingOnlineViolence.pdf.

Premalatha, M., Tabassum-Abbasi, Tasneem Abbasi, and S. A. Abbasi. (2014). "The Generation, Impact, and Management of E-Waste: State of the Art." *Critical Reviews in Environmental Science and Technology* 44, no. 14: 1577–678.

Price, Jenna with Blair Williams. (2021). *2021 Women for Media Report: 'Take the Next Steps'*. Women's Leadership Institute Australia https://www.wlia.org.au/files/ugd/bd298838fee1f77f71481b91ff82163e12f3b1.pdf.

Public Citizen. (2019, August 13). *Foxic: Fox News Network's Dangerous Climate Denial 2019* https://www.citizen.org/article/foxic-fox-news-networks-dangerous-climate-denial-2019/?eType=EmailBlastContent&eId=52dbcd4f-2756-4284-973a-7fe06c039cd5.

Pufendorf, Samuel. (2000). *On the Duty of Man and Citizen According to Natural Law*. Trans. Michael Silverthorne. Ed. James Tully. Cambridge: Cambridge University Press.

Pugh, Tom. (2020, July 30). "Are Young Trees or Old Forests More Important for Slowing Climate Change?" *The Conversation* https://theconversation.com/are-young-trees-or-old-forests-more-important-for-slowing-climate-change-139813.

Putnam, Hilary. (2002). *The Collapse of the Fact Value Dichotomy and Other Essays Including the Rosenthal Lectures*. Cambridge, MA: Harvard University Press.

Quinn, Erin and Chris Young. (2015, January 15). "D. C. Influencers Spend More in Advertising and PR Than Lobbying." *Time* http://time.com/3668128/lobbying-advertising-public-relations/.

Quitián Roldán, David Leonardo. (2013). "La economía del fútbol colombiano: De la ilegalidad y el crimen al glamur globalizado." *Polémika* 10, no. 1: 60–65.

Quitián Roldán, David Leonardo and Olga Luciá Urrea Beltrán. (2016a). "Fútbol, desarrollo social y patria: La violencia como factor de lo nacional en clave de gol." *Revista San Gregorio Especial* 2: 162–70.

Quitián Roldán, David Leonardo and Olga Lucía Urrea Beltrán. (2016b). "Fútbol, radio y nación (1946-1974): Una visión antropológica de la violencia en Colombia." *Espacio Abierto: Cuaderno Venezolano De Sociología* 25, no. 2: 51–66.

Raccanello, Daniela, Roberto Burro, Margherita Brondino, and Margherita Pasini. (2018). "Relevance of Terrorism for Italian Students Not Directly Exposed to It: The Affective Impact of the 2015 Paris and the 2016 Brussels Attacks." *Stress and Health* 34: 338–43.

Rafi Atal, Maha. (2018). "The Cultural and Economic Power of Advertisers in the Business Press." *Journalism* 19, no. 8: 1078–095.

Rafter, Kevin. (2014). "Voices in the Crisis: The Role of Media Elites in Interpreting Ireland's Banking Collapse." *European Journal of Communication* 29, no. 5: 598–607.

Rainforest Action Network. (2018). *Broken Promises: A Case Study on How the Tokyo 2020 Games and Japanese Financiers are Fueling Land-Grabbing and Rainforest Destruction in Indonesia* https://www.ran.org/wp-content/uploads/2018/11/BrokenPromises.pdf.

Ramanathan, Valli Meenakshi. (2013, January 7). "Global IT Spending Pegged at $3.7 Trillion; Gadget Spending Forecast at $1.1 Trillion in 2013." *International Business Times* http://www.ibtimes.com/global-it-spending-pegged-37-trillion-gadget-spending-forecast-11-trillion-2013-996132.

Ramos, Juan Pablo. (2020, June 23). "Amazon, Microsoft y la hipocresía con el medio ambiente." *Cletofilia* https://cletofilia.com/amazon-microsoft-y-la-hipocresia-con-el-medio-ambiente/.

Raphael, Chad, Lori Tokunaga, and Christina Wai. (2004). "Who is the Real Target? Media Response to Controversial Investigative Reporting on Corporations." *Journalism Studies* 5, no. 2: 165–78.

Rathbone. John Paul. (2013, June 3). "The History and Politics of Colombian Media." *Financial Times* https://www.ft.com/content/621bcdfc-9de5-11e2-9ccc-00144feabdc0.

Rathborn, Jack. (2016, August 5). "Leicester City Owners Reward Their Premier League Title Winners With a £105,000 BMW i8 Each." *Mirror* https://www.mirror.co.uk/sport/football/news/leicester-city-owners-reward-premier-8569637.

Rattan, Aneeta, Siri Chilazi, Oriane Georgeac, and Iris Bohnet. (2019, June 6). "Tacking the Underrepresentation of Women in Media." *Harvard Business Review* https://hbr.org/2019/06/tackling-the-underrepresentation-of-women-in-media.

Ray, Manas Ranjan, Gopeshwar Mukherjee, Sanghita Roychowdhury, and Twisha Lahiri. (2004). "Respiratory and General Health Impairments of Ragpickers in India: A Study in Delhi." *International Archives of Occupational and Environmental Health* 77, no. 8: 595–98.

Readfearn, Graham. (2015a, March 1). "Was Climate Science Denialist Willie Soon Funded to do Science or was it Just PR Cash from the Fossil Fuel Industry?" *Desmog* http://www.desmogblog.com/2015/03/01/was-climate-science-denialist-willie-soon-funded-do-science-or-was-it-just-pr-cash-fossil-fuel-industry.

Readfearn, Graham. (2015b, March 5). "Doubt Over Climate Science is a Product with an Industry Behind It." *Guardian* http://www.theguardian.com/environment/planet-oz/2015/mar/05/doubt-over-climate-science-is-a-product-with-an-industry-behind-it.

Readfearn, Graham. (2016, June 21). "Conservative Founders of Climate Denial Are Quietly Spending Millions to Generate More Partisan Journalism." AlterNet https://www.alternet.org/2016/06/conservative-funders-climate-denial-spending-millions-generate-more-partisan-journalism.

Readfearn, Graham. (2022, September 22). "Sky and the *Australian* Find 'No Evidence' of a Climate Emergency—They Weren't Looking Hard Enough."

Guardian https://www.theguardian.com/environment/2022/sep/22/sky-and-the-australian-find-no-evidence-of-a-climate-emergency-they-werent-looking-hard-enough?hsenc=p2ANqtz-8XaluMi2YiPyOjCrOF4jfHiCLFJA9ZDRjX-fSzu-Y3XmwFB1vOm3YivNxWcJF75Ewhdj.

Readfearn, Graham. (2023, May 6). "Climate Scientists First Laughed at a 'Bizarre Campaign' Against the BoM—Then Came the Harassment." *Guardian* https://www.theguardian.com/science/2023/may/07/climate-scientists-first-laughed-at-a-bizarre-campaign-against-the-bom-then-came-the-harassment.

Reed, Sada. (2018). ""I'm Not a Fan: I'm a Journalist": Measuring American Sports Journalists' Sports Enthusiasm." *Journal of Sports Media* 13, no. 1: 27–47.

Reich, Robert. (2023, April 11). "Trump Thinks His Arrest Helped His Presidential Chances. He's Wrong." *Guardian* https://www.theguardian.com/commentisfree/2023/apr/11/trump-arrest-republican-nomination-2024-independents.

Reich, Zvi. (2012). "Different Practices, Similar Logic: Comparing News Reporting Across Political, Financial, and Territorial Beats." *International Journal of Press/Politics* 17, no. 1: 76–99.

Reid, Caroline. (2008, May 3). "For Formula One, Sex Sells; But Not the Way Max Likes It." *The Spectator* https://www.spectator.co.uk/article/for-formula-one-sex-sells-but-not-the-way-max-likes-it/.

Reid, Caroline. (2015, March 19). "20 Brands That Defined F1." *Raconteur* https://www.raconteur.net/20-brands-that-defined-f1/.

Reis de Oliveira, Camila, Andréa Moura Bernardes, and Annelise Engel Gerbase. (2012). "Collection and Recycling of Electronic Scrap: A Worldwide Overview and Comparison with the Brazilian Situation." *Waste Management* 32, no. 8: 1592–610.

Reis Mourao, Paulo. (2018). "Smoking Gentlemen—How Formula One Has Controlled CO_2 Emissions." *Sustainability* 10, no. 6: 1841.

Renda, Andrea. (2018). *The Legal Framework to Address "Fake News": Possible Policy Actions at the EU Level*. European Parliament's Committee on the Internal Market and Consumer Protection http://www.europarl.europa.eu/RegData/etudes/IDAN/2018/619013/IPOLIDA(2018)619013EN.pdf.

Rendall, Steve and Daniel Butterworth. (2004, May/June). "How Public is Public Radio?" *EXTRA!*: 16–19.

Renwick Monroe, Kristen, ed. (2005). *Perestroika! The Raucous Rebellion in Political Science*. New Haven, CT: Yale University Press.

Reporters Without Borders. (2021, May 13). *2011-2020: A Study of Journalist Murders in Latin America Confirms the Importance of Strengthening Protection Policies* https://rsf.org/en/2011-2020-study-journalist-murders-latin-america-confirms-importance-strengthening-protection.

Reporters Without Borders. (2022). *World Press Freedom Index* https://rsf.org/en/index.

Rewilak, Johan M. (2023). "Dictating Paly to the Left Wing? Does Soccer Make You More Democratic?" *Frontiers in Sports and Active Living* https://www.ncbi.nlm.nih.gov/pmc/articles/PMC10076846/.

Reynolds, John. (2012, February 17). "BP's Brand Image Benefits from London 2012 Sponsorship, Claims Research." *Campaign* http://www.campaignlive.co.uk/article/1117665/bps-brand-image-benefits-london-2012-sponsorship-claims-research?srcsite=marketingmagazine.

Rich, Nathaniel and George Steinmetz. (2018, August 1). "Losing Earth." *New York Times Magazine* https://www.nytimes.com/interactive/2018/08/01/magazine/climate-change-losing-earth.html.
Richards, Giles. (2021, November 26). "Climate Emergency Accelerates F1's Efforts to Clean Up Its Image." *Guardian* https://www.theguardian.com/sport/2021/nov/26/climate-emergency-accelerates-f1-efforts-to-clean-up-image.
Richards, Giles. (2023, May 21). "After the Flood, Storms Lie Ahead for Formula One in Race to Hit Carbon Zero." *Guardian* https://www.theguardian.com/sport/2023/may/21/after-the-flood-storms-lie-ahead-for-formula-one-in-race-to-hit-carbon-zero.
Ricchiardi, Sherry. (2006, December/January). "Dangerous Assignment." *American Journalism Review* https://ajrarchive.org/Article.asp?id=4003&id=4003.
Riggio, Olivia. (2022, November 18). "Climate Confusion and Complicity at the *New York Times*." *FAIR* https://fair.org/home/climate-confusion-and-complicity-at-the-new-york-times/.
Rios-Rodríguez, Raul and Ángel Arrese. (2021). "Economic Journalism and the Elitist Approach: A Persistent Pattern in the Use of Sources? The Spanish Press Coverage of the Economic Crisis (2008-2015)." *Brazilian Journalism Research* 17, no. 3: 764–91.
Rodríguez Romero, Carlos Alberto and Edison Jair Duque Oliva. (2007). "Seguimiento a la dinámica competitiva de dos grupos económicos colombianos." *Innovar: Revista de Ciencias Administrativas y Sociales* 17, no. 29: 137–54.
Rojas, Cristina. (2002). *Civilization and Violence: Regimes of Representation in Nineteenth-Century Colombia*. Minneapolis: University of Minnesota Press.
Romero, Mar. (2016, November 24). "Lucía Mbomío: "Una negra periodista! Que aixó sigui notícia em genera." *Crític* https://www.elcritic.cat/entrevistes/lucia-mbomio-una-negra-periodista-que-aixo-sigui-noticia-em-genera-contradiccions-11719.
Ronald, Issy. (2022, December 17). "Brand it like Beckham: How Has This World Cup Affected the 'Brands' Associated with It?" *CNN* https://edition.cnn.com/2022/12/17/football/brands-sponsors-david-beckham-world-cup-2022-spt-intl/index.html.
Ronsse, S. (2019). *Toward a Fairer ICT Supply Chain—Research and fact-finding mission in the context of the project 'Make ICT Fair' in Oruro, Bolivia*. Edinburgh: Make ICT Fair https://www.ed.ac.uk/sustainability/what-we-do/supply-chains/initiatives/make-ict-fair-project/towards-a-fairer-ict-supply-chain.
Roosevelt, Franklin Delano. (1937, January 20). "Second Inaugural Address." https://millercenter.org/the-presidency/presidential-speeches/january-20-1937-second-inaugural-address.
Roper, Dean. (2023, March 9). "Report: World Press Trends Outlook 2022-2023." *World Association of News Publishers* https://wan-ifra.org/insight/report-world-press-trends-outlook-2022-2023/.
Rorty, Richard. (1981). *Philosophy and the Mirror of Nature*. Princeton: Princeton University Press.
Rose, Steve. (2022, June 8). "A Deadly Ideology: How the 'Great Replacement Theory' Went Mainstream." *Guardian* https://www.theguardian.com/world/2022/jun/08/a-deadly-ideology-how-the-great-replacement-theory-went-mainstream.

Rosen, Mike. (2010, July 14). "Soccer is an Un-American Activity." *Denver Post* https://www.denverpost.com/2010/07/14/rosen-soccer-is-an-un-american-activity/.

Rosenblum, Michael. (2017, December 6). "The End of Journalism." *HuffPost* https://www.huffpost.com/entry/the-end-of-journalism-asb8358296.

Roser, Max and Esteban Ortiz-Ospina. (2018, September 20). "Literacy." *Our World in Data* https://ourworldindata.org/literacy.

Ross, Andrew, ed. (1996). *Science Wars*. Durham, NC: Duke University Press.

Ross, Andrew. (2010, October 17). "The Corporate Analogy Unravels." *Chronicle of Higher Education* https://www.chronicle.com/article/the-corporate-analogy-unravels/.

Rowe, David and Raymond Boyle. (2022). "Sport, Journalism, Social Reproduction and Change." *Oxford Handbook of Sport and Society*. Ed. Lawrence A. Wenner. Oxford: Oxford University Press. 1025–043.

Rowe, David. (2007). "Sports Journalism: Still the 'Toy Department' of the News Media?" *Journalism: Theory, Practice & Criticism* 8, no. 4: 385–405.

Rowe, David. (2013, February 21). "On Scandal After Scandal, Sports Journalists Drop the Ball." *The Conversation* https://theconversation.com/on-scandal-after-scandal-sports-journalistsdrop-the-ball-12251.

Rowe, David. (2017). "Sports Journalism and the FIFA Scandal: Personalization, Co-optation, and Investigation." *Communication & Sport* 5, no. 5: 515–33.

Rowland, Christopher. (2013, November 5). "Researcher Helps Sow Climate-Change Doubt." *Boston Globe* https://www.bostonglobe.com/news/nation/2013/11/05/harvard-smithsonian-global-warming-skeptic-helps-feed-strategy-doubt-gridlock-congress/uHssYO1anoWSiLw0v1YcUJ/story.html.

Roxborough, Scott and Agustín Mango. (2018, June 25). "World Cup's Female Reporters Make History While Enduring Harassment." *Hollywood Reporter* https://www.hollywoodreporter.com/news/general-news/metoo-female-reporters-at-world-cup-1122928/.

Ruiz Patiño, Jorge Humberto. (2017). "Balance sobre la historiografía del deporte en Colombia: Un panorama de su desarrollo." *Materiales para la Historia del Deporte* 15: 24–44.

RunRepeat. (2020). *Racial Bias in Soccer Commentary* https://runrepeat.com/racial-biasstudy-soccer.

Ruser, Alexander. (2018). *Climate Politics and the Impact of Think Tanks: Scientific Expertise in Germany and the US*. Cham: Palgrave Macmillan.

Rushkoff, Douglas. (2022). *Survival of the Richest: Escape Fantasies of the Tech Billionaires*. New York: WW Norton.

Rutenberg, Jim. (2000, September 21). "Sydney 2000: Television; NBC's Ratings for Olympics are Worst Ever." *New York Times* https://www.nytimes.com/2000/09/20/sports/sydney-2000-television-nbc-s-ratings-for-olympics-are-worst-ever.html.

Rutenberg, Jim. (2003, March 25). "Newspapers: Words Reflect Changing Report." *New York Times* https://www.nytimes.com/2003/03/25/us/a-nation-at-war-newspapers-words-reflect-changing-report.html.

Ruthrof, Horst. (1992). *Pandora and Occam: On the Limits of Language and Literature*. Bloomington: Indiana University Press.

Saad, Lydia. (2003, July 21). "Public Balks at Obesity Lawsuits." *Gallup News Service* https://news.gallup.com/poll/8869/public-balks-obesity-lawsuits.aspx.

Sacks, Harvey. (1995). *Lectures on Conversation: Volumes I and II*. Ed. Gail Jefferson. London: Blackwell.

Sadeghi, McKenzie and Lorenzo Arvanitis. (2023, May 1). "Rise of the Newsbots: AI-Generated News Websites Proliferating Online." *Newsguard* https://www.newsguardtech.com/special-reports/newsbots-ai-generated-news-websites-proliferating/.
Said, Edward. (1993). "An Interview with Edward Said." *boundary 2* 20, no. 1: 1–25.
Said, Edward. (2003, March 20–26). "The Other America." *Al-Ahram*.
Saint-Simon, Henri de. (2015). *Selected Writings on Science, Industry and Social Organisation*. Trans. and Ed. Keith Taylor. London: Routledge.
Saiya, Nilay. (2016). "Blasphemy and Terrorism in the Muslim World." *Terrorism and Political Violence* 29, no. 6: 1087–105.
Saiya, Nilay. (2020). "Confronting Apocalyptic Terrorism: Lessons from France and Japan." *Studies in Conflict and Terrorism* 43, no. 9: 775–95.
Salazar, Miguel. (2018, September 26). "Soccer and Domestic Violence: When the Beautiful Game Turns Ugly." *The Nation* https://www.thenation.com/article/archive/soccer-and-domestic-violence-when-the-beautiful-game-turns-ugly/.
Salovaara, Inka. (2015). "#Je Suis Charlie: Networks, Affects and Distributed Agency of Media Assemblage." *Conjunctions: Transdisciplinary Journal of Cultural Participation* 2, no. 1: 103–15.
Sampedro, Víctor. (2021). *Comunicación y sociedad: Opinión pública y poder*. Barcelona: Fundació Universitat Oberta de Catalunya.
Sampedro Blanco, Víctor. (2023, January 2). "Desmilitarizar el debate público. Agendas, marcos y relatos para la democracia." *ctxt: contexto y acción* https://ctxt.es/es/20230201/Firmas/41966/Victor-Sampedro-Blanco-Desmilitarizar-guerra-armas-discurso.htm.
Sampei, Yuki and Midori Aoyagi-Usui. (2009). "Mass-Media Coverage, Its Influence on Public Awareness of Climate-Change Issues, and Implications for Japan's National Campaign to Reduce Greenhouse Gas Emissions." *Global Environmental Change* 19, no. 2: 203–12.
Samuel, Martin. (2020, July 2). "Let's Get Down to the Nitty-Gritty … Commentators Must not be Scared to Speak Freely." *Daily Mail* https://www.dailymail.co.uk/sport/football/article-8484997/MARTIN-SAMUEL-Lets-nitty-gritty-commentators-not-scared-speak.html.
Sana, Faria, Tina Weston, and Nicholas J. Cepeda. (2013). "Laptop Multitasking Hinders Classroom Learning for Both Users and Nearby Peers." *Computers & Education* 62, no. 1: 24–31.
Santos Molano, Enrique. (2016, September). "Fútbol: Una pasión incontenible." *Credencial Historia* http://www.revistacredencial.com/credencial/historia/temas/futbol-una-pasion-incontenible.
Sarnoff, David. (1942). "Preface III." *4000 Years of Television: The Story of Seeing at a Distance*. Ed. Richard Whittaker Hubbell. New York: GP Putnam's Sons. xiii–xiv.
Sarnoff, David. (2004). "Our Next Frontier … Transoceanic TV." *Mass Communication and American Social Thought: Key Texts, 1919-1968*. Eds. John Durham Peters and Peter Simonson. Lanham, MD: Rowman & Littlefield. 309–10.
Schäfer, Mike S. (2012). "Online Communication on Climate Change and Climate Politics: A Literature Review." *Wiley Interdisciplinary Reviews: Climate Change* 3, no. 6: 527–43.
Schenk, James. (n.d.). "What is the Most Popular Section in a Newspaper?" *AuthorsCast* https://authorscast.com/what-is-the-most-popular-section-in-a-newspaper.
Scherer, Jay and David Rowe, eds. (2014). *Sport, Public Broadcasting, and Cultural Citizenship: Signal Lost?* New York: Routledge.

Schiffrin, Anya, ed. (2017). *In the Service of Power: Media Capture and the Threat to Democracy*. Washington, DC: Center for International Media Assistance.

Schiller, Dan. (1981). *Objectivity and the News: The Public and the Rise of Commercial Journalism*. Philadelphia: University of Pennsylvania Press.

Schiller, Dan. (2014). *Digital Depression: Information Technology and Economic Crisis*. Chicago: University of Illinois Press.

Schlichting, Inga. (2013). "Strategic Framing of Climate Change by Industry Actors: A Meta-Analysis." *Environmental Communication* 7, no. 4: 493–511.

Schmidt, Hans C. (2018). "Forgotten Athletes and Token Reporters: Analyzing the Gender Bias in Sports Journalism." *Atlantic Journal of Communication* 26, no. 1: 59–74.

Schmidt, Thomas R. (2023). "Challenging Journalistic Objectivity: How Journalists of Color Call for a Reckoning." *Journalism* https://journals.sagepub.com/doi/10.1177/14648849231160997.

Schneider, Christian. (2022, November 26). "Soccer is Unjust and Un-American." *National Review* https://www.nationalreview.com/2022/11/soccer-is-unjust-and-un-american/.

Schoch, Lucie. (2020). "The Gender of Sports News: Horizontal Segregation and Marginalization of Female Journalists in the Swiss Press." *Communication & Sport* 10, no. 4: 746–66.

Schultz, George P. and James A. Baker III. (2017, February 7). "A Conservative Answer to Climate Change." *Wall Street Journal* https://www.wsj.com/articles/a-conservative-answer-to-climate-change-1486512334.

Schulz, Bailey. (2023, February 23). "Gannett Posts Fourth-Quarter Profit After Cost-Cutting." *USA Today* https://eu.usatoday.com/story/money/2023/02/23/gannett-fourth-quarter-profit/11329449002/.

Scott, C. P. (2017, October 23). "A Hundred Years." *Guardian* https://www.theguardian.com/sustainability/cp-scott-centenary-essay.

Scott, Mike. (2013, August 5). "Could Innovation in Formula One Drive Sustainable Technology?" *Guardian* http://www.theguardian.com/sustainable-business/innovation-formula-one-sustainable-technology.

Sedghi, Ami, George Arnett, and Chris Moran. (2014, April 17). "*The Guardian*'s Top 100: Which Articles Have Been Most Popular?" *Guardian* https://www.theguardian.com/news/datablog/2014/apr/17/the-guardians-top-100-which-articles-have-been-most-popular.

Selassie, Habte. (2002, May 28). "Warming Up to Soccer." *Village Voice* https://www.villagevoice.com/2002/05/28/warming-up-to-soccer/.

Self, Will. (2015, February 13). "A Point of View: What's the Point of Satire?" *BBC Magazine* http://www.bbc.co.uk/news/magazine-31442441.

Sen, Amartya. (2000). *Development as Freedom*. New York: Alfred A Knopf.

Sen, Amartya. (2009). *The Idea of Justice*. Cambridge, MA: The Belknap Press of Harvard University Press.

Senchyne, Jonathan. (2020). *The Intimacy of Paper in Early and Nineteenth-Century American Literature*. Amherst: University of Massachusetts Press.

Serlin, David Harley. (1995). "The Dialogue of Gender in Melville's "The Paradise of Bachelors and the Tartarus of Maids"." *Modern Language Studies* 25, no. 2: 80–87.

Serrano-Amaya, José Fernando. (2018). *Homophobic Violence in Armed Conflict and Political Transition*. Cham: Palgrave Macmillan.

Shabecoff, Philip. (1983, October 21). "Haste of Global Warming Trend Opposed." *New York Times*: A1.
Shalala, Amanda. (2020, December 14). "How the ABC News 50:50 Project is Transforming Our Coverage of Women in Sport." ABC https://www.abc.net.au/news/redirects/backstory/2020-12-14/amanda-shalala-on-abc-news-boosting-women-in-sport-coverage/12980472.
Sheffer, Mary Lou and Brad Schultz. (2010). "Paradigm Shift or Passing Fad? Twitter and Sports Journalism." *Journal of Sports Media* 6, no. 2: 43–64.
Shehabi, Arman, Sarah Smith, Dale Sartor, Richard Brown, Magnus Herrlin, Jonathan Koomey, Eric R. Masanet, Nathaniel Horner, Inês Azevedo, and William Lintner. (2016). *United States Data Center Energy Usage Report*. Lawrence Berkeley National Laboratory, Berkeley, California. LBNL-005775 http://etapublications.
Sheppard, Kate. (2010, July/August). "Fair and … Carbon Neutral?" *Mother Jones*: 42–43.
Sherwood, Merryn, Matthew Nicholson, and Tim Marjoribanks. (2018). "Women Working in Sport Media and Public Relations: No Advantage in a Male-Dominated World." *Communication Research and Practice* 4, no. 2: 102–16.
Shils, Edward. (1966). "Mass Society and its Culture." *Reader in Public Opinion and Communication*, 2nd ed. Eds. Bernard Berelson and Morris Janowitz. New York: Free Press. 505–28.
Shor, Eran, Arnout van de Rijt, Alex Miltsov, Vivek Kulkarni, and Steven Skiena. (2015). "A Paper Ceiling: Explaining the Persistent Underrepresentation of Women in Printed News." *American Sociological Review* 80, no. 5: 960–84.
Sibley, Lisa. (2009, August 19). "Cleantech Group Report: E-Readers a Win for Carbon Emissions." *Cleantech* http://cleantech.com/news/4867/cleantech-group-finds-positive-envi.
Siemaszko, Corky. (2021, July 24). "Heat Wave Hits Tokyo as Olympic Organizers Battle to Keep Covid Rates Down." *NBC News* https://www.nbcnews.com/news/olympics/heat-wave-hits-tokyo-olympic-organizers-battle-keep-covid-rates-n1274899.
Silberstein-Loeb, Jonathan. (2014). *The International Distribution of News: The Associated Press, Press Association, and Reuters, 1848-1947*. Cambridge: Cambridge University Press.
Silver, Laura, Aaron Smith, Courtney Johnson, Jingjing Jiang, Monica Anderson, and Lee Rainie. (2019, March 7). *Mobile Connectivity in Emerging Economies*. Pew Research Center https://www.pewinternet.org/2019/03/07/mobile-connectivity-in-emerging-economies/.
Silver, Laura and Elisa Shearer. (2021, June 2). *Americans in News Media 'Bubbles' Think Differently About Foreign Policy Than Others*. Pew Research Center https://www.pewresearch.org/fact-tank/2021/06/02/americans-in-news-media-bubbles-think-differently-about-foreign-policy-than-others/.
Silverman, Alex and John Ourand. (2022, June 14). "MLS Goes with Apple in Landmark 10-Year Global Media Rights Deal." *Sports Business Journal* https://www.sportsbusinessjournal.com/Daily/Issues/2022/06/14/Media/MLS-TV-rights.aspx.
Simmel, Georg. (1949). "The Sociology of Sociability." Trans. Everett C. Hughes. American Journal of Sociology 55, no. 3: 254–61.
Simonton, Ana. (2017). *Out of Struggle: Strengthening and Expanding Movement Journalism in the U.S. South*. Project South https://projectsouth.org/wp-content/uploads/2017/08/Out-of-Struggle-7.26.pdf.

Sin, Ben. (2014, February 12). "All the Modern Olympic Mascots in One Adorable Infographic." *Sports Illustrated* https://www.si.com/extra-mustard/2014/02/12/olympics-mascots-infographic.

Sinclair, Upton. (1919). *The Brass Check: A Study of American Journalism*. Pasadena: The Author.

SINTEF. (2013, May 22). "Big Data, for Better or Worse: 90% of World's Data Generated Over Last Two Years." ScienceDaily http://www.sciencedaily.com/releases/2013/05/130522085217.htm.

Sklair, Leslie, ed. (2021). *The Anthropocene in Global Media: Neutralizing the Risk*. Abingdon: Routledge.

Smith, Adam. (1970). *The Wealth of Nations Books I-III*. Ed. A. Skinner. Harmondsworth: Penguin.

Smith, Anthony D. (2000). *The Nation in History: Historiographical Debates about Ethnicity and Nationalism*. Oxford: Polity.

Snape, Jack. (2023, August 8). "Matildas Break TV Ratings Records, Beating AFL Grand Final and Origin." *Guardian* https://www.theguardian.com/football/2023/aug/08/womens-world-cup-2023-matildas-vs-denmark-tv-ratings-records-afl-state-of-origin.

Snow, C. P. (1987). *The Two Cultures and a Second Look: An Expanded Version of the Two Cultures and the Scientific Revolution*. Cambridge: Cambridge University Press.

Snow, Jon. (2017, August 24). "'I Know Nothing—But I've Experienced a Lot': The MacTaggart Lecture 2017." *iNews* https://inews.co.uk/news/uk/jon-snow-speech-full-i-know-nothing-ive-experienced-lot-86607.

Sobieraj, Katarzyna. (2022). *The Euro Crisis in the Press: Political Debate in Germany, Poland, and the United Kingdom*. Cham: Palgrave Macmillan.

Social Mobility Commission. (2016). *State of the Nation 2016: Social Mobility in Great Britain* https://assets.publishing.service.gov.uk/government/uploads/system/uploads/attachment data/file/569410/Social Mobility Commission 2016 REPORT-WEB1.pdf.

Solidarity. (2001). "Paris May 1968." *Beneath the Paving Stones: Situationists and the Beach, May 1968*. Ed. Dark Star. Edinburgh and San Fracnisco: AK Press/Dark Star. 64–96.

Solnit, Rebecca. (2021, August 23). "Big Oil Coined 'Carbon Footprints' to Blame Us for Their Greed. Keep Them on the Hook." *Guardian* https://www.theguardian.com/commentisfree/2021/aug/23/big-oil-coined-carbon-footprints-to-blame-us-for-their-greed-keep-them-on-the-hook.

Solomon, Norman. (2001, December). "Media War Without End." *Z Magazine* https://znetwork.org/zmagazine/media-war-without-end-by-norman-solomon/.

Song, Yunya, Zeping Huang, Joinathan P. Schuldt, and Y. Connie Yuan. (2022). "National Prisms of a Global Phenomenon: A Comparative Study of Press Coverage in the US, UK and China." *Journalism* 23, no. 10: 2209–229.

Sparks, Robert. (1992). ""Delivering the Male": Sports, Canadian Television, and the Making of TSN." *Canadian Journal of Communication* 17, no. 1: 319–42.

Sports Journalists' Association. (2019, March 20). "BCOMS Founder Mann Calls for Action on Diversity, with Thanks to Raheem Sterling." https://www.sportsjournalists.co.uk/other-bodies/bcoms-founder-mann-calls-for-action-on-diversity-with-thanks-to-raheem-sterling/.

Sreberny, Annabelle. (2016). "The 2015 *Charlie Hebdo* Killings, Media Event Chains, and Global Political Responses." *International Journal of Communication* 10: 3485–502.

Stanton, John, David Lockwood, and Katie Gornall. (2021, November 12). "Premier League: Should Clubs Stop Flying to Domestic Matches for Environmental Reasons?" *BBC* https://www.bbc.co.uk/sport/football/59213173.

Starkman, Dean. (2014). *The Watchdog That Didn't Bark: The Financial Crisis and the Disappearance of Investigative Journalism.* New York: Columbia University Press.

Steen, Rob, Jed Novick, and Huw Richards, eds. (2021). *Routledge Handbook of Sports Journalism.* London: Routledge.

Steinberg, S. H. (1955). *Five Hundred Years of Printing.* Harmondsworth: Penguin.

Stempel, Carl. (2006) "Televised Sports, Masculinist Moral Capital, and Support for the U.S. Invasion of Iraq." *Journal of Sport & Social Issues* 30, no. 1: 79–106.

Stengers, Isabelle. (2018). *Another Science is Possible: A Manifesto for Slow Science.* Cambridge: Polity.

Sterba, James P. (1977, February 2). "Problems from Climate Changes Foreseen in a 1974 C.I.A. Report." *New York Times*: 10.

Stewart, Potter. (1975). "Or of the Press." *Hastings Law Journal* 26, no. 3: 631–37.

Stille, Alexander. (2015, February 28). "Five Lessons About France After *Charlie Hebdo*." *New Yorker* http://www.newyorker.com/news/daily-comment/five-lessons-france-charlie-hebdo.

Stillman, W. J. (1891, November). "Journalism and Literature." *Atlantic Monthly*: 687–95.

St. John III, Burton and Kirsten A. Johnson, eds. (2012). *News With a View: Essays on the Eclipse of Objectivity in Modern Journalism.* Jefferson: McFarland & Company.

Stockton, Ben. (2023, May 30). "Cop28 President's Team Accused of Wikipedia 'Greenwashing'." *Guardian* https://www.theguardian.com/environment/2023/may/30/cop28-president-team-accused-of-wikipedia-greenwashing-sultan-al-jaber.

Stokel-Walker, Chris. (2023, February 13). "AI Chatbots Are Coming to Search Engines—Can You Trust the Results?" *Nature* https://www.nature.com/articles/d41586-023-00423-4.

Stone, Diane. (2013). *Knowledge Actors and Transnational Governance: The Public-Private Policy Nexus in the Global Agora.* Basingstoke: Palgrave MacMillan.

Stoner, Robert and Jéssica Dutra. (2022). *Copyright Industries in the U.S. Economy: The 2022 Report.* International Intellectual Property Alliance https://www.iipa.org/files/uploads/2022/12/IIPA-Report-2022_Interactive_12-12-2022-1.pdf.

STOP and FM. (2021). *Driving Addiction: Tobacco Sponsorship in Formula One, 2021* https://exposetobacco.org/wp-content/uploads/TobaccoSponsorshipFormula-One-2021.pdf.

Streeter, Tom. (2005). "The Moment of *Wired*." *Critical Inquiry* 31, no. 4: 755–79.

Strubell, Emma, Ananya Ganesh, and Andrew McCallum. (2019). "Energy and Policy Considerations for Deep Learning in NLP." *Proceedings of the 57th Annual Meeting of the Association for Computational Linguistics.* Florence: Association for Computational Linguistics. 3645–650.

Sturm, Roland and Ashlesha Datar. (2005). "Body Mass Index in Elementary School Children, Metropolitan Area Food Prices and Food Outlet Density." *Public Health* 119, no. 12: 1059–068.

Sturrock, Leanne. (2018, July 12). "The Environmental Impact of the World Cup—Are FIFA Scoring Sustainability Goals?" *thegreatProjects*.

Suárez Serrano, Chema. (2016). "El periodismo en los conflictos armados del siglo XXI: Entre las nuevas tecnologías y las amenazas de siempre." Revista del Instituto Español de Estudios Estratégicos 8 http://revista.ieee.es/index.php/ieee/article/view/307.

Sudhaman, Arun. (2015, February 13). "Edelman's American Petroleum Institute Assignment Ends." *The Holmes Report* http://www.holmesreport.com/latest/article/edelman%27s-american-petroleum-institute-assignment-set-to-end

Sudhaman, Arun. (2022, February 7). "Resurgent Edelman Reports 15.4% Revenue Increase in 2021." *PRovokeMedia* https://www.provokemedia.com/latest/article/resurgent-edelman-reports-15.4-revenue-increase-in-2021.

Sugden, John and Alan Tomlinson. (2003). *Badfellas: FIFA Family at War*. Edinburgh: Mainstream Publishing.

Sullivan, Margaret. (2013, December 19). "Pledging Clarity, *The Times* Plunges into Native Advertising." *New York Times* https://archive.nytimes.com/publiceditor.blogs.nytimes.com/2013/12/19/pledging-clarity-the-times-plunges-into-native-advertising/.

Sullivan, Walter. (1961, September 11). "Air Found Gaining in Carbon Dioxide." *New York Times*: 29.

Sumiala, Johanna, Katja Valaskivi, Minttu Tikka, and Jukka Huhtamäki. (2018). *Hybrid Media Events: The **Charlie Hebdo** Attacks and the Global Circulation of Terrorist Violence*. Bingley: Emerald Publishing.

Sutton Trust and Social Mobility Commission. (2019). *Elitist Britain 2019: The Educational Backgrounds of Britain's Leading People* https://assets.publishing.service.gov.uk/government/uploads/system/uploads/attachment_data/file/811045/Elitist_Britain_2019.pdf.

Švaňa, Lukáš. (2016). "*Charlie Hebdo* Attacks in the Light of Aquinas' Doctrine of Double Effect and Ignatieff's Lesser Evil Theory." *Human Affairs* 26: 63–72.

Swan, Michael. (2015, January 12). "Charlie Hebdo 'Part of the Situation' That Led to Attack, Says Charles Taylor." *Catholic Register* http://catholicregister.org/item/19513-charlie-hebdo-part-of-the-situation-that-led-to-attack-says-charles-taylor.

Sweney, Mark. (2023, May 5). "'Like Icarus—Now Everyone is Burnt': How *Vice* and *BuzzFeed* Fell to Earth." *Guardian* https://www.theguardian.com/media/2023/may/05/like-icarus-now-everyone-is-burnt-how-vice-and-buzzfeed-fell-to-earth.

Sylt, Christian. (2015, August 25). "Is Formula One the World's Most Sustainable Sport?" *Forbes* https://www.forbes.com/sites/csylt/2015/08/25/is-formula-one-the-worlds-most-sustainable-sport/?sh=5357d4d02952.

Sylt, Christian. (2019, April 23). "Formula One Gender Pay Gap Revealed to be Above UK Average at all but One British Team." *Independent* https://www.independent.co.uk/f1/formula-one-gender-pay-gap-statistics-standings-uk-motorsport-a8882946.html.

Szerman, Nathalie. (2006, April 28). "'Manifesto of Liberties'—A Muslim Association for Freedom in the Arab World." *MEMRI* 271 https://www.memri.org/reports/%E2%80%98manifesto-liberties%E2%80%99-muslim-association-freedom-arab-world.

Tady, Megan. (2008, November 1). "Outsourcing Journalism." *FAIR* http://fair.org/extra-online-articles/outsourcing-journalism/.

Takahashi, Bruno, Juliet Pinto, Manuel Chavez, and Mercedes Vigón, eds. (2018). *News Media Coverage of Environmental Challenges in Latin America and the Caribbean: Mediating Demand, Degradation and Development.* Cham: Palgrave Macmillan.

Talman, Charles Fitzhugh. (1930, May). "Is Our Climate Changing?" *Popular Mechanics*: 817–21.

Tamayo Gaviria, Natalia. (2022, May 20). "Los rostros afros del Congreso 2022-2026." *El Espectador* https://www.elespectador.com/politica/elecciones-colombia-2022/los-rostros-afros-del-congreso-2022-2026/?fbclid=IwAR06E3KycpmFRWhbH4VDwgWqJpx-CL0i9ISD0UMBO2BnP1nOFCJCryBmeY.

Tambini, Damian. (2010). "What are Financial Journalists For?" *Journalism Studies* 11, no. 2: 158–74.

Tao, Rongrong, Baojian Zhou, Feng Chen, Naifeng Liu, David Mares, Patrick Butler, and Naren Ramakrishnan. (2017). "Can Self-Censorship in News Media be Detected Algorithmically? A Case Study in Latin America." *arXiv*:1611.06947v2 https://arxiv.org/abs/1611.06947.

Tarczynska, Kasia, Christine Wen, and Katie Furtado. (2022). *Financial Exposure: Rating the States on Economic Development Transparency.* Good Jobs First https://goodjobsfirst.org/wp-content/uploads/2022/07/Financial-Exposure.pdf.

Tarkov, Anna. (2012, June 30). "Journatic Worker Takes 'This American Life' Inside Outsourced Journalism." *Poynter* http://www.poynter.org/news/mediawire/179555/journatic-staffer-takes-this-american-life-inside-outsourced-journalism/.

Taylor, Louise and David Hytner. (2016, April 10). "Claudio Ranieri Sheds Tears and Dedicates Win to Leicester's Supporters." *Guardian* https://www.theguardian.com/football/2016/apr/10/claudio-ranieri-tears-leicester-city.

Taylor, Luke. (2018, July 3). "Colombians Angry and Bemused by *The Sun*'s Controversial Harry Kane "Cocaine" Front Page." *The Independent* https://www.independent.co.uk/news/world/americas/harry-kane-england-colombia-the-sun-cocaine-front-page-newspaper-three-lions-a8429756.html.

Tell MAMA. (2023). *A Decade of Anti-Muslim Hate: Tell MAMA Report* https://tellmamauk.org/wp-content/uploads/pdf/A-Decade-of-Anti-Muslim-Hate-Tell-MAMAReport.pdf.

The Climate Coalition. (2018). *Game Changer: How Climate Change is Impacting Sports in the UK* https://www.theclimatecoalition.org/gamechanger.

The Lancet. (2023). *The 2023 Report of the Lancet Countdown on Health and Climate Change: The Imperative for a Health-Centred Response in a World Facing Irreversible Harms* https://www.thelancet.com/journals/lancet/article/PIIS0140-6736(23)01859-7/fulltext.

Thiessen, Marc A. (2021, May 14). "An Obama Scientist Debunks the Climate Doom-Mongers." *Washington Post* https://www.washingtonpost.com/opinions/2021/05/14/an-obama-scientist-debunks-climate-doom-mongers/.

Thompson, Graham. (2012). "The "Plain Facts" of Fine Paper in "The Paradise of Bachelors and the Tartarus of Maids"." *American Literature* 84, no. 3: 505–32.

Thompson, Hunter S. (2012). *Fear and Loathing on the Campaign Trail '72.* New York: Simon & Schuster.

Thompson, Peter A. (2013). "Invested Interests? Reflexivity, Representation and Reporting in Financial Markets." *Journalism: Theory, Practice and Criticism* 14, no. 2: 208–27.

Thorpe, Vanessa. (2023, March 18). "'Chat GPT Said I Did not Exist': How Artists and Writers are Fighting Back Against AI." *Guardian* https://www.theguardian.com/technology/2023/mar/18/chatgpt-said-i-did-not-exist-how-artists-and-writers-are-fighting-back-against-ai.

Thurman, Neil, Konstantin Dörr, and Jessica Kunert. (2017). "When Reporters Get Hands-On with Robo-Writing." *Digital Journalism* 5, no. 10: 1240–259.

Timms, Aaron. (2021, August 2). "NBC Paid $7.75bn for its Olympic Rights ... And We Got Televisual Vomit." *Guardian* https://www.theguardian.com/sport/2021/aug/02/nbc-olympic-coverage-peacock-replays-primetime?CMP=ShareiOSAppOther.

Tippet, Anna. (2019, June 24). "Formula 1: There Can Be No Equality in Sport while Women's Bodies are Used for Promotions." *The Conversation* https://theconversation.com/formula-1-there-can-be-no-equality-in-sport-while-womens-bodies-are-used-for-promotions-117443.

Tobitt, Charlotte. (2023, August 21). "Women's World Cup Coverage 'Sparkling Almost as Much as the Lionesses'." *Press Gazette* https://pressgazette.co.uk/publishers/nationals/womens-world-cup-coverage-news/.

Todd, Emmanuel. (2015). *Who is Charlie? Xenophobia and the New Middle Class.* Oxford: Polity.

Tóffano Pereira, Rodrigo Pinheiro, Viachaslau Filimonau, and Gladyston Mattos Ribeiro. (2019). "Score a Goal for Climate: Assessing the Carbon Footprint of Travel Patterns of the English Premier League Clubs." *Journal of Cleaner Production* 227, no. 1: 167–77.

Toffler, Alvin. (1983). *Previews and Premises.* New York: William Morrow.

Tokyo Organising Committee of the Olympic and Paralympic Games. (2021). Update to the Sustainability Pre-Games Report https://gtimg.tokyo2020.org/image/upload/production/cas22cdv09dc0h9yaf5t.pdf.

Tomasik, Emily and Jeffrey Gottfried. (2023, April 4). *U.S. Journalists' Beats Vary Widely by Gender and Other Factors.* Pew Research Center https://www.pewresearch.org/short-reads/2023/04/04/us-journalists-beats-vary-widely-by-gender-and-other-factors/?utmsource=Pew+Research+Center&utmcampa%E2%80%A6.

Tomizawa, Roy. (2016, February 3). "Olympia Cigarettes: How the 1964 Tokyo Olympics Led to Increased Cases of Lung Cancer in Japan Today." *The Olympians From 1964 to 2020* https://theolympians.co/2016/02/03/olympia-cigarettes-how-the-1964-tokyo-olympics-led-to-increased-cases-of-lung-cancer-in-japan-today/.

Tondo, Lorenzo. (2023, June 7). "Sky Italia Suspends FI Commentators After Sexist Remarks On Air." *Guardian* https://www.theguardian.com/media/2023/jun/07/sky-suspends-italian-f1-commentators-after-sexist-remarks-on-air.

Tong, Bing. (2021). *Journalism and Communication in China and the West: A Study of History, Education and Regulation.* Singapore: China Renimin University Press/ Palgrave Macmillan.

Tönnies, Ferdinand. (2000). *Ferdinand Tönnies on Public Opinion: Selections and Analyses.* Trans. and Ed. Hanno Hardt and Slavko Splichal. Lanham, MD: Rowman & Littlefield.

Touré, Hamadoun I. (2008, November 12–13). *ITU Secretary-General's Declaration on Cybersecurity and Climate Change, High-Level Segment of Council* http://www.itu.int/council/C2008/hls/statements/closing/sg-declaration.html.

Tourkochoriti, Ioanna. (in press). "Comparative Law and Philosophy of History: The Case of Free Speech in American and French Legal Thought." *Comparative Legal History: The Value, Purposes and Methods of Historical Comparison.* Eds. Mortimer Sellers and Ioanna Tourkochoriti. Cambridge: Cambridge University Press.

Tranter, Paul J. and Mark Lowes. (2009). "Life in the Fast Lane: Environmental, Economic and Public Health Outcomes of Motorsport Spectacles in Australia." *Journal of Sport & Social Issues* 33, no. 2: 150–68.

Traugott, Michael W. and Ted Brader. (2003). "Explaining 9/11." *Framing Terrorism: The News Media, the Government, and the Public.* Eds. Pippa Norris, Montague Kern, and Marion Just. New York: Routledge. 183–201.

Trenchard, John and Thomas Gordon. (1723). *Cato's Letters, or Essays on Liberty, Civil and Religious and Other Important Subjects (Complete).* N. p.: Library of Alexandria.

Trilling, Daniel. (2021, April 19). "Why is the Right Obsessed with 'Defending' Borders? Because it Sees Citizenship as a Commodity." *Guardian* https://www.theguardian.com/commentisfree/2021/apr/19/conservatives-citizenship-human-right-asylum-seekers-migrants-hong-kong.

Trotsky, Leon. (1977). *Leon Trotsky on Literature and Art.* Ed. Paul N. Siegel. New York: Pathfinder Press.

Trouillard, Stéphanie. (2020, October 24). "Looking Back at France's Long Tradition of Caricature." *France 24* https://www.france24.com/en/france/20201024-looking-back-at-france-s-long-tradition-of-caricature.

Tsavkko Garcia, Raphael. (2020, November 25). "'Jornalismo dos dois lados' no Brasil dá credibilidade a narrativas nocivas." *International Journalists' Network* https://ijnet.org/pt-br/story/jornalismo-dos-dois-lados-no-brasil-d%C3%A1-credibilidade-narrativas-nocivas.

Tuchman, Gaye. (1980). *Making News: A Study in the Construction of Reality.* New York: The Free Press; London: Collier Macmillan.

Tulloch, Christopher and Xavier Ramon. (2017). "Take Five." *Digital Journalism* 5, no. 5: 652–72.

Turner, Fred. (2006). *From Counterculture to Cyberculture: Stewart Brand, the Whole Earth Network, and the Rise of Digital Utopianism.* Chicago: University of Chicago Press.

Tweedale, Alistair. (2018, November 21). "Fifa Talks a Good Game but its Drive for Sustainability Highlights Football's Hypocrisy." *Telegraph* https://www.telegraph.co.uk/football/2018/11/21/fifa-talks-good-game-drive-sustainability-highlights-footballs/.

Tyndall Report. (2003). *On Aftermath of September 11* http://tyndallreport.com/0911.php3.

Tyndall Report. (2019). *2019 Year in Review* http://tyndallreport.com/yearinreview2019/international/.

Tyndall, Andrew. (2021, August 19). "Afghanistan Has Not Been Covered as America's Longest War." *Tyndall Report* http://tyndallreport.com/comment/20/5789/.

Ufarte-Ruiz, María-José, Francisco-José Murcia-Verdú, and José-Miguel Túñez-López. (2023). "Use of Artificial Intelligence in Synthetic Media: First Newsrooms Without Journalists." *Profesional de la información* 32, no. 2: e320203.

UNESCO. (2023a). *Gender Equality in Sports Media* https://webarchive.unesco.org/web/20230104165710/https://en.unesco.org/themes/gender-equality-sports-media.

UNESCO. (2023b, June 29). *What You Need to Know About Literacy* https://www.unesco.org/en/literacy/need-know.
United Nations Conference on Trade and Development. (2022a). *Creative Economy Outlook 2022* https://unctad.org/system/files/official-document/ditctsce2022d1en.pdf.
United Nations Conference on Trade and Development. (2022b). Creative Industry 4.0: A New Globalized Creative Economy https://europaregina.eu/wp-content/uploads/2022/05/creative-industry-4.0-towards-a-new-globalized-creative-economy-unctad.pdf.
United Nations Environment Programme. (2021). *Food Waste Index Report 2021* https://www.unep.org/resources/report/unep-food-waste-index-report-2021.
United Nations Office on Drugs and Crime. (2013). *Global Study on Homicide 2013: Trends, Contexts, Data* https://www.unodc.org/documents/data-and-analysis/statistics/GSH2013/2014GLOBALHOMICIDEBOOKweb.pdf.
United States Atomic Energy Commission. (1954). *In the Matter of J. Robert Oppenheimer. Transcript of Hearing Before Personnel Security Board* http://www.pbs.org/wgbh/americanexperience/features/transcript/oppenheimer-transcript.
U.S. Department of Justice. (2012, December 11). *HSBC Holdings Plc. and HSBS Bank USA N.A. Admit to Anti-Money Laundering and Sanctions Violations, Forfeit $1.256 Billion in Deferred Prosecution Agreement* https://www.justice.gov/opa/pr/hsbc-holdings-plc-and-hsbc-bank-usa-na-admit-anti-money-laundering-and-sanctions-violations.
U.S. Government Accountability Office. (2021, March 19). *Imported Seafood Safety: FDA Should Improve Monitoring of its Warning Letter Process and Better Assess its Effectiveness* https://www.gao.gov/assets/gao-21-231.pdf.
Usher, Nikki. (2013). "Ignored, Uninterested, and the Blame Game: How *The New York Times*, *Marketplace*, and TheStreet Distanced Themselves from Preventing the 2007-2009 Financial Crisis." *Journalism* 14, no. 2: 190–207.
van Creveld, Martin. (1999). *The Rise and Decline of the State*. Cambridge: Cambridge University Press.
van Lienden, Arne and Jacco van Sterkenburg. (2023). "Representations of Race/Ethnicity and the Nation: A Content Analysis of Televised Polish International Football." *International Review for the Sociology of Sport* 58, no. 1: 3–22.
Varoufakis, Yanis. (1998). *Foundations of Economics: A Beginner's Companion*. New York: Routledge.
Venegas, Juan Manuel. (2003, August 2). "¿Yo por qué?, insiste Fox; ¿qué no somos 100 millones de mexicanos?" *La Jornada*: Política 3.
Vernon, James. (2007). *Hunger: A Modern History*. Cambridge, MA: Harvard University Press.
Versi, Miqdaad. (2023, July 29). "Where Were Nigel Farage and His Defenders When Muslim Bank Accounts Were Shut Down?" *Guardian* https://www.theguardian.com/commentisfree/2023/jul/28/nigel-farage-muslim-bank-accounts-coutts-charities-terrorism.
Virilio, Paul. (1989). *War and Cinema: The Logistics of Perception*. Trans. Patrick Cammiler. London: Verso.
Vivar, Roberto Fuentes. (2019, September 24). "Deporte y cambio climático." *Milenio* https://www.milenio.com/opinion/roberto-fuentes-vivar/las-otras-competencias/deporte-y-cambio-climatico.

Volpicelli, Gian. (2023, February 20). "The New Luddites: AI Comes for the Creative Class." *Politico* https://www.politico.eu/article/artificial-intelligence-technology-art-regulation-copyright/.
von der Lippe, Berit and Rune Ottosen, eds. (2016). Gendering War and Peace Reporting: Some Insights—Some Missing Links. Göteborg: NORDICOM.
Voss, Kimberly Wilmot. (2014). *The Food Section: Newspaper Women and the Culinary Community*. Lanham, MD: Rowman & Littlefield.
Wahab, Siraj. (2007, May 17). "Islamophobia Worst Form of Terrorism." *Arab News* http://www.arabnews.com/node/298472.
Wahl-Jorgensen, Karin, Mike Berry, Iñaki Garcia-Blanco, Lucy Bennett, and Jonathan Cable. (2017). "Rethinking Balance and Impartiality in Journalism? How the BBC Attempted and Failed to Change the Paradigm." *Journalism* 18, no. 7: 781–800.
Waisbord, Silvio. (2013). *Reinventing Professionalism: Journalism and News in Global Perspective*. Cambridge: Polity.
Wajcman, Judy. (2004). *TechnoFeminism*. Cambridge: Polity.
Walker, Danna L, Margaretha Geertsema, and Barbara Barnett. (2009). "Inverting the Inverted Pyramid: A Conversation about the Use of Feminist Theories to Teach Journalism." *Feminist Teacher* 19, no. 3: 177–94.
Walker, Mason. (2021, July 13). *U. S. Newsroom Employment Has Fallen 26% Since 2008*. Pew Research Center https://www.pewresearch.org/fact-tank/2021/07/13/u-s-newsroom-employment-has-fallen-26-since-2008/.
Walker, R. R. (1973). *The Magic Spark: The Story of the First Fifty Years of Radio in Australia*. Melbourne, VIC: The Hawthorn Press.
Wallace, Arturo. (2018, May 18). "16 grandes crónicas y reportajes para entender por qué El Faro de El Salvador es un referente fundamental del periodismo latinoamericano." BBC Mundo https://www.bbc.com/mundo/noticias-america-latina-44081293.
Wallace, Juliane Poock, Eric Widenman, and Robert J, McDermott. (2019). "Physical Activity and Climate Change: Clear and Present Danger?" *Health Behavior and Policy Review* 6, no. 5: 534–45.
Wallace, Lewis Raven. (2019). The View from Somewhere: Undoing the Myth of Journalistic Objectivity. Chicago: University of Chicago Press.
Walzer, Michael. (2015). *Just and Unjust Wars: A Moral Argument with Historical Illustrations*, 5th ed. New York: Basic Books.
Ware, Alyn. (2021, July 29). "Tokyo's Games are Harming the Nuclear Weapons Ban Movement." *The Nation* https://www.thenation.com/article/society/tokyo-olympics-nuclear-weapons/.
Washburn, Jennifer with Derrin Culp and Jeremiah Miller. (2010). *Big Oil Goes to College: An Analysis of 10 Research Collaboration Contracts Between Leading Energy Companies and Major U. S. Universities*. Center for American Progress https://cdn.americanprogress.org/wp-content/uploads/issues/2010/10/pdf/bigoillf.pdf.
Waterson, Jim. (2023, May 31). "*Drive to Survive* Commentator Sacked from Formula E Over 'Inappropriate Behaviour'." *Guardian* https://www.theguardian.com/sport/2023/may/31/motor-racing-commentator-sacked-after-complaints-of-inappropriate-behaviour.
Watson, Brenda. (2016). "Belief and Evidence, and How It May Aid Reflection Concerning Charlie Hebdo." *Think* 15, no. 42: 151–61.

Watson, Brendan R. (2014). "When Critical Voices Should Speak Up: Patterns in News Coverage of Unofficial Sources During the BP Oil Spill." *Journalism Practice* 8, no. 6: 842–54.

Watson, Peter J. (2018). "Colombia's Political Football: President Santos' National Unity Project and the 2014 Football World Cup." *Bulletin of Latin American Research* 37, no. 5: 598–612.

Watts, Clint. (2023, February 3). "Iran Responsible for *Charlie Hebdo* Attacks." *Microsoft* https://blogs.microsoft.com/on-the-issues/2023/02/03/dtac-charlie-hebdo-hack-iran-neptunium/.

Watts, Jonathan. (2019, February 25). "Concrete: The Most Destructive Material on Earth." *Guardian* https://www.theguardian.com/cities/2019/feb/25/concrete-the-most-destructive-material-on-earth.

Waxman, Sharon. (2020, June 4). "*Variety* Chief Editor Claudia Eller Takes Leave After Staff Revolt." *The Wrap* https://www.thewrap.com/claudia-eller-exits-variety/.

Webb, Stephen H. (2009, March 12). "Soccer is Ruining America." *Wall Street Journal* https://www.wsj.com/articles/SB123680101041299201.

Webb, Stephen H. (2014, June 12). "Why Soccer is Un-American." *Politico* https://www.politico.com/magazine/story/2014/06/why-soccer-is-un-american-107793/.

Webber, Lawrence and Michael Wallace. (2009). *Green Tech: How to Plan and Implement Sustainable IT Solution*. New York: American Management Association.

Weber, Max. (1946). *From Max Weber: Essays in Sociology*. Trans. and Ed. H. H. Gerth and C. Wright Mills. New York: Free Press.

Weber, Max. (1949). *The Methodology of the Social Sciences*. Trans. and Ed. Edward A. Shils and Henry A. Finch. Glencoe: The Free Press.

Weber, Max. (1976). "Towards a Sociology of the Press." Trans. Hanno Hardt. *Journal of Communication* 26, no. 3: 96–101.

Weber, Max. (2005). "Remarks on Technology and Culture." Trans. Beatrix Zumsteg and Thomas M. Kemple. Ed. Thomas M. Kemple. *Theory, Culture & Society* 22, no. 4: 23–38.

Wells, H. G. (1902). *Anticipations of the Reaction of Mechanical and Scientific Progress Upon Human Life and Thought*, 2nd ed. London: Chapman & Hall.

Wells, Ida B. (2014). *The Light of Truth: Writings of an Anti-Lynching Crusader*. Ed. Mia Bay. New York: Penguin Books.

Wells, Matt and Lisa O'Carroll. (2005, March 24). "Man Bites Man, and That Man is Now the BBC DG." *Guardian* https://www.theguardian.com/media/2005/mar/24/broadcasting.bbc.

Weprin, Alex. (2021, August 11). "Sports Rights' Streaming Wave May Finally End Pay-TV Bundle." *Hollywood Reporter* https://www.hollywoodreporter.com/business/business-news/sports-rights-tv-amazon-disney-viacomcbs-1234995721/.

West, Janet and Brendan Crowther. (2013, April 19). "Sustainability in Broadcast and Digital Media." *BBC* http://www.bbc.co.uk/rd/blog/2013/04/sustainability-in-broadcast-event-summary.

Weston, Phoebe, Julie Richards, and Ben Murray. (2023, November 28). "What Impact Does the *Guardian* Have on the Natural World?" *Guardian* https://www.theguardian.com/environment/2023/nov/28/what-impact-does-the-guardian-have-on-the-natural-world.

Westervelt, Amy. (2021, December 4). "Why Some of Your Favorite Podcasts are Filled with Oil Company Ads." *Guardian* https://www.theguardian.com/environment/2021/dec/04/exxon-podasts-oil-company-ads-climate-crisis.

Westervelt, Amy. (2022a, February 18). "The Great Greenwashing Scam: PR Firms Face Reckoning After Spinning for Big Oil." *Guardian* https://www.theguardian.com/environment/2022/feb/18/greenwashing-pr-advertising-oil-firms-exxon-chevron-shell-bp.
Westervelt, Amy. (2022b, March 10). "How Oil Companies Rebranded Deceptive Climate Ads as 'Free Speech'." *Guardian* https://www.theguardian.com/environment/2022/mar/10/oil-companies-corporate-free-speech-laws-climate-litigation.
Weston Vauclair, Jane. (2015). "Local Laughter, Global Polemics: Understanding *Charlie Hebdo*." *European Comic Art* 8, no. 1: 6–14.
Wetts, Rachel. (2020). "In Climate News, Statements from Large Businesses and Opponents of Climate Action Receive Heightened Visibility." *PNAS* 117, no. 32: 19054–060.
White, Aidan, ed. (2017). *Untold Stories: How Corruption and Conflicts of Interest Stalk the Newsroom*. Ethical Journalism Network https://ethicaljournalismnetwork.org/wp-content/uploads/2017/01/untold-stories-full.pdf.
White, Natasha and Matt Day. (2023, August 14). "Amazon is Removed from Key List of Climate-Conscious Companies." *Los Angeles Times* https://www.latimes.com/business/story/2023-08-14/amazon-carbon-emissions-climate-change.
Whitehead, Sheldon. (2023, June 21). Opening Statement of Chairman Sheldon Whitehouse Senate Committee on the Budget "Dollars and Degrees: Investigating Fossil Fuel Dark Money's Systemic Threats to Climate and the Federal Budget." https://www.budget.senate.gov/imo/media/doc/2023.06.21%20Hearing%20-%20Opening%20Statement%20of%20Chairman%20Sheldon%20Whitehouse%20UPDATED%206.16%20(002).pdf.
Whiten, Jon. (2004, February). "Bad News from Iraq?" *EXTRA!Update*: 3.
Whiten, Jon. (2005, March/April). ""The World Little Noted": CBS Scandal Eclipses Missing WMDs." *Extra!*: 7.
Whiton, Jacob. (2023, July 25). "New Data on Data Center Subsidies, Same Old Problems." *Good Jobs First* https://goodjobsfirst.org/new-data-on-data-center-subsidies-same-old-problems/.
Whitman, Walt. (2004). *Memoranda During the War*. Ed. Peter Coviello. Oxford: Oxford University Press.
Whitten-Woodring, Jenifer. (2009). "Watchdog or Lapdog? Media Freedom, Regime Type, and Government Respect for Human Rights." *International Studies Quarterly* 53, no. 3: 595–625.
Whitwell, Laurie. (2016, February 12). "Polo with Prince Charles, Free Beer for Fans, Caviar for the Players and a £43m Private Jet." *Daily Mail* https://www.dailymail.co.uk/sport/football/article-3444768/Polo-Prince-Charles-free-beer-fans-caviar-players-43m-private-jet-s-Leicester-City-s-Thai-owners-FOXES.html.
Williams, Christopher. (2023, November 30). "Abu Dhabi Takeover of *The Telegraph* to be Investigated Over Censorship Fears." *Telegraph* https://www.telegraph.co.uk/business/2023/11/30/abu-dhabi-takeover-telegraph-investigated-censorship-fears/.
Williams, Raymond. (1970). *The English Novel: From Dickens to Lawrence*. New York: Oxford University Press.
Williams, Raymond. (1977). *Marxism and Literature*. London: Oxford University Press.
Williams, Raymond. (1989). *The Politics of Modernism*. London: Verso.
Williams, Richard. (2019, November 25). "Ferrari's Historic Penchant for a Good Crisis Remains—90 Years Down the Track." *Guardian* https://www.theguardian.com/

sport/blog/2019/nov/25/ferrari-historic-penchant-crisis-90-years-anniversary-maranello.

Williams, Richard. (2020, November 14). "Lewis Hamilton: The Man from Stevenage Who Became the Moral Compass of F1." *Guardian* https://www.theguardian.com/sport/2020/nov/14/lewis-hamilton-the-man-from-stevenage-who-became-the-moral-compass-of-f1.

Williams, Richard. (2021, August 29). "Louise King Obituary." *Guardian* https://www.theguardian.com/stage/2021/aug/29/louise-king-obituary.

Wilson, Harold. (1963). *Labour's Plan for Science: Reprint of Speech by the Rt. Hon. Harold Wilson, MP, Leader of the Labour Party, at the Annual Conference, Scarborough, Tuesday, October 1, 1963.* London: Victoria House.

Wilson, Marisa, ed. (2017). *Postcolonialism, Indigeneity and Struggles for Food Sovereignty.* London: Routledge.

Wilson, Rhoda. (2023, April 17). "IPCC Adjusts Temperature Data to Create the Impression of Catastrophic Global Warming." *The Exposé* https://expose-news.com/2023/04/17/data-adj-to-create-the-impression-of-global-warming/.

Winston, Brian and Matthew Wilson. (2021). *The Roots of Fake News: Objecting to Objective Journalism.* Abingdon: Routledge.

Winston, Brian. (1996). *Technologies of Seeing: Photography, Cinematography, and Television.* London: British Film Institute.

Winston, Brian. (2007). "Let Them Eat Laptops: The Limits of Technicism." *International Journal of Communication* 1: 170–76.

W. K. (1953, May 24). "How Industry May Change Climate." *New York Times*: E11.

Wolfe, Lauren. (2021, July 9). "I'm a Biased Journalist and I'm Okay with That." *Washington Monthly* https://washingtonmonthly.com/2021/07/09/im-a-biased-journalist-and-im-okay-with-that/.

Wolska-Zogata, Irena. (2015). "The Story of Charlie Hebdo: An Analysis of European and American Newspapers." *Mediterranean Journal of Social Sciences* 6, no. 2: 353–62.

Women in Sports. (2018). *Where Are All the Women? Shining a Light on the Visibility of Women's Sport in the Media* https://womeninsport.org/wp-content/uploads/2018/10/Where-are-all-the-Women-1.pdf.

Women's Media Center. (2018). *The Status of Women of Color in the U.S. News Media 2018* https://womensmediacenter.com/assets/site/reports/the-status-of-women-of-color-in-the-u-s-media-2018-full-report/Status-WomenofColorReport2018.pdf.

Wood, Stephen, Paul Shabajee, Daniel Schein, Christopher Hodgson, and Chris Preist. (2014). "Energy Use and Greenhouse Gas Emissions in Digital News Media: Ethical Implications for Journalists and Media Organisations." *Digital Journalism* 2, no. 3: 284–95.

Woodman, Harold D. (1972). "Economic History and Economic Theory: The New Economic History in America." *Journal of Interdisciplinary History* 3, no. 2: 323–50.

Woozencroft, Hugh. (2018, December 14). "Why BBC Sport Can't Escape Sports Journalism's Problem." *BBC* https://www.bbc.co.uk/sport/46571432.

Worswick, Carl. (2023, August 11). "Powerful and Defiant: How Colombia's World Cup Journey Gripped a Nation." *Guardian* https://www.theguardian.com/football/2023/aug/11/colombia-world-cup-journey-england-quarter-final.

Wren-Lewis, Simon. (2018). "'Mediamacro': Why the News Media Ignores Economic Experts." *The Media and Austerity: Comparative Perspectives.* Eds. Laura Basu, Steve Schifferes, and Sophie Knowles. London: Routledge. 170–82.
Wright, C. Edmund. (2014, July 14). "Socialistic Offside Rule Ensures Americans Will Never Catch Soccer Fever." *Breitbart* https://www.breitbart.com/sports/2014/07/14/world-cup-fever-but-how-popular-is-soccer-really/.
Wright, Georgia, Liat Olenick, and Amy Westervelt. (2021, October 27). "The Dirty Dozen: Meet America's Top Climate Villains." *Guardian* https://www.theguardian.com/commentisfree/2021/oct/27/climate-crisis-villains-americas-dirty-dozen.
WWF. (2009, March 11). *Recommendations on Environmental Journalism* http://wwf.panda.org/?158643/Recommendations-on-environmental-journalism.
Wynes, Seth. (2021). "COVID-19 Disruption Demonstrates Win-Win Climate Solutions for Major League Sports." *Environmental Science & Technology* 55: 15609–615.
Wyshynski, Greg. (2023, June 5). "How Vegas, Florida Owners Bring West Point Legacy to the NHL." *ESPN* https://www.espn.com.au/nhl/story//id/37797131/vegas-florida-owners-west-point-legacy-stanley-cup-final.
Yang, Guobin. (2013). "Contesting Food Safety in the Chinese Media: Between Hegemony and Counter-Hegemony." *The China Quarterly* 214: 337–55.
Yankoski, Michael, William Theisen, Ernesto Verdeja, and Walter J. Scheirer. (2021). "Artificial Intelligence for Peace: An Early Warning System for Mass Violence." *Towards an International Political Economy of Artificial Intelligence.* Eds. Tugrul Keskin and Ryan David Higgins. Cham: Palgrave Macmillan. 147–76.
Yardi, Sarita and Danah Boyd. (2010). "Dynamic Debates: An Analysis of Group Polarization Over Time on Twitter." Bulletin of Science, Technology and Society 30, no. 5: 316–27.
Yossman, K. J. and Manori Ravindran. (2022). "Inside the BBC Staff Exodus: Women of Color are 'Exhausted' from Fighting a Broken System." Variety https://variety.com/2022/tv/global/bbc-women-leaving-impartiality-1235221317/.
Youniss, James, Jeffrey A. McLellan, and Miranda Yates. (1997). "What We Know about Engendering Civic Identity: Social Capital, Civil Society and Contemporary Democracy." *American Behavioral Scientist* 40, no. 5: 620–32.
Yuda, Masayuki. (2019, May 31). "Thailand's King Power Wins Bid to Continue Duty-Free Monopoly." *Nikkei Asian Review* https://asia.nikkei.com/Business/Companies/Thailand-s-King-Powerwins-bid-to-continue-duty-free-monopoly.
Zalatimo, Salah. (2018, July 11). "Entering the Next Century with a New *Forbes* Experience." *Forbes* https://www.forbes.com/sites/forbesproductgroup/2018/07/11/entering-the-next-century-with-a-new-forbes-experience/?sh=6ef8accb3bf4.
Zerrenner, Kate. (2019, November 22). "Fasten Your Seat Belts: Formula 1 Racing to the Carbon Neutral Finish Line." *Triple Pundit* https://www.triplepundit.com/story/2019/fasten-your-seat-belts-formula-1-racing-carbon-neutral-finish-line/85706.
Zevin, Alexander. (2019). *Liberalism at Large: The World According to* **The Economist**. London: Verso.
Zimmer, Ben. (2013, September 27). "Did Stalin Really Coin "American Exceptionalism"?" *Slate* https://slate.com/human-interest/2013/09/american-exceptionalism-neither-joseph-stalin-nor-alexis-de-tocqueville-coined-the-phrase-that-is-now-patriotic-shorthand.html.

Zirin, Dave and Jules Boykoff. (2019, July 23). "These Women Have Lost Their Homes to the Olympics in Tokyo—Twice." *The Nation* https://www.thenation.com/article/archive/tokyo-olympics-displacement/.

Zirin, Dave. (2020, January 17). "The Australian Open is the Tip of a Melting Iceberg." *The Nation* https://www.thenation.com/article/environment/australian-open-fires-climate-change/.

Zook, Matthew and Michael H. Grote. (2017). "The Microgeographies of Global Finance: High-Frequency Trading and the Construction of Information Inequality." *Environment and Planning A: Economy and Space* 49, no. 1: 121–40.

Zyvatkauskas, Caz. (2007, February 3). "Theatre Critic." *Economist*: 18.

INDEX

60 Minutes 14–15, 37

ABC 38, 40, 41, 45
Abu Dhabi National Oil Company 70
Acton Institute 69
Adam Smith Institute 69
Adorno, Theodor 97, 114, 125
African Union 50
Air Asia 111
Al Jaber 70
Al Jazeera 131
Alfonso 103
Ali, Tariq 55
Alibaba 85
AlterNet 18
Althusser, Louis 114
Amazon 85, 102, 108, 132
American Coalition for Clean Coal Electricity 84
American Enterprise Institute 69
American Fuel and Petroleum Manufacturers 68
American Journal of Sociology 147
American Petroleum Institute 68
Annheuser-Busch 54
Antena 3 141
Aos Fatos 130
Apple 108, 132, 147
Ardila Lülle, Carlos 98
Armero, Pablo 101
Arnheim, Rudolf 120
Associated Press 105–6, 132, 134, 140

Association of Southeast Asian Nations 50
AT&T 113
Athletic, The 148
Atlantic Council 70
Atlantic, The 127
Atlas Network 69
Attali, Jacques 113
Australian Broadcasting Commission 119–20
Australian Communications and Media Authority 105

Badinter, Élisabeth 61
Bangkok Post, The 111
Bayerischer Rundfunk 131
BBC 18, 19, 21, 23, 85, 102, 109, 110–11, 119, 123, 135, 140–1
Bebel, August 8
Beck, Glenn 95
Beck, Ulrich 114
Beeton, Mrs 51
Benedict XVI 128
Benjamin, Walter 9
Bernstein, Carl 20
Bhagwati, Jagdish 121
Bild 74, 135
Bin Laden, Osama 69
Bira 103
Birth of a Nation, The 119
Black, Hugo 37
Bloom, David 40

Bloomberg 46
Bolívar, Simón 4
Book of Household Management 51
Bowen, Sesalie 24
Boyer, Richard 120
BP 73, 78
Braudel, Fernand 137
Brecht, Bertolt 113, 123, 127
Breitbart 96
British American Tobacco 105
Bruckheimer, Jerry 38
Brunsdon, Charlotte 2
BT Sport 102, 107–9
Bureau of Meteorology 86
Burke, Edmund 7, 141
Burkett, NJ 40
Bush, Vannevar 120
Business Environmental Leadership Council 69
BuzzFeed News 24

Cabral, Amilcar 114
Cairo Declaration on Human Rights in Islam 56–7
Calderón, Felipe 77
Calm 121
Campbell, Naomi 104
Camus, Albert 20
Camus, Renaud 49
Canal+ 101
Caracol 98
Carey, Jim 16
Carlyle, Thomas 4
Carr, David 123
Casablanca 97
Cato's Letters 34
CBS 14, 38, 40, 41, 45, 146
Center for Environmental Research and Earth Sciences 69
Centro de Reflexión y Acción Laboral 82
Chandler, Raymond 100
Charles Koch Foundation 69
Charlie Hebdo 33, 55–62
Chartier, Roger 2
Cheney, Dick 39
Chidbod, Newin 111
Chunichi Shinbun 18
CIA 18–19, 126
Citizen Kane 7
Citizenship 33–63
Claremont Institute 69
Clark, Alan 8

Clark, Jim 103
clientelism 108–13
Clinton, Bill 120
CNBC 46, 135
CNBC Africa 135
CNBC Asia 135
CNBC Europe 135
CNN 20, 38, 39, 61, 131, 135, 140, 141
Cobden Centre 69
Coca-Cola 54
College Fix, The 70
Comedy Central 39
Committee for a Constructive Tomorrow 69
Committee to Protect Journalists 27
Common Dreams 18
Competition and Markets Authority 109, 112
Competitive Enterprise Institute 69
Confederation of European Paper Industries 82
Conversation, The 112
Council of Europe 27–8
CounterPunch 18
Courage, Piers 103
Cowley, Jason 93, 114
Creative Industry 4.0 50
Cumhuriyet 61
Cunard 11
Curtin, John 42
Cyran, Olivier 58

Daily Mail, The 131
Dataminr 131
De Corti, Espera 66
Defence of the Realm 117–18
DeLillo, Don 106
Denver Post, The 96
Dibradoras 148
DiCaro, Julie 101–2
Dilem, Ali 59
Discovery 109
Discovery Institute 69
Döpfner, Mathias 74
Drouyn de Lhuys, Édouard 119
Durkheim, Émile 113
DW 131, 141
Dyke, Greg 23
Dynamo Moscow 97

E Foundation for Oklahoma 69
Eagleton, Terry 5
Eco, Umberto 29, 91, 125

Economist, The 18
Edelman 67–8
El Espectador 11
El Faro 17
El Periódico 18
El Rhazoui, Zineb 59
El Tiempo 99
Engels, Friedrich 133
Englehardt, Tom 122–3
English Premier League 76, 101, 109
environment 64–90
Erdoğan, Recep Tayyip 62
Escobar, Pablo 98
ESPN 94, 95, 103
Europäisches Institut für Klima und Energie 69
European Organization for Nuclear Research 126
European Union 21, 25, 48, 50, 120, 146
Exxon Mobil 68

Facebook 85, 121, 137
Falcao, Radamel 98
Faulkner, William 105
Fédération Française de Football 114
Fédération Internationale de Football Association 77, 148
Fédération Internationale de l'Automobile 77
Ferrari 104
Ferrari, Enzo 103
Ferré, Jean-Luc 148
Ferzat, Ali 59
Financial Times, The 18, 112, 123
Fish, Stanley 36
Food 50–5
Food Network 52
Forbes 123
Ford, Henry 119
Formula One 77–8, 79, 103–5
Forsskåll, Peter 3
Fortune 68
Fourest, Caroline 61
Fox 39, 40, 49, 68, 85–6, 140
Fox, Vicente 44
France 24 141
France Soir 55, 60
Francis 58, 128
Franklin, Bob 137
Fraser Institute 69
Freud, Sigmund 127
Frost, Robert 106
Fuentes Vivar, Roberto 148

Fundación Color de Colombia 141
Fundación para la Libertad de Prensa 26

Gallup 26
Gannett 54, 106, 135
Gans, Herbert 42
García Márquez, Gabriel 17, 148
Gautney, Heather 9
Gawker 24
General Electric 54
General Motors 40
George C Marshall Institute 69
Gibbons, John H 120
Giddens, Anthony 118
Ginsberg, Allen 65
Glanville, Brian 148
Global Warming Policy Foundation 69
Globonews 20
Godin de Beaufort, Carel 103
González, Elián 38
Google 24, 83, 85, 132, 147
Gordon, Thomas 34
Gore, Al 120
Grantham, Bill vii, 33–5
Greenpeace International 85
Greenspan, Alan 46
Griffith, DW 119
Grupo Grancolombiano 11
Guardian, The 18, 85, 122, 123, 140
Guerrero, Andrea 101

Habermas, Jürgen 48
Hall, Stuart 44, 114, 137
Halliday, Fred 91
Hardt, Michael 118
Harvard Business Review 133–4
Hawks, Howard 7
Hawthorn, Mike 103
Headspace 121
Heartland Institute 69
Hegel GWF 2–5
Heidegger, Martin 80–2, 88
Henreid, Paul 97
Heritage Foundation 69
Hewitt, Don 14–15
His Girl Friday 7
Hisense 77
Hobbes, Thomas 44
Hollande, François 55
Hoover Institution 69
Horkheimer, Max 97
HSBC 11–12
Huffington Post 18

Hugo, Victor 119
Hunt, James 103–4
Hunt, Leigh 8
Hussein, Saddam 39

Indian Premier League 93
Indoleft 18
Initiative for Free Trade 69
Innis, Harold 127
Input 24
Insecurity 24–8
Instagram 96, 121
Institute of Economic Affairs 69
Institute of Public Affairs 69
Inter-American Development Bank 50
Inter Miami 96
Intergovernmental Panel on Climate Change 66, 69, 70, 74
International Energy Agency 83
International Federation of Journalists 87
International Telecommunications Union 82–3
International Telegraph Union 119
Isaacson, Walter 38
ITV 109

Je ne suis pas une salope, je suis une journaliste 101
Jefferson, Thomas 3, 7
Jevons, William 84
John of Salisbury 91
Johnson, Boris 20–1
Jota Leaños, John 38–9
junge Welt 18
Just Women's Sports 148
Juvenal 91
JX Press 136
Jyllands-Posten 55

Kaczynski, Tad 69
Kane, Harry 99
Kant, Immanuel 3, 6
Kart, Musa 59
Katzenberg, Jeffrey 119
Keane, Fergal 27
Kellogg 54
Kemp, Jack 95
Kennedy, John F 120
Kerouac, Jak 106
Keynes, John Maynard 117
Khamenei, Ali 62
Kiesling, Barrett C 120
King Power International 110–13

Klein, Naomi 71
Kluge, Alexander 45
Klum, Heidi 104
Knight, Charles 119

L'Association de Manifeste des Libertés 59
L'Équipe 94, 148
l'humanité 18
l'Union des Organisations Islamiques de France 60
La Gazzetta dello Sport 94
La Jornada 18
La República 18
Latour, Bruno 88, 143
Lawrence, DH 7
Le Monde 101, 123, 148
League of Nations 124
Lebeau, Madeleine 97
Legatum Institute 69
Lenin 4
Lennon, John 113
Lewis, Justin 129
Libération 18
Liddy, G Gordon 95
Liebling, AJ 9
Liliana Valencia, Edna 141
Lippmann, Walter 5, 7, 17
Local Labs 136
Lockheed Martin 94–5
London, Jack 37, 119
López-Egea, Sergi 148
Los Angeles Times, The 130
Ludwig von Mises Institute 69
Lukács, Georg 107
Lumet, Sidney 15
Luntz, Frank 67
Luxemburg, Rosa 4, 125

Macaulay, Thomas 4
MacGill Hughes, Helen 16
Magna Carta for the Information Age 120–1
Mail on Sunday, The 104
Major League Baseball 76, 107–8
Major League Soccer 108
Manhattan Institute for Policy Research 69
Manson, Charles 69
Marca 94
Marconi, Guglielmo 119
Marcuse, Herbert 97, 128
Marlboro 104

Marshall, TH 114
Marx, Karl 2, 133, 149
Mattelart, Armand 117
Maxwell, Richard vii, 64
Mbomío, Lucía 141
McDonald's 54
McLaren 104–5
Media Research Center 95–6
Mediapart 18, 147
Melville, Herman 80–2, 83, 88
Ménès, Pierre 101
Mengniu 77
Mercatur Center 69
Merv Griffin Show, The 65
Messi, Lionel 76–7, 96
Meta 132
Microcontos de Futebol 148
Microsoft 84–5, 132
Mill, James 4
Mill, John Stuart 4, 7, 36, 119, 125
Milton, John 3, 36
Mindworks Global Media 135–6
Mobil Oil 71
Moeller, Susan D 39
Mohammed 55, 60
Monsanto 67
Moonves, Leslie 146
Mori, Sayaka 79
Moss, Stirling 103–4
Mother Jones 18
MSN 140
MSNBC 135
Mura, Corinne 97
Murdoch, James 86
Murdoch, Rupert 39, 85–6

Nader, Laura 143
Nation, The 18
National Football League 76, 95, 96, 107, 109
National Geographic 75
National Hockey League 76
National Institutes of Health 126
National Review, The 96
National Science Foundation 126
National Union of Journalists 55, 87
NBC 40, 41, 45, 54, 65, 70, 78–9, 120, 134–5
Nebrija, Antonio de 48
Negri, Antonio 118
Negroponte, Nicholas 121
Netflix 104
Network 15

New Left Review 58
New Statesman, The 18
New York Times, The 17, 22, 38, 40, 52, 53, 54, 61, 65, 71–3, 88, 123
New Yorker, The 104
News Corp 86
Newspaper Death Watch 140
NHK 79
Nielsen 126
Nietzsche, Friedrich 7
NightCafé 131
Nineteen Eighty-Four 97
Nkrumah, Kwame 43
Noticia de un secuestro 148
NPR 22, 23, 141

Obama, Barack 19, 95
Objectivity 11–23
Oborne, Peter 10, 20
Ojo Público 17
Olympics 78–9, 93
Onion, The 96
Open AI 134
Open Europe 69
openDemocracy 18
Oppenheimer, Robert J 124
Opperação Serenata de Amor 135
Organisation for Economic Co-operation and Development 120, 121
Organisation of Islamic Cooperation 55, 58
Orwell, George 97, 113, 13–14
Outline 24

Park, Robert 9
PBS 66
Pepsi 54
Philadelphia Inquirer 52–3
Philadelphia Magazine 52–3
Philip Morris 104
Pius XII 120, 127
Political Prisoners in Thailand 111
Politico 96
Popular Mechanics 64, 65
Postmedia Network 135
Postobón 98
Press On 20, 147
Prieto de Pedro, Jesús 47
Private Eye 39
Profiles from the Front Lines 38
Progressive, The 18

Project South 20
Público 18
Pulvar, Audrey 141

Qatar Airways 77
Qatar Energy 77
Qu'ran 56
Quaker Oats 54

Rainforest Coalition 75
RCA 120
RCN 98–9
Reagan, Ronald 71
Reason Foundation 69
Rebelión 18
Reddit 121, 147
Refinery29 24
Reporters And Data And Robots 135
Reporters Without Borders 25
Reuters 130–1, 135, 136, 141
Rich, Nathaniel 71–2, 88
Ricks, Thomas 39
Rodríguez, James 98
Rolling Stone 86
Rossignol, Laurence 61
Roussel, Henri 58
Rowe, David vii, 91
Rushdie, Salman 62
Ruthrof, Horst 143–4

Sacks, Harvey 137
Said, Edward 91
Saint-Simon, Henri de 4
Salant, Richard S 14
Salud con Lupa 17
Sarnoff, David 120
Saturday Evening Post 64
Schindler's List 119
Scientific American 64–5, 148
Science and Public Policy Institute 69
Scott, CP 6, 30
Seattle Times, The 96
Selassie, Habte 96
Self, Will 59
Sen, Amartya 6
Shell 68
Simmel, Georg 114
Sinclair, Upton 16
Siren Sport 148
Sivanandan, Ambalavaner 48
Sky 61, 102, 104, 107–9
Slate 18
Smith, Adam 132

Snapchat 121
Snow, Jon 26
Society of Professional Journalists 87
Sommers, Mike 68
Soon, Willie 69
Spain, Sarah 101–2
Splinter 24
Sports 75–9, 91–116
Sports Illustrated 95, 106, 136
Springer, Axel 74
Srivaddhanaprabha, Aiyawatt 112
Srivaddhanaprabha, Khun Vichai 111
Steinbeck, John 106
Steinmetz, George 71, 88
Stengers, Isabelle 127
Students and Scholars Against Corporate Misbehaviour 82
Sun, The 99, 104
Sunset & Vine 109
SVT 141
Swiss Fairness Commission 148

Talk TV 86
TaxPayers' Alliance 69
Taylor, Charles 58
technology 105–8, 117–39
Telegraph, The 11–12
Telemundo 148
Televisión Española 141
Thatcher, Margaret 43
Thompson, Hunter S 16
Thompson, Mark 10
TikTok 83, 121
Tillman, Pat 38–9
Time 65, 96, 122
Times, The 126
Toast 24
Tocqueville, Alexis de 4
Todd, Emanuel 57
Toffler, Alvin 134
Tönnies, Ferdinand 1, 9, 148–9
Toronto Star, The 18
Trans Canada 67
Trenchard, John 34
Triângulo do Futebol 148
Tribune 54
Trump, Donald 22, 95, 146
TSN 103
Tuchman, Gaye 16
Twitter/X 107, 121

UN General Assembly 50
Unchained Goddess, The 65

United Nations Conference on Trade and Development 50
United Nations High Commissioner for Human Rights 57
US Army Research Office 126
US Bureau of Labor Statistics 25
US Defense Advanced Research Projects Agency 126
US Department of Defense 126
US Department of Energy 126
US National Mining Association 84
US Navy 126
US News & World Report 38
US Olympic Committee 78
US Student Free Press Association 70
USA Today 96, 106

Vallaud-Belkacem, Najat 61
Viacom 39
Vice 24
Village Voice, The 95
Vivo 77
Vodafone 104

WABC 40
Wal-Mart 68
Wall Street Journal, The 18, 22, 61, 73
Wanda 77

War 37–42, 94–5, 98–9, 125–6
Washington Post, The 39, 54, 73, 86, 131
Weber, Max 4, 7, 9, 19–20, 137
Welles, Orson 7
Wells, Ida B 20
WhatsApp 121
Whitman, Walt 8
Williams, Raymond 16
Williams, Richard 105
Wilson, Harold 120
Wired 128
Woman's Own 43
World Business Council on Sustainable Development 69
World Economic Forum 130–1
WWF India 87

Yaccarino, Linda 121
Yahoo! 106
Young America's Foundation 70
Young, Karen 39
Youtube 56, 83, 121

Zirin, Dave 148
ZNet 18
Zoom 135
Zunar 59

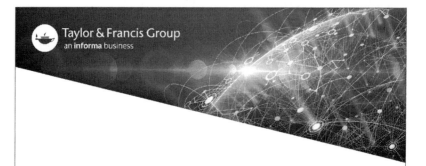

Printed in the United States
by Baker & Taylor Publisher Services